Freedom to Give

The Biblical Truth about Tithing

Daniel Mynyk

CROSSLINK
PUBLISHING

Freedom to Give

CrossLink Publishing
www.crosslink.org

ISBN 978-0-9826215-7-8

Unless otherwise indicated, all scripture quotations are taken from the Holy Bible, King James Version, Cambridge, 1769.

Give thanks unto the LORD, call upon his name, make known his deeds among the people.
— 1 Chronicles 16:8

To my wonderful God and Saviour, my Lord Jesus Christ, from Whom all blessings flow, for His immeasurable, unfathomable, and boundless love, mercy, and grace whereby He redeemed me by His blood through His substitutionary atonement upon the Cross of Calvary, and did for me what I could not do for myself. I am eternally grateful and forever bound to utter His praise, yet I can never begin to repay or prove myself worthy.

To my lovely, endearing, and wonderful wife Chelsea, with whom God has so blessed me in mercy and grace, for her selfless kindness, love, and encouragement to me in this endeavor. Without her care and support, I do not believe I would have ever completed this project.

Table of Contents

FOREWORD

Since the early days of the Reformation the Protestant church has prided itself that its doctrines are based on solid New Covenant principles and practices. This book urges Bible scholars and ordinary Bible students to be approved of God by studying His Word in the context and purposes to whom it was written.

What is so important about tithing? Are there not many much more important issues for the church to study other than tithing? Is not tithing a destructive doctrine which only divides the Body of Christ?

If the Reformers such as Luther, Zwingli, Melanchthon and Calvin had kept quiet, we would all be either cloistered in monasteries or resigned to scholasticism which must agree with Roman Catholic doctrine. There would be no movement forward to explore the depths of Bible revelation and theology.

In my opinion, tithing is the vital doctrine which has kept many churches shackled to the Old Covenant and has prevented the full exploration of God's Word in the area of church finances and growth. Many wealthy Christians give ten per cent and return home confident that they have done what God expects. They attribute their blessings to tithing. On the other hand, many poor Christians have given ten per cent for generations and return home worrying about where they will get enough money from to buy medicine, food, heat and a place to stay. They are afraid that, if they stop giving ten per cent, their promised blessings will never arrive.

Then there are those who have stopped going to church because they simply feel unwelcome or inadequate when the offering plate comes around. Unable to give, they remove themselves from the hearing of the gospel and God's message of salvation.

Jesus preached primarily to Jews who had been instructed for over 1500 years to give tithes from their holy land: tithes to the Temple system—not to Himself—because the Law was still in full force for Jews. He could not and did not command His Gentile disciples to obey the Law and tithe.

Calvary and Pentecost arrived and passed. Both the Temple and its priesthood drastically changed into the doctrine of the priesthood of every believer. Every believer was now a priest before God and the new order of gospel workers followed the pattern of the prophets. Some were full time. Many were self-supporting. All lived by gospel principles of grace and faith.

Paul preached on pagan soil mostly to non-Hebrews and asked for freewill generous and sacrificial contributions. Led by mostly poor women, children, slaves and soldiers, the gospel reached the ends of the Roman Empire by the end of the first century. The keys were a born-again laity, a hunger for lost souls to be saved and freewill generous sacrificial giving. The Hebrew Law, priesthood and tithing were not needed for this revival.

Foreword

Today, the Protestant church of the 21st century stands behind its pulpit and boasts that every one of its doctrines are purely seen in the pages of the New Covenant. This is true with one exception—tithing. It is incomprehensible to me that the modern church can express such great faith in New Covenant principles to teach every doctrine except finances. To act as if God gave better principles for every doctrine except finances is both a sham and a scam.

"Stop it!," I say. Trust God in this too. Go all the way with a God who now functions in the context of His New Covenant.

If you check out every Biblical reference in its context, this book can go a long way to bring peace and truth to your heart and complete the Reformation in the church.

Russell Earl Kelly, PHD

Author of *Should the Church Teach Tithing? A Theologian's Conclusions about a Taboo Doctrine*

www.tithing-russkelly.com

PREFACE

Money talks. Whether in private enterprise or in religious circles, the importance of money and the frequent mention of money is a hot topic; and the subject of money is no less applicable to either area. Likewise, theories of money, methods of handling money, and bookkeeping and accounting practices find their place just as much in public discussion in church polity as in business. The Bible has much to say about money and finances, giving and receiving, and paying dues and taxes in both religious and secular circumstances.

One particular phrase echoed throughout the halls of Christendom may well be one of the most misunderstood phrases at that. The phrase "tithes and offerings," though in word or thought of many alike, will manifest itself differently for every individual. To some, the phrase brings about great joy and confidence; to others, mental anguish, dread, fear, and reluctance. Although "tithes and offerings" is a phrase not met with few acquaintances and little acknowledgment, the number of church "clergy" and "laity" who have committed such a term to serious consideration for deep, practical, Scriptural, and historical study is shockingly minute.

As one who may be picking up this book out of curiosity, no doubt you may have uttered the phrase "tithes and offerings" many times in many contexts. You may have felt with a modicum of confidence that you had a reasonable and safe understanding of this phrase. You may have felt that you have done or continue to do your faithful part in "giving" or "paying your tithes and offerings." You may have felt guilty that you do not perform well enough in this realm. Regardless of your personal experiences, you may have never thought about engaging in a serious study of this topic, including word searches, cross references, geography, and history either to confirm or to challenge your current understanding.

I hope to quench your curiosity, to satisfy your appetite for knowledge, and to develop a greater love and appreciation for the Word of God by presenting an honest, comprehensive, and objective guide. I hope to provide a fascinating commentary of every passage in the Bible covering the subject of "tithes and offerings" and of many commonly regarded passages dealing with "cheerful giving." I endeavor, by comparing Scripture with Scripture, to explain what each of these passages clearly say and what they clearly do *not* say. I do not wish to force you to a specific viewpoint, but I desire to grant you a study that attempts to be complete and unabridged, and allow you to draw your own conclusions. I hope to answer many questions you may have right now, and possibly answer questions that you may encounter in the process of reading this book. It is my sincere desire that after you finish this book, you will never be able to look at the subject of "tithes and offerings" the same way ever again, and that in this subject as well as in any other subject, you will gain a greater love and hunger for the Word of God itself.

INTRODUCTION

From the Author to the Reader

I n the Fall of 2005 I was engaged in a small, informal Bible study group that met regularly on Monday nights. The first task of this Bible study group was a verse-by-verse study and discussion of the Gospel of John. The months that our group spent digging deep into the Word of God transformed me into a serious daily student of the Bible. I realized that not only did I need to assemble faithfully with other believers and hear the preaching of God's Word, but I also needed to study to show myself approved of God. Throughout church history, many martyrs spilled their blood and faced searing flames at the stake to give the common person—me—the privilege of reading the Word of God in the vernacular.

Bible sermons at church provided me with well-studied nuggets of truth from a qualified elder. Personal study and devotions allotted me intimate one-on-one encounters with God and His Word. A group Bible study, however, introduced another method for learning the Bible. An interactive discussion with a group of people—each with different personalities and backgrounds—provides many angles that can lead to the best possible interpretation. This Bible study group included Reformed and non-Reformed alike. Messianic Jewish experience clarified Old Testament laws and traditions. A former Word of Faith proponent shed light on faulty interpretations of problem passages. Some members had a more "fundamentalist" perspective than others. The varied Christian heritages promoted an open evaluation of ideas that most often resulted in interpretations that everyone eventually conceded as true.

After completing a study of the Gospel of John, our group discussed possibilities for another study. Rather than choose another book for a verse-by-verse commentary, we picked a subject. The next study would be entitled "What is the Church?" The goal was to answer this larger question by answering many smaller questions through reading the entire New Testament, using the Old Testament only where New Testament passages used such quotations and concepts. Our group listed nearly 100 questions that we would endeavor to answer through reading assigned portions of the New Testament. Naturally, one of the questions in this list was "Are members obligated to tithe 10% of their income to the church?" After reading the whole New Testament and leaving some questions without written answers, we decided to assign the remaining questions for research and to use the Old Testament as needed. I volunteered to answer the **tithing** question.

Realizing the purpose of this Bible study was both to reveal truth and to encourage everyone to follow this truth, I vowed before this study that I would heed the answer I discovered. If I learned that Christians were obligated to give 10% of their monetary income to the church, I would do just that. If I learned otherwise, I would commit to the pattern, obligation, and example that the Bible demonstrated in the context of the church.

Introduction

I assumed that I would find the quick and easy tithing command for the church. After all, I was taught that such an obligation existed. Surely, the grounds for such a command must exist somewhere in the Bible. I knew what the often-quoted Malachi 3:8-10 passage said, but that was not good enough. I needed to know the context of this passage to determine its bearing on the church. After all, this study was about the church.

The question about "tithes and offerings" for the church became one that had neither a simple nor a straightforward answer. None of the New Testament epistles explicitly mentioned "tithes and offerings" in particular, but surely contained plenty of examples of generosity and praise for giving. I knew that Jesus commended the Jewish religious leaders for their tithing but rebuked them for their neglect of "weightier matters of the law." However, I understood that everything has a context. When Jesus spoke to Jews about *tithing*, He must have been drawing from Old Testament concepts. I knew that the study necessary to answer the question would have to start from the beginning and work its way to the end. Answering this question would require a thorough investigation of the entire Bible.

I spent a few nights reading websites that discussed the matter of tithing and read the passages of Scripture that they referenced. I also engaged in a word study through my Bible software of all forms of the words *tithe* and *tenth*. I was absolutely shocked by what I discovered! What I was reading straight from the Bible simply did not compare with what I was taught. I knew then that most of the sermons that I heard about tithing were simply borne from the same tradition and ignorance that had formed my earlier beliefs. With the exception of some popular televangelists, I truly believe that most pastors and elders who teach "tithing" today are simply honestly ignorant of what the Scriptures themselves teach, and usually bring too many assumptions to common proof texts.

The next Monday night I presented my findings to the group. Every jaw in the room seemed to drop. Obviously everyone in the room had an understanding of tithing from the same traditions that had informed me. Although this question of tithing was only one of 100, the shock of the answer stuck with me and burdened me to research the issue further.

Within one year of this Bible study I began to engage Christian message boards on the Internet. I presented my arguments, findings, and understanding of tithing Scriptures and I faced many of the same arguments and presentations that I would hear in sermons. Most of the arguments against my presentations involved proof texts with assumptions, and arguments from logic, emotions, and practicality. I did not encounter any Scriptural counter-arguments that did not come from certain well-known texts and unproven assumptions about what terms such as *tithes* and *offerings* meant. No one could convince me that I was wrong on these message boards. The only arguments my opponents supplied were ones that I already had answers ready from other Scriptures.

Introduction

Did I ever have slight doubts about my understanding of the subject? Of course! Sometimes I felt the possibility existed that I may have misinterpreted Bible texts or missed the whole "flow" of the Scriptures. To alleviate this concern, I purchased several books about tithing. Although they presented various angles and held different opinions, their premise on the nature of tithing in the Bible agreed with my research.

Over the years since this Bible study I have discussed this subject with many people. I had a friend in seminary who would constantly come to me with questions about Bible doctrines, apparently regarding me as an authority. After we heard a sermon on tithing at church, I explained to him my understanding and he was fully convinced that I was correct.

During one lunch break I joined a table with two seminary student friends. One of them mentioned a sermon about tithing and asked me what I thought about it. Neither of them knew my position, and I was not sure if I even wanted to debate the issue. I asked him, "Are you sure you want my opinion?" He said, "Yes, please." I then barely was able to eat anything as I engaged in a thought-provoking and civil debate where both of these scholarly seminary students drilled me with questions for over a half hour. Absolutely every question they both asked I immediately replied with a thorough answer and Scripture references. They were both stunned at my knowledge of Scripture as I was not a seminary student. One of them said, "You obviously have studied this subject in-depth."

Unsure about if my words meant anything that day, I met one of the two a few weeks later for weekly door-to-door visitation. On the way to a housing community he brought up the issue. He said that my debate during that lunch break caused him to think seriously about the subject and to begin studying it for himself. He said that after careful thought he believed I was correct. He wanted to know why so many are wrong about the issue and how a church could be run otherwise. I simply told him that I believe that many are wrong about it the same way we were both wrong about it before. I also assured him that the Bible provides solutions for church growth in the examples of giving in Acts and in the epistles.

When I learned what I believed was the truth about tithing in the Bible, I found that I had a greater desire to give out of love for God and His Word. There were no longer thresholds to maintain and to hide underneath. The sky was the limit! I began to realize what the Macedonians understood about cheerful and abundant giving as they gave to relieve the Jerusalem church suffering through a famine. They gave abundantly from their poverty. The law of sowing and reaping applied to giving and God blessed those who gave abundantly, cheerfully, and with purpose. I did not have to climb a plateau simply to avoid the judgment of God. He loved all giving and His blessings related to the matter of the heart. If the heart was in the right place, so was the amount. Where my treasure is, there will be my heart also.

This book is the result of my accumulated findings, study, and research about the subject of tithing in the Bible. The fact that scholarly students of the Bible could change their mind to agree with me and the fact that several other books from independent research also agreed with my own staunchly solidifies to me that the Scriptures themselves teach what I have learned by studying them. My intent in writing this book is to engage you with a study that examines the Scriptures in every nook and crevice. If you have never been exposed to a viewpoint that Christians are not required to "tithe" beyond the argument that "we are under grace, not the Law," my hope is that this study will increase your hunger and thirst for the Word of God and aid you in your understanding of it. Perhaps you are a serious "tithing" proponent in pursuit of opposition research. I hope that this book will provide the information you need and that it will cause you to open your heart to the truth of God's Word. If you already come from a position of "grace giving," I hope this book will allow you to defend your viewpoint more effectively and increase your love for God's Word. My greatest hope in writing this book is to see a pursuit of truth in the church of God, and that God will bless the truth and use it to grow and improve His church.

SECTION I: PRE-LAW

Tithing before Moses

In any serious endeavor to study the subject of tithing in the Bible, the most reasonable place to begin would be right at the beginning. In fact, some of the most compelling arguments for modern church tithing come from the fact that the Bible includes instances of "tithing" before God gave the Law to Moses for the children of Israel. These instances of "pre-Law tithing" include the encounter of Abraham and Melchizedek in Genesis chapter 14 and Jacob's vow to God following the vision of the ladder in Genesis chapter 28.

Do these accounts of "pre-Law tithing" demonstrate any command to tithe for the church? As a "father of the faith" (Galatians 3:6-9), do the actions of Abraham in this regard serve as a pattern or example whereby we should or must follow? Does the vow of Jacob form the framework of similar vows that we as New Testament church believers should make to God? If they indeed are examples, patterns, or expressions of commands that we must heed, how do we know how to follow them?

Section 1 will dive into the accounts of tithing before the Mosaic Law—Abraham and Jacob—and will attempt to answer these questions. Studying the "pre-Law tithing" accounts in Genesis will build a solid foundation for understanding the whole of the tithing laws contained in the Mosaic Law. Understanding both the pre-Law and Law tithing passages will then help to explain the context of tithing references contained in the New Testament.

1. Once Upon a Title

Abram and Melchizedek

Genesis 14:18-20

18: And Melchizedek king of Salem brought forth bread and wine: and he was the priest of the most high God.
19: And he blessed him, and said, Blessed be Abram of the most high God, possessor of heaven and earth:
20: And blessed be the most high God, which hath delivered thine enemies into thy hand. And he gave him tithes of all.

The Abram Argument

Any proper research into the realm of tithing appropriately begins with the account of Abram and Melchizedek in Genesis chapter 14. Any search in the Bible for the words *tithe, tithes, tithed,* or *tithing* to study the teaching of these Scriptures will land one in Genesis 14:20. Sometimes the word for the same action may be translated *tenth;* however, the first place this term is found is Genesis 8:5 in which the flood waters receded until "the tenth month."

For some, the issue of "tithing" is utterly important in the structure, function, and operations of the New Testament church. For someone not to support the existing doctrine of "tithing" would be a direct measure to starve the church of its position and effect to influence the world with the Gospel. Some unknowingly blur the terms *tithing* and *giving* so that any argument against the modern doctrine of monetary income "tithing" becomes an argument against giving or an excuse for not giving. Others who understand the distinction between *tithing* and *giving*, but believe that *tithing* and *giving* (often contended as "offerings") are both prescriptive doctrines for the church defend this idea by proclaiming that Abram's *tithe* to Melchizedek proves that *tithing* as a command transcends the Mosaic Law. If "tithing" existed before the Mosaic Law, then, even if the Mosaic Law were canceled in its entirety, "tithing" remains to bind all peoples at all times under the banner of "God's people." Those with whom God covenants at any time He supposedly bestows a divine tithe-tax on income in some form.

Because both Jews and Christians claim Abram (Abraham) as some form of "father" (Romans 4:11-13), the righteous deeds of Abram become the model for which his "children" must follow. Abram blazed the trail of faith and those who claim him must walk the path that he created. If Abram *tithed*, his children subsequently must also "tithe." Abram's deeds that merited him the title "friend of God" demonstrate to his children that they need to find a way to do what he did to gain the same approval from God.

Is such a dogma correct? How does it apply to **other** deeds that Abram did? Do those who claim to follow Abram in "tithing" also follow actions of Abram other than his act of tithing to Melchizedek? Do those who "tithe" because Abram tithed to Melchizedek actually do so according to a model that Abram established? Did Abram do anything deemed "righteous" **before** the Mosaic Law that yet does not apply to God's covenant people **after** the Mosaic Law? If so, how do such facts affect the idea of Abram's "model" tithe? Perhaps a close look at the historical account surrounding Abram's tithe in Genesis chapter 14 can begin to answer some of these questions.

A belligerent battle

Genesis 14:1-11

1: And it came to pass in the days of Amraphel king of Shinar, Arioch king of Ellasar, Chedorlaomer king of Elam, and Tidal king of nations;
2: *That these* made war with Bera king of Sodom, and with Birsha king of Gomorrah, Shinab king of Admah, and Shemeber king of Zeboiim, and the king of Bela, which is Zoar.
3: All these were joined together in the vale of Siddim, which is the salt sea.
4: Twelve years they served Chedorlaomer, and in the thirteenth year they rebelled.
5: And in the fourteenth year came Chedorlaomer, and the kings that *were* with him, and smote the Rephaims in Ashteroth Karnaim, and the Zuzims in Ham, and the Emims in Shaveh Kiriathaim,
6: And the Horites in their mount Seir, unto El-paran, which *is* by the wilderness.
7: And they returned, and came to En-mishpat, which is Kadesh, and smote all the country of the Amalekites, and also the Amorites, that dwelt in Hazezon-tamar.
8: And there went out the king of Sodom, and the king of Gomorrah, and the king of Admah, and the king of Zeboiim, and the king of Bela (the same *is* Zoar) and they joined battle with them in the vale of Siddim;
9: With Chedorlaomer the king of Elam, and with Tidal king of nations, and Amraphel king of Shinar, and Arioch king of Ellasar; four kings with five.
10: And the vale of Siddim *was full of* slime pits; and the kings of Sodom and Gomorrah fled, and fell there; and they that remained fled to the mountain.
11: And they took all the goods of Sodom and Gomorrah, and all their victuals, and went their way.

According to this passage a skirmish occurred among several cities in Canaan. A league of four city kings declared war on a league of five city kings. The city king Chedorlaomer had been holding these five cities in bondage to servitude for twelve years. Chedorlaomer enforced and gained tribute taxes from these five cities. Apparently, after twelve years of being exploited, these kings decided that they had enough and wanted freedom from their slavery. They decided to rebel, causing Chedorlaomer to consolidate his alliance of four cities to quell the rebellion and resume servitude by force of conquest.

It may be important to understand that when Genesis refers to "kings" in this chapter, they are not the kings of large nations that we may understand looking back at history. These were kings of *cities*, and the "nations" at this time were not measured in millions of people. A "nation" at this time had numbers in the hundreds or thousands. A "king" in Genesis 14 was the leader of a city-state and was more of a thug ruler whose "army" was a band of dozens to several hundred armed fighters. A city over which such a "king" would rule would not equal the magnitude of a New York City or a Chicago. These cities were significantly much smaller.

From Genesis 10:22 we read that Elam was one of Shem's sons. Here in Genesis 14:1, Chedorlaomer was king of a city named *Elam*, likely where the descendents of Elam populated after the incident of the tower of Babel. Just because Shem was righteous does not mean that all his sons were. Interestingly, if Melchizedek were Shem as we will examine as an option later in the chapter, Shem and Chedorlaomer, one of Shem's descendents would be on opposite sides of this conflict of city kings.

This battle occurred in a place called the "valley of Siddim" or "valley of flat lands." This valley contained many "slime pits" or pits full of tar or asphalt. This ancient valley of Siddim likely lay adjacent to what would be later known as the Dead Sea.[1] The alliance of five kings under Chedorlaomer apparently obtained the initial victory in the battle, sending the kings of Sodom and Gomorrah into retreat. Even retreat was not possible as they fell hostage to the sticky terrain of the tar pits enabling the alliance to spoil them completely and leave them destitute.

Genesis 14:12-17

12: And they took Lot, Abram's brother's son, who dwelt in Sodom, and his goods, and departed.
13: And there came one that had escaped, and told Abram the Hebrew; for he dwelt in the plain of Mamre the Amorite, brother of Eshcol, and brother of Aner: and these *were* confederate with Abram.
14: And when Abram heard that his brother was taken captive, he armed his trained *servants*, born in his own house, three hundred and eighteen and pursued *them* unto Dan.
15: And he divided himself against them, he and his servants, by night, and smote them, and pursued them unto Hobah, which *is* on the left hand of Damascus.
16: And he brought back all the goods, and also brought again his brother Lot, and his goods, and the women also, and the people.
17: And the king of Sodom went out to meet him after his return from the slaughter of Chedorlaomer, and of the kings that *were* with him, at the valley of Shaveh, which is the king's dale.

Because Lot had chosen to dwell in the area of Sodom (Genesis 13:12), the battle involved his own livelihood. Obviously Lot fought in the army of the king of Sodom. Lot became captive among the spoils

---

1. *Holman Illustrated Bible Dictionary*, rev. ed., s.v. "Siddim."

that the alliance of five kings usurped from the kings of Sodom and Gomorrah. The spoil from these two cities apparently left out at least one single messenger who informed Abram of the incident and especially of what happened to his nephew Lot.

Abram was no simple backwoods sage. Abram was a very wealthy patriarch (Genesis 13:2), so much so that he and Lot could not occupy the same "city" (Genesis 13:6). Abram had servants who oversaw the operation of his possessions (Genesis 13:7). Without a careful study of the Genesis account, one may be tempted to view Abram as a weak old man who, miraculously with a small band of farmer-servants, overthrew mighty armies. Abram's wealth and possessions in reality made his ownership comparable to that of any of the other city kings involved in the battle. Abram hastily prepared a total of 318 of his trained servants for the battle, and these were all ones that came from his own home.

Nevertheless, Abram's worth of a single city could not hope to fight toe-to-toe in a confrontational battle in which both sides prepared in array. Abram had to strategize a surprise attack. The alliance did not know about Abram and his band and were basking in the victory. Abram's army encircled the coalition at night and launched the attack possibly as the foes were sleeping. Abram's army carried out a successful attack and chased the remaining forces away from the spoils. Abram recovered the spoils, including his nephew Lot, and returned them to the region of the defeated cities where they could reclaim them. When the king of Sodom soon discovered that Abram had destroyed his enemy and recovered the goods and people of the city, he approached Abram to congratulate and thank him.

Genesis 14:18-24

18: And Melchizedek king of Salem brought forth bread and wine: and he *was* the priest of the most high God.
19: And he blessed him, and said, Blessed *be* Abram of the most high God, possessor of heaven and earth:
20: And blessed be the most high God, which hath delivered thine enemies into thy hand. And he gave him tithes of all.
21: And the king of Sodom said unto Abram, Give me the persons, and take the goods to thyself.
22: And Abram said to the king of Sodom, I have lift up mine hand unto the LORD, the most high God, the possessor of heaven and earth,
23: That I will not *take* from a thread even to a shoelatchet, and that I will not take any thing that *is* thine, lest thou shouldest say, I have made Abram rich:
24: Save only that which the young men have eaten, and the portion of the men which went with me, Aner, Eshcol, and Mamre; let them take their portion.

This account records a mysterious character named *Melchizedek*, king of a city named Salem, who came to meet Abram. According to the names of the cities and their kings listed in the account previously, Melchizedek and his city apparently was not party to the battle. Melchizedek, king of Salem, did not come to meet Abram for the same reason as did Bera, king of Sodom. Bera came to thank Abram and reclaim spoils. Melchizedek came to bless and praise Abram as a servant of the God Whom he also served. Melchizedek recognized Abram as one who served the same God as he. Melchizedek understood the victory in the battle as a special blessing and recognition upon Abram from his own God. Whereas the king of Sodom was grateful to Abram for material reasons, Melchizedek blessed Abram for spiritual reasons as one whose blessing and power came from his own God. Melchizedek did not just say that Abram mightily won the battle; he claimed that his God "delivered [Abram's] enemies into [his] hand."

Melchizedek blessed Abram in words and by giving him bread and wine. Abram recognized the priesthood of Melchizedek by giving him a customary tenth of all the spoils that he acquired in the battle. These spoils came from the cities of Sodom and Gomorrah. Because these cities lost these possessions in the battle and Abram won them in victory, they were Abram's new possessions by right and he had the legitimate authority to give a tenth of these spoils to whom he so deemed worthy. In fact, the Arab world at the time required giving a tithe of spoils obtained in war to the local priest-king; therefore, Abram likely did not have a choice in the matter![2]

Bera, king of Sodom, felt that since he would have had no possessions at all had not Abram fought to reclaim them, requested that Abram return to him the people of his city but keep the possessions that he won. Bera gratefully acknowledged Abram's merit to keep these goods, but he desired to retrieve his people so that he could rebuild his city. Abram replied that he had already made a vow to his God that he would not keep the spoils that he won. His reason was that he did not want Bera to claim that he enriched Abram. Abram made himself clear that his part in the battle was not a materialistic

---

2. Russell Earl Kelly, *Should the Church Teach Tithing?: A Theologian's Conclusions about a Taboo Doctrine* (New York: Writer's Club Press: 2000), 23-26.

opportunity to increase his own wealth, but rather a goodwill effort to restore them to the cities in which he felt that they belonged. Abram made an exception for the goods that he and his band were already consuming to celebrate and to recover from war fatigue.

Who was the mysterious Melchizedek?

Melchizedek is certainly a mysterious character in the Bible and subject to myth and legend throughout history since records began of his encounter with Abram. Scholarly disagreements and debates as to the identity and nature of this man continue into the present.

A pre-incarnate Christ. Some theologians in early church history and even now believe that Melchizedek was Jesus Christ Himself in the flesh. In other words, Melchizedek was a *theophany.* Early adherents of this view include sects of Gnosticism, and some believed that Melchizedek was a pre-incarnate Son of God while others believed that he was a manifestation of the Holy Spirit.[3]

Particularly, Hebrews chapter 7 verses 3 and 8 provide the problem phrases that give a surface heed to this interpretation. If

Abraham meets Melchizedek

---

3. Ray C. Stedman, *Hebrews,* vol. 15 of *The IVP New Testament commentary series* (Westmont, IL: InterVarsity Press, 1992), 80.

Melchizedek was "without father, without mother, without descent [genealogy]" then, other than the first man Adam, how could any other human embody such apparently non-mortal characteristics? If he had "neither beginning of days, nor end of life" and "abideth a priest continually," how can he be limited merely to the stock of the human race? In fact, proof for Melchizedek being a theophany of Jesus Christ Himself could be in John 8:56 where Jesus declared, "Your father Abram rejoiced to see my day: and he saw *it*, and was glad."[4] Moreover, the bread and wine that Melchizedek gave Abram can symbolize the body and blood of Jesus and the elements of the Lord's Supper.

One apparent problem with the theophany view is that Hebrews 7:3 declares that Melchizedek was "made <u>like</u> unto the Son of God" rather than that he **was** the Son of God. An additional problem is that Psalm 110:4 and Hebrews 7:17 both describe the Messiah as "a priest forever <u>after the order of</u> Melchizedek." Accordingly, in John 8:56 Jesus may just as well have been referring to Yahweh's covenant to Abram in Genesis chapter 17 among other passages.[5] Also, the bread and wine as symbols can be just as compatible with Melchizedek being a **type** of Christ as with being Christ Himself.

---

4. Fred Collier, *Doctrine of the Priesthood Vol 8 No. 1 - New Light on the Ancient Hebrew/Christian Doctrine on Deity — Part 1* (Salt Lake City: Collier's Publishing, 1991), 7.
5. John MacArthur, *The MacArthur Bible Commentary* (Nashville: Thomas Nelson, 2005), 1387.

Another problem with the theophany view is the possibility of earthly descendents of Melchizedek himself. Joshua chapter 10 relays an account during the conquest of Canaan that a league of kings tried to quell the Gibeonite allies of Israel for fear of their strength. Among these kings were Adonizedek, king of Jerusalem. *Jerusalem* (or "Jebu-Salem") is a later name for Salem where the Jebusites dwelt (Joshua 15:63; Judges 1:21; 19:11). King David finally followed the command of God to destroy the Jebusites (2 Samuel 5:6-10; 1 Chronicles 11:4-9) and he established their headquarters named *Jebus*, *Salem*, or *Jerusalem* as the capital city of Israel. Perhaps the name *Jeru-salem* replaced *Jebu-salem* as the name of the city because the Jews rather than the Jebusites now owned the city.

Adonizedek is also another name for the same title as *Melchizedek*. *Adonizedek* means "lord of righteousness" and *Melchizedek* means "king of righteousness." These two titles were synonyms for the same office of being the ruler of the city of Salem or Jerusalem. Likely all kings of this city held a tradition to bear this title or a variation of it[6] similar to how all the kings of Egypt traditionally bore the title *Pharaoh*. Lest one should be tempted to assume, the Adonizedek of Joshua chapter 10 and the Melchizedek of Genesis chapter 14 could not have been the same person. The centuries between these two accounts would eliminate such a possibility. The theophany idea would also fail for Adonizedek because Joshua chapter 10 describes him in a

---

6. Patrick Fairbairn, ed., *The Imperial Bible-Dictionary* (London: Blackie and Son, 1866), s.v. "Adoni-zedek."

negative light as an enemy of the nation of Israel, whereas "the LORD fought for Israel" in his defeat (Joshua 10:14).

A pagan Canaanite priest-king. Another view that attempts to address the problems with the theophany position is that Melchizedek, as king of the city of Salem, was a priest of a pagan Canaanite god. If Melchizedek were a Canaanite priest, he likely would have been a descendent of Ham.[7] Dr. Russell Earl Kelly's extensive treatise on the doctrine of tithing *Should the Church Teach Tithing?* presents Melchizedek in this fashion, arguing that Zedek was the name of a Canaanite god.[8] Indeed, a Canaanite conception of a god named *Zedek* existed[9], and other renditions of the name include *Sydic* and *Sadic*.[10]

The title of Zedek, Sydic, or Sadic likely also represents a title of Noah as being the "righteous" or "just" one.[11] Ancient Asians referred to their god of the planet Jupiter as *Zedek*, corresponding to Shem.[12] The Syrians also traced Shem to the god Jupiter.[13] Northern Africans, on the contrary, regarded Ham as the god Jupiter, Japheth as Neptune, and Shem as Pluto.[14] Perhaps ancient cultures attributed the most

---

7. *Smith's Bible Dictionary*, s.v. "Melchizedek."
8. Kelly, 17.
9. Acharya S, *Suns of God* (Kempton, IL: Adventures Unlimited Press, 2004), 517.
10. Helena Petrovna Blavatsky, *The Secret Doctrine*, vol. 2 of *The Synthesis of Science, Religion, and Philosophy* (Adyar, India: Quest Books, 1993), 392.
11. Ibid.
12. Augustin Calmet, *Calmet's Dictionary of the Holy Bible*, ed. Charles Taylor (London: Holdsworth and Ball, 1832), 640.
13. Budgett Meakin, *The Land of the Moors: A Comprehensive Description* (London: Swan Sonnenschein & Co., 1901), 152.
14. Andrew Tooke, *Tooke's Pantheon of the Heathen Gods and Illustrious Heroes* (Baltimore: Cushings & Bailey, 1851), 141-142.

veneration to the son of Noah from whom they claimed their genealogical heritage, equating him with the god of the sky, or "Jupiter." One can fairly conclude that the Canaanite god Zedek originated from a legendary understanding of Noah or Shem, as many flood legends exist in different parts of the world.

John MacArthur contends that the Scriptures recording Abram and Melchizedek both referring to God by the same titles and descriptions—"The LORD, the most high God (Yahweh El Elyon)" and "possessor of heaven and earth"—intends to convey to the reader that both Melchizedek and Abram understood and regarded the same God.[15] Even if the Canaanites worshiped a god based upon a gossip train from the history of Noah, the text of the account in Genesis provides no clue that *Zedek* should be a proper name for the Canaanite god Zedek or merely the description of "righteousness." To believe that Abram and Melchizedek addressed different deities with the same title with no indication in the Scriptures of such an anomaly would be to argue in a sense that Abram and Melchizedek "talked past each other" regarding such an important matter. One can make a conclusion from this reasoning that Melchizedek being a priest of a pagan Canaanite god cannot withstand careful scrutiny.[16]

---

15. *The MacArthur Bible Commentary*, 34.
16. Christopher R. Little, *The revelation of God among the unevangelized: an evangelical appraisal and missiological contribution to the debate* (Pasadena: William Carey Library, 2000), 72.

Shem. Some believe that Melchizedek was actually Noah's son Shem. According to the years in the Bible giving the life of Shem and the age of him and his descendents when each was born, Shem was still alive during the battle of the kings. In fact, Shem outlived Abram (his great, great, great, great, great, great, great grandson) by thirty-five years! After the flood life spans began to decline sharply from over 600 years to over 200 years and less. A 600-year-old Shem likely provided a grand relic of old age and wisdom also having witnessed first-hand the worldwide destruction from the flood. Shem, having been one of only eight people to repopulate the earth would naturally have worldwide renown to all the city-states that began and grew hundreds of years later. Conclusively, if a Canaanite god was created from a legend of Noah, Shem himself could have simply named his priesthood and city after his father.

Primarily the idea of Melchizedek as Shem comes from traditional Jewish writings.[17] Included in Jewish tradition is the disputed authenticity of a Hebrew manuscript claiming to be the book of Jasher referenced in Joshua 10:13 and 2 Samuel 1:18. This candidate for Jasher 16:11 makes the following assertion: "And Adonizedek king of Jerusalem, the same was Shem, went out with his men to meet Abram and his people, with bread and wine, and they remained together in the valley of Melech."[18] Regardless of the fact that this alleged book of

---

17. James L. Kugel, *Traditions of the Bible: a guide to the Bible as it was at the start of the common era* (Cambridge, MA: Harvard University Press, 1998), 289.
18. *The Book of Jasher*, trans. Mordecai Manuel Noah (New York: M.M. Noah & A.S. Gould, 1840), 45.

Jasher is not found in the Biblical canon, if it's claim of title is truly authentic, it may serve as an historical record of the identity of Melchizedek or "Adonizedek." One possibility of Jewish tradition for Shem in this role as Melchizedek is that it definitively provides a bloodline between the priesthoods of Melchizedek and Levi.[19] Another logical reason, though unsupportable from Scripture, is that, since Shem was living in the land of Canaan, God's call to Abram to leave Ur of the Chaldees and move to the Promised Land of Canaan would be to have him **return** God's favored line of people back to their original land.[20]

One inference from Scripture making Shem a "priest" and identifiable with Melchizedek is the similarity between God's blessing upon Shem (Genesis 9:26-27) and Melchizedek's blessing on Abram (Genesis 14:18-19).[21] Genesis 9:27 reads "God shall enlarge Japheth, and he shall dwell in the tents of Shem; and Canaan shall be his servant." The word *he* in the verse presents a mystery as to its antecedent. Will **God** "dwell in the tents of Shem" or will **Japheth?**

For those who interpret the verse as **God** dwelling in the tents of Shem, the possibility exists for a reference to the priesthood of Shem

---

19. Kugel, 289.
20. Ibid., 290.
21. Fred L. Horton and Fred L. Horton, Jr., *The Melchizedek Tradition: A Critical Examination of the Sources to the Fifth Century A.D. and in the Epistle to the Hebrews*, vol. 30 of *Society for New Testament Studies Monograph Series* (Cambridge, UK: Cambridge University Press, 2005), 117.

himself as Melchizedek.[22] However, the "tents of Shem" does not have to mean Shem himself. As the Hebrew language often refers to descendents by the name of the father, "the tents of Shem" can mean Shem's ancestors. Just as **Japheth** earlier in the verse did not refer to man Japheth himself—unless God meant that He would make Japheth an obese person—so Shem is likely a reference to the **nation** that would form from Shem's ancestors. A reasonable understanding of this verse is that God would make the descendents of Japheth—the Europeans and Asians—large and powerful while also deriving the chosen nation of Israel from the descendents of Shem and living in their tabernacle and Temple. The people of Canaan—the Canaanites— would be the servant of the Semites—the Israelites—when they conquered the land of Canaan.

A compelling reason for **he** being Japheth rather than God is that **Japheth** is closer as a possible antecedent. An interpretation involving **Japheth** dwelling in the tents of Shem expresses the verse as a prophecy for the union of Jew and Gentile in the Christian church.[23] Such an interpretation as a prophecy excludes the descendents of Ham from the church and would hence be demonstrably inaccurate. Possibly a better interpretation regarding **Japheth** in Shem's tents would be that ultimately the Roman descendents of Japheth would occupy the land of Israel and cause the Jews to disperse.

---

22. Kugel, 290.
23. Matthew Henry, *Matthew Henry's Concise Commentary on the Whole Bible* (Nashville: Thomas Nelson, 1997), 21.

Having presented these theories and their support and logical flaws, I rank the idea of Shem or one of Shem's descendents being Melchizedek as most plausible. If "without father, without mother, without descent, having neither beginning of days nor end of life" (Hebrews 7:3) refers only to the record of **priesthood** and not the record of **life**, then Shem remains a possible candidate. However, if these qualifications refer to the record of **life**, then a more probably candidate would be one of Shem's descendents. Although Genesis 10:21-31 appears to provide an exhaustive list of Shem's descendents, naming five sons in verse 22, this list may not be as exhaustive as it appears for Shem or any of his descendents listed. Genesis 11:10-26 provides another genealogy from the line of Shem with a focus on the branch that bore Abram. Between these two genealogies of the line of Shem is the brief account of the tower of Babel in Genesis 11:1-9. Nimrod was the mighty descendent of Ham who ruled the kingdom of Babel and oversaw the tower project (Genesis 10:8-10). Peleg was a descendent of Shem during this time who witnessed the tower of Babel incident, "for in his days was the earth divided." (Genesis 10:25) Genesis 11:11 states that other than Arphaxad, Shem "begot sons and daughters." Likely the names in Genesis 10:21-31 are not exhaustive, and a mysterious descendent of Shem of whom no record exists in the Bible or Jewish tradition of his life receives the title of **Melchizedek** who honors his "zedek" ("righteous") father Noah by naming his family and city after him. Melchizedek's priesthood, however, came from a divine appointment from God and not from a bloodline (see chapter 15 later in this book).

To tithe or not to tithe

One's conception of the person of Melchizedek may or may not determine one's application of Abram's tithe; however, many more who view Melchizedek as a theophany lean toward a binding "principle" or even an outright "obligation" for those who claim Abraham as a spiritual father to pay "tithes" to the living priesthood of Melchizedek. Those who believe that Melchizedek was Jesus Christ Himself often believe that Jesus now "receives tithes" through His church after the manner of Abraham rather than after the Law of Levi.

Some, including popular television preachers like John Hagee, believe that accounts of a "tithe" before the Mosaic Law establish "tithing" as "a divine principle" that yet binds Christians.[24] In other words, the **real** tithe that New Testament believers commit to follow is not the one instituted in the Mosaic Law, but rather the one that Abram gave to Melchizedek before the Law. However, many who make the claim for the Abram tithe upon the church will not shy from quoting verses from the Law to substantiate such an obligation for church tithing. For them, the Abram tithe represents the abiding law of the tithe doctrine, and the tithe commandments found in the Mosaic Law are God's implementation of this doctrine into the code for the nation

---

24. John Hagee, *Financial Armageddon* (Lake Mary, FL: FrontLine, 2008), 111.

of Israel.[25] Although the Mosaic Law does not **directly** command the Gentile church to practice a form of tithing, allegedly it **indirectly** contains the command to tithe by virtue of its supposed relationship to the "pre-Law" tithe to Melchizedek of which the head of the church— Jesus Christ—serves as High Priest after the order of Melchizedek. Therefore, one is free to use passages in the Mosaic Law, such as Malachi 3:8-12, as an application to the church for God's direct blessings and subsequent curses that depend upon the individual's practice of "tithing" according to the current formulation of the perceived "universal" tithing doctrine.

The nature of Abram's tithe

Several questions and issues can arise for one who examines the account of Abram's tithe in detail without merely viewing the presence of the word *tithe* through the lens of modern tradition. Reading the details of this account, one can notice several problems with an attempt to extrapolate Abram's tithe to one's current understanding of the alleged tithing doctrine. These problems shall be analyzed using Abram's tithe as the "tithe that binds."

First, how many times do the Scriptures record Abram giving something in the form of a "tithe"? Genesis chapter 14 and Hebrews chapter 7 are the only accounts of Abram's tithe, and they are both of the same event. As far as we know Abram only tithed to Melchizedek **once**. Accordingly, we can then notice that Abram only tithed to

---

25. Arthur Vergil Babbs, *The Law of the Tithe* (New York: Fleming H. Revell Company, 1912), 107.

anyone once. A legitimate question protrudes from examining this problem: How does Abram's **one-time** tithe to Melchizedek argue a case whereby those who claim him as a "father" must tithe not only once but continually? Read chapter 15 of this book to analyze a possible significance between the priesthood of Melchizedek and the fact that Abram tithed only once.

Second, of what source did Abram tithe? Did Abram tithe of his own "income"? One author claimed: "It is a disputed point whether Abraham meant a tithe of all his property, or of all the spoils of war which he had with him."[26] Although Genesis 14:20 says that Abram gave Melchizedek "tithes of all" and Hebrews 7:2 says that Abram gave "a tenth part of all," Hebrews 7:4 clarifies that he gave "the tenth of the spoils." One could argue that the "tithe of spoils" was only **part** of what Abram gave Melchizedek in the "tithes of all." However, this reasoning fails both logic and Scriptural analysis. Obviously the "all" can mean "all the spoils of the battle." The context of Abram's tithe is directly within the context of winning the battle, returning the spoils, and the king of Sodom requesting a return of his people. Abram gave Melchizedek the tithe after returning from chasing the alliance of Chedorlaomer to Hobah. Abram met both Melchizedek and the king of Sodom in a place called "the valley of Shaveh," which likely belonged to the king of Sodom. Abram was not in his own home when he gave Melchizedek the tithe. It would defy logic and be to argue from silence

---

26. Henry William Clarke, _The History of Tithes from Abraham to Queen Victoria_ (London: George Redway, 1887), 1.

to believe that Abram brought all his many possessions with him to battle. Abram did not have all his possessions with him. He tithed to Melchizedek of the spoils of the battle as Hebrews 7:4 makes clear. If, indeed, Abram tithed only of the spoils of war to Melchizedek—things that were stolen from the kings of Sodom and Gomorrah—and **not** from his own possessions, how does Abram's tithe in this regard present an obligation to those who claim him as "father" to tithe of their own "income"?

Third, of what type of substance did Abram tithe? Did Abram tithe only of money? Did Abram tithe of money at all? Likely, Abram's tithe included money, but was not limited to money. Genesis 14:11 says that the alliance of Chedorlaomer took all the "good" and "victual" from the kings of Sodom and Gomorrah. The "goods" may have included money, but likely also included clothing and weapons. The "victuals" strictly means "food." The alliance stole the food that these kings brought with them to sustain themselves for the battle. In verse 21, the king of Sodom granted Abram to keep the "goods" but requested to return the people. In verse 23, Abram replied that he would not keep a "thread" to a "shoelatchet," which both indicate small portions of clothing. In verse 24, Abram also qualified that he could not return food that his men had already eaten or would need to compensate them for their efforts. If Abram's tithe consisted mostly of material things and food, why do many who attempt to regard Abram's tithe as a model for continual practice for the church dictate that the people only tithe from sources of monetary income or comparable liquidity?

Fourth, what did Abram do with the rest of the spoils after he tithed of them to Melchizedek? Genesis 14:21-24 distinctly records that Abram returned the remnant of the spoils back to the king of Sodom. Abram had to have been aware of the wickedness of the city of Sodom (Genesis 13:13). Abram recognized that the spoils justly belonged to the king of Sodom even though he had the possessive right to keep them. He gave the rest of the spoils of the battle back to the wicked king of Sodom and kept **nothing** from them by which to increase his own estate. If Abram's tithe presents a model for the church, why is not his vow also included in this model? Why should not a Christian today give a tenth to the church and the remainder to the local strip club? If Abram's tithe was only from the spoils of a war, should Christians then seek out war for purposes of tithing? Should Christians who fight in national wars and obtain spoils from the enemy find a local priest-king (or the alleged church equivalent) and then give the rest of the spoils back to a wicked ruler from which they came?

Fifth, Abram's tithe came from an event that arose from less than ideal circumstances. Abram's tithe to Melchizedek was a consequence of rescuing his nephew lot from his own wrongdoing in choosing to dwell in Sodom.[27] If Lot had not committed this selfishness begun by "pitching his tent toward Sodom," Abram would never have fought in the battle at the valley of Siddim. Abram would never have tithed of the spoils of this war to Melchizedek.

---

27. Benny Prince, *Why Tithing is NOT for the Church: The Full Truth About Tithing* (Bloomington, IN: AuthorHouse, 2003), 2.

The Before and After

If the fact that Abram tithed **before** the Mosaic Law presents an obligation to tithe to the church, is the church then obligated to perform other acts that Abram did? An argument for the Abram tithe issuing the church tithe comes from Galatians 3:7-9, among other Scriptures.

Galatians 3:7-9

7: Know ye therefore that they which are of faith, the same are the children of Abraham.
8: And the Scripture, foreseeing that God would justify the heathen through faith, preached before the gospel unto Abraham, *saying*, In thee shall all nations be blessed.
9: So then they which be of faith are blessed with faithful Abraham.

The argument contends that if the Gentile church receives the blessings of Abraham, and Abraham is the example of faith, then New Testament believers should imitate the faithful **deeds** of Abraham. Purportedly, Abraham's deeds and God's institutions before the Mosaic Law reflect His eternal morality, and thus the cancellation of the Law does not nullify faithful deeds and commands in place before Moses. Pastor Bill Winston states: "Notice, God was the one who gave Abram the victory, and Abram gave the tithe to Melchizedek, who was God's representative. Abraham is called the father of the faithful, meaning that we should follow his example."[28] However, the act of Abram's tithe, as examined above, presents many disconnects from the modern

---

28. Bill Winston, *The Power of the Tithe* (Oak Park, IL: Bill Winston Ministries, 1999), 10.

doctrine of perpetual monetary income tithing. Also, many things that Abraham did are not found in the church at all.

First, Abram built altars and performed animal sacrifices before the Law (Genesis 12:7; 13:4,18; 22:9). No attempts to "spiritualize" Abram's altars can avoid the corollary need to "spiritualize" Abram's tithe (which the church today does of a sort). However, Abram's altars and animal sacrifices specifically reflected the mode of Abram's faithful worship to God, and the practice extended as far back as Cain and Abel. Although Abram performed animal sacrifices **before the Law**, Jesus Christ's sacrifice of Himself ended the need to practice burnt offerings (Hebrews 10:1-23).

Second, Abram practiced circumcision before the Law. In fact, not only did Abram practice circumcision, he did so by the very command and covenant of God Himself (Genesis 17:9-14,23-27; 21:4). Although debate exists concerning whether Abram's tithe was a command or a "free will" vow, no dispute is possible regarding circumcision. God **commanded** Abram to circumcise his sons and likewise all his descendents. If Abram's tithe to Melchizedek presents an obligation to the "followers" of Abraham, how much **more** should Abraham's circumcision, being a direct command from God, place such an obligation to the church that claims him as a "father of the faith"! Because the Israelites were descendents of Abraham, God carried the covenant of circumcision to the Mosaic Law. Although circumcision existed **before the Law** and **in the Law**, the New Testament is clear that circumcision no longer applies after Christ's resurrection.[29] If the circumcision in the Law embodied the **whole** of circumcision as it pertained to Abraham and his seed through Moses, then could not the same possibility exist in Scripture for the tithe? If a command that God gave Abraham before Moses is fulfilled and nullified by Jesus Christ, cannot the tithe, which was not even an obvious command to Abraham before Moses be fulfilled in Jesus Christ after the priestly order of Melchizedek? (Hebrews 7:5, 12, 18) Read chapter 15 of this book for the possibility of the priesthood of Melchizedek nullifying the practice of tithing to priests.

Third, Abraham practiced polygamy by conceiving a child through his handmaid Hagar, while his wife was Sarah. Although Sarah encouraged Abraham to do this act, she afterward despised Hagar for it. Despite Sarah's frustration with Hagar, God blessed Hagar and promised a large family from her child Ishmael. The Mosaic Law encoded provisions for polygamy.[30] If one's brother died and left no children, then one had the obligation to marry his brother's wife and raise up seed to his brother. This law did not disregard those who were already married. Also, one could have more than one wife as long as he committed to providing for each of them. Adultery was that of one man lying with another man's wife, and not of an unmarried maiden. If

---

29. See Romans 4:8-13; 1 Corinthians 7:18-19; Galatians 5:1-6; 6:12-15; Ephesians 2:11-16; Philippians 3:3; Colossians 2:9-14; 3:11.
30. See Exodus 21:10-11; 22:15-17; Deuteronomy 22:13-19; 25:5-10.

Abraham practiced polygamy and the Mosaic Law codified polygamy, should New Testament believers also engage in the same?

The fact that Abraham or someone else practiced something before the Mosaic Law does not bind Gentile believers after Jesus Christ fulfilled the Law to do the same, or a variant of the same. The reasoning that actions—faithful and moral or not—prior to the Mosaic Law represent the eternal commands or will of God inclusively binding His church is fatally flawed, and the support is merely conjecture. Although Abraham is the example of faith through which Gentiles can partake in his blessings, by no means is every good or moral action of Abraham or command upon Abraham a proof for such subjection from the church. While Galatians 3:6-9 incorporates the believing Gentiles into the blessings and promises of Abraham by faith, verses 10-29 emphasize that the Gentile church inherited the blessings and faith of Abraham, not the Law. Moreover, most conclusively, the modern income tithe doctrine bears strikingly little, if any comparison to Abram's tithe to Melchizedek.

Conclusion and summary

In conclusion, we have examined several theories to the identity of Melchizedek. These theories may not dictate, but may influence one's view of Abram's tithe as an application to the doctrine of the church. We see that Abram's tithe was a one-time event whereby he gave a tenth of the spoils of a battle to Melchizedek, and not from his own possessions or income. He gave the remainder of these spoils to the king of Sodom. Although Abram performed this tithe act before the

Mosaic Law, the mere presence of a supposed righteous act (rather obedience to the law of a foreign land) before the Mosaic Law cannot of itself determine that the Christian church be obligated to follow suit. Abram practiced animal sacrifices, circumcision, and polygamy before the Law, and all three of these became encoded in the Law. However, clearly none of these practices remain intact in New Testament doctrine after Jesus Christ fulfilled the Law. Moses was a descendent of Abraham and the Mosaic Law specifically applied to the seed of Abraham through the promise of Isaac. Abram's tithe to Melchizedek bears no resemblance to the current teaching of monetary income tithing to the church in any form, function, or timing. The account of Abram and Melchizedek in Genesis chapter 14 cannot possibly support the modern monetary income tithe doctrine.

2. Let's Make a Deal

Jacob's Conditional Vow

Genesis 28:20-22

20: And Jacob vowed a vow, saying, If God will be with me, and will keep me in this way that I go, and will give me bread to eat, and raiment to put on,
21: So that I come again to my father's house in peace; then shall the LORD be my God:
22: And this stone, which I have set *for* a pillar, shall be God's house: and of all that thou shalt give me I will surely give the tenth unto thee.

The Jacob Argument

The argument for the tithe based upon pre-Law accounts in the Bible really includes both the Abraham and the Jacob accounts. These two accounts function as a "tag team" of sorts. If glaring weaknesses exist in the Abraham account, one will swiftly change gears toward the Jacob account. Likewise, if weaknesses exist in the Jacob account, one may leap back into the Abraham account. If one cannot argue a compelling case from both Abraham and Jacob, one may emphasize an overriding "principle" of "tithing" that transcends the Mosaic Law, and therefore binds all God's people who are not under the Law. One may hastily declare: "It does not matter **how** Abraham and Jacob 'tithed;' what matters is that they **did** 'tithe.'" Such a statement assumes that the modern monetary income tithe doctrine must be true by virtue only of the presence of a form of the word *tithe* anywhere in the Bible: especially if this word appears before the life of Moses. In other words, the teaching of the modern monetary income tithe doctrine needs no scrutiny of its details or implementation; the doctrine as a whole is simply assumed. All that is necessary to support its practice and enforcement is the mere presence of someone in the Bible prior to Moses vowing, committing, practicing, or giving a tenth of something somehow to someone.

Nevertheless, the tithe vow of Jacob and Abraham's tithe to Melchizedek exhibit some rather important differences. An advocate of the modern monetary income tithe doctrine may argue these differences as support for the overriding, ambiguous "principle" of "tithing" that church leadership is then free to codify to accommodate the economy and livelihood of New Testament believers. An opponent of the modern monetary income tithe doctrine may conversely argue that these differences present a barrier to needed Scriptural support for the doctrine, and that the assumed details find no grounds in Abraham, nor in Jacob, nor in the Law. This chapter shall examine the account of Jacob's tithe vow in Genesis chapter 28 and determine if this passage yields adequate support for the modern monetary income tithe doctrine.

The background to the vow

Genesis 28:1-5

1: And Isaac called Jacob, and blessed him, and charged him, and said unto him, Thou shalt not take a wife of the daughters of Canaan.
2: Arise, go to Padanaram, to the house of Bethuel thy mother's father; and take thee a wife from thence of the daughters of Laban thy mother's brother.
3: And God Almighty bless thee, and make thee fruitful, and multiply thee, that thou mayest be a multitude of people;
4: And give thee the blessing of Abraham, to thee, and to thy seed with thee; that thou mayest inherit the land wherein thou art a stranger, which God gave unto Abraham.
5: And Isaac sent away Jacob: and he went to Padanaram unto Laban, son of Bethuel the Syrian, the brother of Rebekah, Jacob's and Esau's mother.

The setting and background to Jacob's tithe vow begins following Jacob's deception of his father Isaac into believing that he was Esau. Jacob deprived Esau of the blessing he would receive as firstborn son. Although Jacob and Esau were twins, Esau being the eldest would receive the blessing. At least tradition dictated this practice. In reality, Esau had already forfeited his qualification for the blessing of being the father of the nation by breaking the covenant of Abraham. Abraham made his servant swear not to find a Canaanite wife for Isaac based upon the promise of God to Abraham (Genesis 24:1-7). Esau took two wives of the Canaanite Hittites, upsetting his parents (Genesis 26:34-35).

Isaac likely recognized the roadblock to blessing Esau with the covenant promise; however, he exhibited a superficial favor of Esau based upon his hunting prowess and the wild game that such would bring to his table (Genesis 25:28; 27:1-4). No doubt Isaac also hoped for the success of Esau also according to his status as firstborn. Jacob, having received the blessing from Isaac, now received the commission to follow the covenant of promise by finding a wife from his non-Canaanite kin (vv. 1-2). Isaac pronounced upon Jacob the official blessing of the covenant to be the father of the promised nation (vv. 3-4).

Genesis 28:6-9

6: When Esau saw that Isaac had blessed Jacob, and sent him away to Padanaram, to take him a wife from thence; and that as he blessed him he gave him a charge, saying, Thou shalt not take a wife of the daughters of Canaan;
7: And that Jacob obeyed his father and his mother, and was gone to Padanaram;
8: And Esau seeing that the daughters of Canaan pleased not Isaac his father;
9: Then went Esau unto Ishmael, and took unto the wives which he had Mahalath the daughter of Ishmael Abraham's son, the sister of Nebajoth, to be his wife.

Esau obviously was determined to reclaim the blessing that he had lost to Jacob. When Esau first discovered that Jacob received the blessing from his father, he sorrowfully and hastily begged his father for his own blessing. In a bitter superstition, he desired an **equal** blessing, expecting this his own father who favored him above Jacob could rescind exclusiveness and either grant him the same blessing or revoke the one upon Jacob. Despite the lesser blessing that Esau received from his father, he nevertheless harbored jealousy of Jacob. He did not merely wish to prosper, he wanted the pride of favoritism, dominance, and the legacy of the covenant promise.

The only solution for Esau to reclaim the covenant promise would be to prevent its fulfillment in Jacob. In other words, Jacob would have to die before having a surviving son. A precursory reading of Genesis 27:41 might lead one to think that Esau merely wanted to kill his brother Jacob out of mere rage for his trickery. However, in verse 42 Rebekah tells Jacob that Esau was "comfort[ing] himself" with his plot to slay Jacob. No doubt what brought Esau comfort in killing Jacob would be that the covenant blessing would *de facto* revert to him.

Rebekah informed Jacob of the plot for his death and told him to flee to his uncle Laban's house (Genesis 27:43-45). Rebekah told Isaac that she would rather have Jacob marry a daughter of Laban than one of Heth who dwelt nearby. Although a daughter of Heth would have been the natural choice for Jacob to follow the covenant, Rebekah wanted to persuade Isaac to commission Jacob to retrieve a wife from a remote location to protect Jacob's life from Esau. Most likely Rebekah intended to keep the location of Jacob secret from Esau; however, Esau found out about this commission.

The covenant promise to Jacob was now beginning to unravel before Esau's eyes. The fact that Jacob obeyed to seek a covenant wife and Esau's own Hittite wives frustrated his parents drove Esau to drastic measures. His ability now to kill Jacob conveniently and secretively was thwarted. In a futile effort to qualify himself as worthy of the covenant promise before his parents, Esau added a third wife to his arsenal—a daughter of Ishmael. Ironically, Esau himself could have taken a daughter of Heth to wife, but instead chose a daughter of Ishmael. Perhaps Esau still did not understand that the covenant promise in reality depended primarily on keeping the commandments of the covenant and only secondarily on the status of firstborn. God was the One Who determined the fathers of the covenant—firstborn status was a cultural tradition for inheritance rights, which naturally led some to believe that firstborn status automatically conferred upon one the unconditional blessings of the promise itself. Esau, reasoning that Ishmael was actually Abraham's firstborn son, married a daughter from him. Esau attempted to restore his qualifications for the blessings of the covenant to Isaac by demonstrating that he not only had a wife of kin through which covenant offspring could come, but also that he had a greater right to it by right of firstborn. Esau grossly misunderstood the purpose of the covenant. This type of fleshly view of the covenant rather than the proper spiritual view of godly character and obedience to the righteousness of God's will would ultimately plague the nation of Israel.

The location of the vow

Genesis 28:10-17

10: And Jacob went out from Beersheba, and went toward Haran.
11: And he lighted upon a certain place, and tarried there all night, because the sun was set; and he took of the stones of that place, and put *them for* his pillows, and lay down in that place to sleep.

12: And he dreamed, and behold a ladder set up on the earth, and the top of it reached to heaven: and behold the angels of God ascending and descending on it.

13: And, behold, the LORD stood above it, and said, I *am* the LORD God of Abraham thy father, and the God of Isaac: the land whereon thou liest, to thee will I give it, and to thy seed;

14: And thy seed shall be as the dust of the earth, and thou shalt spread abroad to the west, and to the east, and to the north, and to the south: and in thee and in thy seed shall all the families of the earth be blessed.

15: And, behold, I *am* with thee, and will keep thee in all *places* whither thou goest, and will bring thee again into this land; for I will not leave thee, until I have done *that* which I have spoken to thee of.

16: And Jacob awaked out of his sleep, and he said, Surely the LORD is in this place; and I knew *it* not.

17: And he was afraid, and said, How dreadful *is* this place! this *is* none other but the house of God, and this is the gate of heaven.

Because of Esau's desperate measures of attempting to please his parents with a wife from Ishmael, Jacob indirectly had time to flee to safety before Esau renewed his plot to kill him. Because the journey to Padanaram was greater than one day's travel, Jacob sought a place to sleep on the way. He found no shelter and had to sleep outside on the rough terrain, forming a pillow from stones. Despite the discomfort of such an environment, Jacob's fatigue lulled him into a sleep. While asleep, Jacob had a startling dream.

In Jacob's dream—more appropriately a vision—he saw a tall staircase connecting the ground of the earth to heaven. Angels were ascending from earth to heaven and descending from heaven to earth. This ladder may have symbolized God's very presence to Jacob concerning the promise. God told Jacob that He would give him the very land upon which he slept. The latter, illustrating a direct connection to heaven with angels going up and down, may have been

God telling Jacob that his blessing regarding the promise and the land was not merely an earthly, fleshly promise of father to son, but one directly appointed from heaven itself to Jacob and his seed. Theologians and philosophers can discuss the nuances of the specifics of the vision and to the extent to which this vision was symbolic versus a revelation of supernatural forces at work; however, the

Jacob's vision of the ladder

overriding point appears to be that of a divine confirmation of the covenant promise and that Jacob was the recipient by virtue of the words of Yahweh in verses 13-15.

When Jacob arose, he was frightened. Obviously this dream was no ordinary dream. An encounter with God, whether in a dream-vision or awake, is not normally something that only leaves the recipient in a state of peace and joy. To witness even a fragment of the majesty of God will terrify a mortal human before the blessings therein bring the intended peace and joy. As far as Scripture is concerned, this is the first personal encounter Jacob experienced with God. Abraham, the "friend of God," conversed with God several times throughout his life, and Isaac experienced at least one when he was about to be sacrificed by his own father. The fact that this dream-vision sparked the first personal encounter between Jacob and God serves to emphasize the point that God was now passing the torch of the covenant promise from Isaac to Jacob.

Genesis 28:18-22

18: And Jacob rose up early in the morning, and took the stone that he had put *for* his pillows, and set it up *for* a pillar, and poured oil upon the top of it.
19: And he called the name of that place Bethel: but the name of that city *was called* Luz at the first.
20: And Jacob vowed a vow, saying, If God will be with me, and will keep me in this way that I go, and will give me bread to eat, and raiment to put on,
21: So that I come again to my father's house in peace; then shall the LORD be my God:
22: And this stone, which I have set *for* a pillar, shall be God's house: and of all that thou shalt give me I will surely give the tenth unto thee.

Jacob, then, realizing that God had blessed him in this place and had given him a vision upon the spot where he slept took the stones upon which he slept and built an altar to mark the location. He then made a vow to God which has become a particularly influential statement for forming support for a universal "tithing" doctrine. In response to the vision, Jacob vowed to God that "of all" he received from God, he would "give the tenth" back to God.

Jacob recognized the implications of this vision to his current situation. He was fleeing for his life from his jealous brother who was plotting to kill him. Attempting to obey his father's command to seek a wife from his uncle while simultaneously avoiding the threat of death,

Jacob realized that, from a human standpoint, his life and livelihood had no assurance for tomorrow. However, the vision with direct words of blessing from God Himself served as confirmation that he not only had a promise to live, but also to lead a full life of blessing. If God were to bless him with the promise of the covenant, he would naturally be allotted a wife, surviving children, possessions, a legacy, and peace with his family.

The nature of the vow

Jacob's vow provides a second account where a "tithe" is mentioned. This time, the conditions are very different. Whereas Abraham tithed once, Jacob apparently committed to a continual act. Although Abraham tithed of the spoils of a war, Jacob committed to tithing "of all that thou shalt give me." Abraham gave the rest of the spoils to the king of Sodom, relinquishing ownership back to whom the substance originally came; Jacob, made no such statement and committed no such act. If Abraham's act, standing alone, provides a shaky foundation for the modern monetary income tithe doctrine, then surely Jacob's vow can fill the void. In fact, apologist Thomas Aquinas quoted Jacob's vow as Scriptural proof that one must tithe of all acquired possessions.[31] Jacob's vow appears to provide the perfect proof text for the current teaching on "income" tithing—or does it? As with Abraham's tithe, several issues arise with a presumed link

---

31. Thomas Aquinas, "Whether men are bound to pay tithes of all things?," *Summa Theologica, Volume 2*, trans. Fathers of the English Dominican Province (Charleston, SC: BiblioBazaar, 2008), 312.

between Jacob's vow of a tithe and the teaching of the modern monetary income tithe.

First, Jacob's vow was a **conditional** vow. Jacob did not simply commit a vow to giving a "tithe" to God; his vow depended entirely upon God fulfilling conditions. Thus, his vow constituted a bargain with God. Despite the fact that the conditions of Jacob's vow apparently match the promises that God made to him in the vision, Jacob still crafted a bargain. Jacob would not begin tithing until after, and only after God fulfilled Jacob's parameters. Moreover, God did not promise Jacob peace with his own family, but Jacob added this as a requirement. In fact, Jacob stated that only after God fulfilled his expectations, "then shall Yahweh be my God." If tithing were commanded or expected by custom or tradition in any way, why would Jacob have any right to commit conditionally to follow an already established command? If Jacob's alleged tithe provides a model for Christians in the New Testament church, would not the structure of his vow be included in this model as well? Could not Christians tempt God by withholding tithes until certain blessings occur? Unless one is tempted to ration that Malachi 3:10-12 provides a similar venue, these verses reference the Mosaic Law. Verses 8-9 include a curse for *not* tithing! Under the Law, one had an **unconditional** command to tithe. The difference between tithing and not tithing was blessings and cursings respectively. Chapters 12 and 13 of this book provide an in-depth analysis of the context of the reference to tithing in Malachi as it relates to the Law and the priests.

Second, no specifics in Scripture indicate how Jacob may have performed this ambiguous vow. Did Jacob toss a tenth of his grain into the air and have God sweep it up in chariots of fire? Obviously God has no need for tithes to sustain Himself; therefore, for Jacob to "give to God," he would really have had to give to a person or a group of people of whom God approved. Did he tithe to a priest? Could he have tithed to Melchizedek? If Melchizedek were Shem, he was not alive at this time. No theocratic priestly system existed yet for the nation of Israel. Jacob, as any patriarch at the time, performed his own priestly functions before God by constructing altars personally and performing burnt offerings upon them.[32] One possibility could be that Jacob assumed he would be blessed with the wealth of animals and would use a tenth of them for burnt offerings to God.[33]

Third, no record exists in the canon of Scripture to prove that Jacob actually kept his vow. The only expectation of Jacob keeping his vow is through speculation and tradition. Jacob may have kept his vow by giving his tithe to the poor. According to Jewish tradition, Jacob established the system of tithing for the poor in that he would give a tenth of the food that he acquired to meet the needs of the poor according to his blessings from God.[34] Possibly the altars that the

---

32. Kelly, 31.
33. John H. Walton and Victor H. Matthews, *The Ivp Bible Background Commentary: Genesis-Deuteronomy* (Downers Grove, IL: InterVarsity Press, 2000), 60.
34   Sol Scharfstein, *Torah and Commentary* (Jersey City: KTAV Publishing House, 2008), 97.

patriarchs built became hotspots for giving to the hungry.[35]

Fourth, argument and evidence exists for a link from Jacob's tithing vow to the Mosaic Law itself. Remember that the context presented in this chapter demonstrates that Jacob's vow springs from the covenant promise of God to Jacob that he would be the father of the nation of Israel. In fact, God later renamed Jacob *Israel*, which also became the name of the nation within his womb (Genesis 32:28). Jacob, rather than Abraham, became the father by which his children would claim a name. The people of the nation are often called the "children of Israel" in Scripture. A period of tribulation for the people of Israel is called "the time of Jacob's trouble." (Jeremiah 30:7) If Jacob himself did not tithe, his vow may have been fulfilled in the tithing laws given to Moses.

Another extra-Biblical source of possibility that elaborates upon Jacob's vow is the book of Jubilees. One of Jacob's conditions in the vow was that God would have to return him safely again to his father's house. Jubilees 31:24-32:5 provides an alleged account of Jacob remembering and fulfilling his vow many years later while his son Joseph was in Egypt.[36] In this account, Jacob returned to his father Isaac and relayed his vow at Bethel. Isaac told Jacob to carry out his vow but that he was too old to go with him. He commissioned him to take his mother Rebekah with him to Bethel. As Jacob and his family

---

35. Kelly, 31.
36. *The Book of Jubilees: or The Little Genesis*, trans. Robert Henry Charles (London: Adam and Charles Black, 1902), 189-192.

members with him spent a night at Bethel, Jacob's son Levi dreamed that he and his descendents would become God's segregated priests for Israel. The next morning Jacob performed a "counting" ritual of his sons and discovered that Levi would be the priest and recipient of tithes. He then dressed Levi in priestly clothing and gave him a tenth of everything that he possessed—servants, animals, food, money, clothes, and other goods. If the Book of Jubilees is an accurate historical account of Jacob fulfilling his vow, then it was a direct link to the Levitical priesthood of the Mosaic Law. If the Book of Jubilees is not a reliable account outside the Bible, then the Scriptures themselves provide no useful model by which Jacob's vow itself applies to anyone other than Jacob and its fulfillment remains a mystery. Both Abraham's tithe and Jacob's vow exhibit volitional acts and serve no literal proof of a command to tithe prior to the Mosaic Law.[37] If Jacob's vow demonstrates a pre-Law obligation to tithe, which it could not possibly do, its link to the Levitical priesthood would cancel it per Hebrews 7:5, 12, 18.

Conclusion and summary

In conclusion, we have examined the context and substance of Jacob's vow. We have seen that the events and setting of Jacob's encounter in Bethel relate specifically to the covenant promise of God to Abraham's seed concerning the nation of Israel. We have seen that the details of the vision and the specifics of Jacob's vow also declare the special promise of God for the people of Israel. We have seen that

---

37. Kelly, 31.

the conditional nature of Jacob's vow provides no reliable comparison to the current teaching of unconditional tithing. Although Jacob's vow differed from Abraham's in that the tithe was not of the spoils of a war, the Scriptures do not elaborate on the substance of Jacob's projected tithes. Jacob pledged to tithe of all his possessions, and not simply of sources of monetary income. No record of Scripture exists to prove that Jacob kept his vow. Rational reasons exist for a direct link between Jacob's vow itself and the tithe in the Mosaic Law according to the covenant promise given to Jacob and his name as *Israel*. If the Book of Jubilees supplies reliable extra-Biblical insight into a possible fulfillment of Jacob's commitment, the direct link to tithing under the Law is established as well as the Levitical priesthood, which the epistle to the Hebrews succinctly cancels after Jesus Christ. The account of Jacob's vow in Genesis chapter 28 cannot possibly support the modern monetary income tithe doctrine or any related mandate on the church.

SECTION II: THE LAW

Tithe—It's the Law!

The laws that God dictated to Moses for the people of Israel unquestionably included very clear and stringent commands for tithing. Of course, by *tithing*, those who were subject to these laws were required to give 10% of somewhat of their livelihood to those who were considered their spiritual ministers as well as their authorities. The fact that the Scriptures include blatant commands to tithe is simply not in dispute.

This section of the book will explore all portions of the Mosaic Law that cover tithing particulars and ordinances. The nation of Israel had to obey these laws or face dire consequences. Often churches that teach an obligation to pay 10% of one's income will cite verses from these laws to justify this prerogative.

In studying these laws, we will focus on the specifics of the actual commands and compare them to contemporary teaching. We will examine the thorough and meticulous nature of these laws and use them as a filter to test current prevalent tithing doctrine. We will see from the actual Scriptures that a proper understanding of these laws requires a careful look at context before any attempt to extrapolate or apply them. Will superficial quotations and interpretations of select verses stand up to scrutiny?

3. You Get What You Pay For

Redeeming the Tithe

Leviticus 27:30-34

30: And all the tithe of the land, *whether* of the seed of the land, *or* of the fruit of the tree, *is* the LORD's: *it is* holy unto the LORD.
31: And if a man will at all redeem *aught* of his tithes, he shall add thereto the fifth *part* thereof.
32: And concerning the tithe of the herd, or of the flock, *even* of whatsoever passeth under the rod, the tenth shall be holy unto the LORD.
33: He shall not search whether it be good or bad, neither shall he change it: and if he change it at all, then both it and the change thereof shall be holy; it shall not be redeemed.
34: These *are* the commandments, which the LORD commanded Moses for the children of Israel in mount Sinai.

A primer on the Law

Besides Malachi 3:8-10, no other passage receives as frequent consultations and quotes, whether complete or incomplete, as Leviticus 27:30. For many, the words "all the tithe...*is* holy unto the LORD" settles the matter. The very first mention of tithing in the Mosaic Law from the very first sentence immediately declares it "holy unto the LORD." *Holy,* meaning separate, segregated, devoted, or dedicated, clearly indicates that whatever this "tithe" is, God Himself claims ownership rather than the person who is the caretaker. If the "tithe" is "holy unto the LORD," the readers of these words should take heed to understand just what God intended and stated in the words of His Law. Those who regard the God of the Bible as the One True God do well to respect every word that God said in entirety and examine the context carefully.

With the tithe accounts of Abraham and Jacob as the springboard and the primary argument for the modern monetary income church tithing doctrine, these verses in Leviticus chapter 27 serve as a proof text. Although one less knowledgeable in the Scriptures can be easily persuaded to fall into lockstep with a quote from Leviticus chapter 27, an examination of the actual words of the verses and their context in the chapter can raise significant questions and challenges to the modern doctrine.

Holy unto the Lord

One argument for an enduring or universal "tithe" obligation or "principle" is the phrase "holy unto the LORD." The idea is that if God said something is "holy" unto Himself, He has a special, enduring interest in it. In fact, the inferential present tense of the statement enforces the assumption that the "tithe" or "tenth" is **now** "holy unto the LORD" and has **always been** "holy unto the LORD." One can seem to derive the message that God was "reminding" His people Israel that an obligation to tithe exists and that it is **still** "holy unto the LORD." A statement that would "make good preaching" is that Abraham and Jacob both recognized the importance of the tithe and they also likewise gave to God "all the tithe" that is "holy unto the LORD." However, a study of the context of the tithe in Leviticus chapter 27 and the phrase "holy unto the LORD" and similar occurrences throughout the Law will demonstrate that *tithe* in this passage retains no such distinctly eternal emphasis outside the context of its specified recipients.

The Mosaic Law is not a simple construct. The Jews divide the Law of the Torah into 613 distinct commands![1]

Within the Law, God designates many other things besides the tithe as "holy unto the LORD" or a variant rendering thereof. The annual atonement sacrifice was "most holy unto the LORD." (Exodus 30:10). A special perfume for the tabernacle was "holy for the LORD." (Exodus 30:37) In fact, no one was allowed to replicate it for personal use under penalty of excommunication; it was God's proprietary formula. The Sabbath (seventh) day of every week was "holy to the LORD." (Exodus 31:15; 35:2) The edible portion of meat offerings for priests was "a thing most holy of the offerings of the LORD." (Leviticus 2:3,10; 10:12) The sin offering was "most holy." (Leviticus 6:25) The priestly sons of Aaron were "holy unto their God." (Leviticus 21:6) The wave offerings for the priests were "holy unto the LORD." (Leviticus 23:20) The bread offering that a priest ate on Sabbath days was "most holy unto him of the offerings of the LORD." (Leviticus 24:1-9) Dedicated animals that were given "unto the LORD shall be holy." (Leviticus 27:9) Sanctified houses were "holy unto the LORD." (Leviticus 27:14) Fields dedicated during Jubilee were "holy unto the LORD." (Leviticus 27:21,23) "Every devoted thing *is* most holy unto the LORD." (Leviticus 27:28) During the time of a Nazarite vow, one was "holy unto the LORD." (Numbers 6:8) The firstlings of certain bovine animals were "holy" for burnt offerings "for a sweet

---

1. Walter A. Elwell and Philip W. Comfort, ed., *Tyndale Bible Dictionary* (Wheaton, IL: Tyndale House Publishers, 2001), s.v. "Judaism."

savour unto the LORD." (Numbers 18:17) The Israelites were "a holy people unto the LORD thy God." (Deuteronomy 7:6; 14:2,21; 26:19) There were "holy vessels" in the tabernacle (1 Kings 8:4). The Levites were "holy unto the LORD." (2 Chronicles 35:3) The chief priests were "holy unto the LORD" and the vessels of the sanctuary were "holy also." (Ezra 8:28) The day Nehemiah read the Law to the people of Israel was "holy unto the LORD." (Nehemiah 8:9-10)

Although many things were "holy unto the LORD," they were not necessarily eternal, as the fulfillment and change of the Law through Jesus Christ has made clear. If "holy unto the LORD" marks something as an enduring mandate for the people of God throughout all ages, then should not the church follow the instructions to craft a penetrating perfume for the quarters wherein a local church assembles? Should not the church persist in the practice of yearly atoning burnt sacrifices? If these offerings were "most holy unto the LORD," why did Jesus abolish the practice? If the seventh day of the week was emphatically "holy unto the LORD," then why has much of Christendom switched the "Sabbath" to Sunday? If the priests of Aaron, the chief priests, and the Levites were "holy unto the LORD," why did God establish the destruction of the Temple in A.D. 70, and why did the writer to the Hebrews declare the end of the Levitical priesthood prior to this event? Obviously, the argument for the tithe in Leviticus chapter 27 being "holy unto the LORD" carries no weight of a binding upon the Gentile church, especially when verse 34 states that these commandments, including this tithe, were to "Moses for the children of Israel in mount Sinai."

The chapter of dedicated things

The context of the tithe in this chapter is the entirety of the chapter itself. The whole chapter is about freewill vows of things. These things were dedicated, devoted, or separated volitionally as gifts for God's use through the priestly ministry. Leviticus chapter 27 lists several things that an Israelite could devote for the sanctuary. Such decisions were binding. In most circumstances, one could not retract such a devotion, and in others, one could redeem the thing devoted for a 20% added surcharge upon its value. Different regulations existed for different types of things dedicated. We will examine these regulations for dedicated things to elaborate on the context of the tithe.

Dedicated people

Leviticus 27:1-8

1: And the LORD spoke unto Moses, saying,
2: Speak unto the children of Israel, and say unto them, When a man shall make a singular vow, the persons *shall be* for the LORD by thy estimation.
3: And thy estimation shall be of the male from twenty years old even unto sixty years old, even thy estimation shall be fifty shekels of silver, after the shekel of the sanctuary.
4: And if it *be* a female, then thy estimation shall be thirty shekels.
5: And if *it be* from five years old even unto twenty years old, then thy estimation shall be of the male twenty shekels, and for the female ten shekels.
6: And if *it be* from a month old even unto five years old, then thy estimation shall be of the male five shekels of silver, and for the female thy estimation *shall be* three shekels of silver.
7: And if *it be* from sixty years old and above; if *it be* a male, then thy estimation shall be fifteen shekels, and for the female ten shekels.

8: But if he be poorer than thy estimation, then he shall present himself before the priest, and the priest shall value him; according to his ability that vowed shall the priest value him.

In verses 2-8 the first items presented for dedication were people. The Levitical Law split devoted people into four age groups: 1 month-5 years old, 5-20 years old, 20-60 years old, and 60 years old and older. The 20-60 year old category contained the highest prices for people. Within each category males commanded a higher price than females. The higher price for men versus women within the same age categories likely reflected the perception that men could perform certain required tasks of labor more so than women.[2] Contrary to a political charge of unequal wages, these were actually prices for workers who would then serve the sanctuary without monetary compensation, but rather in adequate food, clothing, and shelter. A dedicated person who may have been perceived as lesser than normal expectations could receive an examination and a lesser price from the priest. Hannah's gift of Samuel to serve Eli is a likely example of devoting a child in the 1-month to 5-year-old range under the prescription of Leviticus 27:6.

Verse 3 provides the monetary denomination for all value estimates in people and things vowed and redeemed: the shekel of the sanctuary. The sanctuary *shekel* was a weight equivalent to twenty *gerahs*.[3] A

---

2. Carol Ann Newsom and Sharon H. Ringe, ed., *Women's Bible Commentary*, expanded ed. (Louisville, KY: Westminster John Knox Press, 1998), 47.
3. See Exodus 30:13; Leviticus 27:25; Numbers 3:47; 18:16; Ezekiel 45:12.

gerah was a weight of approximately one half gram.[4] The shekel as money was a weight in silver. Eventually, under King David, a "king's shekel" or "royal shekel" measure of weight was formed (2 Samuel 14:26). This royal shekel likely weighed twenty-four gerahs instead of twenty.[5]

Dedicated animals

Leviticus 27:9-13

9: And if *it be* a beast, whereof men bring an offering unto the LORD, all that *any man* giveth of such unto the LORD shall be holy.
10: He shall not alter it, nor change it, a good for a bad, or a bad for a good: and if he shall at all change beast for beast, then it and the exchange thereof shall be holy.
11: And if *it be* any unclean beast, of which they do not offer a sacrifice unto the LORD, then he shall present the beast before the priest:
12: And the priest shall value it, whether it be good or bad: as thou valuest it, *who art* the priest, so shall it be.
13: But if he will at all redeem it, then he shall add a fifth *part* thereof unto thy estimation.

Verses 9-13 contain the regulations for vowing or dedicating animals to the sanctuary. The purpose for giving animals was for burnt offerings. Interestingly, animals dedicated through a vow and those required through the tithe underwent similar regulations. The ones giving clean animals were not supposed to check for quality. If one vowed a certain clean animal as a gift and then perceived that a different animal should be brought instead, **both** animals were considered "holy" and had to be dedicated. Apparently, God put these

---

4. Adele Berlin, Marc Zvi Brettler, and Michael A. Fishbane, eds., *The Jewish Study Bible: Jewish Publication Society Tanakh Translation* (Oxford: Oxford University Press, 1999), 290.
5. Ibid.

regulations in place to keep the Israelites to their word. One could not make a vow and then retract it or replace the thing vowed. God bestowed greater import upon the word of promise than that of quality control.

The regulations for unclean animals were much more lenient because unclean animals were not for sacrifices. Most likely, as with dedicated persons, these unclean animals were work force units and thus were traded for a price. Unlike the clean animals, the unclean animals could be later redeemed for their estimated value plus 20%. God most definitely placed this premium on redemption so that the Israelites would treat their vows and the priestly ministry with respect. This surcharge on redemption would prevent frequent recalls of vows and keep the sanctuary from becoming a common trading post. Also, if someone ate dedicated food by accident, that person would have to replace it with 20% extra (Leviticus 22:14-16).

Dedicated real estate

Leviticus 27:14-25

14: And when a man shall sanctify his house *to be* holy unto the LORD, then the priest shall estimate it, whether it be good or bad: as the priest shall estimate it, so shall it stand.
15: And if he that sanctified it will redeem his house, then he shall add the fifth *part* of the money of thy estimation unto it, and it shall be his.
16: And if a man shall sanctify unto the LORD *some part* of a field of his possession, then thy estimation shall be according to the seed thereof: a homer of barley seed *shall be valued* at fifty shekels of silver.
17: If he sanctify his field from the year of jubilee, according to thy estimation it shall stand.
18: But if he sanctify his field after the jubilee, then the priest shall reckon unto him the money according to the years that remain, even unto the year of the jubilee, and it shall be abated from thy estimation.

19: And if he that sanctified the field will in any wise redeem it, then he shall add the fifth *part* of the money of thy estimation unto it, and it shall be assured to him.
20: And if he will not redeem the field, or if he have sold the field to another man, it shall not be redeemed any more.
21: But the field, when it goeth out in the jubilee, shall be holy unto the LORD, as a field devoted; the possession thereof shall be the priest's.
22: And if *a man* sanctify unto the LORD a field which he hath bought, which *is* not of the fields of his possession;
23: Then the priest shall reckon unto him the worth of thy estimation, *even* unto the year of the jubilee: and he shall give thine estimation in that day, *as* a holy thing unto the LORD.
24: In the year of the jubilee the field shall return unto him of whom it was bought, *even* to him to whom the possession of the land *did belong*.
25: And all thy estimations shall be according to the shekel of the sanctuary: twenty gerahs shall be the shekel.

Verses 14-25 contain the regulations for vowing or dedicating real estate. Verses 14-15 set the rules for sanctifying houses and verses 16-25 provide the prescriptions for sanctifying "fields" or land. Sanctified houses for the priesthood required quality control for price. The priest would estimate the price based on the examined quality. Houses could be later redeemed with the trademark 20% surcharge over the estimated value.

One sanctifying a piece of land property was in reality selling the value of the amount of seed that could grow on it.[6] Every fiftieth year was the year of Jubilee in which slaves were set free and dedicated property was returned to the original owners (Leviticus 25). In reality the land that one "sold" for priestly use was actually "rented" until the

---

6. John F. Walvoord and Roy B. Zuck, eds., *The Bible Knowledge Commentary: Old Testament*, vol. 2 of *The Bible Knowledge Commentary: An Exposition of the Scriptures* (Colorado Springs: David C. Cook, 1983), 213.

year of Jubilee. The priest would estimate the appropriate price for the land based upon the length of time remaining until Jubilee. The longer the time until Jubilee, the higher the price for the land. As with houses, one could redeem the land dedicated for priestly use for its value plus 20%. However, if one did not redeem the land before the next year of Jubilee, the land would become permanently "holy" for priestly use.[7]

If one dedicated land for priestly use that one was leasing from another owner, the priest would have to pay the full estimated price for the time remaining for Jubilee on the same day. Possibly the reason that the estimate for land required prompt payment on the same day was to prevent one from selling a piece of land without a proper proof of ownership.[8] Uniquely with property, with the price rules for "leasing" to the priesthood, one would most often be able to redeem the land before Jubilee for a lower price than originally received.[9]

Firstlings are already dedicated

Leviticus 27:26-27

26 Only the firstling of the beasts, which should be the LORD's firstling, no man shall sanctify it; whether *it be* ox, or sheep: it *is* the LORD's.
27 And if *it be* of an unclean beast, then he shall redeem *it* according to thine estimation, and shall add a fifth *part* of it thereto: or if it be not redeemed, then it shall be sold according to thy estimation.

Verses 26-27 describe the rules for firstlings of animals. Unlike the things previously mentioned that people could "vow," "dedicate," or

---

7. Ibid., 213-214.
8. Samuel E. Balentine, *Leviticus*, vol. 3 of *Interpretation Commentary Series* (Louisville, KY: Westminster John Knox Press, 2002), 210.
9. James D. G. Dunn and John William Rogerson, eds., *Eerdmans Commentary on the Bible* (Grand Rapids: William B. Eerdmans Publishing, 2003), 123.

"sanctify" for ministerial use, firstlings were **already** dedicated by default. They were **already** "God's" from the start. Verse 26 states that the firstlings of clean animals are required for the ministry and cannot be redeemed; neither are they sold to the priesthood. Verse 27 states that the firstlings of unclean animals, however, can be redeemed. These animals are "sold" to the priesthood. The Law is much stricter on both vowed and firstlings for clean animals than for unclean animals. Because Israelites could only eat or sacrifice clean animals (except during some annual festivals), God required a reliable source of clean animals both for food and for offerings for the priests and Levites. The unclean animals likely provided a work force for the priesthood.

Firstlings and firstfruits were governed under similar laws. Firstlings were the firstborn of animals during the course of a year. Firstfruits were the first ripened crops from the harvest. Firstlings and firstfruits were both automatically "holy unto the LORD" and were required for certain functions. Many people will confuse firstfruits with tithes or think that firstfruits are the time or manner in which tithes were performed. However, firstfruits and tithes are completely different things in the Law. Their source, time, and regulations are different from tithes. Firstfruits are explained in greater detail in chapter 7 as well as their distinction from tithes.

Devoted for death?!

Leviticus 27:28-29

28: Notwithstanding no devoted thing, that a man shall devote unto the LORD of all that he hath, *both* of man and beast, and of the field of his possession, shall be sold or redeemed: every devoted thing *is* most holy unto the LORD.

29: None devoted, which shall be devoted of men, shall be redeemed; *but* shall surely be put to death.

Verses 28-29 can present a puzzling and disturbing inference for the reader who does not understand the divisions of the chapter, the contexts, and the Hebrew words. Verse 28 includes people, animals and land among "devoted things." Verse 29 then says that any "devoted" **people** cannot be redeemed, but must "surely be put to death." No doubt God was not implementing a policy of human sacrifice. One person did not own another in such a way that one could give another to the tabernacle for the priests to slay for devoted offerings. One commentary suggests that those people were dedicated to service were then required to remain in such service until the day that they died.[10] A keen reader, however, will understand that these two verses are exclusive of the ones above. "Devoted things" are not the same as the things that are "vowed" or "sanctified" in prior verses. If they were, then verses 28-29 would contradict the rest of the chapter because **nothing** "devoted" could be redeemed, whereas certain things "vowed" or "sanctified" could be redeemed.

Several possible interpretations exist for the phrase "shall surely be put to death" in verse 29 as it relates to devoting people in verses 2-8 and 28. One option is that the people "devoted" are those who are

---

10. Daniel Steele and John Wesley Lindsay, *Leviticus and Numbers*, vol. 2 of *Commentary on the Old Testament* (New York: Hunt and Eaton, 1891), 202.

committed to the religious authorities under the sentence of death.[11] Another suggestion is that these people are those whom the Israelites capture in battle and are executed at the command of God.[12] Still, another possibility is that these are killed for breaking the First Commandment and offering sacrifices to a false god.[13] Joshua's conquest of Jericho represents such an example event of things dedicated for death.[14] In fact, the Hebrew word for "accursed" in Joshua 6:17 for Jericho and all its spoils and inhabitants is from the same Hebrew word for "devoted" in Leviticus 27:29, and these words carry the idea of something "banned" or set apart for destruction.

The most probable explanation is that all these "devoted things," including the people, were spoils of war. The account of Achan after the battle of Jericho demonstrates disobedience to these verses. All "devoted" items such as clothes and money were "holy unto the LORD" and belonged in the sanctuary. All "devoted" or "banned" people and animals were to be killed. Often when God would command the Israelites to conquer Canaanite tribes, He would command them to kill all people and animals. Saul disobeyed the command to destroy the Amalekites by sparing King Agag and some

11. A. T. Chapman and A. W. Streane, *The Book of Leviticus in the Revised Version*, vol. 4 of *Cambridge Bible for schools and colleges* (Cambridge: Cambridge University Press, 1914), 155.

12. John Barton and John Muddiman, eds., *The Oxford Bible Commentary* (Oxford: Oxford University Press, 2001), 109.

13. Jacob Milgrom, *Leviticus: A Book of Ritual and Ethics: A Continental Commentary* (Minneapolis: Fortress Press, 2004), 331.

14. Balentine, 210.

of the animals for later burnt offerings. Because God claimed the spoils of His holy battles as "holy" to Himself, no one could redeem any such item. Nonliving things would be treasures for the sanctuary and living things—conquered people and animals—would be sentenced to death.

The tithe in context

Having studied the rest of Leviticus chapter 27, one can begin to understand the significance of the details of the tithe found in verses 30-33. Without the understanding of this context, and fresh with the assumptions and influence of modern tradition and practice, many resort to an extraction of the text without granting the verses the full consideration that they deserve. Understanding that these words were from God Himself, one should believe that every word He uttered to Moses for the Law has purpose and significance. However, until one is willing to commit the study and openness necessary, tradition will dictate both the portion of text quoted as well as the intended meaning or interpretation of the text.

Examples of less than complete or faithful citations of Leviticus 27:30-33 abound, and a select few are provided. Such examples demonstrate the temptation to eisegete or to import one's preliminary understanding rather than to let the text speak for itself. R. T. Kendall quotes Leviticus 27:30 as "All the tithe (NIV: 'a tithe of everything') . . . is the LORD's,"[15] quotes later "The tithe is the LORD's,"[16] and

---

15. R. T. Kendall, *Tithing* (Grand Rapids: Zondervan, 1983), 30.
16. Ibid., 34.

defines the tithe as "10% of our gross salary or wages, or 10% of our net gain if we are in business for ourselves."[17] The cover of a book by Presbyterian Pastor Elmer Bryan Stewart bears the words: "The tithe... is the LORD's; it is holy unto the LORD" with a reference to Leviticus 27:30.[18] George W. Brown presented the tithe as "the tenth part of one's net income, that is, the gross income minus necessary operating expenses." and then justified this by quoting, "The tenth shall be holy unto the Lord" from Leviticus 27:32.[19] A. W. Pink stated that "in Leviticus 27:30-32 we are told that the tithe is holy unto the Lord. That is to say, one-tenth is not **our own personal property** at all: it does not belong to us in the slightest; we have no say-so about it whatsoever it is set apart unto a holy use: it is the Lord's and His alone. [Emphasis added]"[20] J. L. Shuler references Leviticus 27:30, 32 and states: "This means that one tenth **of all the money we earn** is the Lord's tithe. [Emphasis added]"[21] Pastor Eddie Cude quotes Leviticus 27:30 correctly, but then restates: "This scripture states that all the tithe,

17. Ibid., 87.
18. Front cover of: Elmer Bryan Stewart, *The Tithe* (Chicago: The Winona Publishing Co., 1903).
19. George W. Brown, comp., *Gems of Thought on Tithing*, 2nd ed. (Cincinnati: Jennings & Graham, 1911), 38.
20. Arthur W. Pink, *Tithing* (Grand Rapids: Christian Classics Ethereal Library, 2007), 4. http://www.ccel.org/ccel/pink/tithing.html. Also available in print form and as PDF and Microsoft Word eBooks.
21. J. L. Shuler, *Helps to Bible Study* (Hagerstown, MD: Review and Herald Pub Assoc., 1990), 34.

whether it be seed of the land, fruit of the tree, **or one tenth of all that you earn**, is holy unto the Lord. [Emphasis added]"[22]

A lack of focus upon the words of the text of Leviticus 27:30-33 and a study of its context leads many to assume their own definition of the tithe from the standpoint that somehow it must apply to the Gentile church and outside its context of Leviticus 27:34: "These *are* the commandments, which the LORD commanded Moses for the children of Israel in mount Sinai." If the commandments relating to tithing were "for the children of Israel," the means, manner, and source of the tithe spelled in the commandments have purpose and determined the threshold of obedience. If a carpenter or blacksmith gave a tenth of the products that they made to the sanctuary, such things would fall under the laws of "freewill offerings" or "vows" from other passages and not the laws of the tithe.

Yahweh Himself defined the tithe as "of the land." Only things that came from nature that were raised or grown on the soil were subject to the tithe. Weapons, woodwork, pottery, and, of course, money were not subject to the tithe. Anything other than the "tithable commodities" specified in the passages of the Law—including Leviticus 27:30-33— would not fall under the requirements of "tithing." A tithe of crops and livestock was required. Crops and livestock donated to the sanctuary in addition to the tithe would be "freewill offerings" or "vows" depending upon the nature of the items. Anything else given to the

---

22. Eddie Cude, "What Does God's Word Say About The Tithe?," Bible Answers, http://www.bible.com/bibleanswers_result.php?id=161 (accessed January 5, 2010).

sanctuary, including vessels, land, weapons, and money would **always** fall under voluntary gifts because they were not subject to the tithe.

Some try to make "of the land" mean more than the context dictates. The Hebrew word for "land" is *eretz* meaning "soil" in particular. James Scott Trimm in a pamphlet published by the Worldwide Nazarene Assembly of Elohim argues: "In Hag. 2:8 YHWH says 'The silver is mine, and the gold is mine' the point is that everything we know is a product of the ERETZ (land/earth)."[23] Although it is true that gold and silver are products of the *eretz*, this argument ignores the entirety of the requirements of God's statement. God specified **exactly** the **two** "categories" of items that constituted "the tithe of the eretz:" crops that grow in the soil and herd animals raised on its surface. Attempting to derive logical implications of the meaning of a word is meaningless if it does not agree with the context. Also in passing, Haggai 2:8 has nothing to do with **tithing money**, but rather that such wealth for the people would come from God as He proclaimed how He would bless the nation of Israel if they would return to following His commandments.

When God said "of the land" He meant "of the Promised Land." Deuteronomy chapter 12 includes more tithe laws. Deuteronomy 12:1 states: "These *are* the statutes and judgments, which ye shall observe to do <u>in the land, which the LORD God of thy fathers giveth thee to possess it</u>, all the days that ye live <u>upon the earth</u>." The word for *earth*

---

23. James Scott Trim, *The Tithe of YHWH* (Hurst, TX: Worldwide Nazarene Assembly of Elohim, 2009), 9.

in the Hebrew (*eretz*) means "soil" or "terrain." In other words, certain statutes of the Mosaic Law were only intended, required, and enforced for operation within the boundaries of the Promised Land. The tithe of the crops and of the livestock was of only those grown and raised within the parcel of land that God gave the Israelites for their nation. In Deuteronomy chapter 12, God stated that He would designate a place where the people would bring their annual tithes (vv. 5-7, 10-14); this place would be named **only after** the Israelites successfully conquered the Canaanites (vv. 2-4, 8-9). Read chapter 5 for a deeper study of the tithe statutes in Deuteronomy chapters 12 and 14.

If the tithe was "of the land," being "of the seed" and "of the fruit of the tree," then it did not include anything that may have come into the borders of Israel from outside. These items were the "devoted" items that went to the sanctuary, but were not included in the tithe. If the tithe was also "of the herd," "of the flock," and "of whatsoever passeth under the [shepherd's] rod," the tithe of animals could not include things of a class that could not by nature walk under a shepherd's rod for counting. Clean sea animals such as fish (Deuteronomy 14:9) and unclean sea animals such as octopuses, clams and lobsters (Deuteronomy 14:10) would neither be "of the land" nor "of the herd" and would therefore not be subject to the tithe. Therefore, Peter, James, John, and other disciples of Jesus who were fishermen did not tithe of their fish. If they gave fish to the sanctuary, such would fall under "freewill offerings" or "vows."

Interestingly, Leviticus 27:32-33 is the only passage in the entire books of the Law that actually mentions such a tithe of animals.[24] Because of the apparent closure at the end of chapter 26, some theologians believe that Leviticus chapter 26 was actually a preliminary end to the book of Leviticus and that chapter 27 was added later.[25] Some Jewish historians and textual critics believe that the concept of a tithe of animals was a later practice introduced into the reading of Leviticus 27, and that at the actual giving of the Law only the tithe of crops was established.[26] Whenever chapter 27 of Leviticus actually came into existence and its subsequent tithe of animals, it is nevertheless a portion of inspired Scripture, and the practice of tithing animals shows up in Old Testament history (2 Chronicles 31:6).

The Biblical tithe vs. the tithe of money

As is clear from the text of Scripture, the Biblical tithe was of the crops and livestock and only from the boundaries of the Promised Land. Some attempt to explain this fact by assuming that the reason was only that Israel at the time was an "agrarian society." In other words, the tithe was allegedly based upon the prevailing **economy** of each Israelite and that the tithe was essentially equivalent to one tenth of the "income" at the time. A Messianic Jew writes: "Ancient Israel

---

24. *The Oxford Bible Commentary*, 109.
25. Walvoord and Zuck, 213.
26. Aharon Oppenheimer, *The 'am ha-aretz: A Study in the Social History of the Jewish People in the Hellenistic-Roman Period*, vol. 8 of *Arbeiten zur Literatur und Geschichte des hellenistischen Judentums Arbeiten Zur Geschichte Des Antiken Judentums Und Des Urchristentums*, trans. I. H. Levine (Leiden: E. J. Brill, 1977) 25-28.

lived in an agrarian society and thus were given instructions that would be understood by that culture, but we today basically live in an industrial society so we need to adapt our tithing accordingly."[27]

However, references to money in the Scriptures are prevalent, even in Genesis! Abraham was wealthy "in cattle, in silver, and in gold." (Genesis 13:2) When God instituted circumcision for Abraham, He mentioned servants purchased with silver money (Genesis 17:12, 13, 23, 27). Abimelech king of Gerar gave Abraham "a thousand *pieces* of silver" to recompense him for taking his wife Sarah from him (Genesis 20:16). Abraham sought to purchase a cave to bury his wife Sarah when she died "for as much [silver] money as it is worth" (Genesis 23:9) and eventually paid "four hundred shekels of silver." (Genesis 23:15-16) Abraham's servant told Rebekah that God had blessed Abraham with "flocks, and herds, and silver, and gold, and menservants, and maidservants, and camels, and asses." (Genesis 24:35) When Rebekah agreed to be Isaac's wife, the servant gave her "jewels of silver, and jewels of gold, and raiment." (Genesis 24:53) Jacob's wives Rachel and Leah became distressed when their father Laban had "devoured also our [silver] money." (Genesis 31:15) Jacob purchased a field for one hundred pieces of silver money (Genesis 33:19). The Midianites bought Joseph from his brothers for twenty pieces of silver money (Genesis 37:28). Joseph as ruler in Egypt restored silver money to his brothers (Genesis 42:25-44:8). Joseph

---

27. "Tithes and Tithing: A Study, by Yac'ob," Hebrew Messianic Israel, http://www.hmisrael.net/tithes_and_tithing.htm (accessed January 6, 2010).

under Pharaoh gave each of his brothers three hundred pieces of silver money (Genesis 45:22). Joseph alleviated the hunger of the Egyptians during the famine by exchanging their animals and land for bread because "the money failed." (Genesis chapter 47)

These are only references to money found in the book of **Genesis**. As the Scriptures demonstrate, the nation of Israel throughout all their history possessed and used money as a medium of exchange and as a source of income. Even in the New Testament the Jews still tithed only of crops and livestock according to the words of the Law as their economy was served with silver, gold, and copper money. Read chapter 14 of this book for an analysis of the monetary economy of Israel in the New Testament and the persisting practice of keeping the words of the Law by tithing of crops and livestock.

Pastor Bill Winston defines the tithe as "one tenth of all legal incoming cash (earned or unearned),"[28] "ten percent (10%) of all legal and legitimate (justified in scripture) financial increase,"[29] and "ten percent of all our (legal) income, profit, or financial increase."[30] Objecting to the idea of "tithing your time," he writes: "The tithe, in this day, is our medium of exchange—our money. If you read Malachi, chapter three, you will clearly see that God was not talking about talent or time."[31] While Winston is correct that one could not

---

28. Winston, 1.
29. Ibid.
30. Ibid., 3.
31. Ibid., 5.

Biblically tithe of time or talent, he is incorrect in his assumption of what constitutes a Biblical tithe. First, he merely assumes that a Biblical obligation to tithe exists "in this day." Second, he assumes that the Biblical tithe links to the "medium of exchange" in whatever applicable culture.

The Bible neither claims that a tithe applies to a "medium of exchange" nor a "source of income" under any culture—even Israel under the Law. According to Leviticus 27:30-34 the tithe was "of the land," "of the seed of the land," "of the fruit of the tree," "of the herd," "of the flock," and "of whatsoever passeth under the rod." Deuteronomy 14:22 restates: "Thou shalt truly tithe all the increase of thy seed, that the field bringeth forth year by year." Verse 34 of Leviticus chapter 27 clarifies that the commandments in this chapter, including these agricultural tithes were "for the children of Israel."

If one were to throw away all traditions and assumptions and study the text of the Scriptures afresh, one could not arrive at the modern teaching of the monetary income tithe doctrine. To teach today that the tithe applies to the church and is of monetary income, one most certainly received this doctrine through tradition, denomination, or parentage, and not a dedicated personal reading of the Scriptures themselves and in context, free from bias. If one were open and honest to the Scriptures, one would not be tempted to quote Leviticus 27:30 partially as "all the tithe...is the LORD's" and extrapolate this as a command to church members to part with a tenth of all their monetary income for the church treasury. Leviticus 27:30 and 32 clearly specify the **contents** of the tithe, and God did not forget to add anything if He so intended. Because verse 34 declares that all these statutes, including the vows and the tithes, were "for the children of Israel," applying these verses in Leviticus directly to the church is to read into the text of Scripture and ignore the plain words.

Another important nuance of the tithing statutes in Leviticus chapter 27 is the fact that the tithes did not necessarily equal 10% of the annual harvest and born livestock. The tithes were from the **tenth** of each item **counted**; they were not from the "first" tenth. In verse 32, the word for *tithe* and the word for *tenth* are different words. The word for *tithe* means a tenth portion whereas the word for *tenth* means the tenth in a sequence. In other words, the tenth animal counted from every animal that passed under the shepherd's rod was the tithe. If a landowner had 19 sheep born one year of harvest, the tithe would be 1 sheep and not 2 sheep or 1.9 sheep. The tithe of animals was from every tenth one **counted**. If the same landowner instead had 9 sheep born in a year, the tithe would be 0 sheep because he would have not counted any tenth animal. The statutes in Leviticus 27:30-33 regarding tithing do not match the mandate of the modern monetary income tithe doctrine to calculate exactly 10% of one's monetary income.

Although some tithe teachers will harshly preach the modern monetary income tithe doctrine and invoke the curse in Malachi 3:9, others will try to turn the tithe into a general "principle" whereby one receives blessings for following. Larry Burkett attempts to soften the tithe in the law and make it applicable to Christians by claiming the following:

> Although the tithe is mentioned in the law, no punishment was indicated for not tithing. There is a consequence (the loss of blessings), but there is *no* punishment from God for not tithing. The rewards of tithing are described in Malachi 3:10-11, where God promises to pour out a blessing and keep the devourer away. Tithing should always be a voluntary act on the part of God's people. [Emphasis in original][32]

Although no portion of Scripture in the Law that delineates tithes spells punishments in the exact context, the Scripture clearly shows that tithing, like other commands in the Law, carried both blessings for obedience and curses for disobedience. The last verse of Leviticus—27:34—declares that the tithe of the crops and animals mentioned immediately previous, and the other ordinances prior, are "commandments, which the LORD commanded." Deuteronomy 27:26 says "Cursed *be* he that confirmeth not *all* the words of this law to do them. And all the people shall say, Amen." Burkett skipped verses 8-9 of Malachi chapter 3, which demonstrate a curse for failure to follow the tithe laws. Although verse 11 promised blessings, these blessings represented the opposite of the curse that was happening in the land at that time related to the failure to obey the tithing commandments.

Redeeming the tithe

To those who import the idea of monetary "income" into the tithes of the Bible, Leviticus 27:30-33 presents a quandary of interpretations and applications for the concept of "redeeming the tithe." Charismatic

---

32. Larry Burkett, *Giving & Tithing* (Chicago: Moody Publishers, 1998), 29-30.

revivalist Dr. Rodney Howard Browne states the following about redeeming the tithe: "This meant that if someone had skipped out on the tithe they could come back to the Lord and they redeem it by adding one fifth to their tithe. It was a 'back-tithe.'"[33] George W. Brown presented the idea that this was a form of renting the tithe for severe needs and then paying it back later "with interest."[34] However, given God's disfavor of usury in lending funds,[35] the idea that God would exhibit such a type of hypocrisy is rather unlikely.

The *New International Bible Dictionary* explains this tithe redemption law as "a penalty of twenty percent" for eluding "to use the money [conversion medium for traveling to annual feasts] to pay for a substitute."[36] The tithe for annual feasts will be discussed in chapter 5 of this book. Contrary to the assertion of the *New International Bible Dictionary*, when one understands the tithe from the context of the whole chapter 27 of Leviticus, one can comprehend what the Scripture means by "redeeming the tithe" from the context of redeeming other things. If one wished to redeem something that one vowed as a gift to the sanctuary, one would have to purchase it back at its estimated value plus 20%. If one were to redeem a **vowed** unclean

---

33. Rodney Howard Browne, "Redeeming the Tithe,"
http://www.radicalchristiantv.com/2009/01/redeeming-the-tithe/ (accessed January 5, 2010).
34. Brown, 40.
35. See Exodus 22:25; Leviticus 25:36-37; Deuteronomy 23:19-20; Nehemiah 5:7-10; Psalm 15:5; Proverbs 28:8; Isaiah 24:1-3; Jeremiah 15:10; Ezekiel 18:8,13,17; 22:12.
36. J. D. Douglas and Merrill C. Tenney, eds., *New International Bible Dictionary* (Grand Rapids: Zondervan, 1987), s.v. "tithe."

animal back from the sanctuary, one would need to pay 120% of its value. If one were to redeem any of one's tithe of crops from the land back from the sanctuary, one would need to pay 120% of the estimated value. To redeem in this context means to purchase something back. When one purchased something, one obtained the item purchased. If one redeemed a tithe of crops, although that person had to pay extra for it, one would then possess the items that one purchased.

If the tithe were of money, a realistic, plain understanding of redemption would make no sense. If repurchasing a tithe at 20% extra is indeed what the Scriptures teach, then no rational reason would exist for one to pay $120 for the privilege of keeping $100. The reason that an option existed for one to redeem tithes is precisely **because** the tithe was **not** of money. Purchasing money with yet other money of the same currency is absurd. Although for one person the marginal utility of certain prize crops would be greater than 120% of their value in money, prompting the person to redeem them, no logical marginal utility exists to purchase $100 with $120. No idea of "borrowing at interest," "renting," or "late fees" influenced by the false notion of a tithe of monetary income can possibly reflect a correct and honest reading of tithe redemption from these verses. One should not force one's theology into the Scriptures; rather one must derive one's theology from the words of Scripture themselves. The obvious meaning of redeeming the tithe is to purchase the crops back for at premium personal use; thus the laws of redeeming tithes presents a logical bane for the modern monetary income tithe doctrine that would attempt to use any of Leviticus chapter 27 for support.

One might ask what the purpose was for redeeming the tithe and why only the tithe of crops could be redeemed and not the tithe of animals. A 20% tariff on purchasing back one's tithe of crops appears a hefty burden for anyone to pay without a good reason. One possible reason for permitting one to redeem the tithe of crops is to recover seeds to plant for next year's harvest.[37] A logical conclusion for the tithe of animals is that the primary reason this portion of the tithe could not be redeemed was that the priests needed a steady supply of animals for burnt offerings.

Conclusion and summary

In conclusion, we have examined the tithing statutes in Leviticus chapter 27 as well as the context of the whole chapter itself. The tithing statutes exist within the framework of things that are "holy unto the LORD." We have seen that "holy unto the LORD" applies to many things in the Law, and does not automatically consign the tithe to a universal obligation or principle for God's people of all ages. Leviticus chapter 27 specified the rules for things vowed for the sanctuary and which things could be redeemed after the vow for their estimated value plus 20%. Animals and people from spoils of war were sentenced to death, and goods from the spoils were devoted for the sanctuary.

---

37. Andrew Alexander Bonar, *Commentary on Leviticus* (Lafayette, IN: Sovereign Grace Publishers, 2000), 210.

The tithe was only from the boundaries of the Promised Land and only of crops grown and livestock raised therein. The tithe was never of money, nor was it ever of the products of crafts and trade. The people of Israel had money and used it; however, the tithes were not from one's "income," general "production," or the "medium of exchange." Tithes were never of fish or other sea animals either. The tithe falls under similar regulations as firstlings. Both tithes and firstlings were already "holy" and owed to the sanctuary. Like the firstlings of unclean animals, the tithes of crops could be redeemed. Like firstlings of clean animals, the tithe of animals could not be redeemed. These commandments were for the children of Israel. The plain, clear, and honest reading of Leviticus 27:30-34 and its regulations on tithes and their redemption raises many questions and problems for the modern monetary income tithe doctrine and provides no support for it whatsoever.

4. Inheritance Tax

The Levitical Tithe

Numbers 18:20-21

20: And the LORD spake unto Aaron, Thou shalt have no inheritance in their land, neither shalt thou have any part among them: I *am* thy part and thine inheritance among the children of Israel.
21: And, behold, I have given the children of Levi all the tenth in Israel for an inheritance, for their service which they serve, *even* the service of the tabernacle of the congregation.

Numbers chapter 18 is perhaps one of the least cited portions of Scripture from pulpits that references tithing. The reason, perhaps, is the lack of quick, witty, and quotable proof text verses and phrases that can express a general "principle" when divorced from context. Ironically, Numbers chapter 18 also provides some important information: the recipients of tithes and the purpose and reason for these tithes. One would think that an important study of this subject would warrant a careful analysis of the actual prescriptions for the tithes in the Law and their surrounding details. As Dr. Russell Earl Kelly notes: "any legitimate study of tithing should logically begin with the precise wording of the **ordinance** itself. [Emphasis in original]"[38]

Because many are swift to use Leviticus 27:30 or 32 for emphatic general instructions for tithing obligations for the church, and these verses are part of the Priestly Code in the Law, these same people should bear the inherent responsibility of claiming the text of the whole Law regarding tithing and all its nuances. In proper regard they have the further obligation of demonstrating and proving that all specifics of the Law regarding tithes have a reliable and reasonable parallel in the modern church setting. Furthermore, they must also prove these assertions not simply with logic, reasoning, or wishful thinking, but appropriate New Covenant Scripture texts. Failure to sustain any legitimate consultation of Leviticus 27:30,32, Malachi 3:8-10, or other segments of the Law for supporting the modern definition of tithing without fully reconciling these passages with other portions

---

38. Kelly, 32.

of the Law—such as Numbers chapter 18—necessarily fails the teaching. One cannot cherry pick parts of the Law to favor while disregarding other parts of the Law. The Law stands as a whole, and God gave the words of the whole Law for His divine reasons. Just as "all the tithe of the land... is holy unto the LORD" demands the context of the crops and livestock wherein this passage lies, so also any teaching of tithing requires the context of Numbers chapter 18 as bedrock and support. Just as God commanded the tithe in the Law for divine reasons, so also did He ordain its specifics and recipients for divine reasons.

The distinction between Levites and priests

Numbers 18:1

1: And the LORD said unto Aaron, Thou and thy sons and thy father's house with thee shall bear the iniquity of the sanctuary: and thou and thy sons with thee shall bear the iniquity of your priesthood.
2: And thy brethren also of the tribe of Levi, the tribe of thy father, bring thou with thee, that they may be joined unto thee, and minister unto thee: but thou and thy sons with thee *shall minister* before the tabernacle of witness.

Many people under the New Covenant who do not study the Mosaic Law do not realize the rigid distinction between the nature, duties, and privileges of the Levites and those of the priests. Lumping both together as a group of "ministers" in the Old Covenant "ministry," usually from a loose assumption of valid comparison to modern church structure, many fail to understand that the Pentateuch did not treat these two groups of people as anything close to similar. Although some of the duties overlapped, other duties were distinctly apportioned to one group over the other even under the penalty of death.

The Levites were obviously the descendents of Levi, son of Jacob (or "Israel"). As nominal descendents of Jacob, the Levites constituted one of the twelve tribes of the nation of Israel. Levi was the third son of Leah, Jacob's first wife (Genesis 29:31-35). For each of Leah's sons, she named them according to a response to God for his blessing and favor and her relationship with Jacob. Leah named her third son *Levi* because she believed that Jacob would be "joined to her" because God blessed her with three sons at that point (Genesis 29:34). The name *Levi* means "attached" or "joined." Interestingly, in Numbers 18:2, God tells the priests that they were to bring their Levite kin into the tabernacle to assist them "that they may be joined unto thee" (v. 2) and "they shall be joined unto thee." (v. 4) Most perceptively God intended these phrases in the Hebrew to be word plays on Levi's name, declaring that the Levites should be "Levi-ed" to the priests in their ministry.[39]

The priests were also descendents of Levi; however, the priests further branched from this division. The priests were Aaron and his descendents. The Levites who did not come from the family of Aaron could not serve as priests and perform priestly sacrifices on the altar in the tabernacle. Only descendents of Aaron could serve as priests. Conclusively, no man from the other tribes could perform the duties of

---

39. Robert Alter, *The Five Books of Moses: A Translation with Commentary* (New York: W. W. Norton & Company, 1996), 774.

a Levite other than a non-priestly Levite. Further, no man from any tribe except Levi could perform the duties of a priest other than a descendent of Levi through Aaron.

The Aaronic priesthood included an office of *high priest*. The high priest was a sole individual of the priests who performed special priestly functions. The high priest received this office through anointing of oil (Leviticus 21:10; Numbers 35:25) apparently through the collaborative consent of the priesthood as a whole.

God separated the Levites and the priests within the tribe of Levi for sacerdotal ministries in the tabernacle. For this service, these groups of men were to "bear the iniquity" of certain service. The phrase "bear the iniquity" means that the priests and Levites "suffer the consequences for any offense."[40] The Levites and priests as a whole would perform certain duties in the tabernacle and suffer any consequences associated with breaking their duties. However, the priests—Aaron and his descendents—would additionally perform the duties of the priesthood and suffer any consequences for violating those ordinances as well. Because the incident of Korah's rebellion lay fresh in the minds of the Israelites, God may have been emphasizing the graveness of breaking the boundaries of His divinely appointed sacred offices with this phrase.[41]

---

40. Harold W. Attridge and Wayne A. Meeks, eds., *The HarperCollins Study Bible*, rev. ed. (New York: HarperCollins, 2006), 227.
41. Alter, 773.

The privileges and responsibilities of the Levitical priesthood

The priesthood of Aaron was a mixed bag. It was not simply a privileged position of prestige. With the priesthood came both honors and great responsibilities. If the priests or Levites did not perform their duties properly or took them lightly, they would receive severe chastisement from God (Leviticus 10:1-3; 16:1-2; Numbers 18:32).

A common assumption of Jewish priestly practice for the Day of Atonement (Exodus 30:10; Leviticus 16:14-34; 23:26-32) is that the high priest had a rope attached to his leg as he entered to perform the sacrifice. Although the rope idea has no literal Scriptural support, such inference is not without logic. The high priest did have to wear special clothing that included golden bells while performing the atonement so that those outside the holy place could hear (Exodus 28:29-35). The non-Levite people of Israel could not come near or enter the tabernacle under penalty of death (Numbers 18:22). The non-priest Levites could enter the tabernacle but could not enter the holiest of holies where the altar and sacred vessels lay under penalty of death (Numbers 18:2-4). Only the priests could enter the holiest place and perform sacrifices upon the altar (Numbers 18:5,7-10). Thus, logically, the priests would need a method to extract a dead high priest who failed in his duties without themselves dying. Tying a rope upon the high priest's ankle would allow the priests to pull out a dead body if they ceased to hear the sound of the golden bells.

The sacred zones for the Levites and priests

Numbers 18:3-5

3: And they shall keep thy charge, and the charge of all the tabernacle: only they shall not come nigh the vessels of the sanctuary and the altar, that neither they, nor ye also, die.
4: And they shall be joined unto thee, and keep the charge of the tabernacle of the congregation, for all the service of the tabernacle: and a stranger shall not come nigh unto you.
5: And ye shall keep the charge of the sanctuary, and the charge of the altar: that there be no wrath any more upon the children of Israel.

The Levites were to assist the priests in most of the priestly duties in the tabernacle. In their aid and "apprenticeship" for the priests, the Levites had the privilege of serving in almost all areas of the tabernacle. Part of the duties of the Levites was to "keep the charge" of the priests. The word for *charge* in Hebrew most literally means "watch," "guard," "sentry," or "post." Possibly the Levites acted in such capacity in the tabernacle to keep unauthorized persons from entering the holy places. However, the word could have the more general connotation and refer to "maintenance."[42] Perhaps the Levites labored in the upkeep of the tabernacle in keeping it clean and functional, possibly repairing broken structures.

The Levites could serve the priests in every area of the tabernacle except in the most holy place. This area was called the "sanctuary" and only the priests could enter. The sanctuary contained certain priestly vessels and the altar for sacrifices. Whereas verses 3-4 obligate the Levites to "keep the charge" of the tabernacle, verse 5 obligates the

42. Ibid.

priests—and only the priests—to "keep the charge" of the sanctuary itself. Because only the priests could enter the sanctuary that housed the altar, only the priests could perform burnt offerings and sacrifices. The Levites could not perform such sacrifices. Sacrifices were a priestly function and the Levites were not priests. The Levites could possibly herd an animal to a priest near the entrance to the sanctuary, but only a priest could enter with the animal into the sanctuary and offer it upon the altar. God emphasizes the importance of this distinction by stating: "that there be no wrath any more upon the children of Israel." Likely again this reference stands from the heat of the destruction of Korah and his followers.

God granted an exception for a certain family of Levites known as the Kohathites. He permitted them to assist the priests with certain tasks in the sanctuary provided that the priests cover "the holy things" such as the vessels and items for burning incense and the altar for sacrifices (Numbers 4:17-20; 7:4-9). With such precise regulations one can see that God staunchly enforced the privilege of only the Aaronic priests to see the most holy things and that even the Levites could not perform anything that specifically involved mediation between God and the Israelites. The Levites could only assist the priests and help them with tasks that enabled them to perform their priestly duties.

The Levites as gifts to the priests

Numbers 18:6-7

6: And I, behold, I have taken your brethren the Levites from among the children of Israel: to you *they are* given *as* a gift for the LORD, to do the service of the tabernacle of the congregation.

7: Therefore thou and thy sons with thee shall keep your priest's office for every thing of the altar, and within the veil; and ye shall serve: I have given your priest's office *unto you* as a service of gift: and the stranger that cometh nigh shall be put to death.

The Levites were "gifts" to their priestly brethren (Numbers 3:9). They were the servants of the priests when they performed in the tabernacle, and, in essence, were lifelong apprentices. However, the Levites were not allowed to do certain things or attend certain places in the tabernacle. The Levites were servants for the priests and did not act in the capacity of priests themselves. For analogy, the priests were the bosses who performed certain work and the Levites were their employees. The Levites were obligated to act as servants to the priests in the tabernacle between the ages of 25 and 50 (Numbers 8:23-26). The tasks during this age range likely included the heavy labor. Before and after these ages, the Levites still were required to "minister" with the rest, but likely in a less physically demanding manner.

2 Chronicles 34:9-13 lists certain duties that groups of Levites performed in the Temple that later succeeded the tabernacle. Some "kept the doors" of the Temple (v. 9). Others "wrought in the house of the LORD, to repair and amend the house" (v. 10) and were "artificers and builders." (v. 11) Others were "workmen that had the oversight of the house of the LORD" who were "overseers" of the workers above (vv. 10,12,13). Others were musicians (v. 12), and others were "scribes, and officers, and porters." (v. 13) Although the Levites could structure themselves in roles and ranks for maintaining the tabernacle, the image of Levites as prestigious priests quickly fades when one

consults the Scriptures concerning their duties. Many of the Levites who ministered in the tabernacle and the later Temple did so by performing hard physical labor with their hands. New Testament examples of servants of the high priest who were likely Levites include Malchus (Matthew 26:51; Mark 14:47; Luke 22:50; John 18:10,26) the "servants" in the palace (Matthew 26:58; Mark 14:54), and the "maids" who kept the door of the high priest's palace (Mark 14:66; John 18:16).

Many mistakenly view the service of the Levites in the tabernacle with prestige. The Levites were not the ancient equivalent to modern "pastors" or even "assistant pastors" by any stretch of the imagination. The closer equivalent of Levites to the setting of the modern church would be that of janitors, construction workers, maintenance repairmen, secretaries, office workers and typists, service sequence coordinators, deacons, ushers, greeters, and other workers that contribute to the function and harmony of the ministry. Although the Levites assisted the priests in certain functions of the priesthood and tabernacle maintenance, they were servants who carried no prestige that one normally associates with a religious "clergy."

The priests received, burned, and ate the offerings

Numbers 18:8-11

8: And the LORD spake unto Aaron, Behold, I also have given thee the charge of mine heave offerings of all the hallowed things of the children of Israel; unto thee have I given them by reason of the anointing, and to thy sons, by an ordinance forever.

9: This shall be thine of the most holy things, *reserved* from the fire: every oblation of theirs, every meat offering of theirs, and every sin

88

offering of theirs, and every trespass offering of theirs, which they shall render unto me, *shall be* most holy for thee and for thy sons.
10: In the most holy *place* shalt thou eat it; every male shall eat it: it shall be holy unto thee.
11: And this *is* thine; the heave offering of their gift, with all the wave offerings of the children of Israel: I have given them unto thee, and to thy sons and to thy daughters with thee, by a statute for ever: every one that is clean in thy house shall eat of it.

The priests received all the "heave offerings" and had the oversight of stocking them for the time of their consumption. These heave offerings were from "the hallowed things of the children of Israel." Most likely these things were inclusive of all animals and food owed to the sanctuary in some form for priestly activity. These "holy things" that involved offerings, whether voluntary or involuntary, were things of which only the priests and their sons—who were priests in training—could partake. Anything "*reserved* from the fire," including grain offerings, other offerings that were not burned upon the altar, and meat from animals that were burned upon the altar were strictly for the priests and their sons to eat as they performed the associated priestly functions. These men could only eat these "in the most holy place" which was the sanctuary.

In contrast, the whole priestly families could eat "wave offerings" and they could respectively eat them in their homes. The wave offerings were portions of certain animal sacrifices that included the breast and the shoulders (Leviticus 10:14). The priests and their sons could eat certain other portions that were not burned on the altar, but they could take the "wave offering" portion—the breast and shoulders—back home to feed their families. Emphatically, the Levites are not included in any of these provisions and hence could not eat of these holy offerings.

Only members of the priestly families who were "clean" could eat any of the wave offerings. One who was "unclean" could not eat these things during the period of uncleanness. This period of being "unclean" was temporary and resulted from certain actions. A person was unclean if he or she had touched a dead carcass during the same day (Leviticus 5:2; 7:21; 11:1-47); a woman was unclean for seven days after giving birth to a son (Leviticus 12:1-4) and for two weeks after giving birth to a daughter (Leviticus 12:5).

The priests received firstfruits

Numbers 18:12-13

12: All the best of the oil, and all the best of the wine, and of the wheat, the firstfruits of them which they shall offer unto the LORD, them have I given thee.
13: *And* whatsoever is first ripe in the land, which they shall bring unto the LORD, shall be thine; every one that is clean in thine house shall eat *of* it.

Verses 12-13 restate the fact that the firstfruits of things produced from the soil of the Israelite landowners were unconditional property of the sanctuary, as found in Exodus 23:19 and 24:26. Conclusively, only the priests and their families could eat of the holy firstfruits. Their Levite kin could not partake of this privilege. All members of a priest's family could eat of the firstfruits except those who were "unclean." Once again, only those who were officially "clean" could partake of the firstfruits. Deuteronomy 26:1-11 prescribes certain rituals associated with the reception of firstfruits from the people of Israel and is discussed in detail in chapter 7 of this book.

The priestly side of dedicated and redeemed items

Numbers 18:14-19

14: Everything devoted in Israel shall be thine.
15: Everything that openeth the matrix in all flesh, which they bring unto the LORD, *whether it be* of men or beasts, shall be thine: nevertheless the firstborn of man shalt thou surely redeem, and the firstling of unclean beasts shalt thou redeem.
16: And those that are to be redeemed from a month old shalt thou redeem, according to thine estimation, for the money of five shekels, after the shekel of the sanctuary, which *is* twenty gerahs.
17: But the firstling of a cow, or the firstling of a sheep, or the firstling of a goat, thou shalt not redeem; they *are* holy: thou shalt sprinkle their blood upon the altar, and shalt burn their fat *for* an offering made by fire, for a sweet savour unto the LORD.
18: And the flesh of them shall be thine, as the wave breast and as the right shoulder are thine.
19: All the heave offerings of the holy things, which the children of Israel offer unto the LORD, have I given thee, and thy sons and thy daughters with thee, by a statute for ever: it *is* a covenant of salt for ever before the LORD unto thee and to thy seed with thee.

Leviticus chapter 27 discussed in the previous chapter delineated the regulations for dedicating and vowing animals and property for the sanctuary from the perspective of the people of Israel. This portion of Numbers chapter 18 describes the ordinances of dedicated and vowed items from the side of the priests. Remember that Levites are not priests. Animals and other things that the people of Israel devoted, dedicated, vowed, and sanctified were all for the priests specifically and not for the Levites. "Everything devoted," the animals and people "which they [the Israelites] bring unto the LORD," "the firstling," and "the heave offerings of the holy things, which the children of Israel offer unto the LORD" are all sacred gifts to the priests.

This passage in Numbers chapter 18 repeats some of the requirements for devoted items and redeeming them. Of all things that "openeth the matrix" that the people of Israel devote to the LORD are gifts for the priest's use. "Openeth the matrix" simply means things that give birth through the womb. Such a category includes living creatures such as people and animals and excludes plants or nonliving items. From this category, certain things can be redeemed: the firstborn of people and unclean animals. "Shalt thou redeem" means that the priests must allow the people of Israel to redeem these sold sanctuary animals and people from the priesthood on demand. The priests could not legally refuse a valid request for redemption any more than an Israelite could legally refuse to devote a firstling or a tithe. Of course, for any redeemed item the Israelite had to pay a 20% surcharge over the estimated value of these items when redeeming them.

Verse 16 repeats the regulations of Leviticus 27:6. Interestingly, Numbers chapter 18 only lists one category of vowed people—children—and their redemption price; however, such would not conflict with Leviticus chapter 27. Perhaps only listing one regulation in retrospect was a form of index in Hebrew to imply the whole from which the indexed portion comes.

Only firstborn people and unclean animals sold to the sanctuary could be redeemed, or bought back. Only things sold could rightly be redeemed. Firstfruits of crops and firstlings and tithes of animals were automatically required of the people for the priesthood and could not be sold to the sanctuary. Naturally, neither could these items be redeemed. Verse 17 provides some insight into the reason that God especially required the firstlings and tithes of animals to be irredeemable—the priests needed them to perform burnt offerings and sacrifices. According to verse 18, a certain portion of these animals, apart from that required for the fire of the altar, was for food for the priests.

Verse 19 recaps that everything that the Israelites freely grant to the sanctuary are specifically gifts for the priests and their families alone. This was "a statute forever" and metaphorically "a covenant of salt." In other words, this was an enduring covenant that God granted to the priesthood that He would not revoke as long as the Aaronic order remained intact. Salt was a preservative for food; hence, the symbolism is apparent for something that would last. Furthermore, salt is also a seasoning and retains its taste, and God required it as a symbol of covenant in meat offerings (Leviticus 2:13).[43]

Land inheritance vs. tithe inheritance

Numbers 18:20-24

20: And the LORD spoke unto Aaron, Thou shalt have no inheritance in their land, neither shalt thou have any part among them: I *am* thy part and thine inheritance among the children of Israel.
21: And, behold, I have given the children of Levi all the tenth in Israel for an inheritance, for their service which they serve, *even* the service of the tabernacle of the congregation.
22: Neither must the children of Israel henceforth come nigh the tabernacle of the congregation, lest they bear sin, and die.

---

43. *The Bible Knowledge Commentary*, 236.

23: But the Levites shall do the service of the tabernacle of the congregation, and they shall bear their iniquity: *it shall be* a statute forever throughout your generations, that among the children of Israel they have no inheritance.
24: But the tithes of the children of Israel, which they offer *as* a heave offering unto the LORD, I have given to the Levites to inherit: therefore I have said unto them, Among the children of Israel they shall have no inheritance.

In this passage God tells Aaron that he and the priesthood would have no inheritance in the Promised Land. God also reiterates that He told the Levites that they had no inheritance in the land either. God clarifies that He gave all the Levites—which included the priests—"all the tenth in Israel" as an inheritance and as a reward for their service in the tabernacle. The tithes of crops and livestock were to be their inheritance. The tithes **replaced** their inheritance in the Promised Land. They received tithes strictly because God did not even allow them to own land (vv. 20,24). As Matthew Henry explained: "The Levites have the honour of attending the tabernacle, which is denied the Israelites; but then the Israelites have the honour of inheritances in Canaan, which is denied the Levites."[44]

The Levites dwelt in a total of 48 "Levitical cities" throughout the Promised Land, and they were allowed to own the houses and suburbs therein to care for their families (Leviticus 25:32-34; Numbers 35:1-8; Joshua 21:1-3, 41-42). However, they could not own parcels of land sufficient to farm animals. The land on which they worked to farm and

---

44. Matthew Henry, *Matthew Henry's Commentary*, ed. Leslie F. Church (Grand Rapids: Zondervan, 1961), 161.

herd animals for most of the year belonged to people from other tribes. These 48 cities housed certain families of Levites and the priests. The Aaronic priests, who were of the Kohathite Levites eventually dwelt in a total of 13 cities on land that other tribes owned (Joshua 21:4,9-19).[45] The rest of the Kohathite Levites were allotted 10 cities (Joshua 21:5,20-26). The Gershonite Levites dwelt in 13 cities (Joshua 21:6,27-33). The Merari Levites lived in 12 cities (Joshua 21:7,34-40). Prior to settling the Promised Land and building the Levitical cities, when God required the tabernacle to be moved during the wanderings and conquest of Canaan, the Levites had to camp in tents around the tabernacle so that they could dismantle it to carry it to the new location (Numbers 1:48-54).

Contrary to any attempt to relate Old Covenant Levites with New Covenant church ministers, the tithes did not simply replace compensation for labor; the tithe also replaced ownership. Church "pastors," elders, and so-called church "clergy" today take some of the money that they receive from so-called "tithes" of monetary income from members of the church and use this money as any other citizen and church member in the secular marketplace. They will also purchase real estate, including houses, land, and facilities. The children of Levi under the Old Covenant did not possess such a privilege from God.

Mega-church television minister John Hagee, pastor of Cornerstone Church in San Antonio, Texas, who often preaches the

---

45. Kelly, 35.

modern monetary income tithe doctrine, owns a house worth nearly three quarters of one million dollars, a nearly 8000-acre parcel of ranch land in Texas, and another large portion of land that he has yet to exploit fully.[46] Another mega-church television minister Rod Parsley, pastor of World Harvest Church near Columbus, OH, also teaches a similar tithing doctrine and owns a guarded 16-acre portion of land with million-dollar homes for both his family and his parents respectively.[47] He also owns property for getaways, two vehicles worth a total of $120,000, and a private jet.[48] Popular Word of Faith minister Kenneth Copeland, head of Eagle Mountain International Church in Newark, Texas and ministry bases in countries around the world, claims that "tithes" go to "where a pastor, an evangelist, an apostle or some other ministry is in operation."[49] Kenneth Copeland owns a $3.6 million private jet and a $6 million personal mansion among other

46. Lou Dubose, "John McCain's Minister of War," *The Washington Spectator* (April 1, 2008),
http://www.washingtonspectator.org/articles/20080401ministerofwar.cfm (accessed January 15, 2010).
47. Dennis M. Mahoney, "Higher aspirations," *The Columbus Dispatch* (August 21, 2005), http://www.dispatch.com/live/contentbe/dispatch/2005/08/21/20050821-A1-00.html (accessed January 15, 2010).
48. Nate Anderson, "Meet the Patriot Pastors," *Christianity Today* (November 3, 2006), http://www.christianitytoday.com/ct/2006/november/21.46.html (accessed January 15, 2010).
49. "Understanding Tithing," *Kenneth Copeland Ministries*,
http://www.kcm.org/real-help/article/understanding-tithing (accessed January 15, 2010).

things associated with his ministry.[50] Many other such prosperity gospel preachers could be mentioned that own large assets who predictably teach the modern monetary income tithe doctrine with a twist that allows television viewers to owe them their "tithe."

The point of these facts is not to deny these people the right as citizens to own certain properties and obtain measurable wealth if through honest gain. The point is that these ministers have no right to claim a Biblical right to receive tithes and also own property related to real estate. The Scriptures only qualified the Levites and the inclusive priesthood of Aaron to receive tithes of crops and livestock from the Promised Land. Qualifying for these tithes also disqualified them from being able to earn any type of monetary income from a "second job," participate in the marketplace of merchant assets, or own any parcel of land not allotted to them congruent to their houses in the Levitical cities. One has no Scriptural right to claim to be the recipient of Biblical tithes and also purchase and own property that could otherwise belong to one who could not qualify for tithes. Any church "clergy," regardless of their economic status, have no Biblical basis to "have their cake and eat it too" by attaining both the benefits of tithes and property ownership as regular citizens.

Interestingly, the fact that the tithes for the Levites were always only from crops and livestock in the land of Canaan enforces the fact

---

50. "Kenneth Copeland," *Chicago Tribune* (July 27, 2009), http://www.chicagotribune.com/features/religion/chi-kenneth-copeland-080727-ht,0,7366686.story (accessed January 15, 2010).

that they could not own an inheritance of land. Because the tithes were not money, the Levites could not conduct such economical acts of marketplace trading to acquire property. Lest one bring the accusation that the Levites would hence live in poverty, the opposite is the case. Although the Levites and poor were included in classes of people who could partake of certain tithes, the Levites as a class were certainly well-to-do. With the job of ministering in the tabernacle the Levites appreciated a solid and steady standard of living from tithes of food that was guaranteed to keep them from undue hunger. The Levites were the least populous tribe of Israel out of a total of twelve, yet they received one-tenth (rather than one-twelfth) of the produce of the land.[51] Just because the Levites could not freely participate in leisurely marketplace economics nor compound to themselves personal estates does not mean that they were anywhere close to being "poor."

Simply the tenth—the tithe for the Levites

The non-priestly Levites—ones who did not descend from Aaron—received tithes of crops and livestock from the landowners of the other tribes of Israel. These tithes consisted of every tenth item counted. For animals, the tithe was every tenth herd animal that passed under the shepherd's rod in counting. Those who were required to give these tithes were instructed not to inspect them for quality but only to separate every tenth item in counting sequence (Leviticus 27:30-33).

---

51. *Matthew Henry's Commentary*, 161.

The people of Israel were not to tithe the **best**, they were to tithe the **tenth**.

Simply the best—the tithe of the tithes for the priests

Numbers 18:25-30

25: And the LORD spake unto Moses, saying,
26: Thus speak unto the Levites, and say unto them, When ye take of the children of Israel the tithes which I have given you from them for your inheritance, then ye shall offer up an heave offering of it for the LORD, *even* a tenth *part* of the tithe.
27: And *this* your heave offering shall be reckoned unto you, as though *it were* the corn of the threshingfloor, and as the fullness of the winepress.
28: Thus ye also shall offer an heave offering unto the LORD of all your tithes, which ye receive of the children of Israel; and ye shall give thereof the LORD'S heave offering to Aaron the priest.
29: Out of all your gifts ye shall offer every heave offering of the LORD, of all the best thereof, *even* the hallowed part thereof out of it.
30: Therefore thou shalt say unto them, When ye have heaved the best thereof from it, then it shall be counted unto the Levites as the increase of the threshingfloor, and as the increase of the winepress.

Whereas God required the landowners in the Promised Land by His Law **not** to check for the quality of their numbered tithes, but rather simply to yield every tenth item counted, God commanded the Levites to yield to the priests the **best** tenth of these tithes that they received from the people to the priests. This distinction in the nature of the tithes demonstrates yet another difference between the priests and the other Levites. The non-priestly Levites received their tithes directly from the landowners of the other tribes of Israel. The priests received their tithes from the Levites—a tenth of their tithes. Whereas the tithes of the Levites could include "good or bad" items, the Levites had to yield the best tenth of these to the priests. Hence, the Levites could never legally experience what it was like to eat the "best" food available.

Modern tithe teachers attempting to advance the idea of a monetary income tithe doctrine rarely address these nuances. Rarely do they attempt to weave the distinction of the Levitical tithes and the priestly tithes into the doctrine. Often, if they mention the idea of a "best tithe," no true exegesis of Scripture creates a viable similarity between Old Covenant tithes and alleged New Covenant "tithes."

Incidentally, an estimation of quality to identify the "best" of tithes of crops and livestock is possible; however, with monetary income, all units carry equal value.[52] Unless one would resort to claiming an implausible comparison that the "best" tithe of tithes today would be the newest or crispest paper dollars or the shiniest coins, the priestly tithe from this passage carries no realistic application for the New Covenant. Crops and livestock have detectable levels of quality that manifest themselves in texture, flavor, or quantity of edible portions. Fiat money provides no marketable level of quality or value in the matter of exchange whether or not paper currencies are crisp or wrinkled or coins are shiny or culled.

Freedom to eat everywhere

Numbers 18:31-32

31: And ye shall eat it in every place, ye and your households: for it *is* your reward for your service in the tabernacle of the congregation.

---

52. Michael L. Webb and Mitchell T. Webb, *Beyond Tithes & Offerings*, ed. Sharon Y. Brown (Tacoma, WA: On Time Publishing, 1998), 85.

32: And ye shall bear no sin by reason of it, when ye have heaved from it the best of it: neither shall ye pollute the holy things of the children of Israel, lest ye die.

As a reward to the Levites for their work in the tabernacle, the Levites were allowed to eat their tithes anywhere. Reasonably, this meant that they could eat the tithes in the tabernacle while working and also at home with their families. Whereas the priests could only eat certain parts of certain sacrifices that came from their tithes on the job in the tabernacle, the Levites could eat any part of their lesser quality tithes at any place they desired. As a blessing for "heaving the best" tenth of their tithes to the priests, the Levites were allowed more freedom for when and where they could eat them. In keeping with the separation of Levites and priests, God reminded them that they were not allowed to see, touch, or otherwise "pollute" certain things that belonged to the priests and their work.

The Levitical priesthood vs. church ministers

It is important to note that the Mosaic Law required anyone who received tithes to be a descendent of Levi. This means that anyone from the other tribes could not qualify under any condition. The qualification to receive tithes was not derived from a special "calling" associated with skills, talents, desires, or spirituality. Those born under Levi automatically received tithes throughout their lifetimes. Tithes were not part of specific occupations. All Levites received tithes. Both men and women Levites performed some functions in the tabernacle ministry. Both the duty and privilege of receiving tithes was tied to a bloodline, and not from a spiritual occupation that one would achieve upon acquiring a college degree and gathering a group of followers.

Church ministers who teach the modern monetary income tithe doctrine not only have the theological burden to prove that Biblical tithes apply today, that they properly represented "income" in ancient Israel, and that they can truthfully operate from comparable sources of money; but they also must prove that church ministers under the New Covenant have the Scriptural authority to demand or receive such "tithes" pertaining to their position. Most modern tithe-teaching ministers will use 1 Corinthians 9:13-14 as a Scriptural link between the Old Covenant Levitical priesthood and the New Covenant church ministry involving tithes. Read chapter 18 for a lengthy analysis of this passage of Scripture to determine the identity of "they which preach the gospel" and the nature of their livelihood.

Conclusion and summary

In conclusion, we have examined the whole of Numbers chapter 18. This chapter of the Scriptures forms the bedrock for explaining the tithing system of the Mosaic Law. This chapter lists many of the ordinances that make up the Levitical tithes. As well as some important similarities, Numbers chapter 18 explains the stark distinction between the duties and privileges of the priests and those of the other Levites regarding tabernacle ministry and tithes.

The non-Levite people of Israel could neither enter the tabernacle nor get near it. The Levites could enter the tabernacle and minister in it as servants to the priests; however, they could not enter the holiest place—the sanctuary. The priests could enter the sanctuary and perform the required mediatory sacrifices and atonements for the nation. The Levites were "gifts" to the priesthood. The office of a Levite was neither prestigious nor sacerdotal, and often involved much manual labor.

The Levites and priests could not own land. The ministry of the tabernacle and the tithes of crops and livestock replaced their inheritance. They were "separated" from the people of the other tribes and could not acquire personal estates in the marketplace. They resided in certain Levitical cities. They could "own" their houses and adjacent yards as necessary to care for their families, but could not own or purchase other real estate. Many church ministers teach a doctrine of monetary tithes of income for church ministry and that they have the Biblical right to receive from these tithes, yet they ignore the Biblical requirement that those who received tithes could not own land or accumulate estates.

The Levites received tithes of crops and livestock directly from the people of Israel. These tithes could have included "good or bad" items as they were the tenth of everything counted in sequence. The Levites, in turn, had to offer the best tenth of these—a tithe of the tithes—to the priests. They could eat these tithes anywhere they wished or needed. Attempting to extrapolate tithes from the Mosaic Law to the church in a monetary context makes the "best" requirement implausible. Numbers chapter 18 emphatically provides no support for the modern monetary income tithe doctrine.

5. Food, Fun, and Fellowship

The Annual Tithe Festival

Deuteronomy 14:22-23

22: Thou shalt truly tithe all the increase of thy seed, that the field bringeth forth year by year.
23: And thou shalt eat before the LORD thy God, in the place which he shall choose to place his name there, the tithe of thy corn, of thy wine, and of thine oil, and the firstlings of thy herds and of thy flocks; that thou mayest learn to fear the LORD thy God always.

Deuteronomy chapters 12 and 14 are yet more passages that provide actual regulations and purposes for tithing in the Law that rarely, if ever, find their way into sermons propounding a monetary income tithing mandate to church members. In fact, not only do these passages explain tithing in ways that would frustrate proof texting, but also they introduce perplexing allowances that can make many "fundamentalists" squirm.

Although few may dare to attempt to extract Deuteronomy 14:22 as support for church "tithing," those that do ignore the significance of the wording of the verse and especially the passage of verses that immediately follow. These verses explain exactly what to do with the tithe, where to do it, when to do it, why to do it, and with whom to do it. Obviously as mentioned earlier, God did not give the Law for people to cherry pick favorable portions. God gave the Law for its recipients to obey as a whole and to regard every detail. The people of Israel to whom God gave the Law were forbidden from adding to the words or removing from them (Deuteronomy 4:2; 12:32) and had to heed all the words (Deuteronomy 12:28; 17:19; 27:26; 28:58; 29:9; 30:8).

James 2:10 declares that breaking one part of the Law makes one guilty of the whole law. In other words, if one is guilty of violating a statute in the Law, one is officially a Law-breaker. One cannot simply choose parts of the Law to follow and nullify other parts. God did not have such an erroneous principle in mind when He gave the Law. If one in the New Covenant wishes to hold onto certain ordinances in the Law as binding for oneself whereas other ordinances are not, one must have clear Scripture to prove such an assertion regarding the ordinances in question. Likewise, if one wishes to change the terms of an ordinance to extrapolate it into another context, one must have clear Scripture that permits this with the specific ordinance in question. When God gave the Law, He did not merely imply principles, He delineated specifics. Either the ordinance and its specifics apply, or the ordinance itself does not.

Eating the Levitical tithe?

In the previous chapter we observed that the law in Numbers chapter 18 stated that God had "given the children of Levi all the tenth in Israel for an inheritance." The people were required to give the Levites "all the tenth." Now, Deuteronomy chapter 14 commands the people to eat the tithe. For purposes of this discussion, this will be treated as a different tithe from the Levitical tithe—the festival tithe. Many Bible and Hebrew scholars disagree about if these were separate tithes or the same tithe. Arguments exist for the presence of one, two, or three separate tithes in the Mosaic Law. Read chapter 6 of this book for a discussion and evaluation of different arguments for the number of tithes.

The *when* of this tithe—settling in the Promised Land

Deuteronomy chapters 12 and 14 demonstrate a continuity of regulations regarding tithing for the nation of Israel, and both chapters are part of the same block of laws that begins in Deuteronomy 10:11 and ends in Deuteronomy 26:19. Necessarily, the Law provides context for the regulations. This context is just as important to understand the regulations as the regulations are themselves. The following are a list of verses in this passage of laws that clearly denote the context of the laws themselves:

Deuteronomy 11:31-32

31: For ye shall pass over Jordan to go in to possess the land which the LORD your God giveth you, and ye shall possess it, and dwell therein.
32: And ye shall observe to do all the statutes and judgments which I set before you this day.

Deuteronomy 12:1, 8-10, 29

1: These *are* the statutes and judgments, which ye shall observe to do in the land, which the LORD God of thy fathers giveth thee to possess it, all the days that ye live upon the earth.
8: Ye shall not do after all *the things* that we do here this day, every man whatsoever *is* right in his own eyes.
9: For ye are not as yet come to the rest and to the inheritance, which the LORD your God giveth you.
10: But *when* ye go over Jordan, and dwell in the land which the LORD your God giveth you to inherit, and *when* he giveth you rest from all your enemies round about, so that ye dwell in safety;
29: When the LORD thy God shall cut off the nations from before thee, whither thou goest to possess them, and thou succeedest them, and dwellest in their land;

106

Deuteronomy 19:1

1: <u>When the LORD thy God hath cut off the nations</u>, whose land the LORD thy God giveth thee, and thou succeedest them, <u>and dwellest in their cities</u>, and in their houses;

Deuteronomy 26:1

1: And it shall be, <u>when thou *art* come in unto the land</u> which the LORD thy God giveth thee *for* an inheritance, and possessest it, <u>and dwellest therein</u>;

These are some of the verses that plainly demonstrate the temporal context for the laws in this passage. Most, if not all the laws applied to the nation of Israel only as they dwelt in the land of Canaan. God gave all these laws to Moses during their forty-year trek through the wilderness. The nation of Israel was not required to follow these laws in particular until they passed over the Jordan river, overthrew the Canaanites, were safe from invasion, and dwelt in the land. In fact, these laws—particularly the ceremonial ones—only applied to the nation of Israel **within the land of Canaan**. Deuteronomy 12:1 makes this assertion clear: these laws applied to the Israelites "in the land which the LORD your God giveth you." This verse also clarifies that the Israelites were to follow these laws "all the days that ye live upon the earth." The word translated *earth* is the Hebrew word *adamah*, which means "soil." This word still references the land of Canaan. The Israelites were required to follow these laws **when** they obtained the land of Canaan and **as long as** they lived in this land.

The *what* of this tithe—crops and livestock

Deuteronomy 12:17-18

17: Thou mayest not eat within thy gates <u>the tithe of thy corn, or of thy wine, or of thy oil</u>, or the firstlings of thy herds or of thy flock, nor any of thy vows which thou vowest, nor thy freewill offerings, or heave offering of thine hand:

18: But thou must eat them before the LORD thy God in the place which the LORD thy God shall choose, thou, and thy son, and thy daughter, and thy manservant, and thy maidservant, and the Levite that *is* within thy gates: and thou shalt rejoice before the LORD thy God in all that thou puttest thine hands unto.

Deuteronomy 14:22-23

22: Thou shalt truly <u>tithe all the increase of thy seed, that the field bringeth forth year by year</u>.

23: And thou shalt eat before the LORD thy God, in the place which he shall choose to place his name there, <u>the tithe of thy corn, of thy wine, and of thine oil</u>, and the firstlings of thy herds and of thy flocks; that thou mayest learn to fear the LORD thy God always.

As we witness from these tithe laws in Deuteronomy chapters 12 and 14 the tithe still consists exclusively of food products from "the field" of the land of Canaan. The Law painstakingly lists the components of the tithe to indicate that it comprised only food items. John MacArthur comments on Deuteronomy 14:22 that "the tithe (lit. 'a tenth') specified in these verses was only that of the agricultural produce which the land would provide."[53] Corn, wine from grapes, and oil from olives all constituted food items grown from the soil. These were things "that the field bringeth forth year by year."

Naturally, as one would conclude from the requirement of observing certain Mosaic Laws **within the boundaries of the land of Canaan**, that the tithe laws included would only be of food substances linked to these respective boundaries. If the tithe were of money, the

---

53. *The MacArthur Bible Commentary*, 216.

people of Israel could have tithed of their gold and silver that they acquired from the Egyptians in the exodus. They could have tithed during the wilderness wanderings. However, God dictated to Moses that these laws were for the nation of Israel **only** when they conquered the Canaanites and settled in the Promised Land. The tithe laws specifically applied to this land and God required that all tithes be produce **only** from within these boundaries.

The *where* of this tithe—Jerusalem

Deuteronomy 12:5-6, 11, 17-18

5: But unto the place which the LORD your God shall choose out of all your tribes to put his name there, *even* unto his habitation shall ye seek, and thither thou shalt come:

6: And thither ye shall bring your burnt offerings, and your sacrifices, and your tithes, and heave offerings of your hand, and your vows, and your freewill offerings, and the firstlings of your herds and of your flocks:

11: Then there shall be a place which the LORD your God shall choose to cause his name to dwell there; thither shall ye bring all that I command you; your burnt offerings, and your sacrifices, your tithes, and the heave offering of your hand, and all your choice vows which ye vow unto the LORD:

17: Thou mayest not eat within thy gates the tithe of thy corn, or of thy wine, or of thy oil, or the firstlings of thy herds or of thy flock, nor any of thy vows which thou vowest, nor thy freewill offerings, or heave offering of thine hand:

18: But thou must eat them before the LORD thy God in the place which the LORD thy God shall choose, thou, and thy son, and thy daughter, and thy manservant, and thy maidservant, and the Levite that *is* within thy gates: and thou shalt rejoice before the LORD thy God in all that thou puttest thine hands unto.

Deuteronomy 14:22-26

22: Thou shalt truly tithe all the increase of thy seed, that the field bringeth forth year by year.

23: And thou shalt eat before the LORD thy God, in the place which he shall choose to place his name there, the tithe of thy corn, of thy wine, and of thine oil, and the firstlings of thy herds and of thy flocks; that thou mayest learn to fear the LORD thy God always.

24: And if the way be too long for thee, so that thou art not able to carry it; or if the place be too far from thee, which the LORD thy God shall choose to set his name there, when the LORD thy God hath blessed thee: 25: Then shalt thou turn it into money, and bind up the money in thine hand, and shalt go unto the place which the LORD thy God shall choose: 26: And thou shalt bestow that money for whatsoever thy soul lusteth after, for oxen, or for sheep, or for wine, or for strong drink, or for whatsoever thy soul desireth: and thou shalt eat there before the LORD thy God, and thou shalt rejoice, thou, and thine household,

Another indicator that the Israelites could only tithe when they dwelt in the Promised Land is that God declared in the tithing regulations that He would establish one particular location where the people would be required to bring their tithes. The tithe here did not just involve an amount, a source, and a time; it involved a specific place. Notice also that God said that He "shall choose" the place. This is future tense, proving that the requirement to tithe was not until the people conquered the land, thus obtaining possession of the location which God would choose.

The location was very important. The people could perform these tithes to satisfy all other requirements; however, if they did not bring them to God's specific location, God would not consider them legitimate to following the Law. The divided kingdom began after the death of Solomon with Jeroboam over the northern land of "Israel" and Rehoboam over the southern land of "Judah." (1 Kings 11:31-43) Because Jeroboam, ruler of the northern kingdom, understood the requirement of bringing offerings, sacrifices, and tithes to Jerusalem, which resided in the southern kingdom, he broke the Law by establishing two replacement "high places"—one in Bethel and another in Dan—and priests who were neither Aaronites nor Levites to keep his subjects from potentially following Rehoboam (1 Kings 12:26-33). Jeroboam mimicked Aaron's ancient fault by constructing a golden calf for each of these cities and declared that they were "thy gods, O Israel, which brought thee up out of the land of Egypt."

Jeroboam tried to appease the people of the northern kingdom because these two cities had special religious and historic significance. Bethel was where Jacob made his tithe vow to God (Genesis 28:18-22). Dan was the name of a city that the people of the tribe of Dan conquered from the Canaanites for their dwelling place and for certain worship to God (Judges 18). Both these cities would be convenient for the whole populous of the northern kingdom to keep them from having to travel to Jerusalem. All these acts of breaking the law became known as "the sin of Jeroboam" or the acts "that made Israel to sin."[54]

Amos 4:4-5

4: Come to Bethel, and transgress; at Gilgal multiply transgression; and bring your sacrifices every morning, *and* your tithes after three years:
5: And offer a sacrifice of thanksgiving with leaven, *and* proclaim and publish the free offerings: for this liketh you, O ye children of Israel, saith the Lord GOD.

Ironically, the rural prophet Amos lived during the time of Jeroboam II of the northern kingdom (Amos 1:1). Apparently the city of Gilgal became another city where the people of the northern kingdom established a sanctuary for partially following the Law and angering God. Gilgal is the city where the people of Israel offered

---

54. See 1 Kings 13:34; 14:16; 15:30,34; 16:2,19,26; 21:22; 22:52; 2 Kings 3:3; 10:29,31; 13:2,6,11; 14:24; 15:9,18,24,28; 17:21; 23:15.

sacrifices to God to celebrate Saul's coronation as king (1 Samuel 11:14-15). The people of the northern kingdom of Israel were attempting to parade their false observance to the Law by bringing sacrifices and tithes to the cities of Bethel and Gilgal. Although *Bethel* means "house of God"[55] and was where Jacob made a tithe vow, and *Gilgal* means "rolling" to celebrate that God "turned" or "rolled away" the suffering under Egypt,[56] these two cities did not qualify as "the place which the LORD thy God shall choose to set His name there." Only Jerusalem qualified (1 Kings 12:27).

The *how* of this tithe—annual feasts

According to Deuteronomy 14:22, the tithe was an **annual** activity. If one is to use this verse as a proof text for tithing, one would need to observe the requirements. The requirements would be to tithe **from the field** and to do this **once per year**. This requirement served in tandem with the fact that the feasts themselves were held **once per year**. One cannot accurately claim to be following this verse by tithing of **monetary income** and by doing this daily, weekly, biweekly, monthly, or any other non-annual interval.

Deuteronomy 16:5-6, 10-11, 13-15

5: Thou mayest not sacrifice <u>the passover</u> within any of thy gates, which the LORD thy God giveth thee:
6: But <u>at the place which the LORD thy God shall choose</u> to place his name in, there thou shalt sacrifice the passover at even, at the going down of the sun, at the season that thou camest forth out of Egypt.

---

55. Watson E. Mills and Roger Aubrey Bullard, eds., *Mercer Dictionary of the Bible* (Macon, GA: Mercer University Press, 1990) s.v. "Bethel."
56. Ibid., s.v. "Gilgal."

10: And thou shalt keep the feast of weeks unto the LORD thy God with a tribute of a freewill offering of thine hand, which thou shalt give unto the LORD thy God, according as the LORD thy God hath blessed thee:
11: And thou shalt rejoice before the LORD thy God, thou, and thy son, and thy daughter, and thy manservant, and thy maidservant, and the Levite that is within thy gates, and the stranger, and the fatherless, and the widow, that are among you, in the place which the LORD thy God hath chosen to place his name there.
13: Thou shalt observe the feast of tabernacles seven days, after that thou hast gathered in thy corn and thy wine:
14: And thou shalt rejoice in thy feast, thou, and thy son, and thy daughter, and thy manservant, and thy maidservant, and the Levite, the stranger, and the fatherless, and the widow, that are within thy gates.
15: Seven days shalt thou keep a solemn feast unto the LORD thy God in the place which the LORD shall choose: because the LORD thy God shall bless thee in all thine increase, and in all the works of thine hands, therefore thou shalt surely rejoice.

The harvest was used to "fund" several conglomerate annual feasts in Israel. These feasts, described in Deuteronomy chapter 16, include the Passover, the Feast of Weeks, and the Feast of Tabernacles. The tithe, in particular, at the end of the harvest was used for the Feast of Tabernacles. The requirements for the seven-day Feast of Tabernacles correspond to the requirements in Deuteronomy chapters 12 and 14. For each of the three feasts, the people of Israel were to celebrate them "at the place which the LORD thy God shall choose," which became Jerusalem. In these feasts, the people were to eat with their households and share their food with the Levites and poor. The purpose of each of these feasts was to remember the blessings of God and to rejoice before Him. We will seek to understand the significance of rejoicing before God and fearing Him later in this chapter. The Feast of Tabernacles happened at the end of harvest, or "after that thou hast gathered in thy corn and thy wine." If any of the tithe "funded" any of the feasts, most of it likely was used for the Feast of Tabernacles.

The *why* of this tithe—to eat, rejoice, and fear the Lord

Deuteronomy 12:7, 12

7: And there ye shall eat before the LORD your God, and ye shall rejoice in all that ye put your hand unto, ye and your households, wherein the LORD thy God hath blessed thee.
12: And ye shall rejoice before the LORD your God, ye, and your sons, and your daughters, and your menservants, and your maidservants, and the Levite that is within your gates; forasmuch as he hath no part nor inheritance with you.
18: But thou must eat them before the LORD thy God in the place which the LORD thy God shall choose, thou, and thy son, and thy daughter, and thy manservant, and thy maidservant, and the Levite that is within thy gates: and thou shalt rejoice before the LORD thy God in all that thou puttest thine hands unto.

Deuteronomy 14:23, 26

23: And thou shalt eat before the LORD thy God, in the place which he shall choose to place his name there, the tithe of thy corn, of thy wine, and of thine oil, and the firstlings of thy herds and of thy flocks; that thou mayest learn to fear the LORD thy God always.
26: And thou shalt bestow that money for whatsoever thy soul lusteth after, for oxen, or for sheep, or for wine, or for strong drink, or for whatsoever thy soul desireth: and thou shalt eat there before the LORD thy God, and thou shalt rejoice, thou, and thine household,

An overriding theme in the passages of the book of Deuteronomy related to this tithe and the annual feasts is that the people were **to rejoice** before God. Interestingly, although Deuteronomy 16:15 describes the Feast of Tabernacles as "a solemn feast," God commanded the people that they "surely rejoice" (or "only rejoice"). The annual feasts were meant to be a joyous occasion and not merely a command to follow.

The reason that the people were to rejoice was that they were celebrating the fact that God had provided abundantly for them. They were to rejoice "in all that thou puttest thine hands unto." (Deuteronomy 12:18). They were to rejoice recognizing that God had given an abundance through their labors in the field. Why should not they rejoice? They were eating the fruits of their labor. Although God told them to rejoice, it would be absurd to assume that this command was a rigid requirement that resulted in reluctant obedience. Most people enjoy eating, and would have no problem rejoicing in the activity of a feast.

How often do the walls of a church assembly echo with the words of Deuteronomy chapters 12 and 14 in any sermon regarding tithing? For the most part, Christians are told to

A Jewish Passover

"pay" their tithes to the church. They are told to yield their tithes to the church treasury "for God's work." They are told to do this with joy, but they are not informed about the annual feasts of the Law. They are told that they cannot "keep back" any part of their tithe and that they must wholly give it away. If they are lucky enough to hear a monetary application of Deuteronomy 14:22, they most likely would never hear the next verse. They are told that "giving is its own reward," and "paying their tithe" is both a requirement and a cheerful act. Absent is the fact that the Israelites **ate from their own tithe** used for the feasts.

God also told the people that in their practice of segregating tithes for annual festivals was so "that thou mayest learn to fear the LORD thy God." Was God simply telling them to fear Him because He was God and giving a command? Most likely the purpose of "fearing the LORD" meant much more. How would an annual practice of setting apart a tithe of produce only to eat it later in a certain place teach a person to fear God?

One can find a reasonable answer by understanding the fact that the tithes were only of food from the land of Canaan. Because the tithe consisted only of crops and livestock from the land of Canaan, the tithe itself and its source of abundance depended entirely on God's sovereign providence in nature. God controlled the weather—the wind, rain, and temperature—involved in producing the food and its tenth for the feasts. Therefore, the people of Israel realized in eating their feasts that they were celebrating the provision from God in blessing their land particularly. They realized that the food that they depended on for daily sustenance and of that which they ate in a joyous festival came only because God blessed the climate of the land. Peter C. Craigie, Associate Professor of Religious Studies at the University of Calgary, comments that the people would learn to fear God because "their prosperity did not depend on irrigation or advanced agricultural techniques, but on the benevolence and provision of their God."[57]

One can see a link to Malachi 3:10-12 in "learning to fear the LORD" in a tithe of food from the land. During the time of Malachi the appropriate tithes were being withheld from the storehouse in the Temple. According to the words of Malachi, the nation likely was suffering a famine or a drought as a result. God said that if the appropriate tithes returned to the Temple storehouse, He would reverse the course of the weather and return the nation to agricultural blessing. The people did not tithe of monetary income or from anything that could be the product of human skills and trades. They could only tithe of things that God specially provided from the specific portion of land that God gave Israel in which to dwell. The quantity and quality of the harvest and hence the quantity and quality of the tithe itself for the festivals depended solely on God's sovereign control of the weather. Whether the people obeyed God's Law determined how He would control the weather either to bless or to punish them. Thus, with this principle in mind, the yearly act of eating one's tithe in a festival would truly teach one to fear God.

The role of money in the festival tithes

Deuteronomy 14:24-26

24: And if the way be too long for thee, so that thou art not able to carry it; or if the place be too far from thee, which the LORD thy God shall choose to set his name there, when the LORD thy God hath blessed thee:

---

57. Peter C. Craigie, *The Book of Deuteronomy* (Grand Rapids: William B. Eerdmans Publishing, 1976), 233.

25: Then shalt thou turn *it* into money, and bind up the money in thine hand, and shalt go unto the place which the LORD thy God shall choose: 26: And thou shalt bestow that money for whatsoever thy soul lusteth after, for oxen, or for sheep, or for wine, or for strong drink, or for whatsoever thy soul desireth: and thou shalt eat there before the LORD thy God, and thou shalt rejoice, thou, and thine household,

Although strictly none of the tithes in the Law could come at all from a source of money, money did play a vital role in the festival tithe. Money served purely as a conversion medium to make transportation easier. Naturally when God divided the land for inheritance for each of the tribes, many people would dwell in cities and houses far from Jerusalem. Having to horde a full tenth of all crops and livestock for a journey of several days to Jerusalem would be unduly burdensome for wealthy landowners.

To alleviate such a burden, God allowed those who lived a respectable distance away from the sanctuary to convert the tithe to silver money. According to the *New International Bible Dictionary*, money served as a medium to carry tithes to the feasts, at which the people would use this money "to buy **substitutes**. [Emphasis added]"[58] The *HarperCollins Bible Dictionary* explains this requirement that to facilitate distant travel to the Temple, the tithe "could be converted to cash and **replacement** food could be bought for consumption at the Temple. [Emphasis added]"[59] The permission to convert the tithe to money for travel purposes was conditioned on converting the money

---

58. *New International Bible Dictionary*, s.v. "tithe."
59. Paul J. Achtemeier, ed., *HarperCollins Bible Dictionary*, rev. ed. (New York: HarperCollins, 1996), s.v. "tithe."

back to food proper for the feasts. In other words, people would sell titheable commodities for money, bring the money to Jerusalem, and purchase back titheable commodities fit for the feasts. The tithe was always food.

This passage proves distinctly that God specified the tithes as food—and only food—for a reason. The tithe was not of agricultural produce because that was the "money" or "income" of the day and culture. The tithe was not food because Israel was "an agrarian society." The tithe was only of food because it could come only from within the boundaries of the land of Canaan. The source depended upon God's sovereign control of the weather. The tithe was meant to be **eaten** and **to feed** the Levites and poor. The nation of Israel used money, such as in units of silver, for market transactions. The Levitical code established "the shekel of the sanctuary" as a monetary weight for certain functions, including annual sanctuary taxes and selling and redeeming certain dedicated people and items.

Increase vs. income—the profit analogy

The tithe was neither from "money" nor from "income." The tithe was from the annual **increase** of the harvest. New crops that grew during the year and new animals that were born constituted the source of the tithe, not general income from any endeavor. Only landowners tithed. In fact, any landowner during the course of a year would receive monetary income from selling non-holy portions of the harvest and would face costs incurred from fertilizer, wages for hired hands, and storage. A more appropriate comparison—if one could be possible—would be that of tithing from **profit**, not **income**. **Profit = Revenue – Costs**. The tithe was from the **increase** of the harvest, which would include only tangible food assets not owed to anyone. A landowner would have both income and outgo, but the resulting **increase of the harvest** was the source of tithes. No one tithed of anything owed elsewhere. No one tithed from debt. No one tithed from a source that was subject to "bills" or credit. No one in the nation of Israel ever legally tithed from any source of **income**, whether of money or of food.

Replying to a question about withholding "tithing" until debts are paid, R. T. Kendall states: "It is a sin, a high crime, not to pay your 'debt' to God—the tithe."[60] Confusing Biblical tithes with monetary income and confusing *income* with *increase*, most proponents of the modern monetary income tithe doctrine will present such a case that one is obligated to "tithe first" from money that otherwise would be used to pay off debts. Because tithes in the nation of Israel came only from the **increase of the harvest**, and not from the pot of money from which revenues and costs manipulated, any Biblical "model" of tithing from the Law would **not** involve tithing from any source of obligation. Debts, responsibilities, and thrift are a topic for another discussion, but the point exists from proper understanding of the tithe laws that no landowner ever tithed from debt.

---

60. Kendall, 95.

The effects of enlarged borders on festival tithes

John MacArthur explains that "the people would live further and further away from the central sanctuary."[61] The discrepancy between Deuteronomy chapters 12 and 14 regarding "if the place be too far from thee" can possibly be solved from Deuteronomy 12:20. The requirement of Deuteronomy 14:24-26 that those far from the sanctuary must covert the tithe to silver money, bring this money to the sanctuary, and convert it back to food items likely was enforced at the beginning of settlement of Canaan. After God "enlarged the borders" of the nation of Israel, the distance could become too great that the Levitical law could officiate a change in the Law that those farthest away could celebrate their annual tithe festival within their own remote community rather than trek to Jerusalem. Nevertheless, animals required for sacrifices at the sanctuary were unconditionally required for the sanctuary.[62]

Permissions of the festival tithe—drinking wine and strong drink

Deuteronomy 14:26-27

26 And thou shalt bestow that money for whatsoever thy soul lusteth after, for oxen, or for sheep, or for wine, or for strong drink, or for whatsoever thy soul desireth: and thou shalt eat there before the LORD thy God, and thou shalt rejoice, thou, and thine household,
27 And the Levite that *is* within thy gates; thou shalt not forsake him; for he hath no part nor inheritance with thee.

Those who lived far away could sell their tithe for money to make the trip easier, bring the money to Jerusalem, and buy back food for

---

61. *The MacArthur Bible Commentary*, 214.
62. Ibid.

the feasts. Perplexedly, God Himself dictates that those with the monetary medium could purchase "wine" and "strong drink." The Hebrew word for "wine" here is *yayin*, which in most contexts of the Old Testament refers to a fermented juice from grapes or other fruit. A teetotaler (including the author of this book) can reasonably argue that *yayin* is not intoxicating in all occurrences. For instance, *yayin* can generally refer to anything from "the vine," whether fresh or fermented;[63] however, in many instances, the word *yayin* specifically assumes fermentation.[64] The only way to attempt to distinguish between the two is context. Whatever these terms meant, the people were to include the Levites.

Most often when *yayin* ("wine") is associated with *shekar* ("strong drink"), both are implicated as fermented. Thus, when Deuteronomy 14:26 lists both *yayin* and *shekar*, the natural textual assumption is that these terms are conveying the idea of beverages that can potentially intoxicate. For the purposes of alcoholic beverages, *yayin* can be the fermented juice of grapes whereas *shekar* is most likely a fermented drink from other sources, such as grains.[65] "Strong drink" in this passage cannot be dark coffee, ginseng tea, or JOLT.

---

63. See Genesis 49:11-12; Numbers 6:3-4,20; Deuteronomy 28:39.

64. See Genesis 9:21,24; 19:32-35; Deuteronomy 29:6; Judges 13:4,7,14; 1 Samuel 1:14-15; 25:36-37; 2 Samuel 13:28; Esther 1:7,10; Psalm 78:65; Proverbs 20:1; 23:29-35; 31:4-7; Ecclesiastes 2:3; 10:19; Isaiah 5:11-12,22; 24:9-11; 28:1,7,9; 51:21; 56:12; Jeremiah 23:9; 51:7; Daniel 1:5,8,16; Hosea 4:11; Joel 1:5; Micah 2:11; Habakkuk 2:5.

65. Abraham ben Meïr Ibn Ezra, *The Commentary of Abraham ibn Ezra on the Pentateuch*, ed. Jay F. Shachter (Hoboken, NJ: Ktav Publishing House, 2003), 67.

Make no mistake, the Scriptures contain not a few strong statements about the sin of drunkenness and the very likely harm of alcoholic beverages. Is God contradicting Himself in Deuteronomy 14:26? Absolutely not! Although God strictly prohibits drunkenness—abuse of alcohol—He permits responsible use of alcohol for certain activities. Similarly, God strictly prohibits gluttony—the abuse of food—but He does not forbid food itself. Just as gluttony is the **abuse** of food so drunkenness is the **abuse** of alcohol. Some things people need more than others. One needs larger quantities of certain vitamins than that of lipids or fatty acids. In the case of alcohol the average person does not even need any alcohol at all for daily nutrition.

Alcohol, like medicine, possesses certain sedative properties that can be harmful if ingested in more than minute quantities. In fact, one use for alcohol **is** as a medicine (Proverbs 31:6-7; 1 Timothy 5:23). Most medicine is not intended for casual use or to ingest for mere pleasure. Too much aspirin can cause side effects ranging from headaches to a coma.[66] Novocaine can be used as an anesthetic in dentistry with the appropriate doses, but can be harmful if used illicitly. Many people will use counter-top medicines that contain alcohol to treat a common cold or flu and to induce sleeping.

Clearly, the Scriptures as a whole condemn drunkenness and abuse of alcohol, but permit it for special occasions and as a medicine. Even the most ardent abstinence proponent must concede that God at least

---

66. "Aspirin," *Drugs.com*, 2009, http://www.drugs.com/aspirin.html (accessed January 29, 2010).

permitted consumption of alcoholic beverages during the annual tithe festival. *The Student's Commentary on the Holy Scriptures* states that "total abstinence from [fermented] wine is written in the Scriptures from one end to the other."[67] *The Student's Commentary* then proceeds to explain this allowance as follows: "As to the permission of verse 26, the liquors were to be drunk before the Lord. This fact would make excess and drunkenness impossible."[68] In other words, according to the commentary, because God permitted the use of a dangerous substance, He must have sovereignly supervised its use under His commandment to prevent any transgression.

Permissions of the festival tithe—the unclean can eat

In the Mosaic Law several acts, such as touching a dead corpse, could cause an Israelite to become ceremonially "unclean." Depending upon the action, the status of "unclean" could last until the next morning or for several days. While one was "unclean," one could not eat certain permissible portions of animals used in certain sacrifices (Leviticus 7:20). If any food was "holy," only those who were ceremonially clean could eat of it. Although God segregated the tithe for feasts, He clarified that the festivals were not off limits for the ceremonially unclean. The unclean as well as the clean could eat from any permissible food available in the tithe festivals.

---

67. George Williams, *The Student's Commentary on the Holy Scriptures*, 6th ed. (Grand Rapids: Kregel Publications, 1981), 101.
68. Ibid.

The only requirement for both the unclean and the clean was that they could not eat the blood of any permissible animal of which they ate the meat. Distinctly for sacrificial animals the fat, certain organs, and certain portions of the meat were for burnt offerings. The priests could then eat the remaining portion of meat. God expressly clarified in these festival regulations that both the clean and unclean could eat any part of any clean animal available at Jerusalem. No parts were segregated for burnt offerings. The only requirement was that no one was allowed to eat the blood because "the blood *is* the life; and thou mayest not eat the life with the flesh." (Deuteronomy 12:23) They were to strain out the blood from the meat before preparing it.

Conclusion and summary

In conclusion, we have examined the festival tithe as God described in the Mosaic Law in Deuteronomy chapters 12 and 14. We understand that God's Law was given with specific purpose and that no one has a right to divide it or change it without God's permission. The tithing regulations were included in several ceremonial laws that God prescribed specifically for the nation of Israel only for their presence in the land of Canaan. Only when the nation successfully conquered and dwelt in the land, and as long as they stayed in the land, were they obligated to follow these laws. The tithes for the annual festivals were only of crops and livestock and only from within the boundaries of the land of Canaan. The tithes of food were required for several feasts in Jerusalem, and the people were not allowed to eat them elsewhere. The people who tithed ate their own tithes with their households and the nearby Levites. The purpose of the tithe festivals was to rejoice and to fear the Lord, understanding the He blessed them and controlled the climate.

Those who lived far from Jerusalem could ease their travel burden by converting their tithes to money, and converting their money back to food at Jerusalem. At the feasts the people were allowed to drink fermented beverages, and the ceremonially unclean could partake equally in the feasts. The tithes were never of money nor of income. They were from the increase of the harvest. The most accurate possible analogy is that of profit rather than income. Because of the nature of the tithes expressed in these laws, the role of money as strictly a transportation medium, and the fact that tithes were more comparable to profit rather than income, these laws provide absolutely no support for the modern monetary income tithe doctrine.

6. The Third Time's a Charm

The Year of Tithing and the Sabbatical Cycle

Deuteronomy 14:28-29

28: At the end of three years thou shalt bring forth all the tithe of thine increase the same year, and shalt lay *it* up within thy gates:
29: And the Levite, (because he hath no part nor inheritance with thee,) and the stranger, and the fatherless, and the widow, which *are* within thy gates, shall come, and shall eat and be satisfied; that the LORD thy God may bless thee in all the work of thine hand which thou doest.

Deuteronomy 26:12-14

12: When thou hast made an end of tithing all the tithes of thine increase the third year, *which* is the year of tithing, and hast given *it*

126

unto the Levite, the stranger, the fatherless, and the widow, that they may eat within thy gates, and be filled;
13: Then thou shalt say before the LORD thy God, I have brought away the hallowed things out of *mine* house, and also have given them unto the Levite, and unto the stranger, to the fatherless, and to the widow, according to all thy commandments which thou hast commanded me: I have not transgressed thy commandments, neither have I forgotten *them*:
14: I have not eaten thereof in my mourning, neither have I taken away *ought* thereof for *any* unclean use, nor given *ought* thereof for the dead: *but* I have hearkened to the voice of the LORD my God, *and* have done according to all that thou hast commanded me.

The previous chapter of this book discussed the festival tithes. Mysteriously, the final two verses of Deuteronomy chapter 14 inject briefly a very important command for the nation of Israel that raises questions about the nature of tithing and how it was organized. These final two verses denote a "break" from the rest of the chapter. The regulations concerning the tithe in festivals are different from the regulations in these verses regarding the use of the tithe "at the end of three years." The tithe every third year served an entirely different purpose from the festival tithe.

The practice of the year of tithing—wholly given away

According to Deuteronomy 14:28-29 and 26:12-14, this tithe every three years was not for the tithers to eat, unlike the festival tithe. The tither even had to confirm this command with an oath. This oath included that the tither did not use any part of this third-year tithe for anything other than its intended and commanded use—to give to the Levites and poor. In this oath, the tither had to state that he had not eaten any part of it when he was "mourning" (sorrowful from affliction). Likely, the tither vowed that he did not yield to any temptation to eat from this tithe when he was sick or felt "poor." The tither also had to vow that he had not used this tithe "for *any* unclean *use*." This could mean that the tither did not allow a carcass to make someone unclean who shared in the tithe, thereby defiling the entire tithe.[69] Finally, the tither had to vow that he did not give any of the tithe "for the dead." Possibly this meant that the tither did not use any of the tithe as a gift to relieve mourning friends and family of lost loved ones.[70] Another possibility is the prohibition of pagan funeral rites in which one would leave food or money with corpses in their burial so that their souls could use them in the economy of the afterlife.[71] Some Chinese cultures still perform such a practice by issuing "Hell Bank" notes and credit cards for the dead to exchange in the underworld.[72]

Regardless of the charitable possibilities, the third-year tithes were not allowed for any other purpose than to deposit in the local community. One had to bring the tithe as a whole and publicly demonstrate that this contribution represented the entire tithe. Though this tithe was for the Levites and poor, perhaps one was not allowed to segregate any portion specifically for a Levite or poor person outside

---

69. Samuel Rolles Driver, *A Critical and Exegetical Commentary on Deuteronomy*, 3rd ed. (Edinburgh: T & T Clark, 1902), 291.
70. Ibid.
71. Ibid., 291-292.
72. Grant Evans and Maria Tam, eds., *Hong Kong: The Anthropology of a Chinese Metropolis* (Honolulu: University of Hawaii Press, 1997), 244.

this means of depositing in the community bins for that purpose. The Levites and poor needed a reputable source for sustenance.

The recipients of the year of tithing—Levites and poor

Apparently the tithe for every third year—the "year of tithing"—was not for eating at annual festivals but for giving wholly away to the Levites and to the poor. An emphasis seems to be present in this "year of tithing" that, unlike the festival tithes just described, the people yielding this tithe every three years could not eat any of it. They were to "lay *it* up within [their] gates" from which the Levites and poor could glean and eat. Rather than "thou shalt eat there before the LORD," Deuteronomy 26:12 says that this third-year tithe was so that "they [the Levites and poor] may eat within thy gates, and be filled." Clearly, this third-year tithe was not taken to the city of the sanctuary for the annual feasts, but was laid up **at home**. The Levites and the poor, including certain resident foreigners, who lived near a tithing landowner would glean and eat from these tithes available "within thy gates" or within the boundaries of the city where the landowner dwelt. A local storage building may have existed in each city for tithers to bring these tithes so that the Levites and poor had a reliable place to seek food as needed.[73]

Did the poor tithe?

Most who teach a form of tithing for the context of Christians and the church do not heed the specifics of the Law. Because tithes only

---

73. Driver, 167.

came from the **increase** of crops and livestock from the land, naturally only those who **owned** land were responsible to tithe from it. Tailors did not tithe of the clothing that they made, nor of the monetary revenue that they received from sales. Fishers did not tithe of the fish that they caught because the contents of the tithe included crops from the soil, and livestock raised on the soil—flocks and herds. The tithe specifically had to do with the parcel of land that God had promised to the nation of Israel. Only those who owned land had to tithe from food that came from the portion of land that they owned.

The poor were likely among those who owned no land. The "fatherless" were likely orphan children. The "widows" were likely older women who had little possessions and lacked the capacity to work and to feed themselves from their own labor. If the tithe every third year was **for the poor**, naturally it would not also be required **of the poor**. The poor would not be tithing to themselves, and they would not own the land to produce these tithes. The only reasonable and consistent conclusion is that the poor did not tithe—they received tithes.

R. T. Kendall claimed, "It does the poor man no favor to encourage him to think that he is exempt from tithing. Why should he be discriminated against?"[74] In the Law, the poor were "discriminated against" in that the rich were obligated to feed the poor. Because Kendall's entire book *Tithing* teaches the modern monetary income

---

74. Kendall, 94.

tithe doctrine, he would naturally conclude a requirement of the poor to pay "tithes" because most "poor" today possess some amount of money and possibly earn some little money regularly from a source somehow—whether a low-paying job or welfare. Kendall's conclusion results from his own traditional bias rather than a careful reading of the Law itself. His expectation that "the poor" should "tithe" comes from his own logic and that of the "tithing" doctrine that he propounds rather than the actual words of Scripture.

Interestingly, Kendall states that Abraham's tithe "is consistent with all else the Bible has to say about tithes and 'increase' (Deut. 14:28). The tithe comes from the 'increase,' or income."[75] On the contrary, Abraham's tithe was a one-time gift of the spoils of a battle. The tithe in Deuteronomy 14:28-29 was a triannual requirement under the Law for landowners to yield a tenth of the increase of the harvest to the Levites and poor. Neither of these involved "income," and the similarities end at 10% of something to a recipient that included a priesthood.

Many proponents of the modern monetary income church tithing doctrine claim that the tithe universally applies to every individual, and that anything "above" the tithe then was determined by the living standard of the individual. George W. Brown claimed: "The obligation to **pay** the tithe is binding upon the rich and poor alike, but the **gifts** after payment has been made, or, in other words, the freewill offerings of the rich and those in comfortable circumstances should be very

---

75. Kendall, 50.

much greater. [Emphasis in original]"[76] Of course, when one incorrectly extrapolates the tithes and the freewill offerings from the Law into the same source—monetary income—one naturally will arrive at such a conclusion.

Tithes and freewill offerings did not necessarily come from the same source. Tithes came from produce from the land that one owned. Freewill offerings were likely always animals for the purpose of burnt sacrifices.[77] Gifts of monetary contributions in later times were likely called "freewill offerings" as a metonymy of the requirements of the Law (Ezra 7:16; 8:28). The poor could freely give anything that they desired of their meager possessions for a noble cause, but anyone who did not own land did not tithe. Freewill offerings or "gifts" are completely separate from tithes. They are not amounts from the same source.

George W. Brown also claimed: "Do we read anywhere in the Scriptures that God has divided mankind into two classes—one rich and the other poor?"[78] Nevertheless, if God did not "divide" the Israelites into two classes, He most certainly dictated several laws that made a distinction. God specifically commanded not to harm the poor, which included lending money at interest (Exodus 22:22-25; Leviticus 25:36-37; Deuteronomy 24:10-15; 27:19). God commanded

---

76. Brown, 124.
77. See Leviticus 22:17-25; Numbers 15:3; 29:39; Deuteronomy 12:6,17; 16:10; Ezra 1:4; 3:5.
78. Brown, 170.

landowners to leave food in their harvests for the poor to glean (Exodus 23:10-11; Leviticus 19:9-10; 23:22; Deuteronomy 24:19-21). God commanded wealthier Israelites to relieve the poor (Leviticus 25:35; Deuteronomy 10:17-19; 14:28-29; 15:7-11; 26:12-14). One notable thing of which God required exactly from both the rich and the poor was the yearly tax of one shekel of silver for atonement offerings conducted by census (Exodus 30:11-16). Tithes were not a monetary tax on everyone, however; they were an agricultural tax on landowners only. The *Mercer Dictionary of the Bible* further clarifies the landowner-tithe connection by stating that the tithes of the third year were for "the Levites within their towns, the resident aliens, the orphans, and the widows, **since none of them had land of their own**. [Emphasis added]"[79]

Even "wage earners" and "hirelings" were counted among the poor (Leviticus 19:13; 25:39-41; Deuteronomy 15:11-18; 24:14-15; Malachi 3:5; Mark 1:20; Luke 15:17-19). In the culture of Israel, those who earned wages worked for those who owned certain property, such as land. The landowner was the "sower" and the hired servants who "receiveth wages" were the "reapers" (John 4:36; James 5:4). Thus, landowners tithed of the **increase** of the harvest from the land that they owned. The landowner's **hired servants** never tithed because they did not own land from which to tithe. Hirelings never tithed of their **wages** because monetary income was never the source of tithes in the Law. The wage-earning servants likely worked and reaped to gather the

---

79. *Mercer Dictionary of the Bible*, s.v. "tithe."

tithes for the landowner to give or to bring for annual feasts. The understanding of "wage earners" and "hirelings" among the poor also adds proof to the fact that tithes never came from **income** of any kind but rather from the **"profit"** of the land. Only landowners—the "business owners"—tithed of their agricultural "profits." Wage earners did not tithe of their **pay**. Advances in technology and industry have made possible the modern idea of the middle class, who can be considered somewhat "well-to-do," possibly contributing to the false notion of the "poor" who have sustainable income being required to tithe from this income.

How many tithes?

Commentators, theologians, and scholars differ as to how many tithes the Mosaic Law proscribed. Obviously, from the dictates from Leviticus chapter 27, Numbers chapter 18, and Deuteronomy chapters 12 and 14, at least three distinct uses, purposes, or events arise under the banner of tithing. All three of these contexts emphatically present the contents of the tithe, that they were food grown and raised in the land and not money earned in the economy of trade.

Leviticus chapter 27 simply states the two sources of tithes—crops from the soil and new animals raised—and prescribes a 20% tariff on one wishing to redeem any part of the tithe from the crops. Numbers chapter 18 expresses that God gave the Levites "all the tenth in Israel," and that the Levites in turn were to yield a tithe of these tithes to the priests. Deuteronomy chapters 12 and 14 pronounce a use for tithes in which the people brought them to the city of the sanctuary, **ate** them with their households, and **shared** them with the Levites who lived in proximity of them. Now, the final verses of Deuteronomy chapter 14 and several verses in Deuteronomy chapter 26 describe a "year of tithing," making a stark distinction in the procedure and purpose from the context immediately prior.

The different purposes for tithes and the fact that a "year of tithing" existed necessitates the question of whether these laws express different observances and uses for the same single tithe or that they express additional tithes each with a distinct purpose. If more than one tithe existed, did any of the prescriptions overlap and did any one of the tithes serve more than one function? These possibilities will be discussed below.

Arguments and support for one tithe

Some commentators, theologians, and scholars believe that the Mosaic Law commanded only one tithe that had three different uses. In this case, the "Levitical tithe" would be the same as the "Festival tithe," and the Levites would simply be the recipients of the tithe by virtue of sharing them.[80] The year of tithing would also replace the annual feasts every third year.

The *Wycliffe Bible Commentary* calls the idea of Numbers chapter 18 and Deuteronomy chapter 14 expressing two different tithes an "erroneous view" and that Deuteronomy chapter 14 is only expressing a permission to eat "a small part of" the tithe "for a communion feast

---

80. John William Colenso, *The Pentateuch and book of Joshua critically examined* (London, Longmans, Green, and Co., 1873), 223-225.

at the sanctuary."[81] If this commentary is correct, perhaps the tithe that the Levites "inherited" was the right to be included among the class of people—the poor—to receive tithes. During the annual feasts the people who brought tithes were required to treat the Levites as guests and to share their food with them. Moreover, God could have intended that the tithes for the annual feasts have plenty of leftovers that the Levites would receive to take to their homes. Every three years then, the Levites would also receive a greater portion from the tithes because the people would not bring the tithes for a feast and eat portions of them, but wholly give them away for the Levites and poor.

John L. McKenzie's *Dictionary of the Bible* declares of the tithe: "Two years out of three these [tithes] are to furnish the food for the sacred banquet; in the 3rd year the tithes go to the poor."[82] The *Dictionary* further claims that the requirements of Numbers chapter 18 relegating "all the tenth" to the Levites represents a later alteration to the Law in which the tithe in its entirety went to the Levites, and their subsequent tithes of these to the priests.[83] Likewise, the *New International Bible Dictionary* explains that in the earliest form of the Law the tithe was merely "share[d]...with the Levites," but that the later version of the Law, codified once the nation settled in the land of

---

81. Charles F. Pfeiffer and Everett F. Harrison, eds., *The Wycliffe Bible Commentary* (Chicago: Moody Press, 1962), 174-175.

82. John L. McKenzie, *Dictionary of the Bible* (1965; reprint, New York: Touchstone, 1995), s.v. "tithe."

83. Ibid.

Canaan, relegated the same tithe exclusively to the Levites.[84] Although a Biblical historian is alone qualified to determine the truth of such assertion, a mere reader of the text of the Law is left to reconcile all the regulations and uses concerning tithes into a single tenth per tither per year.

Arguments and support for two tithes

If the later tithing regulations were not alterations, but merely extra regulations, some words of the Law can present a problem for the single tithe scenario. In the passage of the "Levitical tithe," God states that He granted "the children of Levi all the tenth in Israel for an inheritance" (Numbers 18:21). Naturally, because the Bible does not contradict itself, if the Levites receive "**all** the tenth," but they only **shared** the tenth in the annual feasts, one could reasonably conclude that the "Levitical tithe" and the "Festival tithe" were two separate tithes. God may have given a special tithe that went wholly for the maintenance of the Levites. The Hebrew *kol maaser* rendered "all the tenth" could also mean "the whole tenth/tithe;" therefore, the Levites could be the legal recipients of "the whole tithe" specifically whereas they also shared the tithes from "the year of tithing" with the poor.

Deuteronomy 12:28 states that the people were to "bring forth all the tithe of thine increase the same year." If "the tithe of thine increase" in verse 28 is the same as the tithe of "the increase of thy seed" in verse 22, one of several possibilities must be true regarding the annual feasts on these years. The year of tithing could preclude

---

84. *New International Bible Dictionary*, s.v. "tithe."

certain annual feasts these years that required tithes for the food. Another possibility is that the year of tithing at least required that the food for these feasts come from some other source than that of the tithes of the same year. Perhaps the priests stored excess food from the previous two years to supply the feasts for the third year. Another possibility is that the feasts every three years were local rather than conglomerate in Jerusalem. The *Believer's Bible Commentary* seems to support the idea of the year of tithing replacing the annual festival tithe for that year by claiming that "[i]n the **third year** he [an Israelite] used the tithe at home to feed **the Levite, the stranger, the fatherless,** and **the widow**. [Bold in original; underlined emphasis added]"[85] Likewise, Professor Peter C. Craigie states: "On every third year in the [Sabbatical] cycle, the tithe was not taken to the sanctuary, but was to be set aside for certain less privileged classes of people. [Emphasis added]"[86]

A reasonable argument for separating the "Levitical tithe" from the "Festival tithe" is the notion of tithes replacing "inheritance." The Levites as a tribe lived from tithes instead of an inheritance. Although the Levites were also numbered among the poor in certain classifications, one would be compelled from Scripture to assume that the Levites received **more** in tithes than the poor for their particular maintenance. Indeed, if the Levites had to yield a tithe of what they

---

85. William MacDonald, *Believer's Bible Commentary* (Nashville: Thomas Nelson, 1995), 214.
86. Craigie, 233-234.

received to the priests, they would appear to be less privileged than the poor who would not have to do likewise. Such a notion would appear to conflict entirely with the idea of the Levites receiving "all the tenth" for "an inheritance" if they, unlike the poor, had to give up some of the same tithes of which they shared with the poor.

The Jewish tradition of the *Mishnah*—the written form of the oral traditions regarding the Torah—argues for two tithes: the *Ma'aserot* ("Tithes") and the *Ma'aser Sheni* ("Second Tithe"). The *Ma'aserot* describes the requirements for determining what foods were subject to tithes and under what conditions (e.g. rotting, ripening). This tithe is the Levitical tithe. Within the Levitical tithe, the tither separates a small portion for the priestly families, then a tithe of what remains for the Levites.[87] After the *Ma'aserot* is fully realized, the *Ma'aser Sheni*—the "second tithe"—is one tenth of **the remaining** produce that the tither reserves for certain purposes.[88] On every first, second, fourth, and fifth years of the Sabbatical cycle, the tither brings these tithes for the annual feasts, whereas every third and sixth years ("the year of tithing") the tither uses the same tithe—now called the *Ma'aser Oni*—**instead** for the poor.[89] Neither the *Ma'aserot* nor the *Ma'aser Sheni* occurred on the Sabbatical year. Although doubting the universal practice of more than one tithe, Archaelogist and historian

---

87. Rabbi Jill Jacobs, "Seder Zeraim (Agriculture)," *My Jewish Learning*, n.d., http://www.myjewishlearning.com/texts/Rabbinics/Talmud/Mishnah/Seder_Zeraim_ Agriculture_.shtml (accessed February 3, 2010).
88. Ibid.
89. Ibid.

Dr. Joachim Jeremias leaned toward the possibility of two tithes as expressed in the Mishnah.[90] The modern Sadducee or Karaite tradition holds this two-tithe interpretation of the Hebrew text of the Torah as well.[91]

Arguments and support for three tithes

Dr. Russell Earl Kelly believes that the two-tithe view has a weakness because "we would have to conclude that there were no feasts every third year if there were no food brought."[92] Indeed, the text of the Law does not literally dictate that the feasts were absent every third year. The regulations for the feasts in Deuteronomy chapter 16 do not distinguish years. The requirement for tithes and the resulting festivals in Deuteronomy chapters 12 and 14 appear to be in conjunction with the "year by year" qualifier in Deuteronomy 14:22. One would scarcely understand a disconnect between the command of the tithes itself and the purpose of the tithes immediately following.

One argument for the possibility of no feasts on the third year is the likelihood of no feasts on the seventh year. Every seventh year— the Sabbatical year—landowners were neither to sow new seed nor to reap and store the harvest (Leviticus 25:1-7). Basically, landowners had to leave the land unattended and simply pick from whatever grew naturally as they needed food. In this Sabbatical year, the people were

---

90. Joachim Jeremias, *Jerusalem in the Time of Jesus*, trans. F. H. Cave and C. H. Cave (London: SCM Press Ltd., 1969), 134-138.
91. Bernard Revel, *The Karaite halakah: and its relation to Sadducean, Samaritan and Philonian Halakah* (Philadelphia: Cahan Printing Co., 1913), 18-20.
92. Kelly, 41.

not to tithe. All that grew that year was to feed the landowner's household. If the Sabbatical year provides a contextual restriction on the annual feasts, then the "year of tithing" could also introduce a similar regulation that limits the number of years upon which the annual feasts fell. Although the Biblical text does not explain clearly if the annual feasts were absent the third and sixth years, strong Jewish tradition and interpretation of the Torah suggests that the "year of tithing" indeed replaced these festivals. However, Jewish tradition has been known to be wrong, leading many Jews to misunderstand the first coming of the Messiah.

Several authorities ascribe to the three tithe idea—that the third-year tithe did not replace the festival tithe. The Jewish historian Josephus believed that the third-year tithe represented an additional third tithe that did not replace the festival tithe.[93] The Apocryphal book Tobit presents three tithes in Tobit 1:6-8. Renowned pastor, author, and Christian commentator Dr. John MacArthur holds that the Israelites paid "three tithes" comprising "23 percent" of their produce.[94]

My preference—two tithes

I believe that the evidence favors two tithes over one or three for several reasons. Although some important names align with the "three tithe" idea, the majority of scholars adhere to the understanding of two full tithes where the third-year tithe replaces the festival tithe in years

---

93. Flavius Josephus, *The New Complete Works of Josephus*, rev. ed., ed. Paul L. Maier, trans. William Whiston (Grand Rapids: Kregel Publications, 1999), 165.
94. John MacArthur, *1 Corinthians* (Nashville: Thomas Nelson, 2007), 110.

three and six of the seven year Sabbatical cycle. Jewish tradition in works such as the Mishnah alludes to the same. Also, the wording of Deuteronomy 14:28 seems to indicate that "all the tithe of thine increase the same year" represents the tithe that otherwise would have gone to the feasts explained in the verses immediately prior. Verses 28-29 seem to be part of the same legal code dictated in verses 22-27.

I do not have any qualms with anyone who would conclude that the Law expresses one tithe or three, as long as one understands the specific contents, uses, purposes, and events associated with the whole of tithing in the Law. Whether one concludes one, two, or three tithes from the whole of the regulations, the regulations themselves present a serious problem to the modern monetary income tithe doctrine. If the Law expresses one tithe, the modern church tithing advocate would have to justify the fact that church members could not bring at least part of their tithes to annual banquets at the church and **eat them** with their households, only **sharing** them with ministers. Only every third and sixth years out of seven would the ministers actually obtain the whole tithe. If the Law expresses two tithes, the modern church tithing advocate would have to justify not teaching these two tithes **and** observing the regulations associated with each. If the Law expresses three tithes, the modern church tithing advocate would have to justify not teaching these three tithes **and** observing the regulations associated with each. Whether one, two, or three tithes, the Law also presents the problem of the Sabbatical year and the year of Jubilee. In both of these years the people **did not tithe**. Cherry picking pieces of the tithing laws while ignoring others and attempting to form a continuity is either ignorance of the text or dishonesty.

The seven-year cycle

Exodus 23:10-11

10: And six years thou shalt sow thy land, and shalt gather in the fruits thereof:
11: But the seventh *year* thou shalt let it rest and lie still; that the poor of thy people may eat: and what they leave the beasts of the field shall eat. In like manner thou shalt deal with thy vineyard, *and* with thy oliveyard.

Leviticus 25:3-7

3: Six years thou shalt sow thy field, and six years thou shalt prune thy vineyard, and gather in the fruit thereof;
4: But in the seventh year shall be a sabbath of rest unto the land, a sabbath for the LORD: thou shalt neither sow thy field, nor prune thy vineyard.
5: That which groweth of its own accord of thy harvest thou shalt not reap, neither gather the grapes of thy vine undressed: *for* it is a year of rest unto the land.
6: And <u>the sabbath of the land shall be meat for you</u>; for thee, and for thy servant, and for thy maid, and for thy hired servant, and for thy stranger that sojourneth with thee,
7: And for thy cattle, and for the beast that *are* in thy land, shall all the increase thereof be meat.

Deuteronomy 15:1-2

1: At the end of *every* seven years thou shalt make a release.
2: And this *is* the manner of the release: Every creditor that lendeth *aught* unto his neighbor shall release *it*; he shall not exact *it* of his neighbor, or of his brother; because it is called <u>the LORD's release</u>.

Several times this chapter has mentioned the seventh year or a seven-year cycle. Every seventh year was a "Sabbath" year of "rest" for the land. Landowners were not allowed to plant any new crops nor gather and store a harvest. Obviously because no gatherings of the harvest occurred on the seventh year no tithing could either. Whatever grew on the land without human attention was specifically there in whole from the household, local poor, and animals to eat leisurely.

The seventh year was also the year in which lenders would cancel debts to borrowers. The people already could not charge interest on loans to each other; however, the seventh year added to the idea that loans were somewhat acts of charity rather than profit-making mechanisms. The question arises that since debts were canceled every seventh year, why would anyone have any motivation to grant a loan on the sixth year with the near possibility of not seeing the funds returned? God specifically forbade people from using the seventh year as an excuse for not lending, and promised to bless those who lent in this condition (Deuteronomy 15:9-10). In this Sabbatical year all servants were permitted to go free if desired (Deuteronomy 15:12-18).

The seventh year, indeed, represented a joyous year for many in Israel. The modern church tithing advocate must justify not including the provisions of the seventh year in the tithing doctrine. In the Law, the seventh year was just as part of the intricate system of tithing as was any other year. In the seventh year the people of Israel **did not tithe**. For even a modicum of consistency, the modern church tithing advocate should teach that every seventh year, church members should not tithe, but should use the tithe for themselves. The doctrine would not be complete without releasing debts. Because many emphasize "the LORD's tithe" (the Levitical tithe) as enduring for the church, consistency would demand that "the LORD's release" (Deuteronomy 15:2) would also endure.

The fifty-year cycle—Jubilee

Leviticus 25:8-12

8: And thou shalt number seven sabbaths of years unto thee, seven times seven years; and the space of the seven sabbaths of years shall be unto thee forty and nine years.

9: Then shalt thou cause the trumpet of the jubilee to sound on the tenth *day* of the seventh month, in the day of atonement shall ye make the trumpet sound throughout all your land.

10: And ye shall hallow the fiftieth year, and proclaim liberty throughout *all* the land unto all the inhabitants thereof: it shall be a jubilee unto you; and ye shall return every man unto his possession, and ye shall return every man unto his family.

11: A jubilee shall that fiftieth year be unto you: ye shall not sow, neither reap that which groweth of itself in it, nor gather *the grapes* in it of thy vine undressed.

12: For it *is* the jubilee; it shall be holy unto you: ye shall eat the increase thereof out of the field.

Not only was there a seven-year cycle, but there was also a fifty-year cycle. After seven sevens, or forty-nine years, the fiftieth year was the year of Jubilee. Similar to every seventh year the fiftieth year included releases of debt and servitude and an absence of farming and tithing. The year of Jubilee then always followed a standard Sabbatical year. Conclusively, there were **two full adjacent years** where the people of Israel did not tithe! The people were to "eat the increase thereof out of the field" (Leviticus 25:12). As chapter 4 of this book explored, the year of Jubilee was unique regarding regulations for buying and selling real estate. God Himself alleviated the concern for the lack of harvest on the seventh year by declaring that He would sovereignly grant that the harvest of the sixth year would abundantly supply food for the same year plus the next two years (Leviticus 25:20-22). The Sabbath years and the year of Jubilee taught the people to fear the Lord in a lack of harvest without tithes just as the other years taught them to fear the Lord in their festival tithes.

Conclusion and summary

In conclusion, we have explored the regulations in the Mosaic Law for the "year of tithing," which occurred every third and sixth years in a seven year cycle. In this "year of tithing," the people of Israel would deposit a whole tithe of their produce into local community bins for the Levites and the poor. The people were to confirm their honesty in this contribution with an oath indicating that the amount they deposited represented a true tenth. We have seen that the poor did not tithe because tithes were required only of those who owned land. The poor partook of the tithes made available every three years.

We examined the possibilities in the Mosaic Law of one, two, or three tithes representing approximately 10%, 20%, or 23% of one's harvest respectfully. Regardless of the number of tithes and their overlap, the regulations for tithes as a whole in the Law present serious problems for those who would quote from the Law to defend the common idea of a tithe of monetary income to the church. Tithes in the Law manifested themselves in three ways: a tithe for the Levites, a tithe for annual festivals, and a tithe for the Levites and poor every three years. For the purposes of the remainder of this book, the Law expresses two complete tithes: the Levitical Tithe for years one through six, and the second tithe that served as the Festival Tithe every first, second, fourth, and fifth years and as the Poor Tithe every third and sixth years.

We observed the seven-year cycle and the Jubilee cycle and their impact on tithing in the Law. Both the Sabbatical year and the year of Jubilee forbade farming the land and subsequently invalidated any requirement for any tithes those years. Both these systematic years of rest required releasing of debts and of servants. All these regulations in the Law conflict with the common teaching regarding tithes. The "year of tithing," the seven-year cycle, the year of Jubilee, and all that pertains to them provides absolutely no support for the modern monetary income tithe doctrine.

7. Two Things That Are Different Are Not the Same

Firstfruits vs. Tithes

Deuteronomy 26:1-2

1: And it shall be, when thou *art* come in unto the land which the LORD thy God giveth thee *for* an inheritance, and possessest it, and dwellest therein;
2: That thou shalt take of the first of all the fruit of the earth, which thou shalt bring of thy land that the LORD thy God giveth thee, and shalt put *it* in a basket, and shalt go unto the place which the LORD thy God shall choose to place his name there.

Proverbs 3:9-10

9: Honour the LORD with thy substance, and with the firstfruits of all thine increase:
10: So shall thy barns be filled with plenty, and thy presses shall burst out with new wine.

How often have you heard a sermon on tithing that included a quip such as the following: "Your tithe ought to be the first check that you write, before you pay any bills"? Often to pad such a statement, the preacher will declare that God commands the tithe **first**. If the preacher defends this assertion with Scripture, he may quote Proverbs 3:9-10. "These two verses," he may stipulate, "present us with both a command and a blessing. If we pay our tithes **first** in obedience to God's command and trust Him with the rest, He will give us more blessings than we can contain."

Firstfruits—noun or adverb?

Are firstfruits and tithes related? Are firstfruits and tithes interchangeable? Do firstfruits and tithes express two aspects to the same practice? Are tithes the amount and firstfruits the timing of the same payment? Are tithes, then, a noun and firstfruits an adverb for the same concept?

All the questions above are important and could leave some modern tithing advocates scratching their heads. The bolder ones may interject an emphatic "Yes!" to all of the above, and then rush to do a word study to prove this answer. A careful and profitable study of these words will test this theory as we will see below.

Nehemiah 10:37

37: And that we should bring the firstfruits of our dough, and our offerings, and the fruit of all manner of trees, of wine and of oil, unto the priests, to the chambers of the house of our God; and the tithes of our ground unto the Levites, that the same Levites might have the tithes in all the cities of our tillage.

Nehemiah 12:44

44: And at that time were some appointed over the chambers for the treasures, for the offerings, <u>for the firstfruits, and for the tithes</u>, to gather into them out of the fields of the cities the portions of the law for the priests and Levites: for Judah rejoiced for the priests and for the Levites that waited.

According to these Scriptures, and several others that are too numerous to list, the firstfruits and tithes appear to be two separate things. In fact, Nehemiah 10:37 demonstrates a post-captivity command concerning both firstfruits and tithes. The *firstfruits* went directly to the **priests** for **the Temple storehouse** whereas the *tithes* went to the **Levites** in their **farming communities**. This passage clearly distinguishes between firstfruits and tithes and their use. Church tithing advocate Dr. Michael Fields admits according to this verse that "we can clearly see that the FIRSTFRUITS, tithes and offerings are three distinct forms of worship. [Emphasis in original]"[95] Are firstfruits and tithes **related?** Yes. They are both parts of the harvest consecrated for certain holy purposes. Are firstfruits and tithes **interchangeable?** Absolutely not. They involve two completely different laws with two completely different functions. Deuteronomy chapter 26 provides more insight into both firstfruit and tithing rituals, demonstrating how completely different they are!

Deuteronomy 26:2, 4, 12

2: That thou shalt take of <u>the first of all the fruit</u> of the earth, which thou shalt bring of thy land that the LORD thy God giveth thee, and shalt <u>put</u>

---

95. Michael Fields, *FirstFruits: Revelation for Increase & Excellence* (Longwood, FL: Xulon Press, 2008), 65.

it in a basket, and shalt go unto the place which the LORD thy God shall choose to place his name there.
4: And the priest shall take the basket out of thine hand, and set it down before the altar of the LORD thy God.
12: When thou hast made an end of tithing all the tithes of thine increase the third year, *which is* the year of tithing, and hast given it unto the Levite, the stranger, the fatherless, and the widow, that they may eat within thy gates, and be filled;

Dr. John MacArthur, commenting on Deuteronomy chapter 26 states: "Moses commanded the people to keep two rituals when they conquered the land and began to enjoy its produce. These two rituals were the initial firstfruits offering (26:1-11) and the first third-year special tithe (26:12-15). [Emphasis added]"[96] Indeed, Deuteronomy chapter 26 clearly and eloquently demonstrates a distinction between firstfruits and tithes in the timing, the means, and the words of their specific vows. Although many other passages elaborate on the distinction between firstfruits and tithes, Deuteronomy chapter 26 most clearly compartmentalizes the two into separate portions of the chapter, complete with their own regulations and vows. Deuteronomy chapter 26 thunders destruction and completely shatters the idea of tithes and firstfruits being two descriptions of the same commandment. Do firstfruits and tithes express two aspects to the same practice? Absolutely not! Are tithes the amount and firstfruits the timing of the same payment? No! Being two different commandments and observances, they cannot be part of the same act. Both the tithes and

---

96. *The MacArthur Bible Commentary*, 227.

the firstfruits dealt with their own amount and also happened on their own distinct timing regarding the harvest.

Firstfruits vs. tithes—different amounts

Deuteronomy 26:2

2: That thou shalt take of the first of all the fruit of the earth, which thou shalt bring of thy land that the LORD thy God giveth thee, and shalt put *it* in a basket, and shalt go unto the place which the LORD thy God shall choose to place his name there.

The *tithe*, of course, is a **tenth** of something. According to the Jewish Mishnah, as the previous chapter of this book explored, the Levitical tithe was the first calculated tenth of the harvest, and the Festival/Poor tithe was the second tenth calculated from the harvest that remained. Regardless of the specific occurrence of any of the three tithing forms, each were a full tenth part of the harvest.

The firstfruits, however, consisted only of a rather small portion: small enough to fit into a basket that a single individual could carry. At the time that firstfruits were required, regardless of the amount of ripe produce present, the one offering the firstfruits would only gather enough to fill a basket. One could assume that God promised to bless in such a way that the firstfruits would always fill the entire basket with much more remaining.

Firstfruits vs. tithes—different times

Not only did firstfruits and tithes represent different portions of a harvest, but also they were observed at different times relative to the harvest. The firstfruits were not even a small portion taken from the tithe or in addition to the tithe. The firstfruits were observed possibly months **before** tithes. According to the *New International Bible*

151

Dictionary, firstfruits "were looked on as a pledge for the coming harvest. [Emphasis added]"[97] Whereas the nation of Israel celebrated the Passover in the wilderness wanderings, God commanded the nation to celebrate the Feast of Firstfruits (Exodus 23:19; Leviticus 23:10-14) and associated proceeding feasts only upon settling the land of Canaan.[98] The Feast of Firstfruits was the **first** annual feast that the Israelites were required to observe in the Promised Land.

Later, after the Israelite landowners gathered their harvest, they brought the Festival tithe to the city of the sanctuary for certain feasts, such as the Feast of Tabernacles.[99] The Feast of Tabernacles (Leviticus 23:34; Deuteronomy 16:13-16; 31:10), also known as the Feast of Ingathering (Exodus 23:16; 34:22), was the **final** annual feast for the nation.[100] The Feast of Tabernacles, or Ingathering, demonstrated God's blessing fully realized at the end of the harvest.

The difference between firstfruits and tithes in their associated feasts makes perfect sense because of the nature of firstfruits and tithes themselves. Firstfruits were of the **first** produce to ripen, signifying God's initial blessing and His promise for a prosperous harvest later in the year. Tithes were a tenth of the **full harvest**—after God's blessing

---

97. *New International Bible Dictionary*, s.v. "firstfruits."
98. John Ritchie, *Feasts of Jehovah: Foreshadows of Christ in the Calendar of Israel* (Grand Rapids: Kregel Publications, 1982), 39.
99. Bert Whitehead and Carrie Wally, *Spirit of the Tithe* (Haverford, PA: Infinity Publishing, 2004), 59.
100. Ritchie, 67.

for the year was actualized in its entirety. Firstfruits pointed to the tithes of the harvest to come.

Firstfruits vs. tithes—different recipients

Not only do firstfruits and tithes occur at opposite ends of the harvest, but also they have different purposes and are for different recipients. Although the Festival tithe of Deuteronomy chapters 12 and 14 served similar functions to firstfruits for certain national feasts, Deuteronomy chapter 26 demonstrates the difference between the firstfruits and the Poor tithe ("year of tithing") in their recipients expressed in their associated vows.

Deuteronomy 26:2-3

2: That thou shalt take of the first of all the fruit of the earth, which thou shalt bring of thy land that the LORD thy God giveth thee, and shalt put *it* in a basket, and shalt go unto the place which the LORD thy God shall choose to place his name there.
3: And thou shalt go unto the priest that shall be in those days, and say unto him, I profess this day unto the LORD thy God, that I am come unto the country which the LORD sware unto our fathers for to give us.

Numbers 18:11-13

11: And this *is* thine [the priests']; the heave offering of their gift, with all the wave offerings of the children of Israel: I have given them unto thee, and to thy sons and to thy daughters with thee, by a statute for ever: every one that is clean in thy house shall eat of it.
12: All the best of the oil, and all the best of the wine, and of the wheat, the firstfruits of them which they shall offer unto the LORD, them have I given thee.
13: *And* whatsoever is first ripe in the land, which they shall bring unto the LORD, shall be thine; every one that is clean in thine house shall eat *of* it.

God granted the privilege of eating the initial firstfruits to the priests at the sanctuary. During the Feast of Firstfruits the Israelites would offer a ram for a burnt sacrifice and a sheaf of the first wheat (Leviticus 23:10-14). The priest would waive the sheaf over the lamb as a dedication before the Lord. The priests could then eat the leftover breast of the ram (Exodus 29:22-28). Therefore, accordingly in Numbers chapter 18, the wave offerings and the firstfruits were for food for the priests.

Deuteronomy 26:12

12: When thou hast made an end of <u>tithing all the tithes of thine increase</u> the third year, *which is* the year of tithing, and hast <u>given *it* unto the Levite, the stranger, the fatherless, and the widow</u>, that they may eat within thy gates, and be filled;

Nehemiah 10:37

37: And that we should bring <u>the firstfruits</u> of our dough, and our offerings, and the fruit of all manner of trees, of wine and of oil, <u>unto the priests, to the chambers of the house of our God</u>; and the tithes of our ground <u>unto the Levites</u>, that the same Levites might have the tithes <u>in all the cities of our tillage</u>.

The firstfruits went directly to the sanctuary as food for the priests. Distinct from this, the Levitical tithe of the Israelites went directly to the Levitical cities for the Levites. The Festival tithe did go to the city of the sanctuary where the

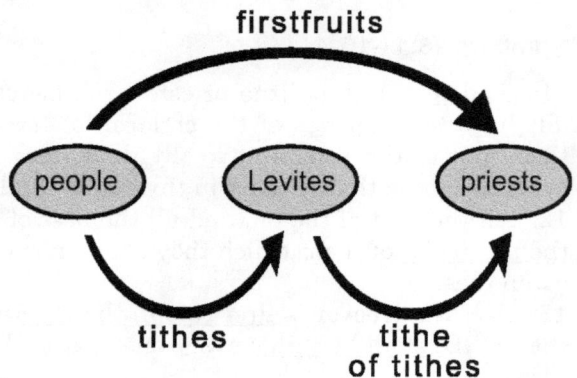

people ate them and shared them with the Levites. The Poor tithe every three years went to storage areas in the local communities for the Levites and poor. However, the people of Israel themselves never tithed directly to the priests or to the sanctuary. As Numbers chapter 18 demonstrates, the only tithes that went into the sanctuary for the priests came from the tithe of the tithes that the Levites brought from their cities. To summarize the distinction between firstfruits and tithes from the people of Israel, the firstfruits were for the priests, but the tithes were for the non-priestly Levites and the poor.

Examples of confusion in tithes and firstfruits

Many who operate from tradition can demonstrate a serious lack of study in their words. Although their literature can contain very valuable spiritual and practical advice, even well-known pastors, theologians, expositors, and Christian authors can misunderstand the distinction between firstfruits and tithes. Popular television preacher John Hagee confuses tithes and firstfruits, thinking that firstfruits are the tempo or manner in which one tithes: "[T]he commandment is this: Tithe first. Give your best to God first; give Him your firstfruits. [Emphasis added]"[101] Prolific author and founder of *Eternal Perspective Ministries*, Randy Alcorn, wondered "[w]hether or not the tithe is still the minimal measure of those firstfruits. [Emphasis added]"[102] One author under the pen name "Bebslin" relays: "I was never taught about giving God a tenth, the first fruits of my labor. [Emphasis added]"[103] Jack Hyles, deceased former pastor of First Baptist Church of Hammond, Indiana, stated concerning a Christian's

---

101. Hagee, 114.
102. Randy Alcorn, *The Treasure Principle* (Sistera, OR: Multnomah, 2001), 60.
103. Bebslin, *Tithing and Winning Souls* (Longwood, FL: Xulon Press, 2009), 27.

money: "The firstfruits belong to God. The first ten percent of our increase is His. [Emphasis added]"[104] Thomas Aquinas, a Catholic Church apologist during the Middle Ages, also confused tithes and firstfruits when he wrote the following:

> Tithes are due on the fruits of the earth, in so far as these fruits are the gift of God. Wherefore tithes do not come under a tax, nor are they subject to workmen's wages. Hence it is not right to deduct one's taxes and the wages paid to workmen, before paying tithes: but tithes must be paid before anything else on one's entire produce. [Emphasis added][105]

The perception that tithes are for the New Covenant contributes to the confusion. Tithes and firstfruits are distinct laws in the Mosaic Code; however, they are often listed together in regulations concerning the sanctuary. The priests received the firstfruits and the tithes from the Levites. Both of these were brought to "the place which God would choose." Therefore, one can miss the distinction.

When one views tithes and firstfruits both as coming from **earnings** of labor—a portion of monetary income—one can then delve into an improper understanding of Scripture that propagates through teaching and tradition. Firstfruits emphasize **timing** whereas tithes emphasize an **amount**. The inference then becomes that one not only must pay "tithes," but must also pay them "first" according to the requirement of "firstfruits." A careful understanding of the Law makes

---

104. Jack Hyles, "Separation of God's Money," in *Jack Hyles Speaks on Biblical Separation* (Hammond, IN: Hyles-Anderson Publications, 1984), par. 4, The Jack Hyles Website, http://jackhyles.net/separate.shtml (accessed February 6, 2010).
105. Thomas Aquinas, "Whether men are bound to pay tithes of all things?," *Summa Theologica, Volume 2*, trans. Fathers of the English Dominican Province (Charleston, SC: BiblioBazaar, 2008), 314-315.

this flawed reasoning an impossible application of any text of Scripture.

A false inference of tithing—Adam and Eve

Some proponents of modern church tithing believe that a prospect of an "eternal principle" can bolster their case that a Christian is required to "tithe" if instances of "tithing" can be drawn from all of Biblical history. Some will go as far as to claim that Adam and Eve "tithed" in the garden of Eden. The idea is that the tree of the knowledge of good and evil was really a form of tithe and that God was making the first parents of humankind "tithe" by having access to all the trees of the garden except this one tree. Marshall B. Spurling claims of this event: "In the Garden of Eden the serpent tricked Adam and Eve to eat from the forbidden fruit. The forbidden fruit was the Lord's tithe."[106] Pastor Jack Hyles described the account as followed: "When Adam and Eve ate of the forbidden tree they were taking that which was sanctified to the Lord. In other words, the sin of Adam and Eve was the sin of not tithing. [Emphasis added]"[107]

Several problems exist with interpreting the forbidden fruit as a "tithe." *First*, the passage nowhere includes any form of the word *tithe*. Assuming "tithing" from this is mere conjecture based on an unsupportable premise that "tithing" must be a universal and timeless "principle." *Second*, for the forbidden fruit to represent a "tithe," it

---

106. Marshall B. Spurling, *Ladder: Math Code 2* (Longwood, FL: Xulon Press, 2006), 112.
107. Hyles, "Separation of God's Money," par. 5.

must be a tenth of something. The forbidden fruit came from a single tree in the Garden of Eden (Genesis 2:9,17; 3:3,6,11,22-24); therefore, one would have to prove that only a total of ten trees existed in the garden. Hyles recalled a horticulturalist informing him that ten trees, each of a different type, could have provided the original seed from which all trees today came.[108] Even if this were true, God guarded the forbidden tree (Genesis 3:22-24). This would mean that one of the types of trees the horticulturalist listed—the forbidden tree—must have "descendents" today of which people eat. _Third_, according to modern tithe teaching, tithes come from the **earnings** of one's labor. Comparing the results of labor used for good purposes to something absent from labor that is forbidden is absurd. The command to abstain from the one tree was just that—a command. It was not a "tithe." Although some Catholic writings claim extra-Biblical stories and traditions of Adam and Eve paying tithes, church historian Henry Clark probes: "Could anything...be more childish and absurd than the story of tracing the payment of tithes to Adam?"[109]

A false inference of tithing—Cain and Abel

An example of confusing or blurring the distinction among offerings, firstfruits, and tithes is another teaching that the sin of Cain was that of not "tithing." Cain was a crop farmer and Abel was a shepherd. Abel offered the firstlings of his flock for a burnt offering,

---

108. Ibid., par. 6.
109. Henry William Clarke, _A History of Tithes_, 2nd ed. (London: Swan Sonnen-schein & Co, 1894), 6.

but Cain offered such an offering from his crops. God "respected" Abel's offering, but not Cain's. Arthur Virgil Babbs in the classic work *The Law of the Tithe* claimed that the Hebrew word translated as "a more excellent" or "greater" really means "more abundant" or "greater in quantity" in Hebrews 11:4 comparing Abel's sacrifice with Cain's.[110] Babbs was proposing that Cain's sin in his sacrifice was not so much the substance of his offering but rather **how much** he offered. Supposedly, Abel gave "more" than Cain, and Cain's sin was that of not giving the **amount** that God required. Babbs then claims that "the germ idea of the tithe is found in their sacrifice."[111]

The Greek word *pleiona* in Hebrews 11:4 does not **have** to mean "greater in **quantity**;" it can mean "greater in **quality**," as most Bible translations render it in some form. Jesus used the word to describe Himself as "greater than Jonah" and "greater than Solomon" (Matthew 12:41-42; Luke 11:31-32). Jesus also used the word to say that loving God with all one's being was "more than" burnt sacrifices (Mark 12:33). Just as the English word **greater** can refer to either quantity or quality depending on the context, so also can the Greek word *pleiona* or any of its forms.

The most natural understanding of Cain's sin was that it was not of the correct **substance**. Cain wanted to offer to God what **he** produced—the fruit of his craft and skills. Cain did not want to ask his

---

110. Arthur V. Babbs, *The Law of the Tithe As Set Forth in the Old Testament: Illustrated, explained, and enforced from Biblical and extra-Biblical Sources*, 2nd ed. (New York: Fleming H. Revell Company, 1921), 25.
111. Ibid., 130.

brother Abel for a sheep. Cain's sin had more to do with **pride**. Hyles claimed that "Abel brought to God that which was sanctified to Him. Cain did not. Cain's sin was that of not tithing."[112] Comparing "the firstlings of the flock" to the Mosaic Law regarding firstfruits and firstlings can also lead to confusion when one already confuses tithes and firstfruits. God required a **blood sacrifice**. Cain disobeyed by offering crops that do not bleed (unless one truly can squeeze blood from a turnip). The practice of the burnt sacrifices at this time was not of **giving** a quantity of what one has, but that of continually offering burnt sacrifices of lambs to signify atonement of sin. God respected Abel's sacrifice because it fit God's message of blood atonement. Cain's sin had nothing to do with not "tithing" or a quantity of any kind; it had to do with pride and breaking God's prescription of atoning sacrifices. Also, if Cain's sin was based on **substance**, this act had nothing to do with tithing; in the Law God required a tithe of livestock **and** a tithe of crops.

A false inference of tithing—Achan

Another less common attempt to inject "tithing" into every facet of history involves the account of Achan's sin at Jericho. Presbyterian pastor Francis Schaeffer claimed that Achan was free to take spoils from Jericho, but his offense was that he took them before the nation

---

112. Hyles, "Separation of God's Money," par. 8.

tithed from these spoils.[113] This is incorrect. Achan trespassed in taking "the accursed thing" (Joshua 7:1). God commanded the Israelites to **destroy** the city of Jericho and all its inhabitants besides Rahab. The people were to kill and burn everything else in the city except for the precious metals, which were to go entirely to the sanctuary (Joshua 6:17-19). The people were not to "tithe" from these spoils; they were forbidden from taking **anything**. Achan kept clothes which should have been destroyed and precious metals which were supposed to go to the sanctuary. Achan's sin was in keeping certain spoils that were either to be destroyed or for the sanctuary treasury. His sin was **not** "tithing" or taking things before "tithes" were extracted.

Jack Hyles also claimed that Achan's sin was that of "not tithing" for a different reason. Because the city of Jericho was the first city that the nation of Israel under Joshua conquered, Hyles considered it the "firstfruits."[114] Hyles then continued by claiming that "in a sense he [Achan] was taking the tithe. This was the first city of the land, the firstfruits of the land, and it was God's! [Emphasis added]"[115] Once again, Hyles, as many church "tithing" advocates, confused tithes with firstfruits. Pastor Bill Winston asserted: "By taking the tithe (the spoil), or robbing God of what belonged to Him, Achan had sinned.

---

113. Francis A. Schaeffer, *A Christian View of the Bible as Truth*, 2nd ed., vol 2 of *The Complete Works of Francis A. Schaeffer: A Christian Worldview* (Wheaton, IL: Crossway Books, 1985), 236.
114. Hyles, "Separation of God's Money," para. 9.
115. Ibid.

[Emphasis added]"[116] Not everything that was "owed to God" is properly called a "tithe." Achan was not supposed to "tithe" the garment; he was supposed to **destroy** it. Achan was not supposed to "tithe" the metals; he was supposed to give them entirely to the sanctuary. Except for the metals, the entire city was **accursed**. Achan's sin had nothing to do with "tithing." It had everything to do with breaking God's commandment regarding conquered cities and "devoting" (Hebrew: *cherem*) or **banning** their spoils (Leviticus 27:28-29).

A false inference of tithing—the resurrection of Jesus

Perhaps the least common false analogy to tithing is that of the resurrection of Jesus Christ. The New Testament often has spiritual analogies to the Law in the Old Testament. Accordingly, the Apostles referred to the resurrection of Christ as "firstfruits" in that His resurrection represented the first of what salvation offered to the church (1 Corinthians 15:20-23; James 1:18; Revelation 14:4). Jack Hyles commented concerning 1 Corinthians 15:23: "Notice especially the words, 'Christ the firstfruits.' Here we go back to the tithe. The firstfruits are God's. The first tenth is God's, and Jesus is called the firstfruits."[117] The *Holman Treasury of Key Bible Words* makes the claim under the definition of *tithe*: "Theologically, the principle of the

---

116. Winston, 16.
117. Ibid., par. 11.

<u>tithe as the first fruits</u> is applied to the resurrection of Jesus Christ as the first fruits of the dead (1 Cor. 15:20-23). [Emphasis added]"[118]

The glaring and obvious problem to the reader by now is the confusion between tithes and firstfruits. The resurrection of Jesus Christ was not a "tithe" to the Father or in any sense. Jesus Christ is called the *firstfruits* of the resurrection from the dead because He rose first under the promise of the New Covenant, and all who become "the children of God" have the promise of this covenant that they will also be raised from the dead. *Firstfruits* in this case is simply a spiritual analogy to the Law in showing the **first** of something offered to God. Jesus Christ is the **firstfruits** of the resurrection from the dead; He is not a **"tithe"** of any kind.

A false inference of tithing—Ananias and Sapphira

In efforts to force tithe teaching into the New Testament post-Calvary, some advocates will resort to using the tragic story of Ananias and Sapphira to bolster fear in the hearts of Christians to follow the modern "tithing" doctrine under penalty of God's wrath. Acts 5:1-11 relays the account in the early church of this couple who sold land but kept back part of the price of this land. They apparently gave a large portion of the proceeds as a gift to the church, yet they found themselves ridiculed by the Apostle Peter for their act of keeping back part of the price. The cost of this action was their lives.

---

118. Eugene E. Carpenter and Philip Wesley Comfort, *Holman Treasury of Key Bible Words: 200 Greek and 200 Hebrew Words Defined and Explained* (Nashville: Broadman & Holman, 2000), s.v. "tithe."

Although the passage does not use the word *tithe*, some contend that a tithe is implicit in the fact that they "kept back *part* of the price" and "brought a certain part." Buddy Hanson, President of the Grace and Law Resource center claims that in their sinful act, Ananias and Sapphira "lied to God in order to keep some extra money for themselves, while hypocritically pretending to pay the whole tithe. [Emphasis added]"[119] In other words, he implies that this couple had an obligation to give a certain amount (a "tithe") and they lied about doing this.

Of course, some will also call their sin that of neglecting *firstfruits*. Dr. Michael Fields in asking "What part of the price did they [Ananias and Sapphira] keep back?" replies: "I believe they kept back **FIRSTFRUITS** [Emphasis in original]."[120] He further declares: "Ananias and Sapphira were not truthful worshippers because they lied to the Holy Ghost and kept back part of the price for the land and that price was **FIRSTFRUITS!!** [Emphasis in original]"[121] Dr. Fields, however, correctly notes that firstfruits and tithes are two completely different things.[122] Therefore, what is the sin of Ananias and Sapphira? Did they fail to give *tithes* or did they fail to give *firstfruits*?

---

119. Buddy Hanson, *What's Scripture Got to Do with It?* (Tuscaloosa, AL: Hanson Group, 2005), 162.
120. Fields, 69.
121. Ibid.
122. Ibid., 72.

A closer look at the details of this passage in Acts demonstrates the fallacies of this contorted support for modern tithe teaching. The correct answer is **neither!** The reasons are as followed:

First, the obvious problem is that no mention of tithing or firstfruits has occurred before or after this point in church history according to Acts and neither term occurs in this passage. The passage only says that the couple kept back a portion of the price and they brought a portion.

Second, most likely others in the church knew this couple and were familiar with the land that they had owned. They claimed to give **all** the money they received from selling the land. If the amount they retained was more than 90% of the proceeds from the sale, the amount they gave would have been obvious to anyone that it would not have been the full amount. Most likely, the portion they **kept back** was a relatively small portion (perhaps a tenth) rather than what they gave.

Third, Ananias and Sapphira clearly had no obligation to give **any** of the price of the land. The Apostle Peter told the couple: "Whiles it [the land] remained, was it not thine own? and after it was sold, was it not in thine own power?" (Acts 5:4) The couple was neither entreated to sell the land at all, nor to give **any** of the proceeds to the church. They were allegedly following the example of others in generosity, not because they were required to do so.

Fourth, the sin of Ananias and Sapphira was purely that of lying, plain and simple (Acts 5:3,4,8-9). In fact, Peter emphasized the severity of this by noting that they had "not lied unto men, but unto

God." (Acts 5:4) Their sin was truly in lying about how much they actually **received** from the sale of the land (Acts 5:8). They gave **X** amount of money to the church and claimed that they sold the land for **X** amount, when they really sold it for **Y** amount. In other words, they lied about the price of the land itself and the fact that what they gave was this full price. Their sin had nothing to do with "greed" in keeping a portion of the sale. Their act of giving was pure generosity, but they were nevertheless punished for lying to the Holy Spirit about this act.

A proper understanding of Proverbs 3:9-10

Proverbs 3:9-10

9: Honour the LORD with thy substance, and with the firstfruits of all thine increase:
10: So shall thy barns be filled with plenty, and thy presses shall burst out with new wine.

As the introduction to this chapter noted, many preachers will cite Proverbs 3:9-10 as a proof text for **tithing** in their sermons and written literature. Dr. Philip Ayers, senior pastor of Glade Creek Baptist Church, preceded a citation of these two verses with the following: "Tithing assures me of success in the financial arena of life. [Emphasis added]"[123] Dr. Daniel A. Biddle quotes this passage and expresses the resulting claim: "By giving ten percent of our income—right off the top—we put God first in the financial area of our lives. [Emphasis

---

123. Philip Ayers, *A Proverb a Day Keeps the Devil Away* (Longwood, FL: Xulon Press, 2008), 164.

added]"[124] Rich Brott and Frank Damazio in their *Family Finance Handbook* quote Proverbs 3:9-10 under a paragraph section titled "Solomon Taught Tithing."[125] Randy Alcorn used Proverbs 3:9 as a support text for tithing and stated: "God's children give to Him first, not last."[126] The list of such mistaken inferences from this familiar Proverb can go on and on.

Proverbs 3:9-10 speaks of **firstfruits** not **tithes**. Although one might believe "honor the LORD with thy substance" refers to **tithing**, this assumption simply cannot be definite. "With the firstfruits of all thine increase," however, is plain and clear. The word *and* is not present in the Hebrew, making these two imperatives parallelisms. Both describe the same act. One honors God with his substance by presenting the **firstfruits** of them.

Solomon is simply referring to the regulations of the Law regarding **firstfruits**. An Israelite honored God with firstfruits by filling a basket with them, going to the sanctuary, presenting them to the priest, and vowing an oath (Deuteronomy 26:1-11). One "honored God" with the firstfruits by giving them to the priests for their **food**. King Solomon, as an executive and arbiter of the Law over the nation, simply restated the requirement of the Law into a poetic proverb. The blessings in verse 10 reflect the blessings that God said that He would

---

124. Daniel A. Biddle, *The Secret of the Seven Pillars - Building Your Life on God's Wisdom from the Book of Proverbs* (Longwood, FL: Xulon Press, 2007), 133.
125. Rich Brott and Frank Damazio, *Family Finance Handbook: Discovering The Blessings Of Financial Freedom* (Portland: City Christian Publishing, 2004), 35.
126. Randy Alcorn, *The Treasure Principle*, 60.

give to the nation of Israel if they follow His Law (Deuteronomy 26:14-19). Proverbs 3:9-10 does **not** teaching **tithing**; it teaches **firstfruits** in the context of the Law. Tithes and firstfruits are two completely different things.

Conclusion and summary

In conclusion, we have examined the difference between firstfruits and tithes in the Mosaic Law. We have seen that firstfruits being distinct from tithes cannot be an adverb for the same action where tithes express an amount and firstfruits express the timing. Firstfruits went directly to the sanctuary for the priests to eat, whereas tithes from the people never went directly to the sanctuary. The people brought tithes to the Levites and the Levites brought their tithe of the tithes to the sanctuary.

Firstfruits occurred at the **beginning** of the harvest and tithes occurred at the **end** of the harvest. Firstfruits were small enough to fit into a basket; tithes were a tenth of the completed harvest. Firstfruits of the people were for the priests, and tithes of the people were for the non-priestly Levites.

Many popular Bible preachers and scholars who have not seriously studied the Law confuse firstfruits and tithes. Adam and Eve's sin of eating the forbidden fruit had nothing to do with tithing. Cain's failure to satisfy God in his offering of crops had to do with blood atonement and firstlings, not tithing. Achan's sin had to do with breaking God's commandment regarding utterly destroying conquered cities, not tithing. The resurrection of Jesus Christ had to do with Him being the firstfruits of the covenant of life, not tithing. King Solomon taught firstfruits according to the Law in Proverbs 3:9-10, not tithes. Confusion about what the Scriptures say about tithes naturally leads to confusion about firstfruits. New Testament allusions to firstfruits have nothing to do with tithes. Confusing firstfruits and tithes most certainly provides no Scriptural proof for the modern monetary income tithe doctrine.

8. Render unto Saul

The Royal Tithe Tax

1 Samuel 8:10-18

10: And Samuel told all the words of the LORD unto the people that asked of him a king.

11: And he said, This will be the manner of the king that shall reign over you: He will take your sons, and appoint *them* for himself, for his chariots, and *to be* his horsemen; and *some* shall run before his chariots.

12: And he will appoint him captains over thousands, and captains over fifties; and *will set them* to ear his ground, and to reap his harvest, and to make his instruments of war, and instruments of his chariots.

13: And he will take your daughters *to be* confectionaries, and *to be* cooks, and *to be* bakers.

14: And <u>he will take your fields, and your vineyards, and your oliveyards, *even* the best *of them*</u>, and give *them* to his servants.

15: And <u>he will take the tenth of your seed, and of your vineyards</u>, and give to his officers, and to his servants.

16: And he will take your menservants, and your maidservants, and your goodliest young men, and your asses, and put *them* to his work.

17: <u>He will take the tenth of your sheep</u>: and ye shall be his servants.

18: And ye shall cry out in that day because of your king which ye shall have chosen you; and the LORD will not hear you in that day.

Understanding the whole nature of tithes in ancient history is critical to comprehending the tithe in the Bible and if it applies to the church. Although the preceding chapters of the book have proven and emphasized that the tithes in the Law were always only from crops and livestock, these tithes were, nevertheless, a form of taxation. They were God's agricultural tax and welfare system for the theocratic nation of Israel.

Observing a form of "tithe" for the maintenance of a king in the passage of Scripture above, one can clearly see the nature of tithes in the Bible. Tithes were a common form of **taxation!** Tithes were not purely religious, as some propose for the context of the church. Tithes always had to do with a **government**. Tithes were always a required contribution for the upkeep of a government. Regardless of if the ancient culture represented a theocracy, a monarchy, an oligarchy, a plutocracy, a democracy, or a republic, tithes were government taxes. Simply because God instituted tithes for the support of a holy Levitical priesthood does not mean that tithes were characteristically a religious ordinance. The Levitical priesthood was the government that God established for the nation of Israel, and the agricultural tithes were the taxes to support this form of government.

The tithe tax in ancient cultures

Tithes were not unique to the nation of Israel and the Levitical priesthood. Tithes existed in ancient cultures prior to the first recorded instance in the Bible. Tithes were not characteristic of religious cultures alone; many non-religious cultures used tithes as a form of taxation.[127] In fact, tithes were prevalent in ancient Arabian lands

---

127. *The Encyclopaedia Britannica*, 11th ed., s.v. "tithe."

where the Canaanite cultures dwelt.[128] Forms of tithe taxation occurred in ancient versions of Babylon, Persia, Egypt, and China.[129] A tithe as a tax for ruling entities and religious functions of theocracies was an established practice in ancient culture, and the patriarch Abraham likely was aware of this common practice when he gave such tithes to the priest-king Melchizedek.[130] The office of Melchizedek as a "priest-king" was not uncommon at the time, as many rulers of city-states exercised such a role.[131]

Although many ancient pagan cultures practiced a form of tithing for religious or priestly functions, these functions were inseparable from the government. As Melchizedek served as a priest-king, Abraham's tithes to him of the spoils of war followed a governmental practice common in Arab lands.[132] Abraham's tithes were both religious and governmental; however, no known ancient religion practiced tithes separate from a ruling entity. Tithes in ancient cultures were clearly a taxation to support the government.

The tithe as a tax in Mosaic Law

In the ancient nation of Israel under the Mosaic Law the government consisted of one of twelve tribes of people. The Levites served many different roles in the theocratic system of government, from officers to laborers. The Levites were civil officers who aided the

---

128. *The HarperCollins Bible Dictionary*, s.v. "tithe."
129. *New International Bible Dictionary*, s.v. "tithe."
130. Ibid.
131. *The Essential Study Bible: Contemporary English Version* (New York: American Bible Society, 2007), 16.
132. Kelly, 23.

priests. Both the priests and their non-priestly Levite brethren—the entirety of the tribe of Levi—constituted the governing body of the nation of Israel.

From a materialistic perspective, the Levitical priesthood would be a form of liability. Their duties did not produce much of anything materially, yet their services consumed material goods. Levites consumed food from the Levitical tithes to perform their duties of aiding the priests. The priests consumed their priestly tithes from the Levites to offer burnt sacrifices to God. From a modern, secular, and materialistic viewpoint, such a form of government would be less than ideal. All governments are liabilities and no government can legitimately create wealth. However, even a government that redistributes wealth would seem more pertinent than one that virtually only exists to consume.

Obviously, God's purpose in establishing the government of a Levitical priesthood for the nation of Israel was to demonstrate His sovereign blessings. God's creation of wealth came from His own control of the weather in the Promised Land. If the people of Israel obeyed God's law and gave certain tithes to this materially unproductive government, God blessed them by giving them an abundant harvest through an ideal climate. If the people of Israel disobeyed God's law and withheld these tithes from the Levites, if the Levites withheld their tithes from the priests, or if the priests kept food from the tithes from the Levites who ministered in the sanctuary, God cursed them by causing famines in the land to suppress the supply of crops and livestock.

Truly, the tithes in the nation of Israel under the Mosaic Law were a form of taxation, albeit from agricultural products alone. No provision or command in Scripture exists for the concept of tithes for independent religious organizations that do not exercise the force of government. When a religion acts separately from government, tithes are not required. History and Scripture provide no such example of required tithes in the context of free worship and voluntary association. When modern churches in free nations teach tithe requirements of their members, they misunderstand the link between tithes and government. Of course, in the United States of America, organizations are free to require membership fees for anyone willing to pay them for the privilege of association. A major purpose of this book, however, is not to challenge such national laws, but to demonstrate that the Scriptures themselves do not communicate a special, universal mandate from God for members of churches to pay tithes for free religious functions.

The sanctuary shekel tax

The tithes were not the only tax God installed in the Law for the nation of Israel. The tithes were a tax on certain sources of agriculture. God also implemented a yearly census in which each Israelite male upon being numbered had to pay a half shekel of silver as "atonement money" for sanctuary maintenance (Exodus 30:12-16). The silver shekel weighed approximately one half troy ounce, worth about what someone in the United States would be paid working minimum wage for one hour. Obviously, this was not meant to be a very burdensome fee. God commanded both the rich and the poor to pay this exact amount. Other than the census for sanctuary tax, God strictly forbade arbitrary censuses because of the temptation to determine military might.

One cannot call this sanctuary tax a "tithe." A *tithe* would be a tenth part of something. The sanctuary tax, however, was not a percentage of anything, but rather a specific quantity. Because of the blurred definition of "tithing" today, some people are tempted to refer to any type of giving of any amount, whether voluntary or compulsory, as "tithing." However, regardless of the economic status of the individual male, the payment was always one half shekel of silver. **Landowners** had to give **tithes** of the increase of their harvest. **All males**, regardless of occupation, owed this annual tax—a small unit of money—to the sanctuary.

God as king

Numbers 23:21-22

21: He hath not beheld iniquity in Jacob, neither hath he seen perverseness in Israel: the LORD his God *is* with him, and the shout of a king *is* among them.
22: God brought them out of Egypt; he hath as it were the strength of an unicorn.

God's established form of government for the nation of Israel was a strict theocracy where He would be King. The laws that the nation would heed would come directly from God Himself, and He would often dictate them through a human mouthpiece. Until after the first king of Israel, the primary means through which God gave His commands, whether codified or situational, was through a human prophet or judge. Nevertheless, God was the true King of Israel. His voice was "the shout of a king" among the people and to the world.

Although Moses was the human servant who led the exodus of Israel out of Egypt, God was the One Who led them out through His mighty power. He hardened Pharaoh's heart, brought the plagues, parted the Red Sea, and sustained the Israelites through the wilderness where even their clothes did not wear out. How often Israel would forget their recent past and the God Who gave them victories!

My horse for a kingdom!

Deuteronomy 17:14-15

14: When thou art come unto the land which the LORD thy God giveth thee, and shalt possess it, and shalt dwell therein, and shalt say, I will set a king over me, like as all the nations that *are* about me;
15: Thou shalt in any wise set *him* king over thee, whom the LORD thy God shall choose: *one* from among thy brethren shalt thou set king over thee: thou mayest not set a stranger over thee, which *is* not thy brother.

Deuteronomy 17:14-20 actually predicts that the people of Israel would eventually reject God's unique theocracy and desire to have a king like other nations even while they were wandering in the wilderness. Included in God's prediction were regulations for the king himself to follow. God did not allow a position as king of Israel to be one of unchecked authority and embellishment. The king had to be of the seed of Israel: the nation could not make alliances with any Canaanite nation by anointing a foreigner as king. The king could not "multiply" wives, horses, or riches. The king also had to have the Law

175

of God present before him to remind him that God was the true ruler of Israel.

The desire for a king manifestly increased over the course of Israel's history as God gave them victory over the Canaanites. God promised Israel the land of Canaan, and they let the results of His sovereign hand go to their heads. Although they conquered the Canaanites with the power of God they eventually wanted these other nations to fear them for the strength of their armies and for the power of a human throne.

The people of Israel were tired of their own God getting the credit for their successes, victories, and prosperity. They were tired of God's name being the focal point of their presence in the land of Canaan. They wanted the might of man to receive the credit for health, wealth, and military gain. Because other nations could boast about the strength of their warriors and the wisdom, power, and riches of their king that acquired them success, the Israelites wanted to join this game with players of their own. Their desire for a king was pure pride—plain and simple.

Another contributing factor to the desire for a king was the false view of the situation of the nation during its hard times. John MacArthur notes that the fact that Israel faced captivities from nations ruled by kings contributed to their desire for a king of their own.[133] The nation of Israel at large forgot both the reason that they faced

---

133. *The MacArthur Bible Commentary*, 314.

problems with their neighboring Canaanites and the reason they were victorious over their enemies afterward. They wanted a king to "fight our battles" (1 Samuel 8:20). Apparently they felt that would have a greater chance of avoiding captivity if they had a designated human king to organize battle strategies. They failed to realize that their captivities happened because of their own sin, not because they had no king to command an army. They also failed to remember the Source of their victories and eventually exalted the human instruments that God used instead of God Himself.

A failed request for a throne—Pretty Please, Gideon!

Judges 8:22-23

22: Then the men of Israel said unto Gideon, Rule thou over us, both thou, and thy son, and thy son's son also: for thou hast delivered us from the hand of Midian.
23: And Gideon said unto them, I will not rule over you, neither shall my son rule over you: the LORD shall rule over you.

The demands of the people during Samuel's life that led to the coronation of King Saul was not the first time the people of Israel expressed a desire for a nominal throne. When God raised Gideon, a lowly farmer, to deliver Israel from the Midianites, the people eventually took their focus from God and placed it onto Gideon.

Despite the fact that God used a mere 300 men to defeat the Midianites for the express purpose of showing His power, the people forgot that God gave the victory. Despite the fact that God didn't even use these men themselves to disarray the hosts of the Midianites, the people lost their focus on God and began to look at man. After further victories with Gideon, the people of Israel desired to establish Gideon as a king and initiate a royal lineage through his descendents.

Gideon had enough of the correct focus to realize that God gave the victories. He may have realized that God did not dictate such a monarchy in the prescriptions of the Law (except where Deuteronomy 17:14-20 provided regulations for the contrary whims of the people). Understanding that God's ordinances defined a strict theocracy, he told the people that "the LORD shall rule over you." The people should have realized that God would continue to grant victories **through people**, but that the source of these victories was the sovereign hand of God, not the might of human instruments.

Unfortunately, Gideon's response was not completely righteous. Although he correctly declined the offer of a throne, he tried to appease the people by creating an ephod, or a memorial garment, from the golden earrings of the spoils of the Ishmaelite cities—the Midianites—that they recently conquered. Perhaps Gideon's intentions were completely just. The high priest wore an ephod according to the Law when performing sacrifices at the altar and other priestly functions in the sanctuary (Exodus 28:1-29:46). Perhaps the intent was to create a memorial that reminded the people that God delivered their enemies into their hands.

Regardless, the people of Israel began to treat this memorial as an idol. The people worshiped the ephod and forsook the legacy of Gideon and their God. When Gideon died, the nation turned over to Baal worship and idolatry. Like the rod of Aaron that budded, the people began to worship an image over the Creator. Like the Ark of the Covenant, the people began to attribute the power of victory to an object instead of the One Whom the object presented. Similarly, when God blesses some churches today with large buildings and large congregations, the temptation creeps to regard the fancy building and the practice of "empire-building" as the source of blessings rather than the God Who gave them.

A failed attempt at a throne—Abimelech's hostile takeover

Judges 9:1-2, 6

1: And Abimelech the son of Jerubbaal went to Shechem unto his mother's brethren, and communed with them, and with all the family of the house of his mother's father, saying,
2: Speak, I pray you, in the ears of all the men of Shechem, Whether is better for you, either that all the sons of Jerubbaal, which are threescore and ten persons, reign over you, or that one reign over you? remember also that I am your bone and your flesh.
6: And all the men of Shechem gathered together, and all the house of Millo, and went, and made Abimelech king, by the plain of the pillar that was in Shechem.

Apparently, Gideon's son Abimelech did not like his father's answer concerning a throne. If Gideon had chosen to become king, he believed that he would likely have inherited the throne. However, because Gideon did not accept the offer, Abimelech could not have the kingdom handed to him. Abimelech determined to take matters into his own hands. He presented a false dichotomy to his family at Shechem that either he should reign or his brothers from all Gideon's sons' mothers should rein, implying that the former choice was superior.

Abimelech was the son of Gideon through a concubine, and he felt that his chances of becoming a king would be threatened if he had surviving brothers of other mothers. His siblings from his mother agreed, and they gave him the funds to hire thugs to help him kill Gideon's other sons. Perhaps Abimelech's immediate family agreed to try to set him up as king knowing that they would receive royal favors if he were to succeed.

Abimelech "slew his brethren...upon one stone" (Judges 9:5). Possibly, this means that he captured them and put them to death together as a public "formal execution."[134] Jotham, the youngest brother escaped and hid himself. When Jotham found out that the people of Shechem made Abimelech king, he stood on Mount Gerazim and proclaimed a parable that allegorized the situation. However, he fled after speaking. Abimelech reigned as king over a region of Israel for three years. Eventually God intervened and caused the people of Shechem to despise Abimelech and to overthrow him.

Have it your way—Saul, the people's king

1 Samuel 10:23-24

23: And they ran and fetched him thence: and when he stood among the people, he was higher than any of the people from his shoulders and upward.
24: And Samuel said to all the people, See ye him whom the LORD hath chosen, that *there is* none like him among all the people? And all the people shouted, and said, God save the king.

Although the people had long desired a king and attempted to establish one in Gideon, they finally got what they wanted during the

---

134. Edward G. Dobson, Charles L. Feinberg, Edward E. Hindson, Woodrow Michael Kroll, and Harold L. Willmington, *King James Version Bible Commentary* (Nashville: Thomas Nelson, 2005), 251.

life of Samuel, the last judge of Israel. Samuel's sons "walked not in his ways" similar to how Eli's sons, Hophni and Phineas, abused their father's office. Perhaps the people of Israel used the wickedness of Samuel's sons as an excuse to cry out for a king. Through Samuel God told the people that He would let them have their king, but that he would be a burden. The burden would eventually be so great that the people would essentially change their mind (1 Samuel 8:18). However, God would refuse to relieve them from the burdens of their own king as He did from the burden of foreign kings.

Despite the warnings from God of the burden that a monarchy would place on the nation, the people desired the burden of human leadership and the prideful status before the Canaanites that a king would afford over the freedom and prosperity that God could give through His personal leadership. The people's choice of Saul exhibited perfectly their focus on outward human appearance over inward qualities. They wanted a king who "looked like" a king. They picked Saul who was likely one foot taller than the average Israelite (1 Samuel 9:2). Likely the people thought that if the Canaanites saw a handsome, strong, and tall king, they would fear the armies that he would command. The choice of Saul was a classic case of "My kung fu is better than your kung fu!"

Examining the history of the life of king Saul in detail is beyond the purpose and scope of this book. Needless to say, the people's choice of Saul reflected where their focus lay, and the flaws of this choice showed. Saul began as a humble leader zealous for following

God's ways. He was even afraid to assume this office at first. As he grew successful and the prestige of the position increased, King Saul forgot that his throne was a privilege from God and thought of it as a divine right. Naturally, he desired a lineage to the throne through his son Jonathan, but God rejected granting Saul this lineage because of his rebellion. God rent the kingdom from Saul, the very first king, and created a perpetual lineage through David.

Better God's way—David, a king after God's own heart

1 Samuel 16:6-7

6: And it came to pass, when they were come, that he looked on Eliab, and said, Surely the LORD's anointed *is* before him.
7: But the LORD said unto Samuel, Look not on his countenance, or on the height of his stature; because I have refused him: for *the LORD seeth* not as man seeth; for man looketh on the outward appearance, but the LORD looketh on the heart.

Even God's servant Samuel did not initially understand the ways of God concerning a king for Israel. As Samuel obeyed God to fetch a king to replace Saul even as Saul remained on the throne, Samuel envisioned in his head a man of comparable outward appearance to Saul. To Samuel's credit, God Himself indicated that Saul was His own choice. Possibly Samuel believed that God included outward strength and height as one of the criteria.

As Samuel came to the house of Jesse and saw his first son Eliab. Samuel may have believed that God providentially led him immediately to the choice for king. Even Samuel viewed a "kingly" quality in the outward appearance of Eliab. He "looked on" this son of Jesse and perceived a king based on his physical presence. God corrected Samuel's perception and told him that the inward qualities were what mattered to God, not simply physical height and might.

To the shock of both Jesse and Samuel, all the "important" sons did not pass God's litmus test. The only remaining son was the lowly youngest who tended sheep. Often the youngest son of any family performed the duties of drudgery while the oldest son, who would inherit the greatest portion of the father's property, received the favorable jobs and training for management. God, however, chose the youngest—the lowly shepherd—to be His king.

David was no weakling, nor was he plain or ugly. He was handsome in his own way. Rather than being good-looking in the hulk-warrior sense, he was probably good-looking in the attractive, baby-faced sense. David was brave, strong, and mighty, however, and performed his duties as a shepherd well. His resume included victories over lions and bears. Despite these qualifications the people of Israel would be unlikely to hire David as a king on these merits alone. A king would need to lead battles, and one who served in an army would likely be a first candidate for king. Eliab may have served in Saul's army according to 1 Samuel 17:28.[135] Perhaps, this fact contributed to Samuel's immediate assessment of him as God's likely choice for king.

David's reign as king was comparatively much more prosperous than Saul's. Although David committed some sins that most people would consider much more serious than did Saul, God called David "a

---

135. Loring Woart Batten, *A Commentary on the First Book of Samuel* (New York: Macmillan, 1919), 133.

man after his own heart" (1 Samuel 13:14). Saul's sins were sacrilegious, but David's sins included adultery and murder. However, David's redeeming quality was that he resolved his sins with true sorrow and repentance. The lesson of God's grace and mercy is not necessarily in the seriousness of a sin, but in the heart of the sinner who sees it through God's perspective.

A bloated bureaucracy

Although Samuel warned that the king would require a tenth of many things for himself, Israel could not **replace** God's theocratic system of government with that of a king. If the people of Israel desired to have a king, they would have to endure **both** the kingship and the Levitical priesthood. This "tithe" for the king was an additional tax; it did not substitute the system of tithes from the Law already in place.[136] Although the temptation may exist among some studying 1 Samuel chapter 8 to assume that the king would usurp the Levitical tithe, no account of Scripture definitively supports such an assumption.[137]

Israel's desire for a king expanded the bureaucracy of the nation. Not only did the nation have to support the Levitical and priestly portion of the government, but also they would have to support a king. The government for Israel through God's law was a theocracy run through a mediatory priesthood. The office of a king simply added to

---

136. Webb and Webb, 104.
137. Henry Landsdell, *Studies in Tithe-Giving, Ancient and Modern* (London: Society for Promoting Christian Knowledge, 1906), 93.

this burden. God required a tithe of the land to support the Levites. Now, with a king, the government would require another tithe of crops and livestock to support the king and his management of the palace and the military.

Any nation that wants their government to perform more services for them will always need more resources to fund these services. Whenever a nation adds another bureaucracy to their governmental roster, the cost will always be higher taxation in some form. People often forget that nothing is truly free of charge. The greater the size and scope of government, the greater the tax burden to fund it. Any government that promises to manage the people's every little need will do so at the expense of their very freedoms. The people of Israel ignored this time-tested law and desired a king anyway. They sacrificed the freedoms that they could have enjoyed under God's form of government for the social status and prestige of human might. Over the centuries after this decision, they suffered dearly for their presumption.

Conclusion and summary

In conclusion, we have examined the fact that tithes represented a form of taxation. Ancient cultures required tithes for their government even before Abraham's tithe to Melchizedek. These cultures, although including religious elements, exacted tithes as a form of governmental tax. Abraham's tithe to Melchizedek actually followed an ancient government custom regarding gifts of the spoils of war.

The tithes in the Mosaic Law were actually a form of agricultural taxation. The nation of Israel was a theocracy and the Levitical priesthood was the government. The tithes of crops and livestock were taxes to support the priesthood government. The Levitical tithes, like the sanctuary shekel tribute, were forms of government taxes; however, the sanctuary shekel was not conversely a "tithe."

God served as the King of Israel and used Levites, priests, prophets, and judges as His servants to mediate between the people and Himself. When the people rejected God and desired a king to be like other nations, they would need to pay an additional tithe tax to support the king. The king did not replace the Levitical government, but was like another branch of government, requiring more "taxes" for maintenance. The larger a government, the more taxes are required to maintain it. The link between tithes as a form of taxation and government entities is indisputable. All tithes throughout history and in the Bible are solely in the realm of government. The Scriptures provide no support for the modern monetary income tithe doctrine that purports to require church members to tithe for reasons that have nothing to do with a nation or a government.

SECTION III: THE LAW RETURNS

It's Still the Law

The southern kingdom of Judah endured 70 years of captivity away from their beloved homeland and away from the ability to keep certain laws that were tied to those borders. God had declared that if the people of Israel did not properly give their land rest and observe the Sabbath days and years and other laws, that He would give the land rest from them by giving them to their enemies in captivity. Because the people disobeyed God in desiring a king, and predictably, wicked kings led the nation astray and into division, God taught them a lesson.

Before the captivity, the northern kingdom of Israel suffered under predominately evil kings whereas the southern kingdom of Judah endured the ups and downs of both good and evil kings. The southern kingdom saw revivals and returns to the Law, departure into idolatry, and further returns to the Law. A notable instance in our study of tithing is the reformation under king Hezekiah following the destruction from his wicked father Ahaz. In restoring the Law, King Hezekiah faces circumstances with the blessings of tithes that lead him to establish his own system of handling and storing the tithes. Although Hezekiah's innovative storehouse system was not required by the Law, it became the bedrock for a future passage of Scripture that seems to be quoted more often than the writer of that passage would ever dream.

9. Back to the Basics

King Hezekiah and the Storehouse Chambers

2 Chronicles 31:11-12

11: Then Hezekiah commanded to prepare chambers in the house of the LORD; and they prepared *them*,
12: And brought in the offerings and the tithes and the dedicated *things* faithfully: over which Cononiah the Levite *was* ruler, and Shimei his brother *was* the next.

A history of forsaking God

God commanded the nation of Israel in the wilderness in Deuteronomy 12:8: "Ye shall not do... every man whatsoever *is* right in his own eyes." After God led Israel victoriously against the Canaanites to settle in the Promised Land, they fell exactly into this trap. The problem was not that God had not provided laws for them to keep. The problem was not that God did not speak through different human vessels to remind them of these laws. The problem seemed to be that the Israelites simply would not commit to following God's laws without coercion or punishment.

Twice the book of Judges sums up the moral condition of the nation of Israel during this period. Judges 17:6 and 21:25 both make the same statement in Hebrew that "in those days *there was* no king in Israel" and "every man did *that which was* right in his own eyes." Obviously, because of the testimony of Scriptures that by desiring a king the nation of Israel forsook God, these verses were not saying that these people **needed** a king to do right. These verses merely portray the sad condition of the nation at that time. Their desire for a king was against God's prescription for their government, yet they could not bring themselves to following God's laws anyway without a central human ruler to provoke them.

With Saul, the nation had the king that they desired. He was tall, strong, commandeering—and totally susceptible to pride, jealousy, breaking God's law, and forsaking God totally. God rejected Saul and chose David with whom He made a covenant that Messiah should sit on his throne. Though David had serious moral weaknesses, he often repented and sought God's mercy and forgiveness. David's son Solomon was generally a God-fearing king and acquired great wealth for Israel; however, his having seven hundred wives and three hundred concubines broke God's laws for kings not to multiply wives and make alliances with pagan cultures. As Deuteronomy 17:17 predicted, a king who would do this would turn away from God.

After Solomon's reign the nation became divided under Solomon's son Rehoboam. The northern kingdom of Israel was almost totally dominated by wicked kings and idolatry. The southern kingdom of Judah experienced a more positive history, but certainly had its share of pagan rulers. During the course of the decline of the kingdom of Judah the people and the government became virtually ignorant of the Mosaic Law, including the tithing laws. After the death of the wicked king Ahaz, his son Hezekiah began to revive God's forsaken Law and Levitical priesthood.

A return to the Law

Hezekiah began to reform the nation immediately upon taking the throne. In the very first month of holding office, he "opened the doors of the house of the LORD, and repaired them" (2 Chronicles 29:3). Apparently, the nation had totally forsaken the operation of the Levitical priesthood and the use of the sanctuary in the temple. The doors were even worn out and needed to be repaired before they were usable again.

King Hezekiah then called in the Levites and priests for a conference meeting. He told them that they had to begin following the priestly laws and use the sanctuary as God commanded. He reminded them of the sorry state that the kingdom was in because it had forsaken the Law. He urged them to follow the Law to restore God's blessing and their prosperity.

Fortunately, the Levites and priests heeded the words of Hezekiah and began a cleaning spree. They restored ministration in the sanctuary and offered sin offerings as atonement for the nation. They followed the solemn sin offerings with thank offerings. Interestingly, the priests needed extra help from the non-priestly Levites because "the Levites *were* more upright in heart to sanctify themselves than the priests" (2 Chronicles 29:34).

After cleansing the sanctuary and restoring the sacrificial system, King Hezekiah began to return the practice of the annual feasts. He placed particular emphasis on the feast of Passover. Possibly Hezekiah wanted to remind the people of Judah of what God had done for them and reinstall the reverence of God that they had lost. The God Who delivered them from bondage by His mighty hand and overthrew the most powerful nation on earth at the time is also the God Who commanded them to observe the feast of Passover every year to commemorate this event.

A return to tithing

2 Chronicles 31:1-3

1: Now when all this was finished, all Israel that were present went out to the cities of Judah, and brake the images in pieces, and cut down the groves, and threw down the high places and the altars out of all Judah and Benjamin, in Ephraim also and Manasseh, until they had utterly destroyed them all. Then all the children of Israel returned, every man to his possession, into their own cities.

2: And Hezekiah appointed the courses of the priests and the Levites after their courses, every man according to his service, the priests and Levites for burnt offerings and for peace offerings, to minister, and to give thanks, and to praise in the gates of the tents of the LORD.

3: *He appointed* also the king's portion of his substance for the burnt offerings, *to wit,* for the morning and evening burnt offerings, and the burnt offerings for the sabbaths, and for the new moons, and for the set feasts, as *it is* written in the law of the LORD.

As 2 Chronicles chapter 30 makes obvious to the context of chapter 31, the annual feasts and tithing under the Mosaic Law were inseparable. As chapters 5 and 6 of this book made clear, the annual feasts and the tithing laws were intertwined together in a Sabbatical cycle. As chapter 7 of this book also added, tithes and firstfruits were two completely different laws observed at completely different times of the year with two completely different recipients. Tithes, firstfruits, and feasts are related like a system of gears in the Levitical laws.

At the appropriate time in the year during King Hezekiah's reforms he made sure that the nation fully prepared for the Feast of Passover and observed it. If you remember from chapter 5 of this book, most, if not all the tithe for annual celebration was used for the Feast of Tabernacles at the end of the harvest. Chapter 7 also explained the difference between firstfruits and tithes and how that firstfruits happened at the beginning of the harvest whereas tithes occurred at the end. There was a Feast of Firstfruits after the priests received their portion at the sanctuary. Later was the Feast of Passover. This feast occurred **before** the tithes.

2 Chronicles 31:4-7

4: Moreover he commanded the people that dwelt in Jerusalem to give the portion of the priests and the Levites, that they might be encouraged in the law of the LORD.
5: And as soon as the commandment came abroad, the children of Israel brought in abundance the firstfruits of corn, wine, and oil, and honey, and of all the increase of the field; and the tithe of all *things* brought they in abundantly.
6: And *concerning* the children of Israel and Judah, that dwelt in the cities of Judah, they also brought in the tithe of oxen and sheep, and the tithe of holy things which were consecrated unto the LORD their God, and laid *them* by heaps.
7: In the third month they began to lay the foundation of the heaps, and finished *them* in the seventh month.

On the heels of observing the Passover, King Hezekiah then began to reinstate the operations of the priests and Levites regarding the sanctuary. He commanded those living in Jerusalem where the sanctuary resided "to give the portions of the priests and the Levites" (2 Chronicles 31:4). This was a reference to both the firstfruits and the tithes of produce required in the Mosaic Law. Interestingly, it appears that Hezekiah simply gave a command for residents of Jerusalem to begin offering firstfruits and tithes. Likely he was trying to start small and gradually reintroduce the entire nation to the requirements of the Law. He ordered the people of Jerusalem to give the priests and Levites firstfruits and tithes "that they might be encouraged in the law of the LORD."

King Hezekiah's reforms worked much better than he expected. His command was exclusively for the residents of Jerusalem who lived in proximity to the sanctuary. However, the hearts of the people of the entire nation became zealous to follow the Law. Likely, the king's command to Jerusalem spread by word of mouth throughout the entire nation of Judah. Even people who had a former alliance with the northern kingdom began to participate in the agricultural laws by bringing their firstfruits to the sanctuary.

Although verses 5 and 6 list the acts of firstfruits and tithes together, these acts were separated over a period of about four months. The firstfruits began in the third month around the time of the Feast of Pentecost and the seventh month was around the time of the Feast of Tabernacles.[1] Tithes and firstfruits were not the same thing. The people did not give their tithes and firstfruits at the same time unless they were late in observing the Law and tried to rush this observance. If they did give "firstfruits" and tithes at the same time in this year of

---

1. Edward Lewis Curtis, Samuel Rolles Driver, Albert Alonzo Madsen, Alfred Plummer, and Charles Augustus Briggs, *A Critical and Exegetical Commentary on the Books of Chronicles*, vol. 10 of *The International critical commentary on the Holy Scriptures of the Old and New Testaments* (New York: Charles Scribner's Sons, 1910), 480.

Hezekiah's reform, they may have simply assigned a certain portion as firstfruits for the priests and the rest as tithes for the Levites.

The courses of priests and Levites

2 Chronicles 31:2

2: And Hezekiah appointed the courses of the priests and the Levites after their courses, every man according to his service, the priests and Levites for burnt offerings and for peace offerings, to minister, and to give thanks, and to praise in the gates of the tents of the LORD.

Hezekiah reinstituted the practice of dividing the priests and Levites into rotating courses of families to minister in the sanctuary. As chapter 4 of this book explained, the Levites and priests dwelt in certain assigned cities throughout the land. The Law did not contain specific regulations for how the priests and Levites would organize themselves to tend the sanctuary. Because the Levites and priests normally dwelt in certain cities, they could not minister in the sanctuary year round.

The original division of Levites and priests into assigned rotating courses began under King David.[2] 1 Chronicles chapters 23-26 describe the structure that David established for sanctuary maintenance. He assigned certain families of Levites to certain tasks. Some were supervisors, some were laborers, some were musicians and singers, and some were politicians. 1 Chronicles chapter 24 delineates a total of 24 courses of Levite families that would rotate for sanctuary ministry. Each course of Levites would serve for a total of one week in

---

2. *Matthew Henry's Commentary*, 475.

the sanctuary.[3] This rotation of 24 courses meant that each family of Levites would minister with the priests an average of two weeks per year. The other 23 courses who were not ministering at the sanctuary were farming in the Levitical cities. This structure of 24 rotating courses of Levites is vital to understanding the events of Nehemiah chapter 13 and the context of the book of Malachi regarding tithes and offerings.

2 Chronicles 31:12-19 explains King Hezekiah's reorganization of the courses of Levites and priests and their assigned duties. These duties included managing the freewill offerings, sacrifices, and sanctification rituals. This system of dividing Levites and priests into courses for duties is prevalent throughout the history of Israel under kingship. David originally established the practice. Hezekiah reintroduced it. Nehemiah later reinstates it after the Babylonian captivity.

The new storehouse chambers

2 Chronicles 31:8-12

8: And when Hezekiah and the princes came and saw the heaps, they blessed the LORD, and his people Israel.
9: Then Hezekiah questioned with the priests and the Levites concerning the heaps.
10: And Azariah the chief priest of the house of Zadok answered him, and said, Since *the people* began to bring the offerings into the house of the LORD, we have had enough to eat, and have left plenty: for the LORD hath blessed his people; and that which is left *is* this great store.
11: Then Hezekiah commanded to prepare chambers in the house of the LORD; and they prepared *them*,

---

3. Kelly, 74.

12: And brought in the offerings and the tithes and the dedicated *things* faithfully: over which Cononiah the Levite *was* ruler, and Shimei his brother *was* the next.

King Hezekiah originally gave the command to the residents of Jerusalem, but the people of the entire nation obeyed zealously. The nation was still divided between the northern kingdom of Israel and the southern kingdom of Judah. However, many people even from the northern kingdom followed the command and brought firstfruits and tithes. The final results in the seventh month around the Feast of Tabernacles were an overwhelming abundance. The priests and Levites ate their fill and the heaps were the remaining food.

The question now was what to do with the remaining food that lay in heaps. Obviously the prudent answer would not be to leave these heaps where they lay. King Hezekiah wisely ordered the construction of storehouse chambers in the Temple to hold this leftover abundance. Matthew Henry suggested that the order to build storehouse chambers to keep the excess food was to prevent it from spoiling or being stolen.[4]

2 Chronicles 31:19

19: Also of the sons of Aaron the priests, *which were* in the fields of the suburbs of their cities, in every several city, the men that were expressed by name, to give portions to all the males among the priests, and to all that were reckoned by genealogies among the Levites.

It is relevant to note that the storehouse practice was not a prescription of the Mosaic Law. God merely commanded the people to

---

4. *Matthew Henry's Commentary*, 476.

bring tithes to the Levitical cities for the Levites and to bring firstfruits to the sanctuary for the priests. The presence of extra food and the separation of Levites into 24 rotating courses established an extra practice of bringing **a portion** of tithes into the Temple storehouse chambers to feed the currently ministering course of priests and Levites. Not all tithes went to the storehouse; only a portion of the Levitical tithe and the priestly tithe went to the storehouse. The reforms of Nehemiah after the Babylonian captivity discussed in the next chapter of this book clearly explain that the people brought their tithes to the Levitical cities for the Levites according to the Law (Nehemiah 10:37). The Levites, in turn, would then give their tithe of these tithes to the priests who would oversee the portion of their deposit in the Temple storehouse (Nehemiah 10:38). The tithes in the storehouse would feed both the priests and the Levites who rotated service in the Temple. These tithes did not feed **all** priests and Levites. This practice is important to understand because Malachi 3:10 does **not** command the people of Israel to bring all their tithes to the Temple storehouse as many modern church tithing advocates incorrectly assert. Only a small portion of the Levitical tithe went to the storehouse.

2 Chronicles 31:19 clearly demonstrates the fact that all priests and Levites did not minister full-time in the Temple. Only a small rotating course of them did so at any time. The rest of the time these priests and Levites lived in their assigned cities. However, the portion of the tithe of the Levitical tithes that went to the storehouse was there to care for

the courses of priests and Levites during the time they ministered in the Temple. Many modern church tithing advocates do not understand this fact from Old Testament laws and history. The Bible contains absolutely no support for the idea of the tithes of all people going to the sanctuary and likely no priest or Levite ministered continually in the Temple. The conception that Solomon's temple or Herod's temple could have possibly had room to store **all** or even a significant portion of a full tenth of annual produce from the land of the entire nation of Israel is utterly absurd. The idea of the church being the New Covenant continuance of the Temple and the storehouse is utterly unsupportable by Scripture. Even if such were the case, the Old Testament does not even support the notion of full-time ministers and all tithes for the storehouse. The next chapters of this book discussing Nehemiah and Malachi will build on this solid foundation and prove that the popular understanding of Malachi 3:8-10 is completely unsound and falls flat on its face.

Conclusion and summary

In conclusion, we have examined the reforms of King Hezekiah to reintroduce the practice of the Mosaic Law to the people of Israel. During the course of Hezekiah's first year he repaired the doors of the sanctuary in the Temple and reopened the sanctuary for Levitical and priestly functions. He counseled these religious leaders to obey the Law, and they sanctified themselves and offered atoning sacrifices for the nation. Hezekiah then concentrated efforts on observing the Feast of Passover. Following the feast of Passover, Hezekiah commanded the residents of Jerusalem to begin the practice of giving the priests their firstfruits and the Levites their tithes.

The command spread throughout the entire kingdom of Judah, and the result was an abundance of food. The priests and Levites ate to satisfaction and a great store of food remained in heaps. King Hezekiah then built storehouse chambers in the Temple to house this leftover food. The practice of storehouse tithing began from this event, but the Mosaic Law itself did not prescribe this means.

King Hezekiah also resumed King David's practice of dividing priests and Levites into courses of families who would take turns ministering in the Temple. The Levites were divided into 24 families who would minister each for one week. The priests would ensure that food from tithes existed in the storehouse to feed the courses of priests and Levites during their ministration in the Temple.

Not all tithes went to the storehouse. Only a portion of the Levitical tithe did. The people brought their tithes to the Levitical cities, and the Levites brought a portion of the tithe of these tithes to the storehouse. Therefore, only a small part of one tenth of the Levitical tithe was present in the storehouse. The fact that the priests and Levites took rotating turns ministering in the Temple, and the fact that less than one tenth of the Levitical tithe went to the storehouse, contradicts modern church tithing practice and teaching. The account of the reforms of Hezekiah in 2 Chronicles chapter 31 provides absolutely no support for the modern monetary income tithe doctrine.

10. Back to the Basics Again

Ezra, Nehemiah, and the Temple

Nehemiah 10:38-39

38: And the priest the son of Aaron shall be with the Levites, when the Levites take tithes: and the Levites shall bring up the tithe of the tithes unto the house of our God, to the chambers, into the treasure house.

39: For the children of Israel and the children of Levi shall bring the offering of the corn, of the new wine, and the oil, unto the chambers, where *are* the vessels of the sanctuary, and the priests that minister, and the porters, and the singers: and we will not forsake the house of our God.

A brief history for a captive audience

Approximately 300 years after Hezekiah's reforms came the reforms under Ezra and Nehemiah. During this period of 300 years several drastic events occurred. Hezekiah's son Manasseh reigned as an evil king who swiftly brought back Baal worship, high places, pantheism, and the heathen human sacrificial practices of Molech. After Manasseh faced captivity from the Assyrians he repented and God reestablished his throne. Manasseh's son Amon inherited the throne at his father's death. He only reigned two years as a king and was even more wicked than Manasseh had been. After only two years, Amon became such a burden that his own servants assassinated him and placed Josiah on the throne.

Josiah began to reign when he was only eight years old, but he returned the nation of Judah to the Law similar to the reforms under Hezekiah. He re-instituted the courses of priests and Levites for work in the Temple and kept the greatest Passover feast in Israel's history. No mention exists of reinstalling the system of firstfruits and tithes during this time, but it may have happened. Josiah died in a battle with Necho, king of Egypt.

After Josiah's otherwise prosperous and reforming reign the seeds of the Babylonian captivity began. The remaining four kings were evil and reigned briefly. Josiah's son Jehoahaz reigned for only three months before Necho brought him captive to Egypt. Jehoahaz's brother Jehoiakim reigned only eleven years before Nebuchadnezzar brought him captive to Babylon. His son Jehoiachin reigned only three months and ten days before Nebuchadnezzar captured him as well. His son Zedekiah reigned for only eleven years during which the prophets Isaiah and Jeremiah prophesied the total captivity of Judah in Babylon. Zedekiah also became captive to Nebuchadnezzar and Judah remained in captivity to the kingdoms of Babylon and Medo-Persia for a combined total of seventy years. This period was considered a rest of Sabbath for the land of Canaan as God has warned would happen in Leviticus 26:33-35 if the Israelites continually broke the Law.

During the seventy year captivity the prophet Daniel prospered in these foreign governments and received special future revelation from God about the date that Messiah would come and further tribulation. Under King Cyrus of Persia whom God predicted would reign, calling him His "servant," his "shepherd" and His "anointed" (2 Chronicles 36:22-23; Ezra 1:1-4; Isaiah 44:26-45:3), the people of Israel were allowed to return to their land to rebuild the Temple. Nehemiah emotionally requested permission from King Artaxerxes of Persia to take with him a band of Israelites to rebuild the Temple in Jerusalem.

Although Artaxerxes granted this partial request, King Cyrus soon later actually commissioned the project permanently and released the remnant of Israel from captivity. The punishment of Israel had been complete, the land had its rest, and the prophecy of Cyrus had been fulfilled.

Rebuilding the Temple and the legacy of Hezekiah

Nehemiah 8:16-18

16: So the people went forth, and brought *them*, and made themselves booths, every one upon the roof of his house, and in their courts, and in the courts of the house of God, and in the street of the water gate, and in the street of the gate of Ephraim.
17: And all the congregation of them that were come again out of the captivity made booths, and sat under the booths: for since the days of Jeshua the son of Nun unto that day had not the children of Israel done so. And there was very great gladness.
18: Also day by day, from the first day unto the last day, he read in the book of the law of God. And they kept the feast seven days; and on the eighth day *was* a solemn assembly, according unto the manner.

Nehemiah once again reintroduced the reforms that kings Hezekiah and Josiah enforced. The difference now was that these reforms were also in conjunction with a large project of building and restoring the Temple in Jerusalem. The group of post-exile Israelites permitted to engage this project in Jerusalem numbered a mere fifty thousand of the entirety of the captives from Judah (Ezra 2:64-65). In Nehemiah chapter 8, Ezra, who was a priest and a scribe, read portions of the Law before the Israelites who were present for the task in Jerusalem. According to the commandment in the Mosaic Law, these Israelites made "booths" and observed a seven-day feast. This feast was none other than the Feast of Tabernacles prescribed in Deuteronomy 16:13-

15. Each family would create and dwell in "tabernacles" or "booths" and eat a feast each day for seven days. The food for the Feast of Tabernacles came from the tithes at the end of the harvest. This passage of reform is an indirect reference to the annual festival tithes.

Nehemiah 10:34

34: And we cast the lots among the priests, the Levites, and the people, for the wood offering, to bring it into the house of our God, after the houses of our fathers, at times appointed year by year, to burn upon the altar of the LORD our God, as it is written in the law:

Nehemiah 10:34 possibly shows that Nehemiah revived the system of courses of Levites and priests who rotate service in the sanctuary. They "cast lots" dealing with burnt offerings "at times appointed year by year." David originally cast lots to determine the order that the 24 courses of Levite families would minister in the Temple (1 Chronicles 24:1-19). Perhaps casting lots also had to do with the order at which the courses priests and Levites would likewise serve. Verses 1-27 list names of certain priests and Levites, and verse 28 lists several professions—porters and singers—to which David originally assigned certain families of Levites.

Firstfruits and tithes reiterated

Nehemiah 10:35-37

35: And to bring the firstfruits of our ground, and the firstfruits of all fruit of all trees, year by year, unto the house of the LORD:
36: Also the firstborn of our sons, and of our cattle, as it is written in the law, and the firstlings of our herds and of our flocks, to bring to the house of our God, unto the priests that minister in the house of our God:
37: And that we should bring the firstfruits of our dough, and our offerings, and the fruit of all manner of trees, of wine and of oil, unto the priests, to the chambers of the house of our God; and the tithes of our ground unto the Levites, that the same Levites might have the tithes in all the cities of our tillage.

These verses provide yet another important confirmation of the difference between firstfruits and tithes. Firstfruits of crops, firstlings of animals, and firstborn of people were all the "firsts" that God required. Notice that **all** these "firsts" were required to go directly to the sanctuary for the **priests**. These "firsts" directly from the people went into the storehouse chambers of the Temple.

In contrast to the means of giving firstfruits were tithes. The people gave **firstfruits** directly to the sanctuary for the **priests**. However, the people gave their **tithes** directly to the Levites who dwelt in the Levitical cities.[5] The people never gave tithes directly to the storehouse. They gave **firstfruits** to the storehouse, but **tithes** to the Levitical cities. To recap, the firstfruits were for priests at the sanctuary; the tithes were for the Levites in their cities.

Only the Levites practiced "storehouse tithing"

Nehemiah 10:38-39

38: And the priest the son of Aaron shall be with the Levites, <u>when the Levites take tithes</u>: and <u>the Levites shall bring up the tithe of the tithes unto the house of our God</u>, to the chambers, into the treasure house.
39: For <u>the children of Israel and the children of Levi</u> shall bring the offering of the corn, of the new wine, and the oil, <u>unto the chambers</u>, where are the vessels of the sanctuary, and the priests that minister, and the porters, and the singers: and we will not forsake the house of our God.

This passage clearly expresses the regulations of the Law regarding the Levitical tithes. Under Nehemiah's and Ezra's leadership, the people of Israel present for the Temple project resolved to follow

---

5. Kelly, 81-82.

the prescriptions of the Law as God dictated and fit them into the structure of Hezekiah's storehouse. Notice that the people gave their tithes to the Levites. Only the tithes of the Levites for the priests went into the storehouse. A portion of this priestly tithe was brought weekly by the ministering course of Levites. Notice also that the high priest was to supervise this process. This tidbit provides important background to the evil of Eliashib the priest in Nehemiah chapter 13. Understanding the specifics of the tithing laws, the Temple storehouse structure, and the priestly oversight of storehouse chambers is absolutely crucial to interpreting the book of Malachi properly.

Remember from the Law that certain offerings from the people of Israel went directly for the priests to use as food for themselves or burnt sacrifices for the nation. Offerings and firstfruits from the people went straight to the sanctuary, but tithes from the people went straight to the Levites. The Levites, in turn, gave the best tithe of their own tithes to the priests. Each ministering course of Levites and priests ensured that they had sufficient food in the Temple storehouse for their duties for the week. Nehemiah reestablished this practice according to the system of the Temple storehouse. The tithes, offerings, and firstfruits were still all agricultural produce alone.

The priestly oversight of the storehouse

Nehemiah 12:44

44: And at that time were some appointed over the chambers for the treasures, for the offerings, for the firstfruits, and for the tithes, to gather into them out of the fields of the cities the portions of the law for the priests and Levites: for Judah rejoiced for the priests and for the Levites that waited.

205

Nehemiah 12:1-26 provides a familiar delineation of names and families of priests and Levites and reiterates a structure of courses according to King David's system. Verses 41-42 lists names of priests and supplies the context for verse 44 above. Some priests were appointed to oversee the chambers and ensure that the offerings and firstfruits of the people and the portions of tithes from the Levites properly went into the storehouse chambers. According to verse 44, the ministering course of Levites and priests brought a portion of tithes that they needed to the storehouse.

The priests and Levites "that waited" were the ones who were ministering in the Temple. "Waited" here means "served" or "ministered" just as we refer to table attendants at a restaurant as "waiters" or "waitresses." Notice that not all priests and Levites ministered in the Temple, nor did they minister continually. The courses who were assigned in their rotations were the ones who "waited" in the sanctuary. Many church leaders who teach monetary income tithing also believe that Levites and priests ministered permanently in the Temple and compare their "full-time ministry" to this incorrect assumption. They likely have never read the passages critically in the Chronicles about the courses of Levites and priests and Nehemiah chapters 10-13. One wrong understanding leads to another.

Are we there yet?

After the Babylonian captivity and an overhaul of the Temple, the Israelites were stilling following the Law **as God gave it**—tithing food items **only**. When God said crops and livestock, He meant crops and livestock. When the people heard this from God, they did not understand Him to mean "whatever your source of 'income' is." They used money—gold and silver—as a medium of exchange for buying and selling goods and services in the market place similar to how we do it today. They gave tithes of the crops that grew on the land and the livestock that they raised at the pinnacle of the harvest to the Levites in their cities. They gave the firstfruits of the beginning of the harvest and the firstlings of their livestock to the priests at the sanctuary. Regarding tithes, they only used money as a convenient medium for travel to bring their tithes of food for the annual feasts—particularly the Feast of Tabernacles. Still, at this point in history, there is no record of the Israelites giving tithes of money, or of any source of "income" such as from labor for hire. There is no record here of them confusing firstfruits with tithes. Even nearly one thousand years after God gave the Law of Moses, the people of Israel never practiced or interpreted them anywhere near the modern church teaching.

Conclusion and summary

In conclusion, we have examined the reforms of Nehemiah and Ezra after the Babylonian captivity. We have briefly analyzed the period in history of the kingdom of Judah between King Hezekiah and Nehemiah. Nehemiah received a commission from King Artaxerxes to bring a group of Israelites to Jerusalem to rebuild the Temple.

Nehemiah implemented reforms similar to those of Hezekiah. He re-instituted the system of courses of Levites and priests to perform the duties of the Law. He re-established the Feast of Passover and the

Feast of Tabernacles. He revived the storehouse system for keeping tithes for Temple ministry.

When the people heard the Law, they began following the Law. Included in following the Law was renewed adherence to the distinct laws of tithes, firstfruits, and offerings, and the duties of the courses of priests and Levites. The people again began giving their firstfruits and food offerings to the priests at the Temple sanctuary. They also resumed giving their tithes of crops and livestock to the Levites in the Levitical cities. The Levites also began giving their tithes of these tithes to the priests, and portions of these to the storehouse to feed the priests and Levites who ministered there. No mention in the Bible at this point yet exists about "tithes and offerings" from monetary income. No mention yet exists of the people of Israel themselves practicing "storehouse tithing." The non-priestly Levites were the only ones who did this. The account of these reforms in Nehemiah chapter 10 provides not even a modicum of support for the modern monetary income tithe doctrine.

11. Power Corrupts

Eliashib Holds His Own

Nehemiah 13:10-12

10: And I perceived that the portions of the Levites had not been given *them*: for the Levites and the singers, that did the work, were fled every one to his field.
11: Then contended I with the rulers, and said, Why is the house of God forsaken? And I gathered them together, and set them in their place.

> 12: Then brought all Judah the tithe of the corn and the new wine and the oil unto the treasuries.

Nehemiah chapter 13 records a startling incident in the history of Israel over which most casual readers of the Bible would brush. Likely, you have not heard any of the text of this account in a pulpit sermon. Ironically, this very account provides the **exact** context of the entire book of Malachi. Nehemiah chapter 13 explains the complaints of God throughout the book of Malachi in veritable detail. Why is this the case? Because strong evidence suggests that the book of Malachi was written during the time that the events of Nehemiah chapter 13 were occurring. The next chapter of this book will explore the evidence of the correlation between Malachi and the events of Ezra and Nehemiah.

Stop in the name of the Law!

Nehemiah 13:1-3

> 1: On that day they read in the book of Moses in the audience of the people; and therein was found written, that the Ammonite and the Moabite should not come into the congregation of God for ever;
> 2: Because they met not the children of Israel with bread and with water, but hired Balaam against them, that he should curse them: howbeit our God turned the curse into a blessing.
> 3: Now it came to pass, when they had heard the law, that they separated from Israel all the mixed multitude.

Verses 1-3 supply a backdrop to the events that occurred during Nehemiah's absence. Levites performed their duty of reading the Law. They read the account of Balaam from Numbers chapters 22-25. Balak, king of Moab, tried to get Balaam to curse Israel, but God turned his attempt at a curse into a blessing. Balak became angry with

Balaam for this. Balaam said that he could only orate what God told him to say.

Balaam rectified this to favor Balak by suggesting that the Moabites intermarry with the Israelites to bring a curse upon themselves (Numbers 25:1-3; 31:16). Reading this account caused the Israelites to separate themselves from their pagan alliances. However, one particular alliance remained unfinished business.

Axis and Allies

Nehemiah 13:4-5

4: And before this, Eliashib the priest, having the oversight of the chamber of the house of our God, *was* allied unto Tobiah:
5: And he had prepared for him a great chamber, where aforetime they laid the meat offerings, the frankincense, and the vessels, and the tithes of the corn, the new wine, and the oil, which was commanded *to be given* to the Levites, and the singers, and the porters; and the offerings of the priests.

Before the Israelites followed the Law after it was read by separating from their pagan alliances and illegitimate marriages, Eliashib the high priest was one of those in the corrupt practice. He was "allied unto Tobiah." His alliance with Tobiah—an Ammonite who was an enemy of Israel—was likely based on a marital relationship within their families. Eliashib's grandson was married to Sanballat's daughter (Nehemiah 13:28). Sanballat and Tobiah together attempted to thwart the reconstruction of the Temple because they feared the resurgence of the nation of Israel. Eliashib as high priest had the oversight of the storehouse chambers to facilitate depositing the tithes (Nehemiah 10:38). Eventually, his alliance with Tobiah through

210

a foreign family relationship (which God strictly forbid for priests) caused him to provide a favor for Tobiah that strictly contradicted his duties.

Eliashib began to abuse his authority and oversight by removing the tithes from the storehouse and using one of the chambers to house Tobiah. Not only had Eliashib broken the Law through forming an alliance with a Canaanite, but he also shirked his responsibility of overseeing the proper use of the Temple storehouse. The fact that tithes were no longer deposited and stored in the chambers was totally the fault of this high priest. Much like Judas Iscariot who criticized Mary's "waste" of a costly ointment yet held the bag of the ministry's treasury, so Eliashib misused his authority over the storehouse. Those who did not know about Tobiah's unlawful quarters in the Temple could not properly be to blame. Those who did know may have been partly to blame, but they may have feared the authority of Eliashib. They may have believed that to oppose Eliashib would be to oppose God.

Verse 5 says that the chamber in the Temple where Tobiah lived was "where aforetime they laid" tithes and other things for the priestly ministry. Evidently this chamber was a primary one used as a storehouse for food for the priests and Levites who ministered. King Hezekiah commanded to build multiple storehouse chambers (2 Chronicles 31:11-12), and Nehemiah resumed this practice whereby tithes, offerings, and other things were stored in more than one chamber (Nehemiah 10:37-39).

Several possibilities exist for what was happening during this evil of Eliashib and Tobiah. Although scholars, historians, and theologians can provide more possibilities, I will present two below.

First, Eliashib may have been feeding Tobiah with **some** of the tithes—namely, the tithes that would normally have gone into this one chamber where Tobiah lived. When Malachi said to bring "**all** the tithes into the storehouse," he could have meant the missing tithes that would have gone into the chamber of Tobiah. Perhaps the chamber of Tobiah was where the tithes for the Levites were deposited and another chamber was where the tithes for the priests resided. Although this assertion is not provable, Nehemiah chapter 13 specifies that the Levites could not receive sustenance, but it says nothing about the condition of the priests. The fact that the "storehouse" comprised more than one chamber in the Temple could have led to assigning substances for certain uses or for certain recipients.

Second, Eliashib may have restrained the practice of bringing tithes into the Temple entirely. The firstfruits may have been enough to feed the priests there and the Levites could not legally eat from the firstfruits. Perhaps the alliance between Eliashib and Tobiah arranged for foreign exports to be brought into the Temple to supply Tobiah. The call, then, of Malachi for bringing the tithes into the storehouse would have been both for the priests and the people, with the brunt of the accusation on the priests for misleading the people and being "partial in the Law."

When the cat's away, the mice will play

Nehemiah 13:6

6: But in all this *time* was not I at Jerusalem: for in the two and thirtieth year of Artaxerxes king of Babylon came I unto the king, and after certain days obtained I leave of the king:

When Nehemiah was in Jerusalem, he governed with an iron hand. He was a purist who did not tolerate blatant disobedience to God's Law. How soon indeed did the Israelites veer from the reforms in Nehemiah's absence! Such had been characteristic of the nation of Israel throughout history. The people were quick to cry out to God during times of oppression from their enemies, yet they were also quick to depart from the Law during peace and prosperity.

This time of wickedness, however, could not be the full fault of the people. The high priest himself misled the people. The priests "caused many to stumble at the Law" and were "partial in the law" (Malachi 2:8-9). The priests introduced the practice of intermarrying with Canaanites (Malachi 2:11-12; Nehemiah 13:23-31), possibly procured by Eliashib's alliance with Tobiah through the marriage between Eliashib's grandson and Sanballat's daughter (Nehemiah 13:28).

Eliashib, the high priest, was responsible in misleading the people about their tithes by keeping them from the chamber where he housed Tobiah. Although any Israelite who knew the Law would have the responsibility to bring it to the attention of violators, the priests and Levites were responsible for preserving and propagating the Law to the nation. The people were to "seek the law at [the priest's] mouth" (Malachi 2:7). It is no wonder that the condemnation of Malachi came

213

down squarely on the priests as the next two chapters of this book will make clear!

The Return of the Governor

Nehemiah 13:7-9

7: And I came to Jerusalem, and understood of the evil that Eliashib did for Tobiah, in preparing him a chamber in the courts of the house of God.
8: And it grieved me sore: therefore I cast forth all the household stuff of Tobiah out of the chamber.
9: Then I commanded, and they cleansed the chambers: and thither brought I again the vessels of the house of God, with the meat offering and the frankincense.

When Nehemiah returned from his obligation before King Artaxerxes in Persia, he learned about the evil practices that were occurring and how the priests were corrupting the people. This realization "grieved [him] sore" (v. 8). Nehemiah must have been heartbroken, because his fiery reforms did not appear to last long outside his direct supervision. Apparently, the sanctification of the priests was only skin-deep. Their hearts were not completely right under Nehemiah. If they were, they would not have needed his abiding presence to continue in the Law. As the situation demonstrated, the priests—the ones who were supposed to be the epitome of righteousness under the Law—were not entirely sanctified and became easily corrupted. Truly, even during the time of Ezra and Nehemiah, "the Levites *were* more upright in heart to sanctify themselves than the priests" (2 Chronicles 29:34).

Nehemiah began his second reforms after returning from Persia. He removed Tobiah and his belongings from the storehouse chamber in the Temple and gave the order to clean the chamber of anything that was unlawful or pagan. Apparently, this chamber was where the vessels of the sanctuary originally resided. It also served as a clearinghouse for priestly sacrifices. This chamber also housed the priestly tithes that would feed both the courses of priests and Levites that ministered. However, the Levites were not getting their portion of the tithes.

Resist Levi and he will flee

Nehemiah 13:10-11

10: And I perceived that the portions of the Levites had not been given *them*: for the Levites and the singers, that did the work, were fled every one to his field.
11: Then contended I with the rulers, and said, Why is the house of God forsaken? And I gathered them together, and set them in their place.

Nehemiah discovered that the Levites were not receiving their portions of the tithes that were originally deposited in the storehouse chamber. Regardless of whether some or all of the tithes that were due for the Temple storehouse were no longer brought there, the major problem was that the course of Levites assigned to minister in the Temple was not getting any. Any Levites who attempted to perform their duties in the Temple could not receive adequate sustenance because they were not receiving their portion of the tithes. To be fed, they had to forsake their duties in the Temple and return to the fields of their Levitical cities. These fields are the homes where the Levites worked the rest of the year to farm the Levitical tithes that the people brought. Each family was supposed to minister in the Temple approximately two separate weeks each year. However, because sustenance from tithes was no longer available for them there, they could not serve these two weeks.

Notably, Nehemiah chapter 13 says nothing about the priests lacking sustenance. The priests were not fled to the priestly cities. Only the Levites were lacking. Either the priests were stealing the portion of the tithes to feed themselves or Tobiah, or their alliance with Tobiah was preventing any tithes from entering the Temple. Remember that the priests had some of their sustenance from firstfruits and offerings. These were inheritance and gifts for the priests alone. The tithes of the people were for the Levites. The tithe of the tithes was for the Levites to give to the priests. King Hezekiah established the practice of bringing a portion of the Levitical and priestly tithe into the Temple and for it to feed both the courses of priests and the courses of Levites as they ministered. Nehemiah resumed this practice with the reconstruction project.

Despite the fact that this Temple storehouse practice did not completely follow the original Law, what the priests did to the Levites was completely wrong and unfounded. The priests broke the Law by forming an alliance with Tobiah, a Canaanite enemy of Israel. The priests broke the Law by marrying Canaanites and teaching the people that they could do the same. The priests broke the sanction of God on Hezekiah's and Nehemiah's practice and shirked God's authority. The priests wronged the Levites by depriving them of sustenance that they needed and that the Temple system organized for their care in ministry. The priests bore the brunt of the iniquity that was occurring in

Nehemiah's absence, and as we shall observe in the next two chapters of this book, the accusations, criticisms, and curses of Malachi.

Why is the house of God forsaken?

When Nehemiah observed what the priests were doing in the temple and how they were stealing tithes from the Levites, he uttered familiar words to these priestly rulers: "Why is the house of God forsaken?" Nehemiah may have directly alluded to the vow that the Israelites made during his initial reforms before he returned to Persia. The Israelites made an oath to follow the Law (Nehemiah 10:29). At the end of this oath, regarding bringing the firstfruits, tithes, and offerings into the Temple storehouse chambers, they said: "We will not forsake the house of our God" (Nehemiah 10:39). Obviously, this vow not to "forsake the house of our God" was broken in whole or in part.

When Nehemiah charged these rulers with the words "Why is the house of God forsaken," they may have begun to lift some of the fog in their brains and remembered the vow that they had made only a few years prior. They may have recalled some of the specifics of the vow and compared them to their current practices. In their vow they promised that they would not marry the Canaanites (Nehemiah 10:30). They promised that they would follow the Sabbath commandments and not buy or sell from foreigners on these days (Nehemiah 10:31). They promised that they would follow the laws of firstfruits, firstlings, and firstborn for the priests (Nehemiah 10:35-37). They promised that they would follow the laws of tithes for the Levites in their cities and that they would bring the tithe of the tithes to the Temple storehouse chambers (Nehemiah 10:37-38). They promised that they would bring priestly offerings to the Temple for priestly ministry (Nehemiah 10:39).

Nehemiah's inquiry is strikingly similar to Malachi's. Malachi asked: "Will a man rob God?" concerning tithes and offerings not being deposited in the Temple storehouse (Malachi 3:8). He then commanded to "bring ye all the tithes into the storehouse" (Malachi 3:10). When one understands the laws of firstfruits, tithes, and offerings in the Law and their recipients and purposes; the historical practice of the Temple storehouse under Hezekiah and later under Ezra and Nehemiah; and the context of Malachi regarding the sins of the priests, one can understand exactly what Malachi was saying. The temptation of taking Malachi 3:8-10 entirely out of context is great when one introduces certain modern traditions into understanding these verses without studying the Law, the history, and the context of these very words. The next two chapters of this book will examine the book of Malachi in detail and expound more on this context as it applies to the situation of the priests and the nation during the time of Ezra and Nehemiah.

Tithes restored

Nehemiah 13:12-14

12: Then brought all Judah the tithe of the corn and the new wine and the oil unto the treasuries.
13: And I made treasurers over the treasuries, Shelemiah the priest, and Zadok the scribe, and of the Levites, Pedaiah: and next to them *was* Hanan the son of Zaccur, the son of Mattaniah: for they were counted faithful, and their office *was* to distribute unto their brethren.

14: Remember me, O my God, concerning this, and wipe not out my good deeds that I have done for the house of my God, and for the offices thereof.

Nehemiah's words seemed to have an effect on the priests and the post-exile Israelites. "All Judah" began to bring their tithes to storehouse. This may be a general term for the Levites. Under Nehemiah's initial reforms the people brought their tithes to the Levitical cities (Nehemiah 10:37). The Levites, in turn, brought the tithe of their tithes to the priests. Each ministering course of Levites and priests brought a portion to the storehouse for their week of service (Nehemiah 10:38). If "all Judah" meant the non-Levite people, it would represent a change from Nehemiah's initial reforms. It could mean the non-Levite people **indirectly** by virtue of the tithes for the storehouse coming from their tithes to the Levites. Dr. Russell Kelly suggests that it was actually tithes from the people, but was a temporary act to supply the storehouse with needed food for the Levites before the traditional structure resumed.[6] This is probably the most reasonable interpretation; otherwise, believing that a full tithe of the kingdom of Judah could fit in several chambers of one building would overestimate the size of the Temple or underestimate the harvest with which Judah was blessed.

Nehemiah obviously no longer trusted Eliashib with oversight of the storehouse chambers. He assigned other priests and even Levites for this duty. These were ones that he "counted faithful" (v. 13).

---

6. Kelly, 87.

Nehemiah attempted to prevent further abuse of the storehouse by assigning Levites with the task of giving the rest of the ministering Levites their portion of the tithes.

The rest of the story

The rest of Nehemiah chapter 13 chronicles Nehemiah's reforms of the Sabbath violations (vv. 15-22) and of unlawful alliances and marriages with Canaanites (vv. 23-31). The background of Eliashib's alliance with Tobiah is exposed in that his grandson was married to Sanballat's daughter. Sanballat was an ally of Tobiah who attempted to disrupt and thwart the Temple reconstruction project. A striking criticism of Eliashib and the priests "defiled the priesthood, and the covenant of the priesthood, and of the Levites" (v. 29). Malachi addresses this same problem in his scathing condemnation of the priests in that they "have corrupted the covenant of Levi" (Malachi 2:8). The next two chapters of this book will exegete the short book of Malachi and explain the striking textual similarities between the words of Malachi and the account of Nehemiah chapter 13.

Conclusion and summary

In conclusion, we have examined the sobering account of the sins of the priests during Nehemiah's absence in Persia in Nehemiah chapter 13 and their effects on the post-exile Israelites. Eliashib's alliance with the enemy Tobiah through a family marriage violated the Law and broke the first reforms under Nehemiah. Eliashib was the high priest who had oversight over the storehouse chambers in the Temple where tithes for Temple ministry were supposed to be deposited. Eliashib emptied a particular chamber and used it to house Tobiah. This sin resulted in tithes not going into the storehouse and the Levites who ministered not getting their necessary portion. The Levites had to flee back to fields of their cities to get sustenance.

Nehemiah returned from Persia and discovered what was happening. He reminded the priests about the Law and the vow that they made to follow it. He removed Tobiah and cleansed the storehouse. He reinstated the practice of bringing tithes into the storehouse to feed the courses of priests and Levites who ministered. The context of the real, historical practice of storehouse tithing helps one to understand what the priests were doing and why the house of God was forsaken. Nehemiah chapter 13 provides no support for the modern monetary income tithe doctrine, nor for the faulty teaching of "storehouse tithing" as is often taught today.

12. Profaning, Perversion, and Punishment

The Priests Exposed

Malachi 2:1-2

1: And now, O ye priests, this commandment *is* for you.
2: If ye will not hear, and if ye will not lay *it* to heart, to give glory unto my name, saith the LORD of hosts, I will even send a curse upon you, and I will curse your blessings: yea, I have cursed them already, because ye do not lay *it* to heart.

If you have been reading this book from start to finish, you may have been thinking that you would never get to a full discussion of the infamous text of Malachi 3:8-10. In fact, the sheer number of times these verses are quoted would make you think that the Bible does not discuss the subject of tithes enough before this point. The fact that this book has covered every passage about tithing thus far in depth and that the content of Malachi has not been discussed until chapter 12 demonstrates that one must read these other Scriptures to get a full understanding of tithing in the Bible. You may have found the previous chapters to be either interesting or tiring. However, studying tithing before Malachi 3:8-10 is absolutely essential to understanding these verses themselves. With a fuller understanding of the regulations of tithes in the Law, the ministry of the sanctuary, the roles of priests and Levites, the history and structure of the Temple storehouse system, and the reforms of Ezra and Nehemiah, you may be in shock as you read the book of Malachi verse by verse and discover how it all makes sense. In fact, knowing the time in history that Malachi was written may be the most important guide to understanding what the words of Malachi mean in context. Prepare for the shock of your life as you may discover that this chapter and the next chapter of this book will totally change your understanding of Malachi 3:8-10 for the rest of your life!

Who was "Malachi"?

Malachi 1:1

1: The burden of the word of the LORD to Israel by Malachi.

The name *Malachi* is a Hebrew word that means "my messenger." A striking similarity between the Hebrew word for *Malachi* (*mal'ākî*) in Malachi 1:1 and "my messenger" in Malachi 3:1 raises some questions. Was the author of the letter prophesying his own reforms? Most theologians believe that the writer and the "messenger" prophesied were different people, especially because the New Testament references Malachi 3:1 as a prophecy of John the Baptist (Matthew 11:7-11; Mark 1:2-4; Luke 1:76; 3:2-4; 7:24-27). A further discussion of the prophesies of Malachi 3:1 occurs in the next chapter of this book.

Some believe that the comparison of 1:1 and 3:1 suggests that "Malachi" was a pen name or a title and not the actual name of the writer.[7] One argument for *Malachi* not being a proper name is that no known historical record or tradition around the time of the letter records anything about the life and person of a prophet named Malachi.[8] Some in the past have accepted the idea of Ezra the scribe being "my messenger."[9] However, this view is becoming less relevant. Whoever was the author of the book of Malachi, the "Malachi" or "messenger" prophesied in the book was a different "Malachi."

The missing link—Nehemiah, Ezra, and Malachi

The correlation of the problems discussed in the books of Malachi and Nehemiah provides the primary evidence that these two writings express the same time period.[10] In fact, the book of Malachi very possibly must have been written during the period of events relayed in Nehemiah chapter 13 before Nehemiah came back to right all the

---

7. Marshall Custiss Hazard and Henry Thatcher Fowler, *Books of the Bible* (Boston: The Pilgrim Press, 1903), 104.
8. Richard A. Taylor and E. Ray Clendenen, *Haggai, Malachi*, vol. 21A of *The New American Commentary* (Nashville: Broadman & Holman, 2004), 205.
9. *Tyndale Bible Dictionary*, s.v. "Malachi, book of."
10. Pieter A. Verhoef, *The Books of Haggai and Malachi* (Grand Rapids: William B. Eerdmans Publishing, 1987), 157.

wrongs. Malachi writes specifically about the very sinful incidents that occurred while Nehemiah returned to King Artaxerxes.[11] The available sources of the Law from which Malachi references can also suggest authorship during this time before Nehemiah returned.[12]

Many prominent theologians, scholars, historians, and reference works derive the inescapable conclusion that the book of Malachi was written during the time of the reforms of Ezra and Nehemiah and proves this with its own content. John MacArthur concurs that the book of Malachi was written "most likely during Nehemiah's return to Persia."[13] *The Chronological Study Bible* arranges the Biblical text in an estimated chronological order and comments that the words of Malachi likely arose during the time of King Artaxerxes of Persia who commissioned Nebuchadnezzar's project, and before Ezra began his later reforms.[14] Stephen Miller's *The Complete Guide to the Bible* estimates that the events in Nehemiah happened "about 445 BC"[15], Ezra's reforms were "in the mid-400s"[16], and Malachi was written "in the 400s BC" confronting the same issues as Ezra did.[17] Warren Wiersbe observed that "Malachi encountered the same religious

11. George Townsend, ed., *The Old Testament: Arranged in Chronological Order*, 2nd ed. (London: C. and J. Rivington, 1826), 923.
12. John Roberts Dummelow, ed., *A Commentary on the Holy Bible* (New York: The Macmillan Company, 1920), 612.
13. *The MacArthur Bible Commentary*, 1077.
14. *The Chronological Study Bible* (Nashville: Thomas Nelson, 2008), 980.
15. Stephen M. Miller, *The Complete Guide to the Bible* (Uhrichsville, OH: Barbour Publishing, 2007), 137.
16. Ibid., 131.
17. Ibid., 292.

situation described in Ezra 9—10 and Nehemiah 8—13."[18] Popular and prolific historian Kenneth C. Davis claims that "historical evidence suggests [Malachi] was written some fifty years after Haggai and Zechariah and the reconstructed Temple but prior to the reforms carried out by Nehemiah."[19] *Halley's Bible Handbook* informs that Malachi "lived nearly a century after Haggai and Zechariah and that he worked with Ezra and Nehemiah in their reforms."[20] The *Zondervan Handbook to the Bible* infers from the content of the book of Malachi that it was "either just before Nehemiah became governor of Jerusalem, or during his absence later on."[21] Matthew Henry noted that whereas Zechariah and Haggai wrote concerning the problems that occurred during the Temple reconstruction project, Malachi wrote about the problems that occurred when the project was already complete.[22] Such an assertion would require historically that Malachi was written during the later time of Nehemiah's reforms, likely during his absence in Persia.

Textual evidences for the correlation of Ezra, Nehemiah, and Malachi exist. When Malachi tells the Israelites to offer sacrificial gifts to their "governor" (Malachi 1:8), he was referring to the office of

---

18. Warren W. Wiersbe, *With the Word: The Chapter-by-Chapter Bible Handbook* (Nashville: Thomas Nelson, 1991), 622.

19. Kenneth C. Davis, *Don't Know Much About® The Bible: Everything You Need to Know about the Gook Book but Never Learned* (New York: HarperCollins, 1998), 255.

20. *Halley's Bible Handbook with the New International Version*, 25th ed. (Grand Rapids: Zondervan, 2000), 485.

21. Pat Alexander and David Alexander, *Zondervan Handbook to the Bible*, 3rd ed. (Grand Rapids: Zondervan, 1999), s.v. "Malachi, Book of."

22. *Matthew Henry's Commentary*, 1194.

"governor" that Nehemiah held (Nehemiah 12:26).[23] Malachi refers to polluted bread on the altar and blemished animals to "offer it now unto thy governor" for acceptance (Malachi 1:7-8), whereas the governor Nehemiah also said that during the time he held this office he had "not eaten the bread of the governor" (Nehemiah 5:14). Likely this governor referenced in Malachi was another governor assigned when Nehemiah returned to King Artaxerxes to report to him (Nehemiah 13:6).[24]

Nehemiah criticizes some Israelites during this time for "marrying strange wives" of Canaanite peoples (Nehemiah 13:23-27), and Malachi revealed that they had "married the daughter of a strange god" (Malachi 2:11). When Nehemiah found out about the sin of Eliashib and the missing tithes for the Levites ministering in the Temple, he said, "Why is the house of God forsaken?" (Nehemiah 13:11). He then removed Tobiah, cleaned out the storehouse, and restored the tithes for the ministering Levites (Nehemiah 13:11-13). Similarly, Malachi states that the priests were "robbing God" by not bringing the tithes into the storehouse (Malachi 3:8-10).

The combined historical and textual evidences overwhelmingly indicate that the book of Malachi was indeed written during Nehemiah's leave of absence before King Artaxerxes, and hence before his second reforms. Understanding that Nehemiah chapter 13 supplies

---

23. Joseph P. Free and Howard Frederic Vos, *Archaeology and Bible History*, rev. ed (Grand Rapids: Zondervan, 1992), 214.
24. Ibid.

the exact historical context of the book of Malachi causes the words of Malachi to explode from the pages of Scripture! Following is a commentary on most of the book of Malachi with references to the proper context.

Name that reader

Malachi 1:1-5

1: The burden of the word of the LORD <u>to Israel</u> by Malachi.
2: I have loved you, saith the LORD. Yet ye say, Wherein hast thou loved us? <u>*Was* not Esau Jacob's brother?</u> saith the LORD: <u>yet I loved Jacob,</u>
3: <u>And I hated Esau,</u> and laid his mountains and his heritage waste for the dragons of the wilderness.
4: Whereas <u>Edom saith,</u> We are impoverished, but we will return and build the desolate places; thus saith the LORD of hosts, They shall build, but I will throw down; and they shall call them, The border of wickedness, and, The people against whom the LORD hath indignation for ever.
5: And your eyes shall see, and ye shall say, The LORD will be magnified from <u>the border of Israel</u>.

Malachi 1:1-5 serves as the essential opening and "greeting" of the letter. Verse 1 clearly identifies the recipients of this letter as "Israel." This is the post-exile nation of Israel after the reconstruction of the Temple. This was the portion of the remnant of Judah that lived in the Promised Land while the governor Nehemiah returned to Persia according to his promise to King Artaxerxes. Because the letter was written "to Israel," one must understand that Malachi 3:8-10 was also written "to Israel." To prove that Malachi 3:8-10 has **other** recipients than the specific ones of the post-exile nation of Israel, one must provide textual or other extant evidence for such a claim. Otherwise, simply reading Malachi 3:8-10 as a command to any hearers is taking the passage out of context, no different from reading 1 Samuel 15:3

227

and commanding that any hearer destroy the "Amalekites" and all their belongings.

In verses 2-3, God reminds the Israelites that His promise was to **them** through Jacob and not through Esau. Though Jacob and Esau were twin brothers, they were not joint-heirs of the promise. In fact, Esau was the firstborn of the two. Despite the patriarchal tradition of blessing the firstborn son, God "loved" Jacob and "hated" Esau. God chose the younger and made the older serve the younger (Romans 9:12-13). The older served the younger by virtue of Esau relinquishing his birthright and blessing to Jacob. God blessed the nation of Israel and made them powerful in history while He "laid...waste" Edom (the descendents of Esau).

In verses 4-5, God declared that the underdog Edomites would resolve to rebuild their cities and obtain power. He dictated that they would indeed obtain a period of power and prosperity, but that it would not last. God would eventually bring Edom back down to impoverishment. When this occurs, the nation of Israel would once again return to praising the One True God. Thus, even though the book of Malachi is full of scathing condemnation for "Israel," the "greeting" of the letter itself provides mercy and hope that Israel will indeed harken to these words.

The priests, the whole priests, and nothing but the priests

Malachi 1:6

6: A son honoureth *his* father, and a servant his master: if then I *be* a father, where *is* mine honour? and if I *be* a master, where *is* my fear? saith the LORD of hosts unto you, O priests, that despise my name. And ye say, Wherein have we despised thy name?

Verse 6 jumps from the general opening of the letter "to Israel" to a specific address to **the priests**. Malachi 1:6 is utterly important to understanding whom **specifically** God addresses in Malachi 3:8-10. In this commentary of the book of Malachi we will follow the pronouns and direct objects. We will follow God's questions and accusations, the futile questions from those whom He addresses, and God's responses to these questions. Is the *entire* book of Malachi addressed specifically to the **priests**? We shall see.

God accuses the **priests** of despising His name. He then quotes their question that challenges the accusation: "Wherein have we despised thy name?" Likely these priests were not conversing directly with God. Either the questions and answers were entirely hypothetical representations of the willful rebellion of these priests against the Law, or they were literal or paraphrased summations of the priests' encounters with the prophets, Ezra, or Nehemiah who contended with them (Nehemiah 13:11). Regardless of the nature of these questions and answers, the target of Malachi 1:6 is the **priests**. Further reading of the book of Malachi will determine if this target ever changes.

Bad karma or bad offerings?

Malachi 1:7

7: <u>Ye offer polluted bread</u> upon mine altar; and <u>ye say</u>, Wherein have we polluted thee? In that <u>ye say</u>, The table of the LORD *is* contemptible.

God accuses the **priests** of offering "polluted bread" on the altar. Remember from the Law that the people of Israel had no access to the inner sanctum of the tabernacle and later the Temple. The people could not go into the sanctuary itself under penalty of death. The Levites could go into the sanctuary to aid the priests in certain ministry, but they could not enter the holiest place. The Kohathite Levites could enter the holiest place where the altar and holy vessels lay, provided that these things were covered from their site. Only the **priests**—the sons of Aaron—could see the altar itself and perform sacrifices upon it. Fittingly, only the **priests** themselves could transgress by "offer[ing] polluted bread upon [the] altar."

The "table of the LORD" was likely another reference to the altar itself.[25] Ironically, the priests answered God's accusation with the question "Wherein have we polluted thee?" while they themselves declared that the altar was "contemptible" or disdained. Likely, the priests forgot about the reverence and respect due them of the altar itself. They believed that it was just another "table" that was as "contemptible" as any other "table."[26] The fact that no one else but they could access the altar of the sanctuary under penalty of death demonstrated that God placed a sacred import on this altar.

The priests were taking their office too lightly. The Law required the people to bring quality products as firstfruits and offerings to the sanctuary for priestly use. The Law also required the Levites to give the **best** tithe of their tithes of crops and livestock to the priests both for their food and for sacrifices. The priests did not lack for quality

---

25. *Matthew Henry's Commentary*, 1195.
26. Ibid.

items for their duties at the altar. They had no excuse for burning "polluted bread" on the altar.

These offerings of "bread" on the altar were the "meat offerings" according to the Law. The priests were required to offer "unleavened cakes of fine flour mixed with oil, or unleavened wafers anointed with oil" (Leviticus 2:4). These "meat offerings" or "bread offerings" were required to be high quality from the high quality grains that they received from the offerings of the people and of the tithes of the Levites. Contrary to the Law, the priests were neglecting their duty to offer to God the **best** of what they received. They kept the best for themselves and offered to God on the altar "polluted bread." Their lack of reverence for the altar led to their lack of reverence for the sacrifices on the altar.

What's good enough for the governor is good enough for God

Malachi 1:8-10

8: And if ye offer the blind for sacrifice, *is it* not evil? and if ye offer the lame and sick, *is it* not evil? offer it now unto thy governor; will he be pleased with thee, or accept thy person? saith the LORD of hosts.
9: And now, I pray you, beseech God that he will be gracious unto us: this hath been by your means: will he regard your persons? saith the LORD of hosts.
10: Who *is there* even among you that would shut the doors *for nought*? neither do ye kindle *fire* on mine altar for nought. I have no pleasure in you, saith the LORD of hosts, neither will I accept an offering at your hand.

Not only did the priests respite their obligations for bread offerings, but also they neglected their obligation for unblemished animal sacrifices. The Law required their animal sacrifices to be "without blemish" (Exodus 29:1; Leviticus 4:3; 9:2; 22:17-25). Any offerings from the people and from the priests for the altar had to be free of detectable defects. In fact, even those of priestly families who had certain physical blemishes themselves were not allowed to come near the altar (Leviticus 21:17-23)!

Obviously, God expected unblemished offerings just as anyone would expect gifts and food to be free of harmful defects. God challenges the priests for their double standard by probing them to "offer it now unto thy governor." He asks if the governor would accept such a contribution from them or hold them in high regard for intending a poor "gift" as something acceptable for one in authority. If indeed the governor would never accept a blemished "gift" at their hands—and they knew this—why then should Yahweh, their supreme ruler, approve of them giving Him garbage for offerings?

The Law itself provided no office of "governor" in the Hebrew government structure. This office and its name came from foreign Persian rule. When Nehemiah requested leave from King Artaxerxes to rebuild the Temple in Jerusalem, the Persian King delegated to him the Persian office of "governor" to supervise this project. Because Malachi was most likely written during Nehemiah's return to Persia and the sins of Eliashib the high priest, the governor that Malachi referenced was likely not Nehemiah himself. This person must have been an interim governor with Persian approval. If Nehemiah had been the governor, one could argue that Malachi likely would have referred to Nehemiah by name. Also, Nehemiah himself said that he never ate "the bread of the governor" (Nehemiah 5:14-18), demonstrating more evidence that another governor would accept gifts from the sacrifices of the priests. The fact that the office of "governor" exists in the book of Malachi gives further proof of its timetable prior to the reforms of Ezra and Nehemiah, with further likelihood of the second reforms during Nehemiah's absence.

God reminds the priests that their sacrifices are not an empty or vain ritual. The purpose of burnt sacrifices is not just to "kindle *fire* on [God's] altar for nought." The purpose was not merely to place **something** on the altar and burnt it with fire to check it off a list of priestly requirements. The sacrifices themselves bore significance, and they were to remind the priests about Who God is and what He expected of them. He expected wholesome offerings because **He** is holy. The doors of the holiest part of the sanctuary were to be shut during sacrifices to keep the activities in the room sacred from those who were not priests and who were not set apart for sacred ministry. It was not a mere vain ritual to shut the doors. Kindling fire on the altar was not an empty custom either. If the priests could not treat the altar and the sanctuary with due reverence and give acceptable offerings, God would take no pleasure in them or their alleged offerings.

Provoked to jealousy

Malachi 1:11

11: For from the rising of the sun even unto the going down of the same my name *shall be* great among the Gentiles; and in every place incense *shall be* offered unto my name, and a pure offering: for my name *shall be* great among the heathen, saith the LORD of hosts.

Time and again Israel would forsake God, and often the priests were responsible for leading the people into idolatry. God predicted yet again that the Gentiles would eventually become members of God's covenant promises. In the Law God declared that He would eventually "move them to jealousy with those which are not a people...[and] provoke them to anger with a foolish nation" (Deuteronomy 32:21; Romans 10:19). God said that He would "call them my people, which were not my people" (Hosea 1:10; 2:23; Romans 9:25-26). God said that the Messiah would be a "stumblingblock" to Israel that would provide salvation to the Gentiles (Isaiah 8:14; 28:16; Romans 9:30-33; 1 Peter 2:6-10). Isaiah prophesied that the Messiah—the "root of Jesse"—would be the One Whom the Gentiles would seek (Isaiah 11:10).

Malachi 1:11 is yet another passage where God predicts the blessings to the Gentiles. "From the rising of the sun even unto the going down of the same" expresses the geographical area that would encompass the Gentiles who would regard the name of Yahweh. Throughout history, empires colonized the world would assume a title such as "the empire on which the sun never sets." A title such as this described the fact that the land of the king and any colonies would expand around the globe wherein the sun always shined on territories under the rule of the empire. God employs a similar expression for the extent to which His followers would exist around the world in Gentile nations. Everywhere the sun shined it would shine upon land where there were Gentile followers who regarded Yahweh as their God. Apparently the sheer volume of these predictions in the Old Testament did not capture the attention of ardent religionists in Israel, such as the scribes and Pharisees of the New Testament, who believed that the covenants and blessings of God were unconditionally upon physical descendents of Jacob merely because of such genetics. This is why, during the period of the apostles and the early church, Paul had to quote these Old Testament prophesies to explain to the Jews why God was rejecting them as a nation and blessing the Gentiles through the Gospel.

The first curse upon the priests

Malachi 1:12-14

12: But ye have profaned it, in that ye say, The table of the LORD *is* polluted; and the fruit thereof, *even* his meat, *is* contemptible.
13: Ye said also, Behold, what a weariness *is it!* and ye have snuffed at it, saith the LORD of hosts; and ye brought *that which was* torn, and the lame, and the sick; thus ye brought an offering: should I accept this of your hand? saith the LORD.
14: But cursed be the deceiver, which hath in his flock a male, and voweth, and sacrificeth unto the Lord a corrupt thing: for I *am* a great King, saith the LORD of hosts, and my name *is* dreadful among the heathen.

In verse 12, God restates the priests' attitude toward the altar of the sanctuary and their "gifts" upon the altar. In verse 13, God elaborates on their dreadful attitude toward their duties by quoting them as treating the duties of the altar as a drudgery. The priests **hated** to offer sacrifices on the altar. To relieve them partly of this "horrible" responsibility, they lazily offered "polluted bread" and blemished animals. They offered "torn," "lame," and "sick" animals as sacrifices, directly in violation of regulations abundant throughout the Law.

Stolen offerings?!

Another point to note is that the word for *torn* in the Hebrew can mean something that was "torn away" or "stolen" from someone else. Every other occurrence of this word in the Old Testament proves such an interpretation. Abimelech's servants "had violently taken away" a well of water (Genesis 21:25). Jacob was afraid that Laban would "take by force" his daughters from him (Genesis 31:31). A thief was required in the Law to return anything that he "took violently away" (Leviticus 6:4). One was not to defraud his neighbor or "rob" him (Leviticus 19:13). If the Israelites refused to keep the Law, they would be oppressed and "spoiled" by their enemies and would have animals "violently taken away" (Deuteronomy 28:29, 31). The men of Shechem set lurkers in place who "robbed" people passing through the mountains (Judges 9:25). The Benjamites took wives of the dancing daughters of Shiloh and "caught" them (Judges 21:23). One of David's mighty men "plucked" a spear out of an Egyptian's hand and killed him with it (2 Samuel 23:21; 1 Chronicles 11:23). Zophar, one of Job's friends, spoke of a wicked man who "hath violently taken away" a house that he did not build (Job 20: 19). In Job's reply, he spoke of the wicked who "violently take away" flocks and "pluck" the fatherless from their mother's feeding, and that drought and heat "consume" the snow (Job 24:2, 9, 19). The Psalmist refers to the poor and the wicked that "spoileth" him (Psalm 35:10). The Psalmist said that he unjustly had to return what he "took not away" (Psalm 69:4). The Proverbs refer to the wicked that are so consumed with harming others that their

236

sleep is "taken away" (Proverbs 4:16). One is instructed in the Proverbs to "rob not" the poor (Proverbs 22:22). One is a destroyer who "robbeth" his father (Proverbs 28:24). Woe is unto one who would "take away" legal rights from the poor (Isaiah 10:2). God commanded Israel to deliver one who is "spoiled" from the oppressor (Jeremiah 21:12; 22:3). God promises blessing to those who have not "spoiled" anyone by violence (Ezekiel 18:7, 12, 16, 18). God accused the Israelites of having "exercised robbery" (Ezekiel 22:29). Woe is unto one who covets fields and will "take *them* by violence" (Micah 2:2). God describes the rulers of Judah as ones who "pluck off" the skin of the people (Micah 3:2).

Given the sheer volume of this word and how it is **always** in the context of removing something by force, one can reasonably conclude that some of the animals that the priests offered on the altar were ones that they robbed or stole from others. The correlation to Nehemiah chapter 13 comes to mind.

Nehemiah 13:4-5, 10

4: And before this, Eliashib the priest, having the oversight of the chamber of the house of our God, *was* allied unto Tobiah:
5: And he had prepared for him a great chamber, where formerly they laid the meat offerings, the frankincense, and the vessels, and the tithes of the corn, the new wine, and the oil, which was commanded *to be given* to the Levites, and the singers, and the porters; and the offerings of the priests.
10: And I perceived that the portions of the Levites had not been given *them*: for the Levites and the singers, that did the work, were fled every one to his field.

In Nehemiah chapter 13—the events that were occurring when Malachi was written—Eliashib the high priest housed Tobiah in one of the Temple storehouse chambers and emptied it of the certain things, including **the tithes that were due the Levites**. The priests were robbing the Levites of the food that they needed to perform their yearly work in the Temple. They had to flee back to their own fields instead of fulfill their time in the Temple. If "torn" offerings indicate **stolen** offerings, then the priests likely could have been taking food by force from the Levites and hypocritically offering it to God.

The issue was quality, not quantity

A key phrase occurs in verse 13. God recaps the actions of the priests regarding the altar: "thus ye brought an offering"! God notes that they did, indeed, bring an "offering." The problem was not that they were derelict in **bringing** an actual offering, but rather that they did not bring a **valid** offering. God asked, "Should I accept this of your hand?" Just as the governor could not accept what they offered as a "gift" because of the poor quality of it, God could not **accept** their "offerings." These statements are absolutely crucial to understanding the role of **offerings** in Malachi 3:8! **Who** was "robbing God" in **offerings** and **how** were they doing so? Were they robbing God by **withholding** offerings or were the robbing God by **bringing** offerings that were **unacceptable**? Perhaps further reading of Malachi will answer these questions. Is the book of Malachi becoming more intriguing and exciting to you?

In verse 14, God pronounces a "curse" upon the "deceiver" who would possess unblemished animals, yet would pretend to offer to God according to the Law a blemished animal. Is God talking about the

people not bringing proper animals to the sanctuary? Obviously, the context thus far in Malachi chapter 1 demonstrates that this "curse" is not on the people. God has given absolutely no change in those whom He is referencing. He is still talking to the **priests**. He is still on the subject of the altar in the sanctuary, to which only the **priests** had access. He is still talking about blemished sacrifices on the altar for which the **priests** were responsible. He is still accusing the **priests** of wrongdoing. The "deceiver" here is the **priest** who received appropriate and quality gifts from the people and tithes from the Levites. The **priests** were not lacking a source of valid grains and animals for burnt offerings. The **priests** demonstrated disdain for the altar and failed in their duties of sanctifying the altar, to which they were fully equipped to do. No rationale can possibly exist from the context of God's condemnations of the **priests** alone in verse 6-14 that the people could be to blame for not supplying the priests with the items that they needed to fulfill their duties; otherwise, God would have condemned the people and held the priests as victims. These verses provide solid proof that the people were not the one's "robbing God"—the **priests** were!

The second curse upon the priests

Malachi 2:1-2

1: And now, <u>O ye priests</u>, this commandment is for <u>you</u>.
2: If <u>ye</u> will not hear, and if ye will not lay *it* to heart, to give glory unto my name, saith the LORD of hosts, I will even send <u>a curse upon you</u>, and I will <u>curse your blessings</u>: yea, <u>I have cursed them already</u>, because <u>ye</u> do not lay *it* to heart.

Malachi 2:1 is not providing a break of any kind, but a further **emphasis**. As we have observed in Malachi chapter 1 beginning at verse 6, God began addressing the **priests** specifically. No break existed anywhere up to this point. God never switched to the people. The accusations have thus far been **solely** upon the **priests**. God now emphasizes **again** that the priests are facing the wrath of His anger. In the previous verse God "cursed" the deceiving priests who offered blemished things on the altar. However, God is not yet done **cursing** the **priests!**

In verse 2, God yet **again** pronounces a **curse** upon the **priests**. God declares that the **priests** did not "hear" or "lay it to heart." They did not "give glory unto [God's] name." God says that if they do not change their ways regarding their duties and office, He would "send a curse" upon them and upon their "blessings." Not only has this, but He further clarified that He has "cursed them already." In other words, the **priests** were already suffering the "curse" of God, and God says that this "curse" would continue as long as they remained in rebellion to the Law. Malachi 3:9 says that "ye *are* cursed with a curse." Is this the same "curse" found in 1:14 and 2:2? The answer to this question depends on whether 3:9 still addresses the priests. Stay tuned for the exciting development!

Corrupting the covenant of Levi

Malachi 2:3-9

3: Behold, I will corrupt your seed, and spread dung upon your faces, *even* the dung of your solemn feasts; and *one* shall take you away with it.
4: And ye shall know that I have sent this commandment unto you, that my covenant might be with Levi, saith the LORD of hosts.

240

5: <u>My covenant was with him</u> of life and peace; and I gave them to him for the fear wherewith he feared me, and was afraid before my name.
6: <u>The law of truth was in his mouth</u>, and iniquity was not found in his lips: he walked with me in peace and equity, and did turn many away from iniquity.
7: For <u>the priest's lips should keep knowledge</u>, and they should seek the law at his mouth: for <u>he *is* the messenger of the LORD of hosts</u>.
8: But <u>ye are departed out of the way; ye have caused many to stumble at the law; ye have corrupted the covenant of Levi</u>, saith the LORD of hosts.
9: Therefore have I also made you contemptible and base before all the people, according as ye have not kept my ways, but <u>have been partial in the law</u>.

Malachi 2:3 is often cited in a list of "strange verses" in the Bible. The strangeness of this verse demonstrates God's fury and utter contempt for the actions of the priests. God would figuratively take the refuse of their vain partying and their empty observances of the annual feasts and spread it on their faces in mockery. In effect, God turned their blessings into a curse.

In verse 4, God says that He would use the curse upon them to teach them that He expects them to honor their special covenant with Him as priests and hold their office sacred. He declared that "my covenant shall be with Levi." He promised that He would eventually right these wrongs and "purify the sons of Levi, and purge them" (Malachi 3:3). As the priests were also sons of Levi, and the context of these verses is still in light of God's words "O ye priests, this commandment is for you," the "covenant of Levi" is a direct reference to the covenant of the Levitical **priests**.

In verses 5-7 and 9, God reminds the priests of their duty to be stewards and protectors of the integrity of His Law. The priests were to keep the Law ever before the nation and the king. The priests were to

241

dictate the words of the Law to teach them to the people. The priests were to be examples of the righteousness of the Law. They were to be the "messenger of the LORD of hosts" or His "Malachi." However, they were "partial in the Law." Like a smorgasbord they picked and chose which parts of the Law they favored and observed them either fully or partially. They obviously did not like performing valid sacrifices on the altar in the Temple and, as we shall observe later, they did not like marrying only of their kin.

In verse 8, God declares that they did not fulfill the requirement of being proper stewards of the Law. Not only did they fail to keep the Law themselves, but also they caused others to do so as well. The priests disobeyed the Law and they taught this disobedience to others as if it were the Law itself. They caused others to partake in their disobedience by thinking that the Law actually condoned these actions. Although the people of Israel broke the Law, the **priests** bore the brunt of this condemnation because they misled the people as to the actual Law itself.

What is this "covenant of Levi" that the **priests** "corrupted"? Because Malachi and Nehemiah chapter 13 correspond, the second reforms of Nehemiah provide the answer.

Nehemiah 13:28-29

28: And one of the sons of Joiada, the son of Eliashib the high priest, *was* son in law to Sanballat the Horonite: therefore I chased him from me.
29: Remember them, O my God, because they have defiled the priesthood, and the covenant of the priesthood, and of the Levites.

Section III: The Law Returns

The covenant of Levi, which included the priests, may have encompassed the entirety of their office and ministry, but the specific subject here is that of holy matrimony. The priests were not allowed to marry Canaanites—only those of their own kin; and they could not marry widows or harlots—only virgins (Leviticus 21:13-15). However, during the time of Malachi—the absence of Nehemiah in Persia—Eliashib the high priest allied to Tobiah and his grandson married the daughter of Sanballat the Horonite. This alliance with Canaanites was strictly forbidden as was the marriage between a priestly son of Aaron and a Canaanite. The priests had "corrupted the covenant of Levi" through unlawful marriage with pagans. Although the people could marry proselyte Canaanites such as was the case with Rahab of Jericho and Ruth of Moab, the priests could only marry direct descendents of Jacob.

Further verses in Malachi chapter 2 show this correlation with Nehemiah chapter 13. In case of observation, if Malachi 2:8 and following corresponds to Nehemiah 13:28-29, both referencing the sins of Eliashib the high priest in foreign alliances through marriage, why cannot Malachi 3:8-10 correspond to Nehemiah 13:4-5 as a reference to the sins of Eliashib the high priest in housing Tobiah in the Temple storehouse and causing the **tithes and offerings** not to be brought into this chamber? Is this not exciting?!

More invalid marriages and offerings

Malachi 2:10-12

10: Have we not all one father? hath not one God created us? why do we deal treacherously every man against his brother, by <u>profaning the covenant of our fathers</u>?
11: <u>Judah hath dealt treacherously</u>, and <u>an abomination is committed in Israel and in Jerusalem</u>; for <u>Judah hath profaned the holiness of the LORD</u> which he loved, and <u>hath married the daughter of a strange god</u>.
12: The LORD will cut off the man that doeth this, the master and the scholar, out of the tabernacles of Jacob, and <u>him that offereth an offering</u> unto the LORD of hosts.

The context up to this point has still been the **priests**. According to Dr. Kelly, the "we" in verse 10 implies that the speaker for verses 10-12 is Malachi himself rather than God, making Malachi possibly a priest.[27] and In verse 10, God is still addressing the **priests** and referring to them violating their covenant. Until the direct object and the pronouns change, the context still demands that God is further talking to the priests.

In verse 11, God declares that "Judah," "Israel," and "Jerusalem," have committed "an abomination" in that they have "married the daughter of a strange god." Although *Israel*, *Judah*, and *Jerusalem* are generic terms, they very well address the priests. Just as we observed that "the covenant of Levi" was the covenant of the priesthood and God was speaking to the **priests** themselves, so also can God be speaking to the **priests** in verses 10-12. In fact, the context of the verses before and the verses after demand this context. Judah is a part

---

27. Kelly, 94.

of Israel. Jerusalem is a part of Judah. Jerusalem is also the holy city where the sanctuary existed. God has not taken the focus away from the priesthood and the sanctuary. Because the priests caused the people "to stumble at the law," any reference to the sins of the people in "Jerusalem," "Judah," and "Israel" are bi-products of the bad influence from the priests.

The sins of the priests in "corrupting the covenant of Levi" was that of intermarrying with Canaanites. This sin spread to the people because the priests were "partial in the Law" and they misled the people. Both the priests and the people as a result "married the daughter of a strange god." Nehemiah 13:28-29 referenced above showed the priests' part in this with the example of the unlawful alliance between Eliashib and Tobiah through their family ties with Sanballat. Nehemiah chapter 13 also shows this influence on the people and how they "married the daughter of a strange god."

Nehemiah 13:23-27

23: In those days also saw I Jews _that_ had married wives of Ashdod, of Ammon, _and_ of Moab:
24: And their children spoke half in the speech of Ashdod, and could not speak in the Jews' language, but according to the language of each people.
25: And I contended with them, and cursed them, and smote certain of them, and plucked off their hair, and made them swear by God, saying, Ye shall not give your daughters unto their sons, nor take their daughters unto your sons, or for yourselves.
26: Did not Solomon king of Israel sin by these things? yet among many nations was there no king like him, who was beloved of his God, and God made him king over all Israel: nevertheless even him did outlandish women cause to sin.
27: Shall we then hearken unto you to do all this great evil, to transgress against our God in marrying strange wives?

These verses in Nehemiah chapter 13 immediately precede verses 28-29 which discuss the source of this problem—Eliashib the high priest. Eliashib's transgression of the Law concerning alliances with foreigners ultimately led to his transgression in stealing tithes from the Levites. When Nehemiah returned from Persia and learned of this sin, his reforms were particularly harsh. He forced these Jews who married unlawfully to repent by pulling out their hair and making them repeat their oath that they would never encourage their families to marry pagan Canaanites. Solomon committed the same sin by making alliances with other kingdoms through many international royal marriages. Although he was originally prosperous, these Canaanite wives turned his heart from God (Deuteronomy 17:17; 1 Kings 11:3-4).

Ezra 10:2-6

2: And Shechaniah the son of Jehiel, one of the sons of Elam, answered and said unto Ezra, We have trespassed against our God, and have taken strange wives of the people of the land: yet now there is hope in Israel concerning this thing.

3: Now therefore let us make a covenant with our God to put away all the wives, and such as are born of them, according to the counsel of my lord, and of those that tremble at the commandment of our God; and let it be done according to the law.

4: Arise; for *this* matter *belongeth* unto thee: we also *will be* with thee: be of good courage, and do *it*.

5: Then arose Ezra, and made the chief priests, the Levites, and all Israel, to swear that they should do according to this word. And they sware.

6: Then Ezra rose up from before the house of God, and went into the chamber of Johanan the son of Eliashib: and *when* he came thither, he did eat no bread, nor drink water: for he mourned because of the transgression of them that had been carried away.

If you remember, Ezra and Nehemiah served together on the reconstruction project. Their ministries overlapped. Nehemiah was the governor approved by King Artaxerxes and Ezra was the priestly scribe. Ezra here encounters priests who admitted to the sin of marrying pagan Canaanites. This sin of the priests spread to the people because the priests who's "lips should keep knowledge" told the people that it was acceptable. Ezra holds the priests responsible. He also discovers the marriage between Johanan, the grandson of Eliashib, and the daughter of Sanballat. Apparently, he and other priests lived in some of the storehouse chambers, and because they had a family relationship with Tobiah, Sanballat's ally, they provided him quarters with them in the Temple.

Further evidence that Malachi 2:10-12 is still directed specifically to the **priests** is that the subject is still the sin of pagan marriages while God refers to the **priests** themselves in verse 12. Just as "the priests' lips should keep knowledge" (v. 7), so are they "the master and the scholar" (v. 12). God said of these **priests** that He would "cut off the man that doeth this" (v. 12); "this" being "[marrying] the daughter of a strange god" (v. 11). No doubt "the man that doeth this" was Eliashib's grandson, and Eliashib was responsible for encouraging this activity.

Verse 12 provides yet more evidence that God is addressing the **priests**. The same "master and the scholar" that "married the daughter of a strange god" was also "him that offereth an offering unto the LORD of hosts." Who else but the priests were the subjects of harsh criticism about blemished offerings?!

Thus, Malachi 2:10-12 provides no change in the recipient. Since 1:6—following the opening of the letter—the entire book of Malachi has been a hypothetical dialog between God and the **priests**. Does this ever change? We will find out.

Malachi 2:13

13: And this have ye done again, <u>covering the altar of the LORD with tears</u>, with weeping, and with crying out, insomuch that <u>he regardeth not the offering any more, or receiveth <i>it</i> with good will at your hand</u>.

In verse 13, God once again reminds the priests of their hypocrisy in their offerings at the altar. They even expressed an outward appearance of sincerity by inducing tears on the altar. Nevertheless, God felt no sympathy for this false humility. God required them to give **righteous** offerings. He required that they **obey** Him by offering unblemished food and animals. They could not take up this slack with tears. Tears could not get God to accept invalid offerings. Perhaps their tears came from the affliction that resulted from their unlawful marriages. Nevertheless, God would not accept their offerings if they could not get their houses in order. Obedience is better than sacrifice (1 Samuel 15:22).

'Til death do us part

Malachi 2:14-16

14: Yet <u>ye say</u>, Wherefore? Because the LORD hath been witness <u>between thee and the wife of thy youth</u>, against whom <u>thou hast dealt treacherously</u>: yet <i>is</i> she thy companion, and <u>the wife of thy covenant</u>.
15: And did not he make one? Yet had he the residue of the spirit. And wherefore one? That he might seek a godly seed. Therefore take heed to your spirit, and let none <u>deal treacherously against the wife of his youth</u>.

16: For <u>the LORD, the God of Israel, saith that he hateth putting away</u>: for *one* covereth violence with his garment, saith the LORD of hosts: therefore take heed to your spirit, that ye <u>deal not treacherously</u>.

In verses 14-16, God further elaborates on the problem with the priests in violating marriage laws and covenants. God honored the marriage vow, and a man who made a vow of marriage promised to care for his wife. Apparently, the priests were not taking their marriage vows seriously. They "dealt treacherously" with their wives. The Hebrew word translated "dealt treacherously" carries the idea of covering offenses or hiding harm. Forgetting that marriage was a **covenant**, the priests broke their covenant by mistreating their wives. They "cover[ed] violence with [their] garment." The likely scenario expressed here was that the priests abused their authority by beating their wives for no good reason. Possibly, if they no longer desired they wives that they had, they secretly beat them and veiled these acts from the people. They looked for any excuse for divorce, possibly even through malice and deceit to justify it. God said that "he hateth putting away" and provided only unfaithfulness through sexual immorality as the sole grounds for divorce (Matthew 5:31-32; 19:3-9).

The attitude of these priests toward marriage and divorce lasted even through the time of Jesus. When the disciples heard the words of Jesus that divorce was not an option for "any cause," they reasoned that "it is not good to marry" (Matthew 19:10). This prevailing culture treated marriage as an option for the pleasure of men and not as a commitment between both the husband and wife of care for each other.

God expressed that the priests' attitude toward marriage was another reason that He did not accept their sacrifices on the altar.

Evil is the new good

Malachi 2:17

17: Ye have wearied the LORD with your words. Yet ye say, Wherein have we wearied *him*? When ye say, Every one that doeth evil is good in the sight of the LORD, and he delighteth in them; or, Where *is* the God of judgment?

Verse 17 ends Malachi chapter 2 with yet another accusation of God against the **priests**. This accusation really sums up the whole problem with these priests as those who supposedly taught and practiced the Law. The priests ask God how they have "wearied" Him with their words. God explains the problem He has with their words: they taught the people that evil is the new good. The priests in their sin and disregard for the Law taught the people that they could commit acts that they knew were against God, yet God would never judge them. God supposedly favored them because they were the blessed children of Israel. Abraham was their father; therefore, God's blessings were upon them unconditionally. The priests taught the people not to worry about doing good and shunning evil because their status as physical seed of Israel made their evil "good in the sight of the LORD."

What was their proof that God accepted or overlooked their evil deeds? They asked, "Where is the God of judgment?" They could find no evidence that God was judging their sin; therefore, they concluded that God really had no problem with their sin. Their question is akin to people today who would make an oath such as "If I am wrong, may God strike me with lightning." If lightning does not strike them that instant, the statement is proven true. The problem with this approach is that it tests or "tempts" God. God is not obligated to act on the whims of His creatures. If one invokes God, He has no obligation to respond to one's words. One should not think that an unfulfilled threat involving the existence, nature, or character of God proves the threat itself. An unfulfilled threat or invocation only proves that a mere human cannot command God to act.

The priests did not understand this truth and believed that the lack of visible judgment proved that God sanctioned their evil. Contrary to their belief, God was indeed judging them. He already "cursed their blessings." They could not detect the judgment of God because they had forgotten what true prosperity really was. Appropriately, the attitude of the priests toward sin reflects the words of Jesus to Nicodemus about being born again. One who does not believe on the Son is "condemned already" (John 3:18). Men "loved darkness rather than light" (John 3:19) and hide from the light "lest his deeds should be reproved" (John 3:20).

Conclusion and summary

In conclusion, we have examined chapters 1 and 2 of the book of Malachi—roughly half its contents. We have explored much evidence without reason for dispute that the book of Malachi was written during the time of the sins of the priests and the Israelites before Nehemiah returned from Persia to perform his second reforms. The historical significance of this causes us to examine any parallels between the words of Malachi and the account of Nehemiah chapter 13. Indeed, the correlation is striking!

The fact that the opening of the letter is specific to Israel as a nation and relays God's promises to the seed of Jacob instead of Edom proves that the recipients were post-exile Israelites and not members of a modern Christian church. Starting in Malachi 1:6, God begins to address the priests, and proclaims His accusations against them despite their objections. Thus far, Malachi has not changed the recipients of the letter—they have been the priests all along.

The priests were responsible for poor offerings that violated the requirements of the Law. They offered polluted bread and blemished animals on the altar and they treated the altar itself with disdain. God said that, although they brought substances for offerings, the priests were giving unacceptable offerings of which neither He nor their Persian governor would approve. The possibility exists that some of what the priests gave as offerings they took from others by force. This correlation may be with the priests stealing the tithes of food from the Levites, causing them to flee back to their fields.

The priests were responsible for "corrupting the covenant of Levi" by marrying Canaanites and encouraging the people of Israel to do the same. This situation is exemplified with Eliashib's alliance with Tobiah and with certain Jews who could only speak Canaanite languages. The priests were "partial in the Law" and neither practiced it with integrity nor dictated it to the people properly. Their intermarriage with pagans caused them to treat the marriage covenant lightly and teach and condone divorce for reasons of convenience. The priests also taught the people that the fact that God apparently had not judged them for their sins was proof that God had no problem with them.

The correlation between Nehemiah chapter 13 and Malachi lays the groundwork for exposing the truest concept of the "tithes and offerings" in Malachi 3:8-10. Amazingly, a passage that is quoted very often is almost never quoted in the value of its context. Thus far, Malachi has been addressed entirely to the priests in their attitude toward the Law and for their dereliction in the sanctity of God's offerings on the Temple altar and of the purity of marriage. The next chapter of this book will finish the commentary of the book of Malachi. Most importantly, it will put Malachi 3:8-10 to the ultimate test of everything that has been observed thus far in the study of Biblical tithing.

13. Provocation and Prophecy

The Priests Exhorted

Malachi 3:8-10

8: Will a man rob God? Yet ye have robbed me. But ye say, Wherein have we robbed thee? In tithes and offerings.
9: Ye *are* cursed with a curse: for ye have robbed me, *even* this whole nation.
10: Bring ye all the tithes into the storehouse, that there may be meat in mine house, and prove me now herewith, saith the LORD of hosts, if I will not open you the windows of heaven, and pour you out a blessing, that *there shall* not *be room* enough *to receive it*.

This is it! In this chapter we will finally examine Malachi 3:8-10. Perhaps, as you have been reading up to this point, you may have already reached some conclusions about what this passage means. We will explore the final two chapters of the book of Malachi and see the heart of God as He exhorts the priests and promises that they will be restored to righteousness. He also makes several prophecies that have been fulfilled in more ways than one. Although the book of Malachi is fraught with harsh criticisms, the overtones include God's covenant promises and His assurance of restoration.

The coming "Malachi's"

Malachi 3:1-5

1: Behold, I will send <u>my messenger</u>, and he shall prepare the way before me: and the Lord, whom ye seek, shall suddenly come to his temple, even <u>the messenger of the covenant</u>, whom ye delight in: behold, he shall come, saith the LORD of hosts.
2: But <u>who may abide the day of his coming?</u> and <u>who shall stand when he appeareth?</u> for <u>he *is* like a refiner's fire, and like fullers' soap</u>:
3: And he shall sit *as* a refiner and purifier of silver: and he shall purify <u>the sons of Levi</u>, and purge them as gold and silver, that they may offer unto the LORD <u>an offering in righteousness</u>.
4: <u>Then shall the offering of Judah and Jerusalem be pleasant</u> unto the LORD, as in the days of old, and as in former years.
5: And I will come near <u>to you</u> to judgment; and I will be a swift witness against the sorcerers, and against the adulterers, and against false swearers, and against those that oppress the hireling in *his* wages, the widow, and the fatherless, and that turn aside the stranger *from his right*, and fear not me, saith the LORD of hosts.

The beginning of Malachi chapter 3 is a prophecy about God's "messenger" who will "clean house" in Israel. Remember that the first two chapters of Malachi have been addressed to the priests. Obviously, because the context has never changed and no indication exists of a different recipient, we should expect that this prophecy is also directed to the priests. God tells the priests to "behold" the coming "messenger" or "malachi." This prophecy seems to involve several things that the "messenger" will do. If we are to regard the whole witness of Scripture, this prophecy can have multiple fulfillments, making several individuals qualify for this "messenger." Each of these possibilities will be discussed.

Nehemiah the messenger

Keeping in mind the correlation of the book of Malachi and Nehemiah chapter 13, we can possibly see Nehemiah himself as one fulfillment of this prophecy of a "messenger." Because the book of Malachi was written soon before the second reforms of Nehemiah, Nehemiah may have represented an imminent fulfillment of some aspect of the prophecy itself.

Nehemiah 13:11-13

11: Then contended I with the rulers, and said, Why is the house of God forsaken? <u>And I gathered them together, and set them in their place</u>.
12: Then brought all Judah the tithe of the corn and the new wine and the oil unto the treasuries.
13: <u>And I made treasurers over the treasuries</u>, Shelemiah the priest, and Zadok the scribe, and of the Levites, Pedaiah: and next to them *was* Hanan the son of Zaccur, the son of Mattaniah: <u>for they were counted faithful</u>, and their office *was* to distribute unto their brethren.

Dr. Russell Kelly notes that the context of Malachi demands that one evaluate Nehemiah as a literal fulfillment of this prophecy.[28] Indeed, the historical and textual correlation of Malachi and Nehemiah

---

28. Kelly, 97.

13 demonstrate the second reforms of Nehemiah as fitting for the actions of the "messenger." According to Malachi, this "messenger" will "purify the sons of Levi." Because the recipients of criticism thus far are still the priests, these "sons of Levi" must be the priests themselves. Priests were descendents of Levi. Also, because one of the actions of this messenger is to restore righteous offerings in Jerusalem (the city of the sanctuary), we must understand this statement in the backdrop of the corrupt sacrifices that the priests were offering in Malachi chapters 1 and 2.

Nehemiah was definitely like a "refiner's fire" in his reforms. He "purged the sons of Levi" when he returned from Persia. According to Nehemiah 13:11, he contended with the "rulers" (priests), gathered them together, and "set them in their place." This action resulted in restoring the requirement of bringing the tithes and offerings back into the storehouse chamber where Tobiah had quartered. Nehemiah also "made treasurers over the treasuries" (storehouse chambers). He "purged the sons of Levi" by overthrowing the priests who abused their oversight and reassigning new priests and Levites to these tasks who "were counted faithful." He "purged" out the bad priests and established the good.

Nehemiah 13:22

22: And I commanded the Levites that they should cleanse themselves, and *that* they should come *and* keep the gates, to sanctify the sabbath day. Remember me, O my God, *concerning* this also, and spare me according to the greatness of thy mercy.

Another of Nehemiah's second reforms was to restore Sabbath keeping in Israel. In Nehemiah 13:22, Nehemiah commanded the Levites to "cleanse themselves." This is another candidate for the "messenger" who would "purge the sons of Levi." The messenger is also "like fullers' soap." Nehemiah acted like a soap when he commanded the Levites to cleanse themselves.

Nehemiah 13:23-25, 28

23: In those days also saw I Jews that had married wives of Ashdod, of Ammon, and of Moab:
24: And their children spake half in the speech of Ashdod, and could not speak in the Jews' language, but according to the language of each people.
25: And <u>I contended with them, and cursed them, and smote certain of them, and plucked off their hair, and made them swear by God</u>, saying, Ye shall not give your daughters unto their sons, nor take their daughters unto your sons, or for yourselves.
28: And *one* of the sons of Joiada, <u>the son of Eliashib the high priest</u>, *was* son in law to Sanballat the Horonite: therefore <u>I chased him from me</u>.

In Malachi 3:2, God asks about the "messenger" two questions: "Who may abide the day of his coming?" and "Who shall stand when he appeareth?" These questions reflect the fact that the "messenger" prophesied will reform with force. He will not come and ask nicely, beg, or plead for these wicked people to turn from their ways. He will **make them** turn from their ways. He will be as a "refiner's fire." The fire has the power over the metal cast into the oven to purify it of alloys and other added elements.

Nehemiah enacts his reforms with the force of a refiner's fire. Who of the Jews could stand when he appeared? He contended with them, cursed them, smote some of them, plucked off their hair, and **made**

them swear that they would not commit the sin that they were doing. They could not abide in their sin when he came. They either changed their actions or faced the consequences. As you may remember, the contributing factor to the sin of these Jews in intermarrying was the alliance of Eliashib and Tobiah through an unlawful family marriage. Nehemiah deals with this in Nehemiah 13:28. He "chased him" away. Truly, Nehemiah was like a "fullers' soap" who "purged the sons of Levi." They could not stand when he appeared.

John the Baptist the messenger

Most often when one reads the prophecy in Malachi chapter 3 about the "messenger," one will recognize the fulfillment in John the Baptist. According to Malachi 3:1, this messenger would "prepare the way before" God. New Testament quotations make John the Baptist an undeniable fulfillment.

Isaiah 40:3

3: <u>The voice of him that crieth in the wilderness</u>, Prepare ye the way of the LORD, make straight in the desert a highway for our God.

Matthew 3:1-3

1: In those days came <u>John the Baptist</u>, preaching in the wilderness of Judaea,
2: And saying, Repent ye: for the kingdom of heaven is at hand.
3: For <u>this is he that was spoken of by the prophet Esaias</u>, saying, <u>The voice of one crying in the wilderness</u>, Prepare ye the way of the Lord, make his paths straight.

Matthew 11:10-11

10: For <u>this is *he*, of whom it is written</u>, Behold, I send <u>my messenger</u> before thy face, which shall prepare thy way before thee.

11: Verily I say unto you, Among them that are born of women there hath not risen a greater than <u>John the Baptist</u>: notwithstanding he that is least in the kingdom of heaven is greater than he.

Mark 1:2-4

2: <u>As it is written in the prophets</u>, Behold, I send <u>my messenger</u> before thy face, which shall prepare thy way before thee.
3: <u>The voice of one crying in the wilderness</u>, Prepare ye the way of the Lord, make his paths straight.
4: John did baptize in the wilderness, and preach the baptism of repentance for the remission of sins.

Luke 3:2-4

2: Annas and Caiaphas being the high priests, the word of God came unto <u>John the son of Zacharias</u> in the wilderness.
3: And he came into all the country about Jordan, preaching the baptism of repentance for the remission of sins;
4: <u>As it is written in the book of the words of Esaias the prophet</u>, saying, <u>The voice of one crying in the wilderness</u>, Prepare ye the way of the Lord, make his paths straight.

Luke 7:27-28

27: <u>This is *he*, of whom it is written</u>, Behold, I send <u>my messenger</u> before thy face, which shall prepare thy way before thee.
28: For I say unto you, Among those that are born of women there is not a greater prophet than <u>John the Baptist</u>: but he that is least in the kingdom of God is greater than he.

John 1:23

23: He [John the Baptist] said, <u>I *am* the voice of one crying in the wilderness</u>, Make straight the way of the Lord, <u>as said the prophet Esaias</u>.

Clearly John the Baptist is without dispute the primary fulfillment of the "messenger" in Malachi 3:1 who would "prepare the way" of the Lord. In fact, John the Baptist fulfilled at least three prophecies—two of which are in the book of Malachi. John the Baptist was the "messenger" who would prepare the way of the Lord and "the voice of one crying in the wilderness." He was also another coming of "Elijah" prophesied in Malachi 4:5-6. We will examine this fulfillment later.

Jesus Christ the messenger

John MacArthur comments that the "messenger of the covenant" in Malachi 3:1 is not the same messenger as the one mentioned before in the same verse.[29] In other words, this verse presents two messengers: the first "messenger" will prepare the way for the arrival of the "messenger of the covenant." The first messenger is John the Baptist. The second messenger is Jesus Christ Himself. He is "the Lord whom ye seek, [who] shall suddenly come to his temple."

According to the words of God recorded in Malachi 3:1, this "messenger of the covenant" who is the Lord is described as one "whom ye seek" and "whom ye delight in." John MacArthur comments that such a description is likely sarcasm.[30] Possibly the sarcasm was not specifically the statement itself but about what this "messenger of the covenant" would do with the priests. Perhaps these wicked priests were legitimately seeking and delighting in the promise of a coming Messiah.

The irony is that this messenger whom these sinful priests anticipated would not be what they expected. The messenger that these priests desired with vain hope and glee would actually come to execute judgment on them. They believed that this Messiah would finally deliver them from the Persian Empire. Several hundred years later the

---

29. *The MacArthur Bible Commentary*, 1084.
30. Ibid.

Pharisees and scribes—the heirs to the seat of these priests—anticipated that the Messiah would deliver Israel from Roman rule and reestablish the throne of David and the kingdom of Israel. The Messiah would not come to give them prominence in the world but to preach repentance to set their houses in order.

Because chapter divisions in the Bible are not inspired, one can see that the prophecy in Malachi 3:1-5 is actually an answer to the question of the priests in Malachi 2:17. The priests asked "Where is the God of judgment?" God says in Malachi 3:5 that the messenger of the covenant whom these priests longingly sought would "come near to you in judgment." The "you" here, of course, must be the priests because the priests asked the question. They were responsible for teaching the people that God would not judge their sin. God answered that He would come to **them** in judgment. Now, we know that up to Malachi 3:5 the ones being addressed are **still the priests**.

Jesus fulfilled the prophecy of "the messenger of the covenant" in several ways. This messenger of the covenant would be "the Lord" who "shall suddenly come to his temple." Jesus "suddenly came to his temple" when He went to the temple and cast out the moneychangers and overthrew their tables (Matthew 21:12-13; Mark 11:15-18; John 2:13-17). Jesus also would institute the practice of offering "an offering in righteousness" in Judah and Jerusalem through the Gospel of His death, burial, and resurrection that would establish a remnant of believing Jews in that He would "turn away ungodliness from Jacob" and "take away their sins" (Romans 11:25-27). The completed prophecy of "the messenger of the covenant" in Jesus Christ will be in the totality of His first and second advents.

Change through an unchanging covenant

Malachi 3:6-7

6: For I *am* the LORD, I change not; therefore ye sons of Jacob are not consumed.

7: Even from the days of your fathers ye are gone away from mine ordinances, and have not kept *them*. Return unto me, and I will return unto you, saith the LORD of hosts. But ye said, Wherein shall we return?

Many preachers will begin the context of the tithing text with verse 6. Whether the text cited for a church tithing sermon is verses 6-12, 8-10, or any other arrangement, the problem of context is not resolved. The context of tithing in Malachi must be everything in the Law about tithing up to this point. The context must include the accounts of Ezra and Nehemiah. The context must invoke the entire book of Malachi and follow the recipients addressed.

Is this too much to ask? To object to this requirement is to contend for the right to ignore the full context and for a license to use Scripture verses apart from their real meaning. One must "study" and "rightly divide the word of truth" (2 Timothy 2:15). The Scriptures are not for one to twist and to abuse for one's own intentions and desires. One who is entrusted to deliver the Word of God to people must make an honest attempt to do so correctly. Scripture is not about pragmatism, but about **truth**. The Word of God is not a tool to manipulate people, but the very words of God and a treatise of His truth.

Some may use Malachi 3:6 in the context of tithing to attempt to prove that it applies to the church. They will use the statement "I am the LORD, I change not" as a proof text that God never changes his requirement to tithe across covenants or dispensations.[31] In other words, the "change not" is supposedly a reference to the **command** to tithe. However, the context that we have seen does not allow this faulty interpretation.

The context still demonstrates that God is talking to the **priests**. No evidence exists yet that the recipients have changed. God explains what He means by "change not" with the independent clause that follows. How does God "change not"? The answer is that "ye sons of Jacob are not consumed." The "change not" has to do with God's covenant with the nation of Israel, not the command to tithe specifically. God will "change not" in that His covenant with Israel is an everlasting covenant. There will always be a remnant of Israel (Isaiah 1:9; 10:21-22; Joel 2:32; Romans 9:27-29; 11:1-5, 25-28). God will never completely eradicate the Israelites. Through His covenant with Abraham, Isaac, and Jacob, He will never "cast away" His people. He will guarantee that there will be some of them who would remain faithful to Him.

God promised the priests that, because of His covenant with Israel, they would not be consumed. "Ye sons of Jacob" is not a reference to the entire nation of Israel, but still to the **priests**. The priests were also qualitatively "sons of Jacob." God has still not stopped addressing the priests, and this verse 6 is still in the context of God's answer to the priests' question of "Where is the God of judgment?" He prophesied

---

31. Kelly, 99.

that He will judge them, but until then, they have not been consumed because of His covenant with Israel.

Although God said He would not change in His righteousness, He demonstrates that the priests themselves have not changed in their wickedness.[32] In verse 7, God states that the priests have "gone away from mine ordinances, and have not kept them." Compare this accusation with that of Malachi 2:8-9 prior in which God said that these priests have "departed out of the way" and "have not kept my ways." God tells the priests to "return unto me, and I will return unto you" just as He told them what He would do in Malachi 2:1 if they "will not hear" and "will not lay it to heart."

The priests inquire to God again by asking "Wherein shall we return?" Just as the priests asked "Where is the God of judgment?" in their teaching that God accepted their sin, they also asked "Wherein shall we return?" because they did not believe that they were doing any wrong from which to return. As we can plainly see, even Malachi 3:6-7 is **still** addressing the **priests**. God's criticisms have been of the **priests** all along. The **priests** have been asking God all the questions about His criticisms, and God has been answering these questions.

Who were robbing God?

Malachi 3:8

8: Will a man rob God? Yet ye have robbed me. But ye say, Wherein have we robbed thee? In tithes and offerings.

---

32. *The MacArthur Bible Commentary*, 1085.

This is it! The text you have been anticipating. Having examined carefully the book of Malachi up to this point, no question is possible that God has been addressing the **priests** all along. Now, we have arrived at the sacred cow of all tithing in the Bible. This is the text most proclaimed in any sermon on tithing. The question now is who was robbing God.

God answers His own question by saying that "ye have robbed me." Who are the "ye" here? This is the "ye" that has been prevalent throughout the book of Malachi. The "ye" are the "O priests that despise my name" in Malachi 1:6. The "ye" are the "O ye priests" in Malachi 2:1. The "ye" are the **priests** who are "the messenger of the LORD of hosts" in Malachi 2:7. The "ye" are the ones who "corrupted the covenant of Levi" in Malachi 2:8.

The "ye" are the **priests** who asked God "Wherein have we despised thy name?"

The "ye" are the **priests** who asked God "Wherein have we polluted thee?"

The "ye" are the **priests** who asked God "Wherefore [does God not accept our offerings]?"

The "ye" are the **priests** who asked God "Wherein have we wearied [thee with our words]?"

The "ye" are the **priests** who asked God "Where is the God of judgment?"

The "ye" are the **priests** who asked God "Wherein shall we return?"

Now, the "ye" are the **priests** who asked God "Wherein have we robbed thee?" Because the recipients have not changed and the priests have asked God all the questions, there is no reason to assume that the criticism and this question has changed to the people. Is there other evidence to prove that the **priests** were the ones who "robbed God"? The plot thickens!

The priests robbed God in tithes and offerings by stealing from the storehouse

God said that the priests were robbing Him "in tithes and offerings." Now, the question remains about what were these tithes and offerings and how they were robbing Him of these. The answer, of course, can be found in the **context** of this verse—the real context that has been proven over and over again. This context is Nehemiah chapter 13, as the accounts very likely represented the same event.

Nehemiah 13:4-5

4:   And before this, Eliashib the priest, having the oversight of the chamber of the house of our God, *was* allied unto Tobiah:
5:   And he had prepared for him a great chamber, where aforetime they laid the meat offerings, the frankincense, and the vessels, and the tithes of the corn, the new wine, and the oil, which was commanded *to be given* to the Levites, and the singers, and the porters; and the offerings of the priests.

Eliashib the high **priest** committed the sin of using one of the Temple storehouse chambers to house the enemy Tobiah. He had "the oversight of the chamber." This chamber was where certain things were brought, including "meat (bread) offerings" and "tithes of the corn, the new wine, and the oil." When the priests allowed the enemy to live in the Temple storehouse, no "tithes and offerings" were brought here. The tithes in particular were those that were "commanded to be given to the Levites."

Nehemiah 13:6

6: But in all this *time* <u>was not I at Jerusalem</u>: for in the two and thirtieth year of Artaxerxes king of Babylon <u>came I unto the king</u>, and after certain days <u>obtained I leave of the king</u>:

Remember that the book of Malachi was written soon **before** Nehemiah's second reforms. It was written during the time that Nehemiah left Jerusalem and returned to the king of Persia out of obligation. Malachi was written before Nehemiah set things right. It was written during the time that Eliashib was committing this transgression of housing Tobiah in the Temple storehouse. It was written during a time when **tithes and offerings** were not being brought into the storehouse. The priests were responsible for this problem.

Nehemiah 13:7-9

7: And <u>I came to Jerusalem</u>, and understood of <u>the evil that Eliashib did</u> for Tobiah, in preparing him a chamber in the courts of the house of God.
8: And it grieved me sore: therefore I cast forth all the household stuff of Tobiah out of the chamber.
9: Then I commanded, and they cleansed the chambers: and <u>thither brought I again</u> the vessels of the house of God, with <u>the meat offering</u> and the frankincense.

When Nehemiah returned from Persia and discovered what Eliashib the high priest was doing, he removed Tobiah and his belongings from the Temple storehouse. He then commanded that things be returned to the storehouse. This included "the meat <u>offering</u>."

Nehemiah 13:10-12

10: And I perceived that <u>the portions of the Levites had not been given</u> <u>*them*</u>: for <u>the Levites</u> and the singers, that did the work, <u>were fled</u> every one to his field.
11: Then contended I with <u>the rulers</u> [priests], and said, <u>Why is the</u> <u>house of God forsaken?</u> And I gathered them together, and set them in their place.
12: <u>Then brought all Judah the tithe</u> of the corn and the new wine and the oil unto the treasuries.

Notice a very important statement in Nehemiah 13:10. Nehemiah discovered that "the portions of the Levites had not been given them." Nothing is said about the priests not receiving their portions of the tithes that were brought to the storehouse. The priests either ate them themselves or fed them to Tobiah. The courses of Levites who were supposed to perform their assigned yearly time in Temple ministry did not have the food from the tithes necessary to feed them for a week. They had to flee back to their fields. The **priests** were **robbing** the Levites of their **tithes!**

Nehemiah then contended with "the rulers" about the situation. These "rulers" were the **priests**, including Eliashib the high priest who had **oversight** of the storehouse chamber. Nehemiah asks a very important question: "Why is the house of God forsaken?" Is this not the parallel of "Will a man rob God?" Is this not the parallel of "Bring ye all the tithes into the storehouse"? The correlation is breathtaking!

Nehemiah then resolved Malachi's question by restoring the **tithes** that were lacking in the storehouse so that the Levites who ministered could receive food. There is no escaping the **correct** interpretation of Malachi 3:8! The **priests** were the ones "robbing God" in "tithes and offerings." The **priests** were the ones responsible for the absence of tithes and offerings in the storehouse. They robbed **God** by robbing **the Levites**.

The priests robbed God in offerings by disdaining the altar

The priests robbed God in offerings in more ways than one. As we observed previously, they robbed both tithes and offerings from the storehouse. They also robbed God in offerings by not giving Him **acceptable** offerings.

The previous chapter of this book covered the sins of the priests in Malachi chapters 1 and 2 in their disdain for the sanctity of the altar of the Temple sanctuary. They offered "polluted bread" on the altar. They offered blemished animals on the altar. God asked them if their governor would accept such things. Because neither the governor nor God would **accept** such things, the priests were robbing the offerings. The priests "brought an offering," but God did not "accept it of their hand." If God did not receive the offerings, He was not getting what was due Him. Therefore, the priests were robbing God of the offerings that He required in the Law. The "messenger of the covenant" who would come to "purge the sons of Levi" (the priests) would ensure that "the offering of Judah and Jerusalem [would] be pleasant unto the LORD" (Malachi 3:4). God would right the wrongs and would then make the priests offer **acceptable** offerings. Then, the priests would no longer "rob God" in **offerings**.

The third curse on the priests

Malachi 3:9

9: Ye *are* cursed with a curse: for ye have robbed me, *even* this whole nation.

Who is cursed with a curse? "Ye" the **priests!** Do not forget that several times prior in the book of Malachi God pronounced a "curse" on the **priests**. God cursed the deceiving priests who had unblemished animals available and "sacrificeth unto the Lord a corrupt thing" (Malachi 1:14). God said that He would "send a curse" upon the priests, would "curse [their] blessings," and even that he had "cursed them already" (Malachi 2:2). God said that the priests were "cursed already" and now he says in Malachi 3:9 that they are "cursed with a curse." Can anyone rightly say that the ones "cursed" in Malachi 3:9 are not the same ones "cursed" in Malachi 2:2?! Especially because the recipients have not changed and the context testifies that the priests were robbing God by robbing the Levites, why would anyone believe that God is now redirecting His words?

One may now object by claiming that verse 9 shifts the criticism to "this whole nation." Is God now addressing the entire nation of Israel and not simply the priests? If "ye" has always been the **priests**, why should it now be any different? From the observation of context and following the pronouns, the idea that "this whole nation" is not a reference to the **priests** can be nothing but illogical.

By referring to "this whole nation," Malachi just as likely can be referring to "this whole nation [of you priests]."[33] Remember that the Levites had no inheritance in the land of Israel, but were allotted 48 cities throughout. Among these Levitical cities were priestly cities. Given that God addressed the corruption of the priests and expressed the totality of this corruption throughout the book of Malachi, God says that "this whole nation" of priests were robbing God. Eliashib the high priest had oversight of the storehouse chamber where he housed Tobiah, but **the whole nation of priests** was part of this scheme. The "whole nation" of priests offered corrupt things on the altar. The "whole nation" of priests colluded in robbing the Levites of tithes and offerings from the storehouse. No evidence exists of any priestly objectors (besides Ezra the scribe) who went against the grain of these transgressions. God condemns the priests in their entirety in the book of Malachi. The "whole nation" of **priests** were responsible for "robbing God"!

Returning the priests to storehouse tithing

Malachi 3:10

10: Bring ye all the tithes into the storehouse, that there may be meat in mine house, and prove me now herewith, saith the LORD of hosts, if I will not open you the windows of heaven, and pour you out a blessing, that *there shall* not *be room* enough *to receive it.*

In Malachi 3:10, God tells the **priests** to bring the tithes into the storehouse. Before Nehemiah's second reforms, Eliashib the high priest, who had oversight of the Temple storehouse, housed Tobiah at

---

33. Kelly, 102.

the expense of storing tithes for the Levites who ministered. Eliashib had a particular chamber used for this purpose emptied so that Tobiah could live there. Naturally, the command to "bring the tithes into the storehouse" required that Tobiah be expelled from the Temple.

Examining common claims—offerings vs. tithes

Now having thoroughly examined the context of Malachi 3:8-10, we arrive at the point of examining common interpretations and applications of this passage. Can these assumptions and claims stand up to any serious scrutiny of the Scriptures?

No doubt you have heard of the term "tithes and offerings." Malachi 3:8 is the only verse in the Bible to use this exact phrase. Likely anyone who refers to "paying" or "giving" one's "tithes and offerings" ultimately obtained this term from Malachi 3:8. Although other verses in Scripture include both **tithes** and **offerings** together, these terms are understood as different substances designated for different purposes.

In Nehemiah 13:5, the storehouse chamber where Eliashib housed Tobiah was formerly used to store **tithes** for the **Levites** and **offerings** for the **priests**. Why were the offerings for the priests? The offerings were grains and animals for the purpose of burnt sacrifices. Only the priests were allowed to perform these on the altar of the sanctuary. Although the priests could eat certain portions of offerings, their purpose was for burnt sacrifices to God **first** and food for them **second**. The tithes were almost always meant for food. Conceivably, the offerings for the priests may have come **from** the tithes that the

Levites brought to the Temple. The priests were robbing God in **tithes** by stealing them from the Levites. The priests were robbing God in **offerings** primarily by giving God unacceptable items for burnt sacrifices. They robbed the former in **quantity** and robbed the latter in **quality**.

Many pastors and theologians today treat the "tithes and offerings" as if they are merely different amounts and portions of the same source—monetary income. Pastor Bill Winston defines *offerings* as "giving over and above the tithe."[34] Likewise, Pastor Stephen Olford indicates that they are "over and above the basic tithe."[35] This assumption does not accurately relay the **real** "offerings" defined in most of the Law, and especially in Malachi 3:8. Tithes were crops and livestock given for the Levites to eat. Offerings were grains and livestock given for the priests to burn on the altar. A tithe is never a tenth of one's **monetary income** in the Bible. An offering is likewise never a voluntary monetary contribution "in addition to" the tithe.

Do tithes precede offerings? George W. Brown declared: "'[G]ive' is not the right word to use until the tenth, God's tenth, has been paid... In other words, pay what you owe before 'giving' anything."[36] Brown suggests that one cannot contribute "offerings" until one has **first** "paid" "tithes." No support for this idea exists whatsoever in Scripture. Several types of offerings existed—sin offerings, freewill offerings,

---

34. Winston, 39.
35. Stephen F. Olford, *The Grace of Giving: A Biblical Study of Christian Steward-ship*, 3rd ed. (Grand Rapids: Kregel Publications, 2000), 29.
36. Brown, 123.

wave offerings, heave offerings, meat offerings, peace offerings, trespass offerings, drink offerings, thank offerings, and possibly others. Each of these had distinct regulations, purposes, and times. **None** of these required that the people of Israel give their tithes to the Levites **first** before they could offer them. The only possible exception would be certain atonement offerings that the priests would perform to cover the sins of the nation each year. However, these offerings would have been of animals **from** the tithe of the tithes that the Levites brought, **not** in **addition** to any tithes. This misunderstanding comes simply from the fact that many **assume** that both "tithes" and "offerings" represent a portion of one's monetary earnings.

Are tithes and offerings both due to the same place? R. T. Kendall, an avid proponent of modern monetary income tithing to the church argues that "'offerings' beyond the tithe are an exception [to the church 'storehouse' requirement], for this way the **tithe** goes directly to the place where the Bible says it belongs. If someone has an offering above the tithe he is inclined to place elsewhere than the church, I could not find much objection. [Emphasis in original]"[37] This idea is common, but represents a fundamental flaw in the understanding of **offerings** in Malachi 3:8, where most derive the idea of "tithes and offerings." As discussed above, the **offerings** to which Malachi 3:8 is referring are **burnt offerings** or **animal sacrifices** of which the priests were offering to God on the altar in the holy place in the Temple. Thus,

---

37. Kendall, 91.

the priestly tithes were for the **storehouse** in the Temple, and the offerings were for the **altar** in the Temple. Both the tithes and offerings were for priestly use in the Temple. Both the tithes and the offerings were of food, and likely the offerings discussed here were **part of** the tithe of animals used for sacrifices. The offerings of Malachi 3:8 were not monetary gifts and they were not "over, beyond, or above the tithe."

In fact, to assume that the command of Malachi 3:10 to "bring all the tithes into the storehouse" applies to the **people** is fundamentally flawed. The people gave their tithes to the **Levites**. The Levites, in turn, gave a tithe of these tithes to the **priests**. It was the tithe from the Levites—**not** the people—that ultimately entered the Temple storehouse. Certain offerings the people brought directly to the sanctuary for the priests, but **never** the **tithes**. The people could not be commanded to bring their tithes to the storehouse because they were already commanded to bring their tithes to the Levitical cities (Nehemiah 10:37). The Levites were required to bring the tithe of these tithes to the storehouse; however, they were not the ones robbing God. The priests were robbing God by robbing the Levites. Either the priests were preventing the tithes of the Levites from going to the storehouse or they were stealing them for themselves or feeding Tobiah.

Although the particular storehouse in which Tobiah lived (from which the priests were "robbing God") was originally designated to store tithes for the Levites and offerings for the priests, these tithes and offerings were for different purposes and had different recipients. Although Kendall is correct that the tithes and offerings in the storehouse were not ultimately for the same deeds, he is, of course, exceptionally wrong in his understanding of what "tithes and offerings" were and what "the storehouse" was.

Examining common claims—the church vs. the storehouse

Because Malachi 3:8-10 is often quoted to command Christians and church members to give their "tithes and offerings" to the church, naturally the "storehouse" must be defined in this assumed new context. Presbyterian pastor Dr. Mark Brewer claims: "The pattern of giving for Christians [in the Bible] is to offer to the Lord our tithes and offerings, which are given to the Church."[38] Is Pastor Brewer correct? Have we seen anything yet in the historical record of the Old Testament that associates the Temple storehouse chambers with the Church? Obviously not. The answer to this question would have to come from the New Testament. The most common passages assumed to provide this link are 1 Corinthians 9:13-14 and 2 Corinthians 16:1-2. Chapter 16 of this book discusses 2 Corinthians 16:1-2 and a modern interpretation of "lay by him in store." Chapter 18 discusses 1 Corinthians 9:13-14 and the assumptions derived in the link between caring for Old Covenant priests and New Covenant gospel preachers.

Pastor Stephen Olford claims that "[t]he New Testament counterpart of this principle [of the Temple storehouse] is that church

---

38. Mark A. Brewer, *What's Your Spiritual Quotient?* (Shippensburg, PA: Destiny Image Publishers, 2008), 190.

members give all tithes to the local church."[39] Obviously this cannot be a correct correlation. The people of Israel never brought their tithes to the storehouse—the Levites did. Another problem is that not "all" tithes went to the storehouse. The people brought the Levitical tithes to the Levitical cities. The Levites, then brought a small portion of these tithes to the storehouse. The festival tithes never went to the storehouse and neither did the third-year tithes for the Levites and poor. Therefore, only a **small portion** of **one tenth** of **some** of the tithes of the people ultimately made it to the storehouse, and not directly from their hand.

In the context of referencing Malachi 3:8-10, Olford continues to claim that "[a] great sin of our time is the robbing and defrauding of the local church by its membership." His statement may, for all intents and purposes, be correct, but **not** in the context of Malachi 3:8-10. The **priests** were the ones that were "robbing God" by robbing the tithes and offerings from the Temple storehouse. Also, no church member can properly "rob" and "defraud" the local church in anything to do with the **real** definition of "tithes and offerings" in the Bible. Truthfully, they could wrongfully deprive the church of adequate funding, but this has nothing to do with "tithes and offerings" nor with the book of Malachi.

R. T. Kendall claims: "The 'storehouse' is a nickname for the Temple of God, or any local synagogue or assembly."[40] This statement

---

39. Olford, 28.
40. Kendall, 79.

is not accurate. The storehouse was not the Temple itself, but a collection of rooms (possibly two) that King Hezekiah built to store food **in** the Temple. No synagogue or assembly constituted a "storehouse." The Old Testament storehouse was not directly linked to the general practice of worship. In fact, the people of Israel did not worship in the storehouse, and only the priests and Levites had access to it. The storehouse existed to feed the Levitical priesthood to support their ministry of **mediation** for the nation of Israel. A Biblical storehouse would not be required if no human priesthood serves.

Many tithe teachers are quick to indicate that one cannot legitimately give a "tithe" outside the confines of the local church budget and be right with God. R. T. Kendall states: "Tithes should not be given to 'charity,' that is, any noble work. When a Christian gives tithes, or any part of them, to non-church organizations—no matter how valuable or useful to society they may be—that Christian robs the church, and therefore God."[41] Pastor Stephen Olford argues: "If we give elsewhere, then it should be over and above the required tithe to our church."[42] Neither Kendall nor Olford understand the system of tithing under the Law. The people never brought their tithes to the storehouse. Every three years the people gave their tithes **directly** to the Levites and the poor, not by proxy of the storehouse (which is not the church). For the Levitical tithe, the people of Israel brought them **to the Levitical cities**. Only the Levites brought the best tenth of

---

41. Kendall, 51.
42. Olford, 29.

this—**their** tithe—to the priests, and only a portion of this went to storehouse for the priests and Levites who ministered there. The festival tithe the people ate themselves and **shared** with the Levites.

R. T. Kendall continues after quoting Leviticus 27:30: "The tithe therefore should go directly and only into the storehouse—the ecclesiastical service of God."[43] To which tithe is Kendall referring? He argues further: "Charitable organizations should be sustained by either non-Christians or Christians who have first given **all** their tithes to the church—and then to that organization. [Emphasis in original]"[44] On the contrary, supposing that Christians had a similar tithing obligation as in the Law, the tithing populous did not bring **any** tithes to the storehouse, which Kendall equates to the church. Moreover, the Levites only brought a small portion of this tithe to the storehouse. Less than one tenth of the people's Levitical tithe was deposited in the storehouse. In other words, if the Law prescribed more than one tithe, only a portion **one tenth** of **one** of the tithes found its way into the storehouse. Later in Kendall's book he correctly lists the three different tithes; however, he erroneously concludes from Malachi 3:10 that all three tithes went directly to the storehouse.[45]

Examining common claims—"spiritual food" vs. real food

Malachi 3:10

10: Bring ye all the tithes into the storehouse, that there may be meat in mine house, and prove me now herewith, saith the LORD of hosts, if I

---

43. Ibid., 52.
44. Ibid.
45. Ibid., 78-79.

will not open you the windows of heaven, and pour you out a blessing, that *there shall* not *be room* enough *to receive it.*

Attempting to wedge Malachi 3:8-10 into the context of the New Testament church is awkward and problematic. Crops and livestock become money. The increase of the harvest becomes the income of wages, regardless of profession. The Levites or priests become church ministers, and sometimes the utter differences between Levites and priests become blurred. Ultimately, the need for Malachi 3:8-10 as a proof text for church tithing involves "spiritualizing" too many elements.

One such element is from the command in verse 10. God said that the tithes should return to the storehouse "that there may be <u>meat</u> in mine house." The word for "meat" simply means "food." It is the Hebrew word *tereph*, which indicates fragments of food. The clear meaning of this is actual, physical food for consumption and bodily nourishment. God was telling the priests to return the tithes **of food** so that, consequently, the storehouse would contain the missing food itself. Predictably, those who are already predisposed to a **monetary** tithe must play gymnastics with the word "meat" or "food."

Pastor Bill Winston quotes Malachi 3:10a and claims: "The 'meat' that God is referring to here is <u>spiritual</u> meat or food. [Emphasis added]"[46] Although the storehouse was a place where certain people were **fed**, this is not the church. How can Pastor Winston dogmatically

---

46. Winston, 39.

make such a statement?! Undoubtedly, he implies the idea of "spiritual food" such as being "fed" with the Word of God. Pastor Stephen Olford concludes from his analysis of Malachi 3:8-10 that "'[s]torehouse tithing,' then, means bringing our tithes to the place where our membership is established, <u>our spiritual life is nourished,</u> and our church privileges are enjoyed. [Emphasis added]"[47]

Statements such as these are an assumption that some necessary correlation must be present. The text of Malachi 3:10 makes no direct or indirect statement about anything "spiritual" whatsoever. God was simply commanding to **return** missing food to the storehouse so that the storehouse would hence have food available. The tithes for the storehouse **were** the food itself. The tithes were not money funds that generated "spiritual food." The tithes were to go **into** the storehouse so that there would be food **in** the storehouse. The priests were to return the **food** to the storehouse so that the very same **food** would be available for the Levites to eat.

Another major problem with the "spiritual food" analogy is that it grossly misunderstands the purpose of this food and the recipients. The people did not bring tithes to the storehouse so that **they** would receive food—physical or "spiritual." Tithes from the people (a portion of one tenth from their tithes to the Levites) ultimately were supposed to be deposited in the storehouse to feed **the priests and Levites—not** the people. The people of Israel did not worship in the storehouse; neither did they receive "food" of any kind from the storehouse. The food was

---

47. Olford, 29.

actual physical food and was for the course of priests and Levites assigned to minister. In Malachi 3:10, God is telling the **priests** to return tithes of **food** to the storehouse so that there would be **food** available for the **Levites** to eat. This verse has nothing whatsoever to do with the **people** at all, neither in tithing nor in receiving "food."

Examining common claims—mysterious blessings vs. "the windows of heaven"

Malachi 3:10

10: Bring ye all the tithes into the storehouse, that there may be meat in mine house, and prove me now herewith, saith the LORD of hosts, if I will not open you the windows of heaven, and pour you out a blessing, that *there shall* not *be room* enough *to receive it.*

When Malachi 3:8-10 is taken from its original context, almost everything must be "spiritualized" or altered to make it fit. The structure of the storehouse, the substance of the tithes, and the ministers must be changed to fit the church setting. The idea of "meat" or "food" must be spiritualized away. Predictably, the same process must happen with "the windows of heaven." What did God mean by this term?

Pastor Stephen Olford compares this with "the outpouring of the Spirit."[48] Pastor Winston adds that these windows of heaven "could even be new inventions or wisdom concerning a matter."[49] R. T. Kendall seems to think that the windows of heaven are primarily "spiritual." After quoting this part of Malachi 3:10, he comments:

---

48. Olford, 32.
49. Winston, 21.

"Were we to stop right there, we might limit the blessing to the spiritual realm.... But Malachi appears to mean more than a spiritual blessing."[50]

Why does he suggest that a "spiritual blessing" is the first and foremost conclusion from this verse? What is the context of this verse that would define for us what opening "the windows of heaven" means? Perhaps a similarity in this phrase exists elsewhere.

Genesis 7:10-12

10: And it came to pass after seven days that the waters of the flood were upon the earth.
11: In the six hundredth year of Noah's life, in the second month, the seventeenth day of the month, the same day were all the fountains of the great deep broken up, and the windows of heaven were opened.
12: And the rain was upon the earth forty days and forty nights.

Part of the flood of Noah's time was caused by rain. The writer of Genesis described the advent of rain by saying that "the windows of heaven were opened." Obviously, one would not conclude that God would be blessing Israel with a destructive flood. He was promising rain.

Deuteronomy 11:13-15

13: And it shall come to pass, if ye shall hearken diligently unto my commandments which I command you this day, to love the LORD your God, and to serve him with all your heart and with all your soul,
14: That I will give *you* the rain of your land in his due season, the first rain and the latter rain, that thou mayest gather in thy corn, and thy wine, and thine oil.
15: And I will send grass in thy fields for thy cattle, that thou mayest eat and be full.

---

50. Kendall, 83.

One of the blessings of following God's commands was that He would ensure that the weather would consistently accommodate an abundant harvest. If the nation of Israel obeyed, they would receive adequate rain for their crops and it would be always on time; if they disobeyed, they would undergo famine. Malachi 3:11-12 indicates that the land was experiencing famine conditions.

As a result of sufficient and abundant rain, God promised that the blessing would be so large that the people would not have enough room to receive it. If the blessings were monetary returns in today's economy, no condition would occur where we would not be able to receive it all. A number in a bank account can be arbitrarily high. The blessing of Malachi 3:10 is not money or "spiritual blessings." It is an abundant harvest. It is food and **only** food!

Examining common claims—Satan vs. the devourer

Malachi 3:11

11: And I will rebuke <u>the devourer</u> for your sakes, and <u>he shall not destroy the fruits of your ground</u>; neither shall your vine cast her fruit before the time in the field, saith the LORD of hosts.

Obviously the context of Malachi 3:11 is still concerning harvest, crops, and food. It is referring to famine, the lack of rain, and anything that God caused or allowed to occur to the harvest because of disobedience. The devourer is something **physical** that devours physical **crops**. The only reasonable understanding is that of some kind of insect or animal that enters the field unauthorized and eats crops before they are ready for harvest.

Those, such as John Hagee, who do not look at the exact context and specifics of this passage and the laws themselves that this passage references will be forced to interpret "the devourer" as Satan rather than the obvious intention of locusts or other creatures that would literally destroy the crops of their harvest by **devouring** them.[51] Although Pastor Stephen F. Olford correctly noted that "[t]he locusts had eaten the crops," he makes the same effort to "spiritualize" and apply this passage out of its context by claiming that "[t]oday they symbolize the forces of Satan that are arrayed against the church."[52] No indication or inference of such alignment exists in the text. These are purely the ideas of those who believe that some way, somehow, Malachi 3:8-12 **must** be both a command and a promise to Christians today to "test God" in the imaginary idea of the monetary income tithe doctrine.

Examining common claims—the church vs. the nation

Malachi 3:12

12: And all nations shall call you blessed: for ye shall be a delightsome land, saith the LORD of hosts.

Assuming that Malachi 3:8-12 applies to the church also assumes that a "nation" and a "land" can be converted to a diaspora of Christians. God promised the nation of Israel that they would be "a delightsome land." The weather would affect a mass of land, not individual people. If the **nation** of Israel as a whole obeyed God's

---

51. Hagee, 114.
52. Olford, 32.

commands, He would guarantee that the weather would be proper for an abundant harvest. This weather could not be divided according to individual people. The Gentile nations would observe God's blessings on the nation of Israel. This promise was a national promise, not an individual promise.

Evil is the new good, part II

Malachi 3:13-15

13: <u>Your words</u> have been stout against me, saith the LORD. Yet <u>ye say</u>, What have we spoken *so much* against thee?
14: Ye have said, It *is* <u>vain to serve God</u>: and <u>what profit *is it* that we have kept his ordinance</u>, and that we have walked mournfully before the LORD of hosts?
15: And now we call the proud happy; yea, *they that* work wickedness are set up; yea, they that tempt God are even delivered.

Is God still taking to the priests? The verses above appeared to be addressed to the nation. Do not forget that God was speaking to the priests in verse 10. He referred to them as "this whole nation" in verse 9. Up to this point, the priests clearly have been asking all the questions. Why would there be a break now?

It is true that the whole nation was suffering a famine because of the sins of the priests and the people. The priests were responsible for misleading the people in the Law. The whole nation suffered, but the priests were the proxy. Any indirect address to the nation here is through a direct address to the priests.

Another evidence for the continued recipients here being the priests is that the questions asked here are similar to the question earlier of "Where is the God of judgment?" In a similar vein, the priests are questioning the worth of serving God because they could not detect any blessings or merit. They, like King David and King Solomon observed that the righteous appeared to suffer and the wicked appeared to prosper (Psalm 73:12-14; Ecclesiastes 7:15-16) However, both of them realized that this apparent paradox was temporary (Psalm 73:16-19; Ecclesiastes 7:17-19).

The promise of restoration

Malachi 3:16-18

16: Then they that feared the LORD spake often one to another: and the LORD hearkened, and heard *it*, and a book of remembrance was written before him for them that feared the LORD, and that thought upon his name.
17: And they shall be mine, saith the LORD of hosts, in that day when I make up my jewels; and I will spare them, as a man spareth his own son that serveth him.
18: Then shall ye return, and discern between the righteous and the wicked, between him that serveth God and him that serveth him not.

God promised these wicked priests that they would ultimately return to Him. A possible immediate fulfillment of this was the second reforms of Nehemiah. However, if this promise is linked to the prophecy of the coming Messiah, then the ultimate fulfillment would be that of the remnant of Israel who would be saved. Malachi chapter 4 makes this promise a connection with the events surrounding the coming "messenger of the covenant."

The day of the Lord

Malachi 4:1

1: For, behold, the day cometh, that shall burn as an oven; and all the proud, yea, and all that do wickedly, shall be stubble: and the day that cometh shall burn them up, saith the LORD of hosts, that it shall leave them neither root nor branch.

287

Joel 1:15

15: Alas for the day! for <u>the day of the LORD</u> *is* at hand, and as a destruction from the Almighty shall it come.

Malachi prophesies of a "day" that would come, similar to the "day of the Lord" prophesied in Joel 1:15. This "day of the Lord" was prophesied as a dreadful day. This "day" was not a 24-hour period, but rather a **starting point** for a series of events. The "day of the Lord" from these two prophets began with the coming of the Messiah and His death on Calvary. Some would face destruction while those who sought the True God would be spared.

Malachi 4:2

2: But unto you that fear my name <u>shall the Sun of righteousness arise with healing in his wings</u>; and ye shall go forth, and grow up as calves of the stall.
3: And ye shall tread down the wicked; for they shall be ashes under the soles of your feet in the day that I shall do *this*, saith the LORD of hosts.

Joel 2:17-19

17: Let <u>the priests, the ministers of the LORD</u>, weep between the porch and the altar, and let them say, Spare thy people, O LORD, and give not thine heritage to reproach, that the heathen should rule over them: wherefore should they say among the people, Where *is* their God?
18: <u>Then will the LORD be jealous for his land, and pity his people</u>.
19: Yea, the LORD will answer and say unto his people, Behold, I will send you corn, and wine, and oil, and ye shall be satisfied therewith: and I will no more make you a reproach among the heathen:

With the prophecy of the destruction that would come with the events of the coming of the Messiah also came a promise to the priests and to the people of Israel. They could escape the wrath if they returned to God. The moniker for the Messiah as "the Sun of righteousness" is likely a comparative allusion to the Persian sun god

288

as having "healing in his wings [or rays]" parallels the Persian kingdom's symbol of a son with extruding rays at the top sides.[53] Of course, Malachi knew that Yahweh is the only true God and that the Messiah is also God Himself.

The second coming of Elijah

Malachi 4:4-6

4: Remember ye the law of Moses my servant, which I commanded unto him in Horeb for all Israel, with the statutes and judgments.
5: Behold, I will send you Elijah the prophet before the coming of the great and dreadful day of the LORD:
6: And he shall turn the heart of the fathers to the children, and the heart of the children to their fathers, lest I come and smite the earth with a curse.

In verse 4, God makes one last reminder to the priests to follow the Law. In verse 5, He then prophesies that "Elijah the prophet" would return to set things right. This Elijah must be the same as the first "messenger" who would "prepare the way of the Lord." Jesus and others in the New Testament referred to this prophecy of Elijah's second return and noted John the Baptist as the fulfillment (Matthew 11:13-14; 17:10-13; Mark 9:11-13; Luke 1:11-17). Obviously John the Baptist was not literally Elijah returned from the dead or reincarnate, but one would be like Elijah and act with the same spirit.

Conclusion and summary

In conclusion, we have examined the second half of the book of Malachi. These final two chapters of Malachi cover a provocation of

---

53. Leland Ryken, Jim Wilhoit, Tremper Longman, Colin Duriez, Douglas Penney, and Daniel G. Reid, *Dictionary of Biblical Imagery* (Downers Grove, IL: InterVarsity Press, 1998), 827.

the priests and a prophecy of the Messiah and restoration. Perhaps an immediate partial fulfillment is that of Nehemiah. The obvious fulfillment involves John the Baptist and Jesus Christ Himself.

We have observed that the rest of Malachi provides no realistic break in the recipient. The entire book of Malachi is addressed directly to the priests, with indirect references to the nation under their care. The priests were asking all the questions and God was giving them all the answers.

We have examined Malachi 3:8-12 in extensive detail. The priests were robbing God in tithes and offerings. They were robbing the offerings from the storehouse and giving God poor offerings. They were robbing the storehouse tithes from the Levites. We have examined the weight of common opinion, interpretation, and application of terms and phrases in Malachi 3:8-12 to the church setting and have found them all wanting. The overwhelming testimony of context and logic for Malachi 3:8-12 provides absolutely no proof for the modern monetary income tithe doctrine.

SECTION IV: NEW TESTAMENT TITHING

Is This Still the Law?

The Mosaic Law in the Old Testament contains extensive rules and regulations for how the nation of Israel had to conduct their personal lives and their theocratic government. God established a Levitical priesthood who would have no inheritance in the land and would instead live from the agricultural tithes of the people of Israel. As part of the conditions of the priesthood, the priests would intercede to God on behalf of the people of Israel. The priests would perform specific sacrifices that would cover their own sins as well as the sins of the people. Every year the priests had to perform a solemn sacrificial ritual to cleanse the nation of sins for that same year. Only the priest could enter the holiest place containing the altar, and anyone else attempting to do the same would die.

Coming to the New Testament, we observe that only a few mentions of tithing exist. In fact, the only individuals to dictate the act of tithing by name are Jesus Christ Himself and the writer to the Hebrews. Since we consider ourselves members of the New Testament church and not of the former theocratic nation of Israel, we need to examine these instances of tithing carefully to understand them in context. Since Jesus is the mediator of the New Covenant, does the fact that Jesus Himself mentioned tithing place such a command upon His New Covenant people? Does the writer to the Hebrews recalling the account of Abraham's tithe to Melchizedek and declaring Jesus Christ "a priest forever after the order of Melchizedek" bind tithing as an ordinance upon the church? Let us dig deep into the Word of God and attempt to understand these verse important passages of Scripture to obtain yet a further grasp upon the Biblical concept of tithing.

14. The Pharisees Rebuked

Weightier Matters

Matthew 23:23

23: Woe unto you, scribes and Pharisees, hypocrites! for ye pay tithe of mint and anise and cummin, and have omitted the weightier *matters* of the law, judgment, mercy, and faith: these ought ye to have done, and not to leave the other undone.

Luke 11:42

42: But woe unto you, Pharisees! for ye tithe mint and rue and all manner of herbs, and pass over judgment and the love of God: these ought ye to have done, and not to leave the other undone.

Jesus had a bone to pick with the hypocritical religious leaders. Matthew chapter 23 and Luke chapter 11 supply the account of Jesus' woes upon the scribes, Pharisees, and lawyers. Amid these scathing remarks, Jesus mentioned their acts of tithing to the extreme while ignoring the matters of the Law that really made the difference—love, justice, faith, and mercy. Even though they were going overboard, Jesus did not tell them to cease their tithing and **replace** it with the "weightier matters." He told them to do **both**. By virtue of Jesus "commending" the religious leaders for their tithing, are we obligated to do the same?

A matter of Law

Some dismiss the absence of tithing as church doctrine in the New Testament as an argument from silence. In essence, the fact that tithing does not exist in the epistles proves that further reaffirming it would be redundant. Retired pastor Robert T. Kendall claims that "[t]ithing was so deeply imbedded in the Jewish conscience, moreover, that it needed virtually no mention in the New Testament. Tithing was an assumption when Jesus came on the scene."[1] Of course tithing was "deeply imbedded." It was **the Law!** Approximately four hundred years prior to this time, the people understood the curse upon the land when they forsook the Law. The priests knew all too well as they had been misleading the people. The priests faced God's curse and burning criticisms in His words through Malachi. The people suffered. The priests suffered. The land suffered. Tithing, like other commands and ordinances in the Law, was much more than merely a matter residing "in the Jewish conscience." It was much more than "an assumption."

Another argument stemming from a misunderstanding of the Law and the covenants is that Jesus dismissed his "opportunity" to drop the tithing laws in His accusation. Accordingly, the fact that He "commended" their acts of tithing proves that such portion of the Law lives on while many other portions became obsolete under the New Covenant. Kendall claims that "[i]t is striking that our Lord endorsed tithing in this verse [Matthew 23:23]."[2] The fact that Jesus "endorsed

---

1. Kendall, 29.
2. Ibid.

tithing" should not be surprising, as the One Who made the statement is the Law-Giver.

To understand the context of Matthew 23:23, we need to look at the words of Jesus to the people and His disciples:

Matthew 23:1-7

1: Then spake Jesus to the multitude, and to his disciples,

2: Saying, The scribes and the Pharisees sit in Moses' seat:

3: All therefore whatsoever they bid you observe, *that* observe and do; but do not ye after their works: for they say, and do not.

4: For they bind heavy burdens and grievous to be borne, and lay *them* on men's shoulders; but they *themselves* will not move them with one of their fingers.

5: But all their works they do for to be seen of men: they make broad their phylacteries, and enlarge the borders of their garments,

6: And love the uppermost rooms at feasts, and the chief seats in the synagogues,

7: And greetings in the markets, and to be called of men, Rabbi, Rabbi.

Jesus told these people that "[t]he scribes and Pharisees sit in Moses' seat." The scribes and Pharisees were the ones who preserved the Law. God gave the Law through Moses, and the scribes and Pharisees were the nominal sect who kept the Law in tact and promoted its practice. Therefore, as the maintainers of God's ordinances, Jesus told the people and His disciples to keep what they say as pertains to the Law.

The people were still under the Law during Jesus' earthly ministry. Kendall continues by claiming that "[i]f tithing was a part of the law that would or could be dropped under the New Covenant this is the place our Lord would have done it. He did not."[3] Kendall grossly misunderstands when the New Covenant began. The New Covenant began not with the birth or the earthly ministry of Jesus, but with His death and resurrection. Paul said that the act of Calvary removed the requirement of the ordinances of the Law "against us" (Colossians 2:13-14). Paul also said that Christ "abolished" the ordinances of the Law, calling them "the enemy," and "slew them" **by the cross** (Ephesians 2:13-16). Christ's death and resurrection established the New Covenant. During Jesus' earthly ministry, He and the nation of Israel were still under the Old Covenant—the Law. Jesus had no intention of dismantling the Law in His ministry. He taught obedience to the Law and He fulfilled the Law.

Will the real hypocrites please stand up

Although today the term *Pharisee* is a synonym for "legalistic religious hypocrite" because of the record of New Testament Scripture, the virtually universal understanding of the religious sect during their time was one of high regard.[4] Accordingly, the Apostle Paul, as a qualification for outward righteousness to people and "confidence in the flesh," identified himself as a former Pharisee (Philippians 3:4-6). The Pharisees were a vocal, yet relatively small body with high clout upon a nation of people that sought to maintain their theocratic identity.[5]

---

3. Ibid., 30.
4. *Zondervan Handbook to the Bible*, s.v. "Parties and movements in 1st-century Judaism."
5. Ibid.

The Pharisees were essentially Law politicians through example rather than as actual officials during the time of the Roman government, acting as a form of "right wing" representatives for the executive sect in the puppet Jewish provincial government allowed to thrive under Roman rule. The Pharisees were the "separatists" of their day as their title may imply.[6] The Pharisees were one of two major religious parties, with the Sadducees as the other "left wing" party. The Pharisees were the stronger and most pronounced of the two parties, whereas the Sadducees existed as an alternative, less popular viewpoint.[7] Interestingly, although the Sadducees were less spiritually-oriented in their dogma than the Pharisees, no Scriptural record exists of Jesus exhuming heavy accusations on them. The Pharisees—the religious sect with the highest adoration and respect for the day—bore the brunt of condemnation from Jesus' ministry.

While the Pharisees of Jesus' day were mostly legalistic hypocrites, their roots were much nobler, perhaps attributing to their widespread regard before the accusations from Jesus. The Pharisees may have begun as a religious sect among the Maccabean revolt to free the Jews from foreign rule.[8] As respectable liberators with a fierce loyalty to Jewish cultural tradition and the Law and Prophets (Old Testament) the demise of the integrity of the Pharisees largely went

---

6. *Vine's Complete Expository Dictionary of Old and New Testament Words* (Nashville: Thomas Nelson, 1996), s.v. "Pharisees."
7. Ibid.
8. *Holman Illustrated Bible Dictionary* (Nashville: Holman, 2003), s.v. "Jewish Parties in the New Testament."

understandably undetected and unnoticed. Their evolution from staunch purity to excess legalism and hypocritical moral character was a slow and unfortunate progress.

The history of their zeal transitioned from a legitimate and balanced adherence to God's Law to one comprising two extremes: an outward rigor and epitome of righteousness (Matthew 5:20; 23:5-7) and an inward corruption of legal loopholes and hypocrisy (Matthew 23:4,14,27). Therefore, when Jesus clashed with the Pharisees during His earthly ministry, His disciples had to face the shock and scratch their heads as they gradually learned the significance of their Saviour's words. The resurrection of Jesus Christ proved His Person and work, and the disciples later understood the full impact of the truth behind these religious zealots as they faced persecution by their own countrymen as Apostles. The Pharisees even resorted to acts of loyalty to the pagan Roman Empire to quell the rising tide of the ministry of the early Christian church.[9] According to the accusations of Jesus, the Pharisees obviously were aware of their double standards and accepted their position and influence because of the prestige and surface-level fulfillment such an arrangement provided them.

The scribes were largely among the number of the Pharisees.[10] They copied the Law precisely to keep it available. God commanded

---

9. See Matthew 22:15-22; Mark 12:12-17; Luke 20:19-26; 22:66-23:2; John 19:6-12; Acts 25:7-8.
10. *Zondervan Handbook to the Bible*, s.v. "Parties and movements in 1st-century Judaism."

the people of Israel to observe and keep His statutes.[11] Keeping the Law completely intact—every jot and every tittle—was vitally important for the nation of Israel so that they could know God's Law and thus receive His blessings and not His cursings. The scribes "sat in Moses' seat" by preserving the words of the Law that God gave to Moses. They also guided the Pharisees who then carried out the assumed acts of the Law in the public realm.[12]

Although the scribes never assumed a nominal legal office, they apparently acted as such indirectly.[13] Their copying and teaching of the Law affected the actions and directions of the Jewish government, and hence the people of the land.[14]

The "lawyers" were from the number of the Pharisees who interpreted the law.[15] In fact, the lawyers likely thrived from among the scribes, who were mostly Pharisees.[16] Whereas the Pharisees as a body of religious leaders promoted the Law and practiced the Law (allegedly), the lawyers among them were the ones who interpreted the Law for them and for the people who would observe them. Although the scribes and Pharisees influenced Jewish Law indirectly through example, the lawyers as legal scholars may have served officially in

---

11. See Leviticus 19:37; Deuteronomy 5:31-6:3; 6:24-25; 8:1; 11:32-12:1; 12:28,32; 15:5; 28:1-68; 31:12; 32:46.
12. *Vine's Complete Expository Dictionary*, s.v. "Pharisees."
13. Ibid., s.v. "scribe (-s)."
14. Ibid.
15. See Matthew 22:34-35; Luke 7:30; 14:1-4. Compare Luke 11:44-46,52-54 to Matthew 23:2-4,15.
16. *Vine's Complete Expository Dictionary*, s.v. "lawyer."

the legal entity known as the Sanhedrin.[17] Along with the scribes and Pharisees, Jesus singled out the lawyers for certain rebuke and condemnation (Luke 11:45-52).

Did Jesus tithe?

According to Jesus Christ, He came to "fulfill" the law (Matthew 5:17). What did He mean when He said that He would "fulfill" the law? Did He mean that He would engage absolutely every command in the Torah?

Jesus fulfilling the law does not mean that He followed every ordinance in the law. Indeed, as a Jewish male carpenter, many ordinances did not apply to His person. His gender, nationality, occupation, and social status dictated which ordinances from the Mosaic law concerned His earthly life. In other words, Jesus "perfectly obeyed all the commandments, the judgments, and the ordinances which applied to Him."[18]

Some believe that Jesus Himself tithed and set this example by His statement in Matthew 23:23.[19] If Jesus rebuked the scribes and Pharisees, He would not have told them to do something that He did not have to do, right? Not necessarily. If certain laws applied only to certain groups of people, then the group wherein Jesus existed would ostensibly determine if Jesus tithed.

---

17. Ibid.
18. Kelly, 117.
19. Hagee, 112.

First, as we determined previously, not all Israelites tithed. Only landowners who grew crops and raised livestock within the national bounds of Israel tithed of them.[20] Jesus was a carpenter with His earthly father Joseph and did not own land. He traveled around and claimed no official residency to His name during his ministry (Matthew 8:20; Luke 9:58). The poor did not tithe; they **received** tithes. Jesus was not born wealthy (Leviticus 12:1-8; Luke 2:7,21-24), did not grow up wealthy (Matthew 2:23; John 1:46; 7:40-42,52), and neither ministered nor died wealthy (Isaiah 53:2; Zechariah 9:9; Matthew 17:24-27; Mark 8:34; 2 Corinthians 8:9). For these reasons, no convincing and supportable argument exists for Jesus to have tithed as a man. Jesus as the Law-Giver had the right to criticize the scribes and Pharisees for petty extremes in their tithing while disregarding the weightier matters.

Follow the money

Returning to the text of this chapter, of particular note is the nature of the act of the scribes and Pharisees in their tithing. Notice yet again that their tithes consisted of food items and not money. We know that Israelites had access to money throughout their existence as a nation. Especially even during the Roman captivity, if the tithing laws depended upon the nature of the Jewish economy, the people of Israel could have surely adopted coinage for their tithes and derived them

---

20. See Leviticus 27:30-32; Deuteronomy 14:22-29; 26:12-14; 2 Chronicles 31:5-6; Nehemiah 10:37; 12:44.

from sources of monetary income. According to Matthew 23:23 and Luke 11:42, this simply was not the case.

The people and the religious leaders were still tithing "of the seed of the land, or of the fruit of the tree" (Leviticus 27:30), and "all the increase of [their] seed, that the field bringeth forth year by year" (Deuteronomy 14:22). They were still tithing "of the herd, or of the flock, even of whatsoever passeth under the rod" (Leviticus 27:32). Money was still only involved in the acts of tithing only if one wanted to redeem the tithe of the crops (Leviticus 27:31) or needed a medium of exchange to bring the tithes of food to Jerusalem (Deuteronomy 14:24-26). The tithing laws did not require food items for purposes of tithes because Israel was an "agrarian society;" the tithing laws required **only** food items grown or raised within the boundaries of the Promised Land specifically so that the people only tithed of things that God specially provided Himself through the weather in His care of the land that He promised His people Israel. The land would be "flowing with milk and honey" (food) because **God** provided it, not through the crafts and skills of people. They could only tithe of things that totally depended on God's handiwork in nature.

Israel was never an "agrarian society" and had plenty of supply of sound money upon their exile from Egypt as they "spoiled the Egyptians" (Exodus 3:20-22; 11:1-2; 12:35-36; 20:22-23). They had enough wealth in gold and silver to construct the tabernacle according to God's specifications (Exodus 25-40). They had enough gold to construct a golden calf idol from their earrings (Exodus 32). They knew about money because God made a covenant of circumcision with Abraham and mentioned silver money (Genesis 17:9-27; 31:14-16). Abraham purchased a cave with silver money to bury his wife Sarah (Genesis 23; Acts 7:16). Jacob bought real estate with 100 pieces of silver money (Genesis 33:18-20). The Egyptians and Joseph's brothers used silver money even during the famine (Genesis 42:25-44:34). As Joseph's family resided in Egypt during the famine, the silver money suffered inflation because food commodities became scarce (Genesis 47:13-20).

The Israelites during the time of Jesus and the first century had many uses for money. They paid the temple tax with money (Matthew 27:24-27). They gave donations freely for the temple (Mark 12:41-44). They paid taxes to the Roman government in Roman coin, which they had to use for the market (Matthew 22:17-22; Mark 12:12-17; Luke 20:19-26; 23:2; Romans 13:6-8). They bought and sold real estate with money (Acts 4:34-37). Jesus cast out the moneychangers who profited by required silver shekels for sacrificial animals and being dishonest with currency conversions (John 2:14-16). Jesus referenced money in His parables (Matthew 20:1-16; 25:14-30; Luke 15:8-10; 19:11-27). The Jewish religious leaders bribed the Roman soldiers with money (Matthew 28:11-15). Jesus commissioned His disciples not to bring a supply of money as missionaries (Matthew 10:5-10; Mark 6:7-8; Luke 9:1-3). Judas Iscariot betrayed Jesus for silver money (Matthew 26:14-16; 27:3-10; Mark 14:10-11; Luke 22:3-6). Monetary units included the *mite* or *lepton* (Mark 12:42; Luke 12:59; Luke 21:2), the *farthing* or *kodrantēs* or *assarius* ("quadrant") (Matthew 5:26; 10:29; Mark 12:42; Luke 12:6), the *penny* or *denarius* (Matthew 20:1-16; 22:19; Mark 12:15; Luke 20:24; Revelation 6:6), and the *pound* or *mna* (Luke 19:11-27). The New International Bible Dictionary observes that although Israel under captivity was subject to the coinage of the Roman government, "that the laws regarding the tenth were still observed is shown by the fact that the Pharisees tithed even the herbs that were used in seasoning food."[21]

Variety is the spice of tithes

The scribes and Pharisees practiced tithing according to the Law, and they even stretched the Law beyond its original intention. Although the tithing laws required tithes "of the seed of the land" and "of the fruit of the tree," the scribes and Pharisees taught more than the general spirit. Arthur V. Babbs clarified: "The Pharisees of our Lord's day paid not only tithes of grain and fruits, but also of pulse, herbs, in gardens, which the law did not require [Emphasis added]."[22] The Law obviously referred to farm lands and substantial crops and fruit, not small personal garden patches and seasonings. If one cannot see what "seed" here implied, one could arrive at an absurd idea that one must tithe of the grass that grows wild on every parcel of land. Clearly the intention of the Law was to rejoice before the Lord in His blessings and to feed the Levites, the poor, and the foreigners who sojourned. The scribes and Pharisees drove the focus and intent of the Law away

---

21. *New International Bible Dictionary*, s.v. "tithe."
22. Babbs, 35.

from feeding the hungry to meticulous labor and calculations. If the scribes and Pharisees truly intended their giving of spices to meet needs, they could have extracted a generous visible portion of their gardens instead of spending unnecessary time and energy to calculate and pick a precise tenth of these small items. Their actions in this regard were clearly intentional to demonstrate excessive piety in following the letter of the Law to the extreme to make others who did not do likewise feel guilty.

I favor a "formal equivalency" method of Bible translation over a "dynamic equivalency" approach. "Formal equivalency" requires as much a word-for-word translation as possible to favor the actual text itself over attempting to explain what the writers "meant." "Dynamic equivalency" attempts a thought-for-thought translation approach, attempting to express what the translators feel the writers "meant" without transferring every word to the target language. Such an approach can possibly introduce biases, assumptions, and traditions into the resulting "paraphrase" that may not accurately reflect the idea expressed in the source itself. An example is Eugene Peterson's rendition of Matthew 23:23 in *The Message*, in which he paraphrased the actions of the religious leaders: "You keep meticulous account books, tithing on every nickel and dime you get... Careful bookkeeping is commendable, but the basics are required." Likewise, Luke 11:42 in *The Message* similarly states: "You keep meticulous account books, tithing on every nickel and dime you get... Careful bookkeeping is commendable, but the basics are required." Obviously, Peterson's own bias influenced his **paraphrase** of the text of Scripture, replacing the garden herbs with his traditional understanding of a tithe of monetary income. In his efforts to communicate "the message" of these verses to his readers, he assumed that the tithing of the religious leaders applies to them and communicated this assumption by adapting the substance of the tithe to his own preferences.

A. W. Pink acknowledged the nature of the tithe from the scribes and Pharisees, but did not extrapolate the bearing that this has upon the words of Jesus themselves:

> In that verse Christ is rebuking the scribes and Pharisees because of their hypocrisy. **They had been very strict and punctilious in tithing the herbs,** but on the other hand they had neglected the weightier matters such as judgment, or justice, and mercy. But while Christ acknowledged that the observance of justice and mercy is more important than tithing—it is a "weightier matter"—while, He says, these they ought to have done, nevertheless He says, **these other ye ought not to have left undone.** He does not set aside the tithe. He places justice and mercy as being more weighty, but He places His authority upon the practice of tithing by saying, "These ought ye to have done, and not to leave the other undone." It is well for us if we by the grace of God have not omitted justice and mercy and faith: it is well if by the grace of God those things have found a place in our midst: but the tithing ought not to have been left undone, **and Christ Himself says so.**[23] [Emphasis added]

Arthur Pink, and most others who read Jesus' rebuke to the scribes and Pharisees miss a very important point about the words of Jesus. They ignore the **mint, anise, and cummin** and the **mint, rue, and all manner of herbs** in the tithing that Jesus said that they were "not to

---

23. Arthur W. Pink, *Tithing* (Grand Rapids: Christian Classics Ethereal Library), 4.

leave... undone." R. T. Kendall does mention the nature of their tithes briefly:

> Our Lord, I say, might have made light of their tithing "of mint and anise and cummin," or as the New International Version translates it: "You give a tenth of your spices—mint, dill and cummin." It would have been an apt place for Jesus to magnify such meticulous care to tithe—which He did—but also to leave it at that so we could see the humor, as it were, in His assessment of them. But He *took the care Himself* to sanction such bother to tithe, provided that it was done in the context of judgment, mercy, and faith.[24] [Emphasis in original]

However, Kendall does not seem to grasp the full extent of what the words of Jesus entail, nor the connection that the tithes "of mint and anise and cummin" had to the specifics of the Law even with the nit-picking extremes of these religious leaders. At first this point may appear to be splitting hairs. After all, if Jesus is referring to the conventional livelihood of these people, why should these specifics matter to us?

The problem is that these specifics **do** matter immensely. Not to engage in "hyper-red-letterism" and invoke the wrath of Dr. James White, but these are the words of Jesus, and what He said matters! We cannot simply cherry-pick some words from His single statement and apply them the way we want, yet simultaneously ignore other words that actually define the terms. When Jesus uttered these words, He uttered them for a purpose, and I suppose that the God-Man never used his breath in speech superfluously.

---

24. Kendall, 30.

Jesus told the scribes and Pharisees that their tithing **of herbs** was something that they were "not to leave... undone." The words of Jesus present a conundrum for the thoughtful income tithe teacher. Does what Jesus said to the scribes and Pharisees apply to us today? Regardless of if the answer is a **yes** or **no**, it will raise more questions.

If the answer is **yes**, then we need to obey the words of Jesus and tithe **of mint, anise, cumin, rue, and all manner of herbs**. If the "ye" (scribes and Pharisees) includes you and I, then we need to do what He said and do **exactly** what He said. There is no way around this command. What authority do we have to divide, reinterpret, or reapply the words of Jesus in the inspired Word of God? If this command to the scribes and Pharisees applies to us, then we are in serious trouble! In fact, Jesus told them "woe unto you"! Where the Son of God speaks of woe, all do well to take heed. If we are tithing of our monetary income, and not of our **herbs**, as Jesus plainly said, then we are disobeying the command of our Saviour. I have met many who profess Christianity in my life, but I have yet to meet a single one who tithes **of mint, anise, cumin, rue, and all manner of herbs**. Are we all under the curse of God?

If the answer is **no**, then Jesus' statement is not telling New Testament Christian church-goers *to tithe*. He is not telling Christians to tithe of their **herbs**, and He is certainly and obviously not telling Christians to tithe of their **monetary income**. We must not do violence to the words of Jesus and the inspired words of God. Either what Jesus said applies as a command to us or it does not. If what Jesus said applies to us as a command then we must do what He said—**exactly** what He said! If what Jesus said does not apply to us as a command, then these passages are yet others that neither teach the monetary income tithe nor obligate Christians to follow such teaching. If we are obligated to tithe, and to do so from our monetary income, then we must find this command elsewhere. The words of Jesus here do not appear to qualify.

Beauty and the beast

Jesus also referenced tithing in the New Testament through a parable. In the same vein as the accusations against the scribes and Pharisees, He compared a boasting, hypocritical self-righteous Pharisee to a sinful, but humble publican. The tithe comes in the same context of being a nit-picking excess while the more important matters fall by the wayside.

Luke 18:9-14

9 And he spake this parable unto certain which trusted in themselves that they were righteous, and despised others:
10 Two men went up into the temple to pray; the one a Pharisee, and the other a publican.
11 The Pharisee stood and prayed thus with himself, God, I thank thee, that I am not as other men *are*, extortioners, unjust, adulterers, or even as this publican.
12 I fast twice in the week, I give tithes of all that I possess.
13 And the publican, standing afar off, would not lift up so much as his eyes unto heaven, but smote upon his breast, saying, God be merciful to me a sinner.
14 I tell you, this man went down to his house justified *rather* than the other: for every one that exalteth himself shall be abased; and he that humbleth himself shall be exalted.

Here, the Pharisee boasts about his supposed righteousness. He prays to God, but in reality he prays to himself. He makes a statement regarding his tithing that one can easily misunderstand without having studied the issue in Scripture: "I give tithes of all that I possess." The Pharisee was not making a simple statement saying "I pay my tithes as I am supposed to do according to the Law." The Pharisee, like the ones Jesus accused in Matthew 23:23 and Luke 11:42, was making a statement of **exaggeration**.

Likely, this statement bears appropriate similarity to the previous accusation. The Pharisees not only tithed according to the Law, they tithed **of mint, anise, cummin, rue, and all manner of herbs**. They went out of their way to show themselves sticklers for the letter of the Law to make everyone else feel guilty or not as righteous. They expended time and energy to pick and calculate a tenth of spices from their gardens. Their actions said, "I give tithes of **all** that I possess." The Pharisee in the parable tithed **of mint, anise, and cummin**. He tithed **of his spices**. He exceeded the intent of the Law and bragged about it. He tithed **of "all" that he possessed**.

However, the publican who did not "tithe of all that he possessed" went to his house justified because he recognized his state. He recognized that he was a sinner and that God was holy. He saw his sin for what it was and knew that he needed mercy and grace. The Pharisee thought that he was righteous and that his excesses in the Law gave him approval from God. According to Jesus the Pharisee was wrong, and the publican received mercy and grace. The self-righteous

Pharisee was unjustified and the publican was justified. Clearly, this account of "tithing" does not prove the monetary income tithe doctrine.

Render unto Caesar

Another account in the New Testament that some use to argue monetary income tithing is that of the encounter between Jesus and the Pharisees and Herodians regarding taxes to Caesar. The Pharisees were the Jewish loyalists to the Mosaic Law. The Herodians were the Jewish loyalists to the Jewish government as established under Roman rule, and hence loyalists to Caesar. They banded together to try to ask Jesus a baited question. If Jesus answered to the affirmative, the Pharisees could accuse Him of defying the Torah. If Jesus answered to the negative, the Herodians could ensnare Him as a rebel to Caesar. The situation would be sure to be win-win for those who wanted to destroy Jesus and lose-lose for the Perfect One Who was heeding both the Law and the Roman regulations.

Matthew 22:15-22 (cf. Mark 12:12-17; Luke 20:19-26)

15: Then went the Pharisees, and took counsel how they might entangle him in *his* talk.
16: And they sent out unto him their disciples with the Herodians, saying, Master, we know that thou art true, and teachest the way of God in truth, neither carest thou for any *man*: for thou regardest not the person of men.
17: Tell us therefore, What thinkest thou? Is it lawful to give tribute unto Caesar, or not?
18: But Jesus perceived their wickedness, and said, Why tempt ye me, ye hypocrites?
19: Show me the tribute money. And they brought unto him a penny.
20: And he saith unto them, Whose *is* this image and superscription?

21: They say unto him, Caesar's. Then saith he unto them, <u>Render therefore unto Caesar the things which are Caesar's; and unto God the things that are God's</u>.
22: When they had heard *these words,* they marveled, and left him, and went their way.

Many simply gloss over the precise wording of this account and make assumptions based on their traditional understanding of Biblical tithing. The common understanding is that Jesus was saying that from one's monetary income, one has the obligation to pay the government tax owed, and from the same monetary income pay the religious tenth owed to the church.[25] The idea is that from one's finances, one has obligation to both a secular tax and a religious tax. A closer examination of the texts, coupled with our current understanding of the nature of tithing according to the Mosaic Law, will reveal exactly what Jesus meant in His statement about "the things that are Caesar's" and "the things that are God's."

Because we understand what the tithing laws entailed even during the time of Jesus, we know that both His and the leaders' understanding of tithing was the same. If the tithing laws were of the crops and livestock of the land of Israel, then Jesus obviously was not referencing tithing with the Roman penny. He was not implicitly endorsing a new concept. His statement about "the things that are God's" may or may not imply tithing. If He did imply tithing here, it was not in terms of the Roman coin.

---

25. Stan Wangenye, *God's Will still is Prosperity* (Longwood, FL: Xulon Press, 2009), 99.

The question of "Is it lawful to give tribute [taxes] to Caesar?" involved an understanding of the Mosaic Law. In other words, the question of "Is it lawful?" was not one of Roman law, but of the Torah. By way of "lawful," the question was if the action was **permissible** under the Law. The Pharisees and Herodians were attempting to trap Jesus between the accountability of two loyalties. Regardless of the fact that the "good" Jewish citizens paid their taxes to Caesar, these Jewish leaders desired to take a current non-issue or assumption and raise a stir. Since many regarded Jesus as a master of the Law and taught its stated and moral principles, His answer to the question would create a popular enigma.

Jesus replied to the plot by asking the Pharisees and Herodians a rhetorical question about the profile and superscription on the face of the penny. They replied that it was Caesar's. In other words, the coin rightfully belonged to Caesar as he so dictated. The Roman government minted the coins likely from silver under its jurisdiction. The Roman government stamped the profile of Caesar's face and placed his name above it, indicating his rightful ownership. If Caesar, therefore, who owned the mint and created the silver for circulation regulated taxes of them, the coins were "the things that are Caesar's." In other words, if Caesar owned the coins in circulation and wanted them back, he was entitled to them. By virtue of the official stamp upon the coins, the "things that are Caesar's" were **the coins themselves**, not simply the taxes of them that he required.

What are "the things that are God's"? Since Jesus specified that the coins belonged to Caesar, then He would also not claim that the coins belonged to God (in the general sense of one's obligation). **All** the *pennies* or *denaria* in circulation bore the stamp of Caesar, claiming his ownership. "The things that are God's" denoted something else that was not denominated in Roman coinage. "The things that are God's" may have included several items and sources. In this phrase, Jesus may have implicitly included the temple tax (Matthew 17:24-27), which was a *didrachma* or two drachma piece. These were ancient Greek coins that the Jews may have possessed and adopted for their purposes after the Roman conquest. A silver *didrachma* coin was equal in weight to a *half shekel,* the required poll tax for the tabernacle (later the Temple) according to the Law (Exodus 30:11-16). The Jewish equivalent to a Greek *didrachma* was a *bekah* or *beqa',* which was also a half shekel (Genesis 24:22; Exodus 38:26). The Jews did not pay the temple poll tax in Roman coins, but rather in Greek *didrachmas* circulating as weight in silver or in traditional Jewish *half shekel* units of silver, which would be a weight and monetary equivalent. The coin that Peter found in the fish's mouth was a *tetradrachma* (Matthew 17:27) or four drachma piece, enough to cover Peter's and Jesus' tax exactly.

Jesus could also have implied the Jewish money required for sacrificial animals during Passover. However, He also drove out the moneychangers twice (John 2:13-17; Luke 19:45-46). The moneychangers were robbing the people through a process of coin clipping. The Greek word for *money* in John 2:15 means "clipping" or "bit." As coins of the day exhibited a smooth rounded edge that could wear out through circulation, a dishonest merchant could "clip" coins for trade by shaving small, virtually undetectable portions around the edges and use the shavings to cast new coins. This practice was a way of robbing those who needed currency conversion to purchase animals for sacrifice. The buyer would unknowingly trade in a weight of silver in the foreign currency for a slightly less weight in Jewish currency. The result would be theft from the buyer through inflation and reduced purchasing power. Meanwhile, the moneychangers could take the free money from the coin clippings and increase their wealth. The Law strictly forbade a "false balance" of weights and measures.[26] Today, the milled edges around legal tender coins prevent clipping by making it detectable. Ironically, inflation now occurs through other means such as metallic alloys of lesser worth, paper currency through a printing press, and electronic accounting.

Jesus most certainly could have also implied that "the things that are God's" are the tithes according to the Law. This was likely the thrust of His statement. The coins with Caesar's image were "the things that are Caesar's" and belonged to him if he so taxed. The crops and livestock from the boundaries of the land of Israel were "the things that are God's." Thus, with the reply of Jesus to the Pharisees and Herodians, no conflict arose. He proved that paying "tribute" to Caesar

---

26. See Leviticus 19:35; Deuteronomy 25:15; Proverbs 11:1; 16:11; 20:23.

in his own money was "lawful" as well as giving God the things—temple taxes, Passover sacrifices, and agricultural tithes—that belong to Him. Both represent the lawful right to property ownership.

Conclusion and summary

In conclusion, we see that the accusations of Jesus were not delectable for the religious leaders. His endorsing of their acts of tithing—despite their excess—is not proof that Christians have a Scriptural obligation to tithe of their monetary income to the church. Their acts of tithing extrapolated from the Mosaic Law, which they were still under during the time of Jesus' ministry. Jesus commended their tithing as it pertained to the Law. Only upon Calvary did Jesus eliminate the obligation to tithe. These New Testament instances of tithing provide no proof for the monetary income tithe doctrine.

15. The Law Repealed

Abraham and Moses

Hebrews 7:1-4

1: For this Melchizedek, king of Salem, priest of the most high God, who met Abraham returning from the slaughter of the kings, and blessed him;
2: To whom also Abraham gave a tenth part of all; first being by interpretation King of righteousness, and after that also King of Salem, which is, King of peace;
3: Without father, without mother, without descent, having neither beginning of days, nor end of life; but made like unto the Son of God; abideth a priest continually.
4: Now consider how great this man *was*, unto whom even the patriarch Abraham gave the tenth of the spoils.

The writer of the epistle to the Hebrews recalls the account of the encounter between Abraham and Melchizedek. Despite the details of the tithing requirements in the Mosaic Law, Abraham's act of tithing to Melchizedek constitutes both the first and the last mentions of tithing in the Bible. This fact easily leads some to believe that Abraham's "pre-Law" act of tithing fortifies the modern understanding of the concept of tithing as an "eternal moral principle" or some other binding construct. Because Abraham tithed to Melchizedek "before the Law" and a New Testament epistle recalls this incident, it is argued that the law of tithing, like the laws against murder, stealing, and adultery, transcend the bounds of the Mosaic Law. The fact that no visible **command** is present in Abraham's actions does not invalidate a moral prescription for the church; for it allegedly expounds the mind of God and obligates those who are His people in any covenant or dispensation to commit perpetual tithes to the current divine priesthood. Does the account of the tithe of Abraham in the Old and New Testaments form the covers on a proverbial book that directs the Christian church to an ordinance and obligation of monetary income tithing? This chapter will attempt to shed light on this issue and argument. It will attempt to answer this question by exposing both the fate of the tithe in the Mosaic Law and explaining the application of Abraham's tithe to the priesthood of Jesus Christ after the order of Melchizedek.

The authorship of the epistle to the Hebrews

Yet another cordial debate that has reigned throughout the halls of Christendom—and even today—is the authorship of the book of Hebrews. While such a debate should not enrage the constituents at opposite ends and falls within the negligible squabbles of orthodoxy, one's idea of the author of the epistle to the Hebrews could slightly affect one's interpretation of its doctrine. If one believes that Paul wrote the epistle, one may attempt to correlate statements to other Pauline epistles and apply the emphasis of Hebrews through this lens. Likewise, if one believes that Luke or some other writer who composed other canonized portions of the New Testament wrote this epistle, one may be tempted to evoke a similar bias. If one believes that someone else, such as Apollos, wrote this epistle, one may be free to speculate on the style, doctrine, and emphasis of the letter's teachings by attempting to match it with an historical or traditional understanding of this person whom the Bible otherwise grants no exhaustive exposure.

The foremost possibility for the authorship of the epistle to the Hebrews by way of tradition is the apostle Paul. Although tradition has extended through the centuries to suggest Pauline authorship, and many in the church of the first few centuries held this view, such support for the Apostle Paul as author is waning.[27] Arguments for Paul as author include the fact that Paul was a highly scholarly student of Gamaliel and a former Pharisee. These qualifications express that Paul knew the Mosaic Law intimately and could explain it against the backdrop of his conversion on the road to Damascus. The epistle to the Hebrews consists entirely of an *exposé* of Jewish law and customs

---

27. William MacDonald, *Believer's Bible Commentary* (Nashville: Thomas Nelson, 1995), 2155.

from a Christian perspective. The writer also expressed praise for the recipients' material support of him in prison (Hebrews 10:34) similar to the way Paul did to the Philippians (Philippians 4:10-12).

Doubts about Paul as author include the fact that the epistle to the Hebrews is absent the conventional trademark greeting that exists in every other epistle that Paul wrote in the Biblical canon. Paul always identified himself at the very start of his epistles and ended them with a similar closing. In addition, if Paul who identified himself as an "apostle," "minister," or "teacher" to the Gentiles (Romans 11:13; 15:16; Galatians 2:1,8; 1 Timothy 2:7; 2 Timothy 1:11) wrote the epistle to the Hebrews, it would be the only one which he did not write to Gentile-dominant churches according to his special ministry. One remedy to suggest the uniqueness of the epistle to the Hebrews with Paul as the writer is that Paul may have intentionally masked his identity in writing to these Jews to attempt to avoid exposing himself to persecution from Jewish religious leadership that opposed the gospel.[28] Although such an argument may have a weight of persuasion, it is nevertheless an educated guess at best and merely speculation. Another related idea is that the epistle was heavily influenced by Paul though composed by another in some way subject to his teachings.[29]

Other ideas for the writer of this epistle are that of Luke, Paul's companions Barnabas or Silas, Aquila and Priscilla who explained the

---

28. Ibid.
29. William Smith, *Smith's Bible Dictionary*, s.v. "Hebrews, Epistle to the."

gospel to Apollos (Acts 18:24-28), or Philip the evangelist.[30] Another suggestion is that Apollos wrote the epistle because he was very articulate in Greek and the Septuagint as an Alexandrian, and the epistle demonstrates articulate style of the Greek while quoting the Septuagint frequently.[31] As Apollos was a learned scholar and zealous in the message of John the Baptist before Aquila and Priscilla explained to him the full Gospel, He may have expressed this sentiment to Jews who needed the same conversion of message that he originally did. Regardless of the possibilities of the writer of the epistle to the Hebrews, what is significant is the message of the epistle and the fact that God Himself knows whom He inspired.

The temporal setting of the epistle to the Hebrews

Although no definite date can be stamped on the epistle to the Hebrews, several reasonable arguments can confine the possible date to a certain range. An obvious parameter to limit the date of the epistle to the Hebrews is the destruction of the temple in A.D. 70. The fact that the writer to the Hebrews explained the Aaronic priesthood and the Melchizedek priesthood throughout the epistle in detail and never recalled a past event as major as the destruction of the temple demonstrates the unlikelihood of a date after A.D. 70. The writer refers to Levitical temple activities in the present tense as if they persisted at the time without such an interruption (Hebrews 7:5, 8,28; 8:3-5; 9:13-

---

30. William MacDonald, 2155.
31. Ray C. Stedman, *Hebrews*, vol. 15 of *The IVP New Testament commentary series* (Westmont, IL: InterVarsity Press, 1992), 11.

14,22,25). Also, the writer of the epistle seems to assume that Timothy is still alive (Hebrews 13:23). Clement of Rome apparently quoted from it in his *1 Clement* epistle commonly dated A.D. 95.[32] The epistle would likely have required time to circulate before Clement possessed it and read it enough to quote it. If the epistle was written to Jews at Rome, Hebrews 12:4 may indicate that it was written prior to any major event of persecution under Roman authority.[33] The latest event of such nature before the fall of Jerusalem would have been the persecution under Nero in A.D. 65.[34] Possibly, if the epistle must have a pen date before this event, an appropriate year would be A.D. 64. However, with such minor interpretation of one verse, preclusion of a major persecution event is not completely necessary. A possible date range is A.D. 64 to A.D. 67.[35]

The quality of a new priesthood

Hebrews chapter 7 contains several "proof text" verses that, without further investigation into context, lead some into believing an ideology that Christians have an obligation to give perpetual tithes to the current functioning priesthood. Primarily, those who teach modern church income tithing read verses 1-12 or a selection of these verses to attempt to prove their point. The basic premise is that the Levitical

---

32. Edgar Johnson Goodspeed, *The epistle to the Hebrews* (New York: Macmillan, 1908), 19.
33. Frederick Fyvie Bruce, *The Epistle to the Hebrews*, rev. ed. (Grand Rapids: William B. Eerdmans, 1990), 21.
34. Ibid.
35. Doremus Almy Hayes, *The New Testament epistles: Hebrews, James, First Peter, Second Peter, Jude* (New York: The Methodist book concern, 1921), 164.

priesthood had flaws and the Melchizedek priesthood is better. Abraham gave tithes to Melchizedek who was Jesus Christ incarnate. The Levitical priesthood ended, but the work of Christ confirms that the Melchizedek priesthood lives on. Because Abraham gave a tithe to the Melchizedek priesthood **before the Mosaic Law**, and the Melchizedek priesthood is perpetual, Christians need to pay tithes to Jesus after the order of Melchizedek instead of Levi. Jesus receives these tithes through His church for the work of the gospel ministry. In other words, tithing did not change, but the recipient of tithes changed.

While much of the preliminary idea is true, the logical conclusion is incorrect according to the context and thrust of Hebrews chapter 7, and, more precisely, the entire epistle. As the epistle was likely written to Jewish Christians to keep them from succumbing to the pressure of Judaism, the writer explains to the recipients as those who understood the Mosaic Law and Jewish customs.[36] However, these recipients were ones who likely did not understand the full spirit of the Law and its consummation in Christ. They may have believed that Christ's sacrifice was the one necessary to pay the final sin debt, yet they did not comprehend how Christ's sacrifice qualified the end of the Levitical priesthood and the temple services. Judaizers who professed faith in Christ also pressured and convinced weak converts that following the whole Mosaic Law was still necessary to be God's people.

---

36. Albert Barnes, *Notes, Explanatory and Practical, on the Epistle to the Hebrews* (London: Routledge, Warne, and Routledge, 1860), 7.

Melchizedek being "without father, without mother, without descent" does not necessarily mean that he had no biological ancestors, making him divine rather than human. Many who read verse 3 misunderstand the intention of these phrases. Verse 3 stating that Melchizedek had no father or mother meant that he had no record of a priestly lineage whereby he would receive the office of priesthood through a bloodline. His parents are not on record and are not recorded as being of renown. The thrust of Hebrews in comparing Jesus Christ as a Priest after the order of Melchizedek with the Levitical priesthood is that the Melchizedek priesthood is not defined in terms of a physical lineage. Those serving as Levites had to come from the seed of Levi. Those serving as priests had to come from the seed of Aaron, who came from Levi. The priests had Aaron as their father and Elisheba as their mother (Exodus 6:23).

The Levitical priesthood also required a surviving bloodline. The Greek word translated "without descent" is *agenealogētos*, which literally means "without genealogy." In other words, not only did Melchizedek not have a record of priestly **parents** to qualify him physically as a priest, but he also had no line of priestly **ancestors** that would qualify his status according to record and carry out "the order of Melchizedek." The qualification for the order of the priesthood of Melchizedek is not one of bloodline, but one of the quality and characteristics of the person to fulfill such an order. If one were to ask Melchizedek for his qualification to be "priest of the most high God," his answer would not be "My father was Priest Jones, as I am sure you have heard of him. He came from the late, great Priest Smith." His qualification did not come from surviving legal records that authorized him to claim the same rites through his father. He had no known father and mother; his priesthood did not need them.

Verse 3 also describes Melchizedek as "having neither beginning of days, nor end of life." No record exists of the event in history whereby Melchizedek assumed the role of "priest of the most high God." No record exists of him being anointed with the office during his lifetime. The Mosaic Law required a ritual for those of the line of Aaron who were of age to become official ministering priests (Exodus 29). The non-priest Levites would serve from the age of 25 through 50 (Numbers 8:24-26). No record exists of Melchizedek undergoing a ritual to establish the days of his priesthood nor of a time when his priesthood began. No record exists of the time Melchizedek died, passing his priesthood to a successor of his offspring.

Hebrews 7:4-7

4: Now consider how great this man *was*, unto whom even the patriarch Abraham gave the tenth of the spoils.
5: And verily they that are of the sons of Levi, who receive the office of the priesthood, have a commandment to take tithes of the people according to the law, that is, of their brethren, though they come out of the loins of Abraham:
6: But he whose descent is not counted from them received tithes of Abraham, and blessed him that had the promises.
7: And without all contradiction the less is blessed of the better.

Verse 4 implores the reader to "consider how great this man [Melchizedek] *was*." In the minds of Jews and Jewish Christians, Abraham was the model man. Abraham was the "friend of God" (2 Chronicles 20:7; James 2:23). Abraham was the one through whom the promises of God come (Galatians 3:29; Hebrews 7:6). Verse 17 declares that Melchizedek was "great" by comparing him to "even the patriarch Abraham." Melchizedek "blessed" Abraham, and verse 7 emphasizes that "the less is blessed of the better." In other words, Melchizedek was greater than Abraham because he gave the blessing and Abraham received the blessing. Melchizedek was also greater than Abraham because he received tithes from Abraham that demonstrated credibility to his priesthood. Most especially, Melchizedek was great in that he blessed Abraham, who was the ancestor of Levi through which came the Levitical priesthood. Abraham who "had the promises" submitted himself to a priest and acknowledged him as such who came from no official priestly line. Abraham treated Melchizedek as a priest similarly to how an Israelite descendent of his would treat a Levitical priest.

Verses 4-7 emphasize the point that Melchizedek's priesthood was unique and different from the Levitical priesthood in that Melchizedek received tithes, yet he was not of the children of Levi. According to the Mosaic Law, the Levites had a commandment from God to live from the agricultural tithes of the people of Israel, as they had no inheritance in the land. However, Abraham followed no encoded law from God to give the priest Melchizedek tithes from the spoils of the war. Melchizedek was neither a priest by divine law nor received tithes by divine law. However, Melchizedek was a priest by divine appointment. The account of Abraham's tithe to Melchizedek legitimizes the priesthood of Melchizedek in the eyes of those intimately involved in Jewish laws and traditions.

The superiority of a new priesthood

The writer to the Hebrews refers to the Melchizedek priesthood as superior to the Levitical priesthood (Hebrews 7:21-24) to which they were accustomed. The writer quotes the Old Testament to demonstrate that Jesus Christ was a Priest after this superior order (Psalm 110:4; Hebrews 5:9-10; 7:17). To many Jews who knew nothing but Jewish laws, traditions, and customs, the idea of a "better" priesthood would be absurd. They were the people of the Self-Sufficient God, and this God instituted to them the Levitical priesthood. How could God have given them something that He Himself would determine to improve? By simply following the prescriptions for the sacrificial system, the people appeared to have all they needed to obtain God's approval. God declared that without the shedding of blood no remission for sins would be possible (Leviticus 17:11; Hebrews 9:22). However, many did not realize even from their own Law and Prophets that these laws were a temporary picture and but a shadow of things to come (Colossians 2:13-17; Hebrews 8:1-6; 10:1). They were forward-looking illustrations of what Messiah would do on their behalf, and they should have instilled in the minds of the Jews the high and awful price of their sins.

Hebrews 10:1-3

1: For the law having a shadow of good things to come, *and* not the very image of the things, can never with those sacrifices which they offered year by year continually make the comers thereunto perfect.

2: For then would they not have ceased to be offered? because that the worshipers once purged should have had no more conscience of sins.
3: But in those *sacrifices there is* a remembrance again *made* of sins every year.

The Levitical and Melchizedek priesthoods have very important similarities; however, they exhibit stark contrast in their implementation and effectiveness. The purpose of the Levitical priesthood was to act as mediators between God and the Israelites. Only the Levites and priests could come into the holy place in the house of God (Numbers 18:1-7, 22-23). Only the priests—those of the family of Aaron—could go into the holiest place and perform sacrifices upon the altar. Only the priests of the family of Aaron could eat of the burnt offerings used for atonements (Exodus 29:32-34). Whenever any Israelite committed a known sin or a transgression of the law, he or she would have to bring an animal to the priests for a sacrifice. A priest then performed the sacrifice to God as intercessors between God and the sinner. Once per year also, just in case any sins were missed, the priests had to make a solemn atoning sacrifice on behalf of the entire nation of Israel (Exodus 30:10; Leviticus 16). However, all these sacrifices at these different times could never pay the sin debt. They could also never cover any subsequent sins.

Hebrews 10:4-8

4: For *it is* not possible that the blood of bulls and of goats should take away sins.
5: Wherefore when he cometh into the world, he saith, Sacrifice and offering thou wouldest not, but a body hast thou prepared me:
6: In burnt offerings and *sacrifices* for sin thou hast had no pleasure.
7: Then said I, Lo, I come (in the volume of the book it is written of me,) to do thy will, O God.

8: Above when he said, Sacrifice and offering and burnt offerings and *offering* for sin thou wouldest not, neither hadst pleasure *therein*; which are offered by the law;

The atonement sacrifices could not take away sins; they only provided a temporary cover for them. Although God commanded the nation of Israel to perform the atoning sacrifices and sin offerings, He never recognized them as sufficient to remove the stain of sin. Even in the Old Testament God expressed His disfavor of them when His people performed them simply out of ritual. When King Saul performed a burnt offering of things in disobedience to God's command to destroy the Amalekites, Samuel scolded him and asked, "Hath the LORD as *great* delight in burnt offerings and sacrifices, as in obeying the voice of the LORD?" Burning things upon an altar did not appease God; justice and purity did.

God condemned the people of Israel through the prophet Isaiah by comparing them to Sodom and Gomorrah (Isaiah 1:9-11). He reminded them of His promise to preserve a remnant, and without this promise they would have been eradicated as was Sodom and Gomorrah. He

A Levitical high priest sacrificing a goat

then called them "rulers of Sodom" and "people of Gomorrah." He asked them the following: "To what purpose is the multitude of your sacrifices unto me?... I am full of the burnt offerings of rams, and the fat of fed beasts; and I delight not in the blood of bullocks, or of lambs, or of he goats." Even if the people of Israel accurately kept the laws of sacrifices and offerings, they could not appease God. Sin requires justice, and this justice requires a perfect sacrifice.

Hebrews 10:9-12

9: Then said he, Lo, I come to do thy will, O God. He taketh away the first, that he may establish the second.
10: By the which will we are sanctified through the offering of the body of Jesus Christ once *for all*.
11: And every priest standeth daily ministering and offering oftentimes the same sacrifices, which can never take away sins:
12: But this man, after he had offered one sacrifice for sins forever, sat down on the right hand of God;

Contrary to the Levitical priesthood established in the Mosaic Law, the priesthood of Jesus Christ after the order of Melchizedek is superior. With the priesthood of Jesus Christ an extant sacrifice is not necessary to atone for each individual sin. The sacrifice of Christ on the Cross of Calvary atoned for **all** the sins of His people. Jesus, our High Priest is in heaven (Hebrews 4:14; 9:24) and seated at the right hand of the throne of God (Hebrews 8:1; 12:2). The sacrifice of Christ was **once** and its application is effective **for all time**.

Notice also the wording of verse 9. Of Jesus Christ the writer said "He taketh away the first, that he may establish the second." Jesus did not simply "tweak" the Law and change it a little. Jesus **took away** the priestly laws of atoning offerings and sacrifices and **replaced** the whole system with His priesthood. The whole purpose of the Levitical priesthood was to function as a medium between God and His people Israel. Now, as Paul told Timothy, "For *there is* one God, and one mediator between God and men, the man Christ Jesus; Who gave himself a ransom for all, to be testified in due time." (1 Timothy 2:5-6) By virtue of the perfect sacrifice of Christ, **He** is now our high priest and **He** is our mediator between the Father and us, not a priesthood of sinful, mortal people.

What sustained the former mortal Levitical priesthood? **Tithes!** The priests and Levites had no inheritance in the land of Israel and thus could not grow their own crops and raise their own livestock or acquire wealth for themselves. The tithes were only of food, and part of the reason for these tithes was to feed the Levites and priests. Does our High Priest Jesus Christ require food to sustain His priesthood? **No!** He performed His sacrifice **once for all** and is seated in the heavenlies. He does not need tithes of food to act as mediator between God and man.

Not only did the tithes feed the Levites and priests, but they also supplied the animals needed for burnt offerings and sacrifices. The reason the people of Israel could redeem their tithes of crops but not of livestock (Leviticus 27:30-34) was that the priests and Levites needed the sheep, goats, bullocks, rams, and other animals to perform burnt offerings according to the Mosaic Law. Does Jesus need tithes of animals to perform burnt offerings as a high priest? **No!** Jesus Christ as our High Priest has already performed the one-time **perfect** sacrifice of His own body on the Cross. He is the Lamb of God Who takes away the sin of the world. He is the spotless Lamb. He was both Priest and Sacrifice. Because Christ performed a perfect sacrifice of Himself for sins to atone for them once for all time, He does not need animals for intercessory offerings. He also does not need tithes to supply these animals.

The role of tithes in both priesthoods

Hebrews 7:8-10

8: And here men that die receive tithes; but there he *receiveth them*, of whom it is witnessed that he liveth.
9: And as I may so say, Levi also, who receiveth tithes, paid tithes in Abraham.
10: For he was yet in the loins of his father, when Melchizedek met him.

Returning to Hebrews chapter 7, we observe that the writer of Hebrews compares the nature of the Levitical and Melchizedek priesthoods regarding tithes. In verse 8, the writer refers to the Levites as "men that die." The Levites who lived and died received their sustenance from tithes according to the Law (v. 5). Their priesthood was marked by a beginning and an ending that depended on the lifespans of moral individuals. However, Melchizedek received tithes from Abraham in a priesthood that has no end. The priesthood of Melchizedek ever lives because no record of the mysterious Melchizedek exits to state his death and successor.

Some have mistakenly concluded that verse 8 proves a **perpetual tithe** to Jesus Christ. By verse 8 saying that "there he *receiveth them*" referring to Melchizedek receiving the tithes from Abraham, Jesus Christ after the order of Melchizedek *receives* (present tense) tithes as "he liveth." However the *"receiveth them"* is in **italics**, which means that the translators added these words. Most likely the rationale was to make the compared phrases parallel: "here [the Levites] receive tithes; there Melchizedek receives tithes." Since the subject is Melchizedek and the account of Abraham's tithe was in the past, the writer was neither intending to claim that Melchizedek nor Jesus after his order **continually** receives tithes. Attempting to prove a doctrine from inserted words in a translation that were not present in the source texts ultimately fails. The verse is simply stating that the Levites who die receive tithes, but Melchizedek received tithes from Abraham and the order of his priesthood is not limited to the lifespan of one man.

Since the Levites also were commanded under the Mosaic Law to tithe of their own tithes to the priests—descendents of Aaron—they tithed to the order of Melchizedek by virtue of their father Abraham acknowledging his priesthood. Through a connection of bloodline, one can perceive that even the Levitical priesthood ultimately recognizes that it owed its significance and existence to the superior Melchizedek priesthood. The writer of the Hebrews is demonstrating that the Levitical priesthood was not an end unto itself. The Levitical priesthood receiving tithes was but a shadow of the perfect Melchizedek priesthood that received tithes even from the Levites and priests themselves through Abraham, the father of the nation of Israel. The role of tithes in the Levitical priesthood was to sustain them. The role of tithes in the Melchizedek priesthood was to acknowledge its significance.

Hebrews 7:11-17

11: If therefore perfection were by the Levitical priesthood, (for under it the people received the law,) what further need *was there* that another priest should rise after the order of Melchizedek, and not be called after the order of Aaron?

12: For the priesthood being changed, there is made of necessity a change also of the law.

13: For he of whom these things are spoken pertaineth to another tribe, of which no man gave attendance at the altar.

14: For *it is* evident that our Lord sprang out of Judah; of which tribe Moses spake nothing concerning priesthood.

15: And it is yet far more evident: for that after the similitude of Melchizedek there ariseth another priest,

16: Who is made, not after the law of a carnal commandment, but after the power of an endless life.

17: For he testifieth, Thou *art* a priest forever after the order of Melchizedek.

The writer asks the reader that if the Levitical priesthood was complete, why do the Hebrew Scriptures acknowledge the significance of a priest who was not of the sons of Aaron according to the Law. Why would Jesus come as a High Priest after the order of Melchizedek if the Levitical priesthood could atone for sins? If Jesus Christ is a priest after the order of Melchizedek and performed a sacrifice of Himself that the readers regarded as significant, then the natural conclusion would be to understand that the priesthood changed therein from that of Levi to that of Melchizedek. This priesthood did not require a genealogy.

The writer explains that Jesus Christ came from the tribe of Judah and not Levi. Jesus Christ claims his priesthood from the order of

Melchizedek by divine appointment, not from a natural order of being a son of Aaron. The Law required priests to come from the tribe of Levi, and specifically from the family of Aaron. However, since Jesus came from the tribe of Judah, his priesthood could not have come from the prescription of the Mosaic Law. Interestingly, the tribe of Judah is the one from which came the **kings!** Therefore, among the people of Israel the Law did not provide for one to qualify both as a priest and a king. If one were a candidate for kingship, one would have to trace his lineage to Judah. If one were a candidate for priesthood, one would have to trace his lineage to Levi. As Judah and Levi were sons of Jacob—brothers—one could **not** fulfill the requirements for **both** offices.

Jesus Christ, however, fulfilled the requirements for the offices of both priest and king. He is King of Israel by virtue of being from the tribe of Judah. God promised that the Messiah would be a king from Judah (Genesis 49:10). God promised that the Messiah would come from the lineage of David (Isaiah 11:1-10). Jesus fulfilled the legal requirement for kingship by being a descendent of Judah. He also fulfilled the prophecy that the line of David would be preserved.

Jesus also fulfilled the requirement of priesthood by receiving the divine appointment to carry out the priestly order of Melchizedek. Jesus was not made a priest "after the law of a carnal commandment" (the Mosaic Law prescription for Aaronic priesthood), but rather "after the power of an endless life" which Melchizedek typified. Uniquely, King David also acted as a prophet by foretelling of Jesus that He is "a priest forever after the order of Melchizedek." Jesus fulfilled the roles

of Prophet, King, Priest, and Sacrifice.

One tithe canceled and the other completed

Hebrews 7:18-28

18: For there is verily a disannulling of the commandment going before for the weakness and unprofitableness thereof.
19: For the law made nothing perfect, but the bringing in of a better hope *did*; by the which we draw nigh unto God.
20: And inasmuch as not without an oath *he was made priest*:
21: (For those priests were made without an oath; but this with an oath by him that said unto him, The Lord swore and will not repent, Thou *art* a priest forever after the order of Melchizedek:)
22: By so much was Jesus made a surety of a better testament.
23: And they truly were many priests, because they were not suffered to continue by reason of death:
24: But this *man*, because he continueth ever, hath an unchangeable priesthood.
25: Wherefore he is able also to save them to the uttermost that come unto God by him, seeing he ever liveth to make intercession for them.
26: For such a high priest became us, *who is* holy, harmless, undefiled, separate from sinners, and made higher than the heavens;
27: Who needeth not daily, as those high priests, to offer up sacrifice, first for his own sins, and then for the people's: for this he did once, when he offered up himself.
28: For the law maketh men high priests which have infirmity; but the word of the oath, which was since the law, *maketh* the Son, who is consecrated forevermore.

Prolific author and Reformed theologian Dr. R. C. Sproul reasoned: "I would say that if the tithe were abrogated, we would expect to have an explicit teaching in the New Testament that says tithing is no longer in effect."[37] In reality, no need for a specific statement declaring "tithing is no longer in effect" is necessary if all

---

37. R. C. Sproul, *Now, That's a Good Question!* (Wheaton, IL: Tyndale House Publishers, 1996), 437.

the parameters for a cancellation of tithing are laid in place. Below, we will see what amounts to as close to a direct statement as one will find in the Bible. Dr. Sproul argues: "Tithing was a responsibility central to the old-covenant economy and would be carried over, particularly when you understand that the new-covenant community was established principally among Jews, who would obviously continue that practice unless they were told that it was no longer necessary."[38]

Dr. Sproul is correct that the Jews would continue the practice of tithing; however, they would continue to tithe to **the Temple** and not to **the church**. Converted Jewish landowners, who, like Paul, strove to observe Jewish ordinances, would continue to follow the Law of tithing to "the place where God set His name" which would have been the Temple in Jerusalem at the time. Jewish Christians under the influence of Judaism still regarded the Levitical priesthood as authentic and necessary even following the resurrection of Christ. They continued to tithe their crops and livestock to the storehouse chambers of the Temple and observe the nuances of the seven year cycle.

Conversely, the fact that the apostles did not mention tithing is not proof that it switched operation from the Jewish Temple to disparate Christian churches. Jews continued to follow the tithe ordinances in the Law regarding the Temple. Because no apostle writing under the inspiration of the Holy Spirit never mentioned tithes in church doctrine and never specifically declared that tithes were to go to the new church

---

38. Ibid.

of Jesus Christ instead of to the Temple proves that the Scriptures do not mandate a tithe of any form to the churches. Jesus predicted the destruction of the Temple, which was fulfilled in A.D. 70, ending the Levitical priesthood. The apostles never told the Gentile believers in Scripture to tithe. The Gentiles (who were not under the snare of Judaism) did not tithe to the temple. The faithful Jews continued to do so until A.D. 70. Nothing in Scripture told them what to do with the Levitical priesthood, as it was tied specifically to God's singular sanctuary. The destruction of the Temple as prophesied by the One Himself Who would be the High Priest forever proves the official end of the Levitical priesthood. The Levitical priesthood was sustained through tithes. The priesthood of Christ needs no tithes to mediate to the Father, and no Scripture claims that the superiority of Christ's priesthood carries the perpetual practice of tithing over from the terminated Levitical priesthood.

Hebrews chapter 7 clearly teaches directly or indirectly that the system of tithing under the Mosaic Law is no longer operative. Verse 18 declares that "there is verily a disannulling [or **cancellation**] of the commandment going before." Something changed and, either way, affects the Mosaic laws of tithing. Two possibilities exist for the "commandment" in verse 18.

First, the "commandment" may be a reference to "the carnal commandment" in verse 16, which likely means the commandment prescribing how one becomes a priest. The commandment is "carnal" in that it is based upon the flesh. One must have a **physical** qualification to become a priest—be a descendent of Aaron. When the writer describes the commandment as "going before," he could be referring to the fact that the law, having already changed, renders the commandment a relic of the past.

Second, the "commandment" may be a reference to the Levitical "commandment to take tithes" in verse 5. When the writer describes the commandment as "going before," he could be saying "not the commandment I just mentioned (in verse 16), but the one **before** that." By virtue of Jesus Christ changing the priesthood from that of "men that die" to that of one that "ever liveth," the commandment of Levi to take tithes is no longer in effect, because the Levitical priesthood is unnecessary.

Regardless of which of the two verses the "commandment" in verse 18 references, the effect is the same on the laws of tithing according to the Mosaic Law. Since the priesthood has changed to the everlasting order of Melchizedek, indeed, no further need exists for the Levitical priesthood to mediate through sacrifices; nor is there a need of the commandment for them to take tithes to sustain themselves. The destruction of Jerusalem and the leveling of the temple soon afterward—as Jesus Himself prophesied—solidified the fact that the Levitical priesthood ended.

Now, what of tithing? Verse 19 said that the law of the Levitical priesthood was not sufficient, but the hope of the priesthood of Jesus Christ is "by the which we draw nigh to God." We no longer need a line of human priests to go to God on our behalf. We **ourselves** can draw nigh to the Father through Jesus Christ. Moreover, the tithes that were previously required to draw nigh to God through the Levitical priesthood are not necessary either. According to verse 27, Jesus does not need to offer continual daily sacrifices, but His one-time sacrifice of Himself completed the atonement for sin forever.

Contrary to what some argue, Hebrews chapter 7 provides no contextual or textual room for a prescriptive system of tithing to the Melchizedek priesthood. The account of Abraham tithing of the spoils of war to Melchizedek supplies no divinely codified **law** for Abraham's tithe. Hebrews 7 merely elaborates that Abraham's tithe to Melchizedek proved that Melchizedek was a real priest. Because Melchizedek blessed Abraham and received the blessing, Melchizedek was a priest. Because Abraham gave tithes of the spoils of war to Melchizedek and Melchizedek accepted them, Melchizedek was a priest.

Furthermore, many miss the stark facts regarding Abraham's tithe. Abraham tithed **once** to Melchizedek. He tithed of the **spoils of war**. He gave **all the rest of the spoils** to the king of Sodom. Abraham's **one-time** tithe clearly presents no tangible model for Christians to follow as a system of "tithing." Do Christians need to go to war and get spoils for the purposes of tithing? Do they need to give these tithes only to a priest-king who is a party to the same war? Do they also need to give away the remainder of the spoils to someone else? If **Jesus Christ** is indeed the Priest after the order of Melchizedek, why do some churches virtually extract these tithes for the elders who minister there as if they were **Levitical** priests?

Because Abraham tithed **once**, how can we derive a command, obligation, or "moral principle" to tithe **continually**? If Abraham tithed of **the spoils of war**, how can we derive a necessity to tithe **of monetary income**? If Abraham gave **the rest of the spoils away**, how can we derive the idea that we **do not** have to do the same? If even under the Levitical priesthood the Israelites only gave their tithes wholly away **every third year**, how can we derive from either the Levitical or Melchizedek priesthoods the idea that we must tithe of **all monetary income** and at **all times**?

Principally, Abraham's **one-time** tithe bears significance to the nature of the priesthood of Melchizedek. Under the Levitical priesthood, the people of Israel were required to tithe continually to the Levites so that the priests could offer sacrifices **continually**. Under the Melchizedek priesthood, Jesus Christ offered the sacrifice of Himself **once for all**. Abraham's tithe to Melchizedek merely legitimized the Melchizedek order of priesthood. Conclusively, Abraham's **one-time** tithe was all that was "needed" to legitimize Christ's **one-time** sacrifice. Abraham **completed** the tithing "requirement" for the Melchizedek priesthood. Abraham tithed **once for all**, and Jesus Christ sacrificed **once for all**.

Conclusion and summary

In conclusion, we see that Hebrews chapter 7 clearly declares that Melchizedek was superior to Abraham and his descendent Levi. The

Melchizedek priesthood is superior to the Levitical priesthood. The fact that no record exists of Melchizedek's genealogy of priesthood proves that he was a priest by divine appointment from God. Melchizedek was a type of Christ, and Jesus Christ is a priest after the order of Melchizedek. By virtue of the sacrifice of Christ on Calvary, He has canceled the Levitical priesthood and its need for a sustaining system of tithes for a system of sacrifices. Abraham's tithe proved that Melchizedek was an authentic priest. Abraham's one-time tithe of the spoils of war matches Christ's one-time atonement for sins. Hebrews chapter 7 cannot teach an obligation for a perpetual monetary income tithe to the church by any stretch of the imagination.

SECTION V: NEW TESTAMENT GIVING

Commands and Principles of Generosity

Now that we have seen every verse in the entire Bible that explicitly mentions tithing, we can approach passages in the writings to the churches—the epistles—concerning giving with a clear understanding and a firm grounding upon the context of the tithing laws. Although we have covered the direct, our study of tithing still is incomplete. Some people will contend that certain New Testament passages that teach "cheerful giving" or "proportionate giving" do teach tithing *implicitly*.

We will now make an effort to examine all these passages carefully and with great scrutiny of their context to determine if these passages do teach "tithing" implicitly as some have claimed. Some verses have very important "key words" to understand, and the debate exists over the intention of these key words. However, the context of these verses and in other passages related to the events of the context of these verses must play a primary role in deducing precisely what these "key words" truly say from the writer to the reader.

The New Testament Acts of the apostles and the epistles to the churches contain livid examples of the spirit of the early church in Godly giving and meeting needs. We do well to study them in depth as a challenge to our own lives and way of thinking. We do need to study them carefully to eliminate the baggage of unwarranted assumptions, but we also need to inject into our hearts the clear intent and message that God gives through His Word about these historical passages.

16. A Famine Foretold

Instructions for Meeting Remote Needs

1 Corinthians 16:1-2

1: Now concerning the collection for the saints, as I have given order to the churches of Galatia, even so do ye.
2: Upon the first *day* of the week let every one of you lay by him in store, as *God* hath prospered him, that there be no gatherings when I come.

A superficial analysis of 1 Corinthians 16:1-2

No doubt you have seen envelopes in the pews or chairs within your church or a church you have visited. Upon these envelopes the words were engraved "Tithes and Offerings" in red or black lettering as a title to make the reader clear that these envelopes are not for mailing personal notes or love letters. Below the title is the proof text of Scripture to support the title provided: 1 Corinthians 16:1-2! Possibly, the envelope included the actual text along with the reference, just in case any doubt existed in the heart of the reader.

Here, you see it for yourself! Paul, the greatest apostle in the early church, and the most prolific writer in the New Testament, elaborates on something called "the collection for the saints." What else could this be than "tithes and offerings" for the church? If it is a "collection," obviously we must put our mites in the "collection plate." Since this collection is "for the saints," our contributions to this collection plainly go into the church budget, which then distributes appropriately to the

342

ministers and the saints in need. This "collection for the saints" is obviously the "tithes and offerings" that I need to put into the plate, right?

Not only that, but Paul also clarified that he had given this order to the church of Galatia before and also now to the church of Corinth. Apparently, this command was not just a one-church deal. As any serious student of the Word, "ye" most often stands out as more than just the immediate recipients of the actual, physical epistle. Clearly, this order is to **every church**, as the Scriptures are written for **everyone!**

As we continue to read these verses, nothing appears to be rosy for the "tithe denier." Verse two continues with another important phrase: "Upon the first [day] of the week." Apparently, not only do we need to give our "tithes and offerings" to our church, but we must do it weekly—every Sunday to be exact! Conclusively, we must tithe, and we must tithe every Sunday—the Lord's day!

Yet another key phrase stares you in the face: "let every one of you." This phrase does not single out the rich, the healthy, the well-to-do, or the young. This phrase is for **everyone** in the church! No one is exempt! God requires our "tithes and offerings," and He requires them of **every** single church member! Still, we have only begun.

The subsequent phrase makes the law even more clear (as if we had any doubt until this point). "Lay by him in store" sounds strangely similar to a passage that you may have seen on other envelopes: "bring ye all the tithes into the storehouse." Surely, the "store" in this verse

343

references the "storehouse" in Malachi 3:10, because people do not store things, storehouses do! The plight for the greedy non-tither still does not end with this phrase.

The next phrase, "as God has prospered him," now screams into your ear. What else could this be besides "tithes and offerings"? This phrase clearly speaks of a proportion of what you earn, and what other proportion does the Bible emphasize besides "tithes and offerings"? You figure that if one cannot see "tithes and offerings" so far, he or she must have a hole in the brain large enough through which to drive an eighteen wheeler.

Finally, to sum up this clear and blunt command, Paul concludes with the phrase "that there be no gatherings when I come." You now have the definitive proof. If we do not prepare ourselves, determine what our "tithes and offerings" are proportionate to our income, and have them ready to place in the collection plate, the church would be forced to be subject to "gatherings." It would be far easier to give your "tithes and offerings" on Sunday at church than inconveniently with a knock at the door. It is better to give your "tithes and offerings" freely at the appropriate time than to need to have God come to you and "gather" them when you least expect.

The envelope has more than proved its point. It has quoted a passage in the New Testament in clear support of tithing. Not only is the passage in the New Testament, but it is also addressed specifically to **churches!** The envelope has successfully matched its title—"Tithes and Offerings"—to the verses immediately below. We see the proof text for New Testament church "tithes and offerings"—or have we?

Context is king!

We can read these two verses of Scripture until we are blue in the face and miss what they are really saying. We can examine each of these words in the Greek, exegete them, and diagram the grammar, but still not understand the **message**. What are we missing when we have just examined each phrase in detail? The answer is simple—context!

Examining individual words in a sentence cannot guarantee deciphering the correct message without context. Context may determine what a particular word or phrase means where the sentence itself provides no such definition or clarification. Context can include sentences immediately before or after the sentence in question. Context can also include somewhat distant passages within the same epistle or volume. Context may even reside within other works by the same author in which the author assumes the reader is familiar.

We will now examine these two often quoted verses of Scripture in light of context to elaborate on the meaning and message of the key phrases found in these two verses. In the case of these two verses, context will be in all the sources mentioned above. Context for these verses will be found in the same chapter of this epistle, in another epistle written to the same church, in another epistle written to a different church, and even in another letter written by a different person! All of these contextual passages together will shed light on the message of these two verses as a whole, as well as the meanings of each of the key phrases.

The immediate context—verse 3

Naturally, the first place to look for context is immediately surrounding the passage in question. Since these two verses appear at the beginning of a chapter, we can look at the verse following:

1 Corinthians 16:3

3: And when I come, whomsoever ye shall approve by *your* letters, them will I send to bring your liberality unto Jerusalem.

Verse 3 includes a contextual key phrase that seems to clarify some of what the previous two verses progress. Paul said that he intends this "liberality" to go "unto Jerusalem." Clearly, the "liberality" is what the previous two verses dictate. However, this liberality is going to **Jerusalem**. Why? Is this because Jerusalem is the "mother church"? Does this verse support a denominational structure in which member churches need to send their "tithes and offerings" to a network church? Obviously, before we assume too much, we need to see some more context.

The historical context—Acts 11:27-30

Since each epistle in the New Testament has an historical context, we should see if any history will provide us some understanding about the events that transpired during the time that Paul wrote this epistle. For such history, we shall turn to one of the New Testament's books of history—the book of the Acts of the Apostles—written by Luke.

Gaining a firm grasp of history can help us to understand the context of orders to churches during the same time frame.

Acts 11:27-30

27: And in these days came prophets from Jerusalem unto Antioch.
28: And there stood up one of them named Agabus, and signified by the spirit that there should be great dearth throughout all the world: which came to pass in the days of Claudius Caesar.
29: Then the disciples, every man according to his ability, determined to send relief unto the brethren which dwelt in Judea:
30: Which also they did, and sent it to the elders by the hands of Barnabas and Saul.

Around the time of this prophesy, Paul (then known as Saul of Tarsus) was just beginning his missionary journeys. In fact, this task of bringing famine relief to Judea was the very first thing that Paul and Barnabas did as a missionary team! Acts chapter 12 narrates a parenthesis of the accounts of Peter's imprisonment and deliverance and Herod's death. The end of this chapter concludes with Paul and Barnabas finishing this assigned task (Acts 12:25) before they begin their missionary journey together in chapter 13.

Verse 28 in our contextual passage gives a prophesy about a "dearth" or famine. Although it says "throughout all the world," it only meant the area of Judea (v. 29). The word translated *world* is not the usual Greek word *kosmos*, but is *oikoumenen*, which specifically has to do with land or an empire. As the prophets, including Agabus, resided in Antioch (v. 27), the prophesy concerned the land, or empirical region in which Antioch resided. Thus, "all the world" meant "all the land [of Judea]." The prophecy was about a famine that covered the land of Judea, and the prophets came from Jerusalem to Antioch to inform the church there about the difficulties that the church of Jerusalem would face. The disciples then gathered sustenance to send "unto the brethren which dwelt in Judea." This phrase most specifically applies to the church at Jerusalem as 11:27, 12:25, and other passages will make clear.

The political context—Hebrews 10:32-34

The famine foretold was an induced famine through persecution as the writer to the Hebrews makes clear.

Hebrews 10:32-34

32: But call to remembrance the former days, in which, after ye were illuminated, ye endured a great fight of afflictions;
33: Partly, whilst ye were made a gazingstock both by reproaches and afflictions; and partly, whilst ye became companions of them that were so used.
34: For ye had compassion of me in my bonds, and took joyfully the spoiling of your goods, knowing in yourselves that ye have in heaven a better and an enduring substance.

Some believe that the writer to the Hebrews may have been Paul. This passage seems eerily similar to Philippians 4:10-14 where Paul, being in prison, thanks the Philippians for ministering to him in his suffering while they gave to him out of a position of not having much to give themselves. However, Paul is not the only possibility for authorship as he was not the only apostle who suffered imprisonment. Some suggest that Barnabas wrote the epistle to the Hebrews, and, as we read earlier, Barnabas was involved with Paul in the initial famine relief efforts. He knew and understood the famine situation and its nature.

The writer to the Hebrews reminds them of the time that they suffered at the hands of their enemies shortly following their conversion to the Gospel. The writer notes that these Hebrews were notable not only for the afflictions that they suffered, but also for their alliance and support of others who faced the same persecution. In verse 34, the writer elaborates on the afflictions that the Hebrews suffered. It was "the spoiling of [their] goods." This verse as well as others provides insight into the nature of the famine as being a persecution upon the the Christians of Judea, namely the church of Jerusalem, in which the empire either destroyed their crops or robbed them.

The epistolary context—1 Corinthians 16:15-17

So far we have seen a narrative passage that speaks of a famine in Judea that would affect the church of Jerusalem. We have seen that Paul and Barnabas brought famine relief to Jerusalem. We have also seen verse 3 of the 1 Corinthians 16 passage that spoke of Paul intending to bring "liberality" to Jerusalem. Obviously, in 1 Corinthians 16:1-3 Paul was not referencing the same trip that he and Barnabas took in Acts chapters 11-12, because this trip was before any of his missionary journeys. As we will discover through some other passages in Paul's epistles, the famine did not end with the relief ministry in Acts chapters 11-12. Part of Paul's missionary journeys involved telling churches along the way to become involved in this serious famine situation and to send aid through Paul to Jerusalem.

Now, continuing the context in chronological order, we need to look at more of 1 Corinthians chapter 16. If we read down to verses 15 through 17, we will see more of the context of verses 1 and 2:

1 Corinthians 16:15-17

15: I beseech you, brethren, ye (know the house of Stephanas, that it is the firstfruits of Achaia, and *that* they have addicted themselves to the ministry of the saints,)
16: That ye submit yourselves unto such, and to every one that helpeth with us, and laboreth.
17: I am glad of the coming of Stephanas and Fortunatus and Achaicus: for that which was lacking on your part they have supplied.

Paul points out in verse 15 that people of the region of Achaia were primary contributors toward relief of this famine. They were likely the first people after the ones in Antioch to provide such famine relief. The region of Achaia began with the household of Stephanas, whom were a few notable believers that Paul baptized (1:16). We will see that the region of Achaia receives more mention from Paul about this specific famine in other passages.

In verse 16, Paul tells the Corinthian church to follow the example of Achaia and contribute to this famine relief project. Apparently, the Corinthian church needed the special instructions given in verses 1 and 2 because they were not as rich and able to give spontaneously as did other churches. Paul must have let them know about the famine before this first epistle, because he mentions their "lacking" aid in verse 17.

An exegetical analysis of 1 Corinthians 16:1-2

In this epistle, Paul supplies the church of Corinth as he did the churches of Galatia a plan so that they can contribute meaningfully to this effort despite their current lack of abundance. If all church members save up a portion of income or produce on the first day of each week, they would have enough set aside so that when Paul arrived, they could fill the ships with supplies. Paul would not have to waste time and "gather" the aid from them.

Do we now see what some of the key phrases in 1 Corinthians 16:1-2 mean? From the context, "the collection for the saints" does not seem to denote a collection plate of "tithes and offerings" from one's **monetary income** to go into one's own church's budget. The "collection for the saints" refers to famine relief project for the saints in Jerusalem (v. 3). No "tithes" or "offerings" are mentioned in this passage whether directly or indirectly.

What about "the first [day] of the week"? Does this phrase assume that these collections happened within the confines of a Sunday "worship service"? Regardless of if the early church did conduct formal worship services each Sunday as a regular practice (that subject would be a debate for a different book), reasons exist for the collections not being during a worship session. The "first [day] of the week" could just as well signify the first day after one receives weekly wages, and thus has sustenance to give. However, another reason exists for why the collections are not corporeal in a worship service.

The next part of the verse says "let each of you lay <u>by him</u> in store." The phrase says that each one who gives lays "by him" in store. It does not say that each one adds to a corporate collection. Each person should lay "by him" (*par heautw* or "near oneself") "in store"

351

(*thesaurizwn* or "reserving," "amassing," "storing," or "treasuring"). Thus, Paul tells each one to "lay up near himself, amassing" what God has prospered him. There is no possible way to infer from this verse a corporate collection. The only corporate collection occurs when Paul arrives, not on the first day of each week.

Paul's order to "lay by him in store" is more akin to a charge to set up a personal savings account (minus the compound interest element). Each person was to designate a portion of each week's earned income to his or her own personal savings. Then, when Paul arrived, each person would take the total accumulated and present it to Paul to deliver to Jerusalem.

The phrase "as *God* hath prospered him" would refer to earned wages or possibly other forms by which one's wealth is increased. Most likely it is weekly wages, as Paul provides a weekly frequency to store up for this aid. Paul possibly did not expect each member of these churches to continue this practice after he arrived to collect the famine relief; however, the practice was still a pragmatic and worthy discipline for saving up for a rainy day or another potential famine.

The subsequential context—2 Corinthians chapter 9

Now, we shall look further to see other passages of Scripture in the context of this famine. Later on within a year from the first epistle, Paul wrote a second epistle to the Corinthian church. If we begin looking at chapter 9, Paul wrote the following:

2 Corinthians 9:1-5

1: For as touching the ministering to the saints, it is superfluous for me to write to you:

2: For I know the forwardness of your mind, for which I boast of you to them of Macedonia, that Achaia was ready a year ago; and your zeal hath provoked very many.

3: Yet have I sent the brethren, lest our boasting of you should be in vain in this behalf; that, as I said, ye may be ready:

4: Lest haply if they of Macedonia come with me, and find you unprepared, we (that we say not, ye) should be ashamed in this same confident boasting.

5: Therefore I thought it necessary to exhort the brethren, that they would go before unto you, and make up beforehand your bounty, whereof ye had notice before, that the same might be ready, as *a matter of* bounty, and not as *of* covetousness.

Now, we can spot a familiar phrase. We can easily determine what "ministering to the saints" means. It is referring to the same famine relief project in the first epistle. Paul said that it is really unnecessary for him to write to them again concerning this project. Now, Paul uses the zeal wherewith the church of Corinth has responded to encourage the churches of the region of Macedonia to participate in the project. He makes mention of Achaia having prepared to give for the last year, and the zeal from the Corinthian church has inspired the people of Macedonia to share in the blessing of giving (v. 2).

Paul assumes, based on his knowledge of the hearts of the Corinthian church that, if they received word of a need, they would do all in their power to fill it (v. 2). He assumes that "the forwardness of [their] mind" or their "predisposition" would compel them to act accordingly as Paul gave them instruction in the first epistle. However, Paul takes a precaution of sending contributors and their gifts from Macedonia to Corinth if somehow the Corinthian church did not live up to Paul's expectations (vv. 3-5).

With this context out of the way, let us approach the next very familiar passage:

2 Corinthians 9:6-9

6: But this *I say*, He which soweth sparingly shall reap also sparingly; and he which soweth bountifully shall reap also bountifully.
7: Every man according as he purposeth in his heart, *so let him give*; not grudgingly, or of necessity: for God loveth a cheerful giver.
8: And God is able to make all grace abound toward you; that ye, always having all sufficiency in all *things*, may abound to every good work:
9: (As it is written, He hath dispersed abroad; he hath given to the poor: his righteousness remaineth forever.

Paul proceeds to attach blessings from God to those who give for His ministry. He does not specify an amount or exactly what those blessings would be; he only matches them with the proportion of which one gives (v. 6). He provides a promise of a nominal match that if one gives a little, one will receive a little in blessings; conversely, if one gives a lot, one will receive a lot in blessings.

The analogy Paul supplies is one of farming. If a farmer plants only a few seeds into the ground, he or she should not expect that the entire field would produce crops. Likewise, if the farmer plants seeds all across the field, he or she should reasonably expect that a much larger area of field would produce edible crops. The proportion of yield is relative to the proportion of effort expended to produce a yield.

However, following Paul's farming analogy, he tells each person to give what that person determines in his or her own heart to give (v. 7). He did not just say that each person should give "a lot," which would still be rather ambiguous. Rather, after laying the principle of sowing and reaping before the church, he instructs each member simply to give as one desires to give. He clears away the roadblocks by leaving the amount and the proportion to the individual.

He tells them not to give "grudgingly" or "out of sadness or grief." In other words, Paul did not want the members of the church of Corinth to strive to give an amount that would bring them harm or sorrow. He wanted them to give, but to give responsibly and realistically. Paul also told Timothy that anyone who did not provide for his family is worse than an infidel (1 Timothy 5:8). Therefore, for one to give "not grudgingly," one needs to balance his or her own needs with the needs of others. Although God wants us to give to meet needs, He also expects us to be reasonable. We cannot act upon "blind faith" and expect Him to intervene for our good. We are not allowed to tempt or test God with unreasonableness, even if we think that we are doing something good (Deuteronomy 6:16; Matthew 4:7; Luke 4:12; Acts 15:10).

Paul also tells the Corinthians not to give "of necessity" or "under compulsion" or "by restraint." Paul clarifies that whatever they give should not be some kind of individual requirement. If one were to say that a "tithe" of one's monetary income were a Scriptural requirement to meet remote needs, then that assertion would contradict this verse. "Necessity," "compulsion," or "restraint" would include **any kind** of nominal or proportional requirement, and Paul instructs the Corinthians not to give this way.

Paul then explains **why** he does not want the Corinthians to give "grudgingly" or "of necessity." "For God loveth a cheerful giver," he declares. By deriving a contrast between "cheerful giving" and giving under grief or compulsion, Paul presents a dichotomy. **Either** one gives out of pain or requirement, **or** one gives freely and cheerfully. One does not give cheerfully **and** out of necessity. Cheerful giving **requires** that the nominal or proportionate amount of the gift be at the sole discretion of the giver. If cheerfulness is a feeling unique to an individual person, likewise the gift must be unique to the individual person. An outside constraint is incompatible with an inside quality.

Paul defends his admonition by assuring the Corinthians that God will bless them if they follow it (v. 7). He supports his assertion in verse 8 by quoting from Psalm 112:9. This passage is a reference to something that **God** does. Paul is telling the Corinthians to give freely and then saying that their action is actually God meeting the needs of the poor. Therefore, Paul attaches a promise to his order to give freely. He lets the Corinthians know that, if God promises to take care of the poor, then, if their free giving contributes toward this work of God, He will naturally keep them from wanting in this work as well.

Paul, then continues by explaining that this free giving is more than just meeting the intended needs:

2 Corinthians 9:10-15

10: Now he that ministereth seed to the sower both minister bread for *your* food, and multiply your seed sown, and increase the fruits of your righteousness;)
11: Being enriched in every thing to all bountifulness, which causeth through us thanksgiving to God.
12: For the administration of this service not only supplieth the want of the saints, but is abundant also by many thanksgivings unto God;

> 13: While by the experiment of this ministration they glorify God for your professed subjection unto the gospel of Christ, and for *your* liberal distribution unto them, and unto all *men*;
> 14: And by their prayer for you, which long after you for the exceeding grace of God in you.
> 15: Thanks *be* unto God for his unspeakable gift.

Now, after Paul gave the principle of sowing and reaping (v. 6), he explains that God is the One Who both supplies the seeds themselves and the crops that they produce (v. 10). Since the "sowing" in this case is giving to meet needs, Paul is elaborating that God supplies the abundance that we possess whereby we give freely. Paul is requesting to God on behalf of the Corinthians that if they give what God has given them, then, like planting seed, God would return them abundance and reward their giving as well.

In the next verse, Paul continues that reaping an abundance from the giving of "sowing," we will thank God for supplying our needs. No doubt, Paul still believed that we ought to thank God regardless of the circumstances (Philippians 4:11; 1 Timothy 6:8; 1 Thessalonians 5:18). Nevertheless, the natural response of a Christian to God's obvious and abundant blessing is to thank Him for it. A continuous cycle should result, whereby, if we give and receive blessings from God, we should then, from those blessings, give again.

Not only do we thank God for His rewarding our giving, but the recipients of our gifts, the poor saints, will thank God as well (v. 12). Paul declares that not only does the giving relieve the needs, but it also produces a sweet smelling savor of thanksgiving to God. If the Corinthians give as Paul anticipates, they will not only be talkers but walkers (v. 13). Not only would the saints in Jerusalem have cause to praise God about the Corinthians' "professed subjection unto the gospel," but they would also see that their words have backing, for they also demonstrate commitment in their "liberal distribution" in the cooperative "experiment of this ministration." Finally, Paul thanks God for the total contributions toward the famine relief, calling it "his [God's] unspeakable gift" (v. 15).

The geographical context—Romans 15:24-33

Finally, having covered the epistles to the Corinthians, we will conclude with another account from the epistle to the Romans. As Paul visited the Corinthians, he likely wrote the epistle to the Romans here.[1] Naturally, since he went to Corinth to collect their bounty for famine relief, he mentioned this incident when writing Romans:

Romans 15:24-26

24: Whensoever I take my journey into Spain, I will come to you: for I trust to see you in my journey, and to be brought on my way thitherward by you, if first I be somewhat filled with your *company*.
25: But now I go unto Jerusalem to minister unto the saints.
26: For it hath pleased them of Macedonia and Achaia to make a certain contribution for the poor saints which are at Jerusalem.

As Paul is bringing his third missionary journey to a close by bringing the famine relief from several churches to Jerusalem, he mentions his plans to make a journey to Rome to visit the church of the Romans. Although he is writing from Corinth, he still needs to travel back southeast to Jerusalem before going west to Rome. Once

---

1. Geoffrey W. Bromiley, *The International Standard Bible Encyclopedia*, vol. 7. s.v. "Romans, epistle to."

again, we see a familiar phrase to describe this famine relief: Paul will go to "minister unto the saints." (v. 25)

Paul mentions the regions of Macedonia and Achaia again as we have seen that those two regions are the foremost contributors of famine relief. Both of these regions represented the Greek peninsula with Achaia on the south and Macedonia on the north. Corinth is a city in the region of Achaia, but contributors of Macedonia were going to join Corinth ahead of Paul as he traveled southward from when he wrote his second epistle.

Now, having resided in Corinth for about three months, Paul writes his epistle to the Romans and notes this project.[2] The "poor saints which are at Jerusalem" (v. 26) are those in the Jerusalem church who are suffering from the famine in Judea. Paul is accumulating the contributions from the regions of Macedonia and Achaia, including from the Corinthian church.

Now, we shall observe the rest of Romans chapter 15:

Romans 15:27-33

27: It hath pleased them verily; and their debtors they are. For if the Gentiles have been made partakers of their spiritual things, their duty is also to minister unto them in carnal things.
28: When therefore I have performed this, and have sealed to them this fruit, I will come by you into Spain.
29: And I am sure that, when I come unto you, I shall come in the fullness of the blessing of the gospel of Christ.
30: Now I beseech you, brethren, for the Lord Jesus Christ's sake, and for the love of the Spirit, that ye strive together with me in your prayers to God for me;

---

2. Ibid.

31: That I may be delivered from them that do not believe in Judea; and that my service which *I have* for Jerusalem may be accepted of the saints; 32: That I may come unto you with joy by the will of God, and may with you be refreshed.
33: Now the God of peace *be* with you all. Amen.

Paul notes that the churches of Macedonia and Achaia are giving to Jerusalem in a sense out of gratitude, for out of Jerusalem came Paul himself (Acts 9:26-28). Paul later established his headquarters at Antioch (Acts 11:26-27), but the Jerusalem church informed him of the famine (Acts 11:28-30). Because the churches in Judea were humanly responsible for bringing the "spiritual things" of the glorious Gospel to the Gentile churches of Macedonia and Achaia, then the churches of those regions felt obligated as "debtors" to meet the needs for "carnal things" of these largely Jewish churches (v. 27).

Paul assures the Roman church that he intends to visit them after performing this famine relief project (v. 28). He then asks for their prayers of protection. Paul often faced persecution from the non-believing Jews, namely those of the ruling religious elite. He asks them to pray that the Jewish elite do not hinder him (vv. 30-31), and that the famine relief that he brings there will be sufficient to meet their needs: that it "may be accepted of the saints." (v. 31) If the religious elite, such as the Sanhedrin, attempt to arrest him, or if the famine relief is found to be insufficient, Paul may not be able to have the "joy" and "be refreshed" as he attempts to journey to Rome (v. 32).

Conclusion and summary

In conclusion, we see very clearly that 1 Corinthians 16:1-2 is **not** talking about tithing of monetary income. It is not even talking about giving to one's own church. Although I am not saying that one has no obligation to support the work of one's own church, I am clarifying that a proper reading of these verses in context shows that these verses are not the proof text for such a requirement. The context of these verses has specifically to do with a prophesied famine in Judea. Acts 11:27-30, 1 Corinthians 16, 2 Corinthians 9, and Romans 15:24-33 all support this view. A valid applications from these passages would be to save up income every time one receives a wage and use these savings to generously meet needs.

17. Double Honor for Elders

Two Wages for Two Jobs

1 Timothy 5:17-18

17: Let the elders that rule well be counted worthy of double honor, especially they who labor in the word and doctrine.
18: For the Scripture saith, Thou shalt not muzzle the ox that treadeth out the corn. And, The laborer *is* worthy of his reward.

Perspective from the modern church

Perhaps you have heard a sermon preached that based its message upon, or included, the above passage to argue a point. The message may or may not have included the subject of "tithes and offerings." For those that **did** include "tithes and offerings" the premise was that the elders (or "pastors") received their salaries from the "tithes and offerings" that the people gave out of obligation to the church. For those that **did not** include "tithes and offerings" the argument was ultimately the same as the one above and led to the seemingly inescapable conclusion: God, through the apostle Paul, commanded the church that they should pay the elders **twice as much** as the wages everyone else received for their jobs.

A pastor preaching these verses may elaborate on the passage and explain the rationale behind paying him twice as much as everyone else earns. After all, Paul under the inspiration of the Holy Spirit would not give such a commission to the church via Timothy unless some sound reasons existed. Paul likely was not commissioning this church to do something that they were **already** doing. He was likely telling them to start practicing something that was expedient.

One reason that one preaching this passage may present for paying elders twice as much as everyone else is that God places such a value and premium on His work of the ministry. Exposition of the Word of God has a substantially greater effect and profit on people in the eyes of God than any other endeavor. The largest business, the greatest employer, and the enterprise that provides more jobs and higher quality jobs in the market pales in comparison to the importance God places on an occupation that reaps the souls of men and women for His kingdom. Why should not elders who preach the Word of God and edify and equip the saints receive **twice as much** in remuneration as they do in their less profitable jobs? In fact, since their work is **priceless**, twice the pay is the **least** the church congregation could do for them. Getting twice as much in the world's wealth is but a shadow of what they deserve, much to the effect of writing a simple "thank you" note to a millionaire who generously paid for a surgery that saved your life. You would feel forever indebted, and your note could only express the sentiment of thanks. Should not elders receive twice the pay as everyone else as merely a modicum of their worth?

Another reason that one preaching this passage may present for this idea of "double honor" is that the amount of labor and effort involved in the work of an elder is equivalent to the work of two jobs on the same terms and level as the congregation. Today, pastors carry a large burden and perform a long laundry list of duties with their time that the members of the congregation could never hope to do fully. In fact, congregations often expect pastors to do many things, and therefore are willing to offer a high price for one to do this work for them.

For the modern church, pastors will preach three one-hour sermons per week and spend hours studying the Bible in English and Greek, craft alliterated outlines for each of these, and research statistics and illustrations from outside sources to support the points of their outlines. Pastors will also organize and lead soul-winning endeavors such as door-to-door visitations on Thursday evenings and Saturday mornings. Pastors will organize outreach programs and social church functions on the calendar. Pastors will oversee bus ministries for city children and may even drive a bus themselves. Pastors will attempt to visit anyone in the church who is ill at a home or in the hospital.

Pastors will attempt to minister to those facing death and share the Gospel with them or encourage them in the Lord.

Modern churches often do not simply involve the confines of the worship services and related activities; they may also act as the hub for other organizations that function as arms of the central church ministry. A church may run a private Christian school and the pastor acts as a school principal. When the teacher cannot get a message through to a child in a classroom and requires further acts of punishment besides a scolding that interrupts the class lecture, the teacher will send the rebellious child to the pastor-principal. Accordingly, the pastor must be available in the assigned office during the bulk of school hours and may be doing sermon preparation during that time. The pastor then needs to know how to counsel rebellious children and make appropriate provisions with the parents to enact sufficient extra-curricular punishments.

A modern church may also run a non-profit ministry organization that manages funds for mission work and also maintains its own schedules and updates. The ministry, the school, and the church will all have separate, but affiliated web sites in which the pastor will provide input for content and approve all updates before they are released into the wild. A pastor may not only function much as a CEO, but the CEO of more than one organization. Obviously, the burdens expected of modern pastors demand many hours of labor and reasonable and appropriate compensation. When asked about the time spent fulfilling all their expectations, pastors may readily describe their work load in terms of 80 to 100 hours. In this case, receiving twice the pay as one who works 40 hours per week would be not only reasonable but a moral obligation.

While the truth may be that many modern church elders who claim the title of "pastor" may labor such many hours and perform such many tasks, we do need to understand what the Scriptures are actually saying. After all, the Scriptures were not written in the twenty-first century. Paul was writing to Timothy in the first century and was structuring his argument based on the events and activities surrounding the first century church. To understand the exact message of this passage, we need to understand the structure of the church during this time. We also need to study the Scriptures in light of the context and in light of other passages.

Perhaps some modern pastors do not perform the lengthy list of assumed duties, or perhaps many in the congregation are unaware of what their pastor actually does. The Scripture passage above many shock or outrage some and lead them to rationalize an understanding of "double honor" other than the conventional definition. Regardless, several theories exist to explain what Paul means by "double honor." We will examine several of these theories, and I will present my own theory as to its possible definition.

The double pay theory

In my experience, the most common interpretation of "double honor" is that it means "double pay" in some form. However, the question becomes one of logistics. In first-world countries like the

United States of America where concepts such as "lower class," "middle class," and "upper class" exist to describe the income levels and standard of living for certain citizens, the definition of "double pay" has no recognizable metric from the Scripture to apply to modern church practice. A logical method of determining the base from which to double is to calculate the average of something and then double the result. One suggestion is to pay the "senior pastor" of the church by calculating the average salary of the other members of the church staff and doubling the result.[3] Another idea is to pay an elder twice the average of what one of the church members earns.[4] Yet another option for the average income method is to calculate the average of the income from the congregation and double this result.[5] The major problem with the latter approach is that the members of the congregation would have an obligation to reveal their income information to the church staff.[6] Some members may object to such a required invasion of sensitive aspects of their private lives.

---

3. David Pollock, "Worthy is the Pastor", Resource Ministries, http://www.resourceministries.net/articles_details.php?articlesID=8 (accessed December 1, 2009).

4. Patric Knack, "Lesson Six: Faith Working Through Love" in From God to Divine Brussels Sprout—Paul's Letter to the Galatians, Naperville Presbyterian Church, http://www.npchurch.org/adulted/studies/galatians_npcu/GalLesson6.pdf (accessed December 1, 2009).

5. govols, comment on "Is your Pastor a millionaire?", The Fighting Fundamental Forums, comment posted March 25, 2008, http://www.fundamentalforums.com/the-fighting-forum/46265-is-your-pastor-a-millionaire-3.html#post978066 (accessed December 1, 2009).

6. cilrel, comment on "Money and a Pastor's Example to his Flock!", The Fighting Fundamental Forums, comment posted April 16, 2009,

Section V: New Testament Giving

The double respect theory

In an effort to discount the obvious justification for embellishing pastors with wealth, and with painful memories or regard for scam artist religious leaders and popular prosperity preachers, some will contend that the "honor" in this passage refers to types of honor **other than** monetary or material compensation. Double honor, then, does not refer to pay, but rather to recognition, a "pat on the back," or some other form of cordial respect for a position of spiritual authority. In other words, the word translated as *honor* in 1 Timothy 5:17 is translated as *honor* for good reason in many Bible translations so as to be distinguished from material compensation or earned wages.

Some who have researched and seriously challenged the conventional and ignorant modern understanding of tithing and have witnessed the destructive effects of "kingdom-building" fundamentalists and multimillionaire prosperity evangelists have good reason to see a red flag in regard to using Scripture to teach that God has commanded modern church members to embellish their pastors with unprecedented material and carnal blessings. Dr. Russell Earl Kelly, a southern Baptist theologian, has written his Ph.D. dissertation on the subject of tithing. In his book based upon his dissertation research *Should the Church Teach Tithing?*, Dr. Kelly presents an array of reasons that "double honor" in 1 Timothy 5:17 should not mean double pay or wages. He argues that the verses prior and following

http://www.fundamentalforums.com/the-fighting-forum/66518-money-and-a-pastors-example-to-his-flock.html#post1381366 (accessed December 1, 2009).

367

verses 17 and 18 demonstrate the context of rebuke and scrutiny of wrongdoing.[7] This honor, in turn, for elders that study and teach God's Word is twice that of elders that do not serve in this capacity because these elders should receive honor for their age and proven experience, and also more honor for labor and spiritual value of teaching and edifying with God's Word.[8]

Not only does the context provide a case for "double honor" not referring to some form of salary, but also the word *honor* itself can raise this objection. Dr. Kelly argues that the uses of the Greek word for *honor* in the context and elsewhere in other New Testament passages do not denote forms of material compensation, and that if Paul meant such, he could have used a Greek word that more specifically supplied the intended meaning.[9] Indeed, as the Greek word *timē* ambiguously refers to anything due one's position or work, whether wages, respect, esteem, or dignity, it most likely does not mean "wages" or "pay" in its forms and translations in many passages.[10] Also, the Greek word *kopiaō* translated as "labor" meaning "to grow tired or weary" is not the one commonly used for working for reward or wages. A word in the Greek more fit for such a definition is

---

7. Kelly, 211.
8. Ibid.
9. Ibid., 212.
10. See John 4:44; Romans 2:7,10; 9:21; 12:10; 1 Corinthians 12:23-24; Colossians 2:23; 1 Thessalonians 4:4; 1 Timothy 1:17; 6:16; 2 Timothy 2:20-21; Hebrews 2:7,9; 3:3; 5:4; 1 Peter 1:7; 2:7; 3:7; 2 Peter 1:17; Revelation 4:9,11; 5:12-13; 7:12; 19:1; 21:24,26

ergazomai as other passages of Scripture exemplify.[11] Clearly, for one to argue that "double honor" refers to a double portion of wages or salary, one must endeavor to provide careful proof against the support for the contrary.

The respect plus pay theory

Another theory about the meaning of "double honor" is that one should really see it as "two honors." The two honors are different types of honors—both of them due elders who labor in God's Word. Since the word *honor* can mean either material remuneration or respect, perhaps what Paul meant by "double honor" is that an elder should receive both: one honor in the form of respect for the spiritual office and experience, and a second honor in the form of wages due the labor.[12] This theory seems appealing as a compromise between the views that *honor* means respect versus material or monetary wages. Especially for those who may have had troubling experiences with authoritarian or manipulative church leaderships, they may not see how the Scripture can reasonably expect them to embellish elders with material wealth who also openly revel in the same.

---

11. See Matthew 7:23; 21:28; 25:16; 26:10; Mark 14:6; Luke 13:14; John 3:21; 5:17; 6:27,28,30; 9:4; Acts 10:35; 13:41; 18:3; Romans 2:10; 4:4-5; 13:10; 1 Corinthians 4:12; 9:6,13; 16:10; Galatians 6:10; Ephesians 4:28; Colossians 3:23; 1 Thessalonians 2:9; 4:11; 2 Thessalonians 3:8,10-12; Hebrews 11:33; James 2:9; 2 John 8; 3 John 5; Revelation 18:17
12. Ray C. Stedman, "Help for Elders", The Ray C. Stedman Library, http://www.raystedman.org/timothy/3778.html (accessed December 1, 2009).

My "two jobs" theory

The theory that I shall now present envelopes portions from the other theories that I have listed above. After studying the context carefully, along with trying to understand both the culture of the first century A.D. and passages in the Bible detailing early church history and structure, I have built my theory about what Paul meant by "double honor." I believe that he did indeed refer to some form of material or financial care, maintenance, or remuneration. Elders should be counted worthy of "double honor" and both these honors refer to compensation for labor. However, I do not believe that the "double honor" as a whole comes from the church itself—only the second one does. Paul told Timothy and his church to consider the elders worthy of "double honor" or "two honors:" the first honor already coming from their existing occupation, and the second honor coming from the church for their labor in the Word of God.

Now, my theory may at first appear to be a stretch from a superficial reading of the verse. How in the world could I arrive at such a premise when the verse itself does not even mention the elders having another occupation? How could I possibly "divide" the "double honor" into two parts when the verse does not make this assumption apparent? Is not Paul telling the church itself to give the elders "double honor"? I will attempt to answer these questions by laying the foundation for my theory from other Scriptures and let the Bible interpret itself.

A working definition of "honor" for widows and elders

First, we need to establish the basis that the word *honor* itself does indeed imply some form of material care, maintenance, or wage. To do this we need to examine the context to determine what connotation the *honor* reflects. Verses 3 through 16 all speak of how to treat widows in the church.

1 Timothy 5:3-16

3: <u>Honor widows</u> that are widows indeed.
4: But if any widow have children or nephews, let them learn first to show piety at home, and to requite their parents: for that is good and acceptable before God.
5: Now she that is a widow indeed, and desolate, trusteth in God, and continueth in supplications and prayers night and day.
6: But she that liveth in pleasure is dead while she liveth.
7: And these things give in charge, that they may be blameless.
8: But if any provide not for his own, and especially for those of his own house, he hath denied the faith, and is worse than an infidel.
9: Let not a widow be taken into the number under threescore years old, having been the wife of one man,
10: Well reported of for good works; if she have brought up children, if she have lodged strangers, if she have washed the saints' feet, if she have relieved the afflicted, if she have diligently followed every good work.
11: But the younger widows refuse: for when they have begun to wax wanton against Christ, they will marry;
12: Having damnation, because they have cast off their first faith.
13: And withal they learn *to be* idle, wandering about from house to house; and not only idle, but tattlers also and busybodies, speaking things which they ought not.
14: I will therefore that the younger women marry, bear children, guide the house, give none occasion to the adversary to speak reproachfully.
15: For some are already turned aside after Satan.
16: If any man or woman that believeth have widows, let them <u>relieve them</u>, and let not the church be <u>charged</u>; that it may <u>relieve them</u> that are widows indeed.

Verse 3 begins by saying to "honor widows that are widows indeed." The word for *honor* is the same Greek word for *honor* in verse 17 for the "double honor" for elders. Naturally, one would conclude that such contextual proximity would dictate that both uses reflect the same meaning.

A "widow indeed" is Paul's way of distinguishing the textbook definition of a widow—one whose husband has died and is currently unmarried—with a widow for whom appropriate "honor" is due. First, a widow that deserves "honor" is "desolate" or truly alone. If the loss of a husband currently represents a loss in care, she has need of "honor." Second, according to verses 4, 5, 6, 10, and 13, the widows should only receive this "honor" if they demonstrate godliness and train their children to be godly. Third, according to verses 9, 11, and 14, the widows should only receive this "honor" if they are at least sixty years old, demonstrating that they are incapable of supporting themselves, nor of marrying again a husband who can support her and bearing more children. Finally, according to verse 16, the widows should only receive this "honor" if they do not have close friends or relatives who can provide for them without having to bring the matter to the church for consideration. These friends and relatives can "relieve" or help the widows.

We can reasonably draw the conclusion from the qualifications above that the "honor" for widows relates to maintenance or care for material needs. Following the discourse of this "honor" for widows, verse 17 then commissions that the elders that "rule well" or "lead well" should be "counted worthy of double honor." Apparently, the "honor" for elders is the same type of "honor" for widows. This "honor" is a form of maintenance or upkeep to meet needs. Verse 18 provides the reason for this "honor" by stating that "the laborer *is* worthy of his reward." An obvious inference indicates that the "honor" is material or financial care in return for the labor in God's Word.

Do other occurrences of the Greek word *timē* indicate such an idea of compensation for work? Some occurrences of this word refer to the "price" of something.[13] Dr. Kelly in his analysis of this word in the New Testament draws a distinction between the ideas of "price" and "wage."[14] In economics "price," or ("value") and "wages" are not necessarily different. Both of them represent a form of measure between two things. Although "wages" may carry more the idea of a contractual agreement between two parties, both "wages" and "price" dictate a negotiable market value for goods and services offered or performed.

A working definition of "labor"

Does the word *kopiōntes* for "labor" in verse 17 indicate work for hire? Well, no, at least not upfront. In fact, for purposes of my theory for the meaning of "double honor," I completely agree that Paul intended to use a form of *kopiaō* rather than *ergazomai* in verse 17 distinctly to indicate that the elders who "labor" in God's Word were exhibiting toil unto fatigue and that this "labor" was **not** in itself a work for hire. The elders who "labor" in God's Word did not sign any contract or agree to some form of compensation for their contributions

---

13. See Matthew 27:6,9; Acts 4:34; 5:2-3; 7:16; 19:19; 1 Corinthians 6:20; 7:23
14. Kelly, 212.

as elders in the church. If this statement is true, then why is verse 18 stated the way it is? Why does verse 18 use the word *ergatēs* for "laborer" in its justification for "honoring" an elder? Why does it use the word *misthou* which most properly means "pay for service"? Dr. Kelly points that Paul could have used *misthos* ("pay for service") in verse 17 instead of *timēs* ("honor/respect/dignity") if he intended to convey this notion.[15] My contention is that Paul intended to convey the idea of toil or weariness without specified compensation in verse 17, and that he also intended to convey the idea of one who works for pay in verse 18 as support for the "honor" in verse 17.

According to my theory, the elders in the church may have been exerting time and energy into the Word of God for **no pay**. They may have been performing their leading as elders in the church as a service, yet receiving **no compensation**. Paul instructed Timothy to "honor" the elders that lead well for their labor in God's Word, and this honor, indeed, is a wage, pay, maintenance, or some form of material remuneration.

Now, what of "double honor"? As I explained previously, my theory is that the "double honor" or "two-fold honor" or "two honors" are **both** forms of "pay" for work: the first one already coming from their current source of living. The objection to my idea would come from the common notion (and modern practice) of church eldership being one's primary or designated vocation in life.

---

15. Kelly, 212-213.

Is the office of an elder a vocation?

Many people simply **assume** that a position as an officer of the church is designed as a vocation in itself. One who pursues the position of an elder or "pastor" of a church then also chooses to give up other career endeavors to enter "full-time ministry" as a member of the "clergy." A church, then, consists of "clergy" and "laity." The "laity" are regularly attending members of the church who work "secular" jobs and volunteer time for "sacred" church-related tasks. The "clergy," in turn, are the ones in church authority who have a calling from God to devote their entire lives to "the ministry" and cast aside the influence of "the world" by placing their care and deriving their livelihoods from funds raised for the church.

What I have just described may be the model for most churches **now**, but was it the model of the early church when Paul wrote his epistle to Timothy? Was an "elder" or "pastor" one's livelihood? Was one person a farmer, one a blacksmith, one a tailor, one a fisher, and one an "elder" or "pastor"? Was being an "elder" really a full-time recognized occupation for livelihood? Could one be **both** a farmer by trade **and** serve as an elder in a church? Was this common and would it have been overbearing?

Senior elder or multiple elders?

One element that would determine if an elder possibly worked in the manner that a common church member would is the nature of the position as the Scriptures detail. Did the apostolic churches have a single elder or multiple elders? If a church had a single elder, did it have multiple subservient elders? Did the church have a plurality of elders who were equal in authority to each other? We will need to search the Scriptures to answer these questions.

Searching for any form of the word *presbuteros* ("elder"), we observe some interesting facts:

⅄ The church at Jerusalem had "elders" (Acts 11:29-30).

⅄ The disciples "ordained elders in every church" (Acts 14:22-23).

⅄ The church at Jerusalem had "apostles and elders" (Acts 15:2,4,6,22-23).

⅄ The "apostles and elders" at the Jerusalem church ordained decrees (Acts 16:4).

⅄ Paul contacted "the elders of the church" at Ephesus (Acts 20:17).

⅄ Paul consulted with the "elders" of the Jerusalem church (Acts 21:18).

⅄ Paul told Timothy not to rebuke "an elder" in his church, to honor "the elders that rule well," and to try an accusation against "an elder" with two or more witnesses (1 Timothy 5:1,17,19).

⅄ Paul told Titus to "ordain elders in every city" (Titus 1:5).

⅄ James told told a sick person to "call for the elders of the church" (James 5:14).

⅄ Peter exhorts "the elders which are among you" (1 Peter 5:1).

Searching for any form of the word *episkopos* ("bishop" or "overseer"), we observe some interesting facts:

⅄ Paul told the elders at Ephesus as "overseers, [to] feed the church of God" (Acts 20:28).

⅄ Paul and Timothy address "all the saints, ... the bishops and deacons" at the church at Philippi (Philippians 1:1).

⅄ Paul tells Timothy the qualifications for "the office of a bishop" (1 Timothy 3:1-2).

⅄ Paul tells Titus, after commissioning him to ordain "elder**s** in every city" that "if any be blameless... for a bishop must be blameless." Apparently, a bishop/overseer is the same as an elder (Titus 1:5-7).

Searching for any form of the word *poimen* ("shepherd" or "pastor"), we observe some interesting facts:

⅄ Paul says that Jesus gave "some pastor**s**... for the perfecting of the saints" (Ephesians 4:11-12).

⅄ Peter calls Christ "the Shepherd and Bishop of your souls" (1 Peter 2:25).

⅄ Peter, telling elders to be "example**s** to the flock" refers to Christ as "the chief Shepherd" (1 Peter 5:3-4).

Apparently, being an elder, overseeing as a bishop, and shepherding a flock (the saints in a church) are all titles and duties of the same office. An elder is a bishop is an overseer is a pastor is a shepherd. Since these are all the same office, the Bible only defines two "offices" in the church: the elder-bishop-pastor (1 Timothy 3:1; Titus 1:7) and the deacon-servant (1 Timothy 3:10,13).

From what we have seen, any given church in the New Testament had a plurality of elders and deacons. No mention existed of any church having a single leader or a "senior pastor" or elder who held the reins. No mention existed of an elder "board" that served under one chief overseer. The structure of an apostolic church, according to

377

the New Testament account, is one of a plurality of leaders ("elders" or "bishops" or "pastors") who minister in the Word of God, and a plurality of servants ("deacons") who "wait tables" or perform other service-related functions in the church. No single man has the ultimate authority over what happens, and in turn, the burden of responsibility for everything that happens.

If our analysis of the Scriptures is correct, how did the structure of the church evolve from the specifics of the New Testament scriptures to the form that we know today? Obviously, according to the Scriptures the church did not embrace such a structure immediately. Primarily, the idea of a single elder with final authority over the church was an idea that led to the development of the official Catholic Church. Church government with the highest authority being a single elder (now commonly called "pastor") having subservient "elders" instead of a plurality of equal elders began to take precedence at the close of the second century.[16] Jerome, having first defended the notion that Peter was the head elder and apostle upon which the church was based later denounced this teaching by declaring that all the apostles oversaw the early church and contributed "equally."[17] Jerome later also explained that a selection of one elder to oversee the others, like the

---

16. Thomas Martin Lindsay, *Church and the Ministry in the Early Centuries* (London: Hodder and Stoughton, 1903), 366.
http://www.ccel.org/ccel/lindsay/early_church.html (accessed December 2, 2009).
17. Richard Frederick Littledale, *Plain reasons against joining the church of Rome* (London: Society for Promoting Christian Knowledge, 1886), 243.

selection of Peter to be the ultimate authority for the church, was to keep the church from dividing or splitting.[18]

The same argument against multiple "elder-led" church polity continues today. What most Protestants, Baptists/Congregationalists, and non-denominationalists that argue for single "pastor-led" church polity do not realize is that their reasoning for "final decision-making" and "schism prevention" was the identical reasoning that created the structure of the Catholic Church that they much despise. The logic that created the formal pyramid of cardinals, bishops, and priests serving ultimately under one pope is the same logic that creates the single pastor personality who oversees a "board" of elders or deacons. Some churches apparently even blur the distinction between an *elder* and a *deacon*, where the "deacon board" functions as the group of elected individuals who make decisions under the final authority of the one pastor.

The early church structure demonstrated in the New Testament is one of the apostles starting churches and ordaining elders. The elders then would plant other churches and ordain elders. Each church had a plurality of elders with equal and collective authority in affairs. Each church also had a plurality of deacons who were servants. The deacons did not rule in any way, but performed service functions such as "waiting on tables" (Acts 6:1-6). However, both elders and deacons had spiritual gifts. The apostles, elders, and deacons would all preach the Gospel in the towns and cities. Women could also be deacons, as

---

18. Ibid.

this was a servant office (Romans 16:1), but they did not exercise preaching ministry.

Dividing the burden of leadership responsibilities

A simple deduction of a multiple elder church polity is that the burden of church leadership is divided among multiple persons, and is thereby lessened for each one. One elder does not have to study, plan, and preach a minimum of three sermons every week. One elder does not have to dictate, oversee, and orchestrate all outreach activities. One elder does not have to try to visit all the ill. One elder does not have to make all decisions in church discipline. One elder does not have to wear many hats. With a multiple elder polity, the so-called "full-time" job of a "pastor" becomes less of a formal sacerdotal occupation. The responsibilities are a lighter burden and can take less time with many hands.

Full-time ministry or extra work?

With the above rationale in mind, were elders then "employees" of a church "organization" in the apostolic era? Was being an elder one's "occupation" just as being a carpenter was another's occupation? Was the house of God a source of priesthood jobs where "clergy" members worked "full-time" in ministry instead of working a "secular" job?

Obviously, we know that the Roman empire during the time of the apostles did not recognize the Christian church the same way that modern "Free World" countries such as the United States of America recognize churches. Churches during the Roman empire suffered persecution from the government. The government did not recognize them as independent organizations with the power of association. The Roman empire did not confer 501(c)(3) status to "religious organizations" to function as "non-profit" entities. The Roman Empire did not recognize the Christian "clergy" as a formal occupation for tax purposes. The early church met in houses and even caves to escape persecution. Certainly the employment structure for positions in "religious organizations" did not exist during the time Paul wrote his first epistle to Timothy.

If no formal employment organization for church elders existed in the first century, and churches themselves had to struggle with persecution from both the Roman government and Jewish religious leaders, a reasonable assumption would be that the elders, deacons, and saints in the churches all worked a livelihood apart from the church. The church was not the source of someone's occupation; the church was the ministry of the assembly of believers **apart** from the livelihood of all involved.

Did the elders work just as non-elders did? First, we have seen nothing in Scripture to prove that being a church elder was an occupation on par with production occupations. Also, the Scriptures mention the idea of elders working. In Acts 20:34-35 Paul commissioned the elders at the church of Ephesus to do as he did in that "[his] hands have ministered unto [his] necessities." He told them to do this "to support the weak" and that by this physical labor "it is more blessed to give than to receive." This commission was in addition to Paul's earlier commission in verse 28 "to feed the church of

God." The work of being an elder was an **additional** labor in the ministry to that of the elder's livelihood, just as the work of being a deacon and "serving tables" was not what the church-servant did for a living.

The second "honor"

Returning to 1 Timothy 5:17-18, we can now examine "double honor" in light of the historical and Scriptural information that we explored. If "honor" is upkeep, maintenance, sustenance, wages, or pay, then what of "double honor"? If we have eliminated the presupposition of eldership being one's full-time job, then my theory of "double honor" begins to make sense. Paul compares the "honor" for elders to the "honor" for widows. The widows that are "widows indeed" and have no adequate means of self-sustenance are worthy of the "honor" of relief through family or otherwise through the church. The "honor," maintenance, or wages for elders are two-fold. The first "honor" or wage is the one that they already receive in their current livelihood. The second is what Paul is instructing that they receive for their labor in the Word of God as an elder.

Paul did not tell Timothy to **give** the elders "double honor." He said to "count them <u>worthy</u>" or "consider them <u>worthy</u>" of "double honor" because of their labor in the Word of God. Paul justified this consideration by citing the law that one who works should receive payment. Paul used the word *kopiaō* for the "labor" of the elders in verse 17 to say that they "grew weary" or "became fatigued." Paul then compared this "labor" to one who works for a wage by using the word *ergatēs* in verse 18. Paul, in effect, told Timothy that the elders who lead well and minister in the Word should not do this for **nothing**; one who works should be paid!

Because the elders already earned a livelihood outside the ministry was no excuse for the saints who fed from the ministry of the elders to expect them to do all this work without any kind of compensation. They should "count them worthy" of "double honor." They should recognize the worth of the elders in receiving a second wage of some kind atop their livelihood for their secondary work in the ministry. If one who works should be paid, then elders who already receive their "honor" or wages from their "labor with their hands" should receive a second "honor" from their "labor in the word and doctrine." They should be considered worthy of "double honor" because what they do in their lives amounts to two jobs. The "double honor" is not "twice the pay" for the work of being an elder; it is one "honor" that already exists and the second "honor" for working as an elder.

Think for a minute: why would Paul tell Timothy to pay elders **twice as much** as the average person receives for the job of being and elder, and that not doing so would be equivalent to "muzzling an ox"? In other words, while the ox is pulling the weight of the plow, one should not place a barrier on the ox's mouth to keep it from eating as it performs the work. The idea of not muzzling an ox has to do with expecting the ox to work **for nothing**. One should not treat the ox as **slave labor**. Compensating an elder for the particular work of being an elder less than **twice as much** as most other people would hardly be an argument for "muzzling an ox." Combining the ox-muzzling idea with the worth of a laborer to receive a wage, Paul explains that an elder who labors in the Word should receive compensation for doing this, and not to do it necessarily **for free**. Because elders who labor in the Word work what amounts to a second job, the church should "count them worthy of double honor" by supplying the second honor for this labor.

Conclusion and summary

In conclusion, we see that the conception of church structure has changed drastically since the early church. We see that one's conception of church polity can affect how one interprets Scriptures regarding church polity. Based on the text of 1 Timothy 5:17-18, the immediate context of this passage, the context of other New Testament passages, and the history of the early church, I believe that my theory of the intention and meaning of "double honor" provides a substantial measure of sense. It also quells the outrage that can result from an indoctrination or a superficial reading of these verses. I believe, and I feel that I have proven, that "double honor" means "two wages." The elder receives the first honor already in his current livelihood. Since one who works should be paid, the elders who labor in the Word of God should receive adequate payment—the second honor—for this labor as well. They should be considered worthy of receiving "double honor" for the entirety of their labors.

18. They that Preach the Gospel

Compensation for Evangelists and Missionaries

1 Corinthians 9:13-14

13: Do ye not know that they which minister about holy things live *of the things* of the temple? and they which wait at the altar are partakers with the altar?
14: Even so hath the Lord ordained that they which preach the gospel should live of the gospel.

1 Corinthians 9:13-14 is another passage often cited as an attempt to link the tithe from the Mosaic Law to the New Testament church either as a binding obligation or as an "eternal moral principle." The passage appears to claim that church ministers should receive support in the same way that Levites and priests ministering in the temple received it. Is this passage the "missing link" that proves that God ordained "tithes and offerings" as we understand them by current church tradition?

Before we can answer that question for sure, we need, as always, to examine the context of this passage. We need to define several terms. Who are "they which preach the gospel"? What exactly does "even so" imply? What is the overall emphasis or "principle" invoked in this passage according to context? The answers to these questions will determine if this passage proves the modern monetary income tithe doctrine.

Out with the old and in with the new

Some have argued that this passage means that Paul commanded Christians as from the Law to render the "tithes and offerings" to the functioning of the Gospel ministry as did the nation of Israel for the

385

Levites and priests.[19] The argument from this passage is that though it does not explicitly say so, it **implicitly** states that God ordained "tithes and offerings" for New Testament Gospel ministers as He did Old Testament Levitical ministers.[20] Do New Testament Gospel ministers hold the same "office" or replace the bloodline of the Levites? What were the functions of the Levites and priests, and do New Testament ministers fulfill the same functions?

Thomas Aquinas claimed that "the clergy are the successors of the sons of Levi in the New Testament. Therefore tithes are due to the clergy alone."[21] According to our current understanding of Old Testament theocracy and tithing laws, the descendents of Levi included the priests (the descendents of Aaron) and the Levites (the other descendents of Levi). None of the Levites could own property besides their houses in the Levitical cities (Numbers 35:1-5). They lived in the Levitical cities which were farm communities within the land of the other tribes. The people of the other tribes owned the land, but the Levites resided in the Levitical cities. The Levites could sell their houses, but could not conduct other transactions in property (Leviticus 25:32-34). If the Scriptures link the so-called "clergy" of the

---

19. Lansdell, 171.

20. Davis W. Huckabee, "Tithing: Established by Law" (Lawton, OK: Watchman Press, n.d.).
http://www.pbministries.org/Theology/Davis%20Huckabee/Sermons%20To%20Bap
tist%20Churches/ch22_tithing_established_by_law.htm (accessed December 7, 2009).

21. Thomas Aquinas, "Whether men are bound to pay tithes of all things?," *Summa Theologica, Volume 2*, trans. Fathers of the English Dominican Province (Charleston, SC: BiblioBazaar, 2008), 315.

church to the Levites and priests of the Old Covenant, the "clergy" in parallel should not be allowed to purchase and own property.

Among the so-called "clergy" of the church, which ones fulfill the equivalent of the Levites and which ones conversely perform the functions of their priestly brethren? Professor Dan Moseley makes the following claim: "The Levites are Israel's equivalent of the associate minister. The priest is the senior minister and the Levite is the associate."[22] However, the Scriptures contain no explanation for such an assumption for linking the priests and Levites to New Testament ministers in such a manner to transfer their specific duties and position. Claiming a direct correlation between these physical descendents of Levi with their mediatory roles to positions crafted by modern local churches is purely an imaginary construct. Only **some** of the priests and Levites ministered in the tabernacle or the temple continuously; the other Levites spent most of the year **farming**. When the priests did minister in the temple they performed intercessory sacrifices to God on behalf of the people (Leviticus 14:19-20). Therefore, to argue that so-called "clergy" perform the same role that Old Testament Levites and priests performed would also be to argue that one man, or a conglomeration of men, act as "mediators" between God and Christians. Also, to argue that the "clergy" function as the "sons of Levi" presents a conundrum for the division between priests

---

22. Dan Moseley, *Joyful Giving: Sermons on Stewardship*, ed. (St. Louis, MO: Chalice Press, 1997), 70.

and other Levites. 1 Corinthians 9:13-14 refers to "they which wait at the altar," which **only** the priests could do under penalty of death!

The Scriptures are clear Who the Mediator of the New Testament is: "For *there is* one God, and one mediator between God and men, the man Christ Jesus." (1 Timothy 2:5) The Scriptures are clear Who our Priest is: "Seeing then that we have a great high priest, that is passed into the heavens, Jesus the Son of God, let us hold fast *our* profession. For we have not a high priest which cannot be touched with the feeling of our infirmities; but was in all points tempted like *as we are, yet* without sin." (Hebrews 4:14-15) The Scriptures are clear Who our Advocate is: "My little children, these things write I unto you, that ye sin not. And if any man sin, we have an advocate with the Father, Jesus Christ the righteous." (1 John 2:1) The Scriptures are clear Who is a priest after the order of Melchizedek Who has also eliminated the need for the priesthood of Aaron (Hebrews 7:11-25). The link between "they which wait at the altar" and "they which preach the gospel" clearly is not one of a succession of priesthood, but simply one of a principle of work and reward.

They which preach the gospel

Most often, a sermon reference to 1 Corinthians 9:13-14 derives an implication that "they which preach the gospel" are church elders (or "pastors"). In other words, Paul is mentioning the "clergy." Most often a precursory reading of this passage leads people to believe that pastors who head the church are "they which preach the gospel." In fact, even prolific Christian author Randy Alcorn believes this as he states that "[p]astors are paid to free them for ministry" and then claims 1 Corinthians 9:14 as support.[23] Are church elders indeed what Paul meant? Shall we examine the context?

Paul clearly is referencing **himself** in the phrase "they which preach the gospel." Observe verse 16: "For though <u>I</u> <u>preach the gospel</u>, <u>I</u> have nothing to glory of: for necessity is laid upon me; yea, woe is unto me, if <u>I</u> <u>preach not the gospel</u>!" (1 Corinthians 9:16) In verses 1-6, Paul establishes his power and rights as an **apostle**. In verses 7-14, Paul provides several analogies to prove a point that anyone who labors does so in hopes of a return from the labor. In verses 15-27, Paul declares that he is obligated to labor in the Gospel regardless of if he receives remuneration for the labor.

Because Paul was referencing **himself** as among "they which preach the gospel," was he a church elder? What do elders do? Elders apparently ministered in a church and **stayed** in the church. They were to "feed the flock of God." (1 Peter 5:1-3) They were to "feed the church of God." (Acts 20:28) Were elders specifically "they which preach the gospel" in nominal terms?

To determine who are "they which preach the gospel" we need to examine similar phrases and terms throughout the New Testament and observe their context.

Jesus "<u>went about all Galilee</u>...**preaching the gospel**" (Matthew 4:23)

---

23. Randy Alcorn, *Money, Possessions, and Eternity*, rev. ed. (Wheaton, IL: Tyndale House Publishers, 2003), 247.

⋏ Jesus "went about all the cities and villages...**preaching the gospel**" (Matthew 9:35)

⋏ Jesus declared that "the poor have **the gospel preached** to them" (Matthew 11:5)

⋏ Jesus said that the "**gospel...shall be preached** in all the world" (Matthew 24:14)

⋏ Jesus said that the "**gospel...shall be preached** in the whole world" (Matthew 26:13)

⋏ Jesus "came into Galilee, **preaching the gospel**" (Mark 1:14)

⋏ Jesus said "**the gospel must first be published** among all nations" (Mark 13:10)

⋏ Jesus said that the "**gospel shall be preached** throughout the whole world" (Mark 14:9)

⋏ Jesus told His disciples to "go...into all the world and **preach the gospel**" (Mark 16:15)

⋏ Jesus said that He would "**preach the gospel** to the poor" (Luke 4:18)

⋏ Jesus declared that "to the poor **the gospel is preached**" (Luke 7:22)

⋏ The disciples of Jesus "departed, and went through the towns, **preaching the gospel**" (Luke 9:6)

⋏ Jesus "**preached the gospel**" to the Jews in the temple (Luke 20:1)

⋏ The apostles "**preached the gospel** in many villages of the Samaritans" (Acts 8:25)

⋏ Paul and Barnabus "**preached the gospel**" in Lystra and Derbe (Acts 14:6-7)

390

⅄ Paul and Barnabus "**preached the gospel** to that city [Derbe]" (Acts 14:20-21)

⅄ Peter declared that "the Gentiles... should hear **the word of the gospel**" (Acts 15:7)

⅄ Paul relayed that God had called him to "go into Macedonia...to **preach the gospel** unto them" (Acts 16:10)

⅄ Paul said that he had "gone **preaching the kingdom of God**" (Acts 20:25)

⅄ Paul said that he was "an apostle, separated unto **the gospel of God**" (Romans 1:1)

⅄ Paul spoke of serving "**in the gospel of his Son**" and hoping for "a prosperous journey" (Romans 1:9-10)

⅄ Paul said that he was "ready to **preach the gospel** to you that are at Rome" (Romans 1:15)

⅄ Paul asked "how shall [preachers] **preach**, except they be sent?" He said that their feet are beautiful and that they "**preach the gospel** of peace, and bring glad tidings of good things!"

⅄ Paul said that he was "to the Gentiles, **ministering the gospel of God**" (Romans 15:16)

⅄ Paul declared that "from Jerusalem, and round about unto Illyricum, [he had] fully **preached the gospel of Christ**" (Romans 15:19)

⅄ Paul said that he "strived to **preach the gospel**, not where Christ was named, lest [he] should build upon another man's foundation" (Romans 15:20)

⅄ Paul said that Christ "sent [him]...to **preach the gospel**" (1 Corinthians 1:17)

⅄ Paul said that he "came to Troas to *preach* **Christ's gospel**" (2 Corinthians 2:12)

⅄ Paul said that Titus "whose praise *is* in **the gospel**" was "chosen of the churches to travel with [him]" (2 Corinthians 8:18-19)

⅄ Paul said that he was "come as far as to [the Corinthians] also in *preaching* **the gospel of Christ**" (2 Corinthians 10:14)

⅄ Paul hoped "To **preach the gospel** in the *regions* beyond" the Corinthians (2 Corinthians 10:16)

⅄ Paul warned about someone "that cometh [who] **preacheth another Jesus**" (2 Corinthians 11:4)

⅄ Paul recalled that he "went up by revelation, and communicated unto [Jerusalem] that **gospel which [he preached]** among the Gentiles" (Galatians 2:2)

⅄ Paul said that he "**preached the gospel** unto [the Galatians]" (Galatians 4:13)

⅄ Paul told the Ephesians to have their "feet shod with the preparation of **the gospel of peace**" (Ephesians 6:15)

⅄ Paul said that he was to "open [his] mouth boldly, to make known the mystery of **the gospel**, for which [he was] an ambassador" (Ephesians 6:19-20)

⅄ Paul said that Timothy "hath served with [him] **in the gospel**" (Philippians 2:22)

⚐ Paul declared that "in the beginning of **the gospel** [he] <u>departed from Macedonia</u>" (Philippians 4:15)

⚐ Paul reminded the Colossians of "the truth of **the gospel** which <u>is come unto</u> [them]" (Colossians 1:5-6)

⚐ Paul encouraged the Colossians of "the hope of **the gospel... which was preached** <u>to every creature which is under heaven;</u> whereof <u>[Paul was] made a minister</u>" (Colossians 1:23)

⚐ Paul told the Thessalonians that the "**gospel** <u>came...unto [them]</u> in power, and in the Holy Ghost" (1 Thessalonians 1:5)

⚐ Paul said that the Thessalonians "**sounded out the word of the Lord**...<u>in Macedonia and Achaia</u>" and that their faith "<u>is spread abroad</u>" (1 Thessalonians 1:8)

⚐ Paul reminded the Thessalonians of his "<u>entrance unto</u>" them "to **speak unto [them] the gospel of God**" (1 Thessalonians 2:1-2)

⚐ Paul said that Timothy, who had <u>traveled with him</u>, was "a fellow laborer in **the gospel of Christ**" (1 Thessalonians 3:2)

⚐ The writer of the epistle to the Hebrews declared that "<u>unto us</u> was **the gospel preached**" (Hebrews 4:2)

⚐ Peter reminded the Jewish believers in his epistle about the apostles "that have **preached the gospel** <u>unto [them]</u>" (1 Peter 1:12)

⚐ John in his vision of the Revelation saw an angel have "**the everlasting gospel to preach** <u>unto them that dwell on the earth, and to every nation, and kindred, and tongue, and people</u>" (Revelation 14:6)

From this comprehensive list of verses we can decipher a trend about what "preaching the gospel" meant at that time. Jesus "preached the gospel." He was a traveling evangelist—a missionary. Paul "preached the gospel." He was a traveling evangelist—a missionary. In the context of these passages, "preaching the gospel" meant leaving one's post or home base and delivering it to those who have not heard. Preaching the gospel was associated with being a **traveling minister**. Those who "preach the gospel" are "**sent**." They **"go"** into a region, a city, or a village and "preach the gospel." They **"come"** into a place and "preach the gospel." When the Holy Spirit called Paul and Barnabas to "preach the gospel" He said "Separate me Barnabas and Saul for the work whereunto I have called them." (Acts 13:2) Those who "preach the gospel" are **separated** to a special work. They no longer act as a full-time member of a particular local church. They are **separated** unto a ministry of "preaching the gospel."

Were church elders also "they which preach the gospel"? Apparently the New Testament never refers to the work of a church elder as one who "preaches the gospel." An elder of a church is one who has authority over **the people of God** in church matters. An elder's job is to **feed the flock** and **feed the church**.

The church is the body of **believers** in Christ. One does not "preach the gospel" to believers or to the church. The word translated as "church" in the New Testament is the word *ekklēsia*. This word has sort of a double meaning. One aspect of it means "called out ones." The other aspect of it means "assembly." Properly, a *church* is "an assembly of called out ones." A church is not a building, nor is it a social gathering of believers and non-believers. According to Acts

2:41, those who **believed** and **were baptized** were "added to the church." A local church is properly an assembly of gospel believers, and an elder's role is to teach them the Scriptures to **edify** them in the faith. An elder does not "preach the gospel" to his congregation of gospel believers.

Today, churches have turned the truth on its head. The thrust is now to "invite lost people to church" so that they can hear a "gospel message" from the "pastor." Nowhere can one find this model of ministry in the Bible. The Biblical model is one where the church is foremost an assembly of believers who meet for edification and worship to the God Whom they all believe. The church commissions and **sends** "evangelists" or "missionaries" who "preach the gospel." The people of the church also **go out** into their cities and convert people to the gospel. Once people are converted, then they join the **assembly**. When the gathering of a church itself functions as a place for "preaching the gospel," the saints lose further teaching in the meat of the Word and edifying. They are not further **equipped** in the faith. If churches would follow the model exhibited in the Bible, more people would be bringing the gospel **to** the lost, and the saints would be receiving more grounding in sound doctrine, not merely hearing the baby steps repeated.

Am I saying that only "evangelists" or "missionaries" can "preach the gospel"? Of course not! Stephen, who was a **deacon** (one who served tables in the church) **preached the gospel** to the Jewish religious leaders. All Christians have an obligation to share the gospel with those around them in their vocation. Church elders should likewise share the gospel with those around them in their vocation. However, "preaching the gospel" is not a unique job description for church elders. It is a unique job description for **evangelists** and **missionaries**. Church elders are not what Paul meant in 1 Corinthians 9:14 by "they which preach the gospel." He was referencing himself and those likewise who did the same work that he did—**travel** around and present the gospel to regions beyond.

Even so

Because we have established that "they which preach the gospel" are traveling gospel ministers, we also need to determine what Paul meant concerning the manner in which God has ordained that these people receive their support. Do these traveling ministers receive their support from "tithes"? 1 Corinthians 9:13-14 is the "missing link" passage that provides a last resort for New Testament ministers being the official successors of the Levitical priesthood, and thereby receiving their support through a similar program.

To answer the question of whether traveling ministers receive their support through "tithes," we need to examine several factors. _First_, the passage itself does not state anything about "tithes" **explicitly**; therefore, an inference of a "tithing" structure must be **implicit**. _Second_, verse 13 is not the only statement to compare to verse 14. Verse 7 provides parallel rhetorical questions that reflect the same principle as does verse 13. _Third_, the only **law** that Paul stated was that of not "muzzling an ox." This law is the legal support from which Paul grounds all the comparisons: a soldier receiving support for his war efforts, a husbandman planting a vineyard and expecting to eat the grapes from it, a shepherd expecting to receive sustenance from his flock, and a priest who ministers at the altar eating from the food at the altar.

Paul quoted the same law here to justify support for traveling ministers (like himself) as he did to justify support for church elders. Those who work should receive compensation. The elders should receive the second honor for their secondary labor in the Word of God. The traveling ministers should receive compensation for their ministry of "preaching the gospel." Notice that Paul did not say of the traveling ministers to "count them worthy of double honor." As we established in the previous chapter, the "double honor" or "two honors" for elders were the compensation for both their "secular" vocation and their labor in the Word of God. Since traveling ministers cannot establish themselves in one location to obtain a full-time occupation, their full-time solitary occupation **is** traveling and "preaching the gospel." For this single job, they receive an appropriate "honor" through support from the churches.

Has God ordained that this support come in the form of "tithes"? Jim Voss of the Fundamental Baptist Institute paraphrases 1 Corinthians 9:14 as follows: "As the priests of Israel lived by the tithes of the people, EVEN SO (by the tithes of Christians) God has ordained (appointed) that preachers of the Gospel live [Emphasis in original]."[24] The problem with this assessment is that this paraphrase does not accurately represent the original verse. The verse does not mention **tithes** at all. The supposition is that "even so" implies that as the Levitical priesthood received its support from **tithes**, God has also ordained that "they which preach the gospel" receive their support from **tithes**.

A. W. Pink wrote regarding 1 Corinthians 9:13-14:

> The emphatic words there are, "Even so" in the beginning of the fourteenth verse. The word "tithe" is not found in these two verses but it is most clearly implied. In verse 13 the Holy Spirit reminds the New Testament saints that under the Mosaic economy God had made provision for the maintenance of those who ministered in the temple. Now then, He says, in this New Testament dispensation "Even so" (v. 14)—the same means and the same method are to be used in the support and maintaining of the preachers of the Gospel as were used in supporting the temple and its services of old. "Even so." It was the tithe that supported God's servants in the Old Testament dispensation: "even so" God has ordained, and appointed that His servants in the New Testament dispensation shall be so provided for.[25]

Many weaknesses exist with this precursory understanding of 1 Corinthians 9:13-14. If Paul intended to imply that "they which preach the gospel" receive their support from **tithes**, then the church today is not following the Biblical prescription for tithing. Clearly, Paul was referencing the Mosaic Law in his comparison of the Levitical

---

24. Jim Voss, "WHY I TITHE," Fundamental Baptist Institute, http://www.fbinstitute.com/Voss%20Jim/WHY%20I%20TITHE.htm (accessed December 14, 2009).

25. Arthur W. Pink, *Tithing* (Grand Rapids: Christian Classics Ethereal Library, 2007), 6-7, http://www.ccel.org/ccel/pink/tithing.html.

priesthood (a function of the Law) to traveling ministers. If Paul was linking the tithes **according to the Law** regarding support for the Levitical priesthood to the traveling ministers, then the church is not following the Biblical mandate for the system in which God prescribed tithing. Several points of examination can hold Pink's "the same means and the same method" contention to the fire to determine if he properly understood what Biblical **tithes** were.

First, the tithes that went to the Temple were not a full tithe of the people of Israel. The people brought their tithe to the Levitical cities (Nehemiah 10:37), and the Levites brought one tenth of their tithes to the priests. Only a small portion of the Levitical and priestly tithes went weekly to the Temple storehouse (Nehemiah 12:44). If the church is indeed the storehouse—which it is not—and church members fulfill the same role as the people of Israel, only one hundredth **maximum**— not one tenth—should actually go into the church. Otherwise, if the local church represents the local community bins for the Levites and poor—which they do not—a full tithe would go into the local church every third and sixth years in a seven-year cycle. Either way, no valid Scriptural support exists for a full tithe to go into the place of ministry at all times.

Second, tithes were always **only** of the crops grown and livestock raised within the boundaries of the land of Israel. Tithes were not of money. Money was only in reference to tithing if one wanted to redeem the tithe of the crops for their value plus 20%, or for the annual feasts if one needed an easier medium in which to carry the tithes of food to God's chosen location. If "even so" implies "tithes" and "they which preach the gospel" receive their support by "the same means and the same method," then the church must support traveling ministers with food, and this food must come from the boundaries of the nation of Israel (Deuteronomy 12:1-11).

Third, these tithes of food came in an intricate seven-year cycle. Every first, second, fourth, and fifth years out of every seven, those who tithed came to the place of God's choosing, brought a second tithe, and **ate their own tithes**. While the families ate their own tithes, the Levites could receive sustenance by the people sharing it with them. If "even so" implies "tithes" and "they which preach the gospel" receive their support by "the same means and the same method," then the church must host feasts every first, second, fourth, and fifth years out of seven years in a place where they know God has approved, and the traveling ministers must go to this place if they wish to partake of the tithes. They would not receive the whole tithes, but would only get what the tithers shared with them in the feast.

Fourth, every third and sixth years in the seven-year cycle the second tithes of food were wholly given away. In fact, the people of Israel were commanded to give these tithes to the Levites and poor. The people would deposit these third-year tithes in local communities for the Levites and poor to eat as needed. These tithes did not go to the Temple storehouse, but to "local storehouses." If "even so" implies "tithes" and "they which preach the gospel" receive their support by "the same means and the same method," then the church members who

400

own land in Israel must give these second tithes of food wholly away every third and sixth years in a seven-year cycle. The traveling ministers would also have to accept having the poor in the land glean from the same trough.

Fifth, every seventh year was a Sabbatical year. In this year was no "year of tithing." In this year, **no one tithed**. If "even so" implies "tithes" and "they which preach the gospel" receive their support by "the same means and the same method," then the traveling ministers would have to understand that they would not receive tithes every seventh year. The sixth year tithes would have to be sufficient to sustain them for the seventh year.

Sixth, the tithe laws in the Mosaic Law did not stand on their own. They were part and parcel of other laws. The tithing laws were intertwined with dietary laws (Deuteronomy 12 and 14). Ceremonially unclean people could not eat in the congregation at any other time, but during the tithe feasts they could eat the animals, provided that they did not eat the blood. The tithing laws were also intertwined with a seven-year cycle that involved releasing debts and freeing servants (Deuteronomy 15). If "even so" implies "tithes" and "they which preach the gospel" receive their support by "the same means and the same method," then would not other laws in the Torah necessarily apply? Where is the justification for changing the tithe laws in the Mosaic Law to one of wholly giving away a tenth of **all monetary income** at all times and ignoring the specifics of the Law? If the support for traveling ministers is "the same means and the same method" as that for the Levitical priesthood, then how does one justify totally changing the terms of the law and cherry-picking what applies and what does not? Either the support is "the same means and the same method" or it is not. Obviously, Paul was not referring to **tithing** in particular; otherwise, the church today is in trouble for disobeying God's commands in the Law.

If Paul was not referring to **tithing** in 1 Corinthians 9:13-14, what did he mean? Several verses in context can shed light on what he truly meant, and why he neither stated nor implied "tithes."

1 Corinthians 9:7-12

7: Who goeth a warfare any time at his own charges? who planteth a vineyard, and eateth not of the fruit thereof? or who feedeth a flock, and eateth not of the milk of the flock?

8: Say I these things as a man? or saith not the law the same also?

9: For it is written in the law of Moses, Thou shalt not muzzle the mouth of the ox that treadeth out the corn. Doth God take care for oxen?

10: Or saith he *it* altogether for our sakes? For our sakes, no doubt, *this* is written: that he that ploweth should plow in hope; and that he that thresheth in hope should be partaker of his hope.

11: If we have sown unto you spiritual things, *is it* a great thing if we shall reap your carnal things?

12: If others be partakers of *this* power over you, *are* not we rather? Nevertheless we have not used this power; but suffer all things, lest we should hinder the gospel of Christ.

Paul's message in this chapter appears to be that one who labors in a venue has just expectations to receive remuneration from the same venue. If one goes to war by commission from authority, that person should justly expect to receive support for the endeavor rather than have to fight in the war and pay for all the effort from that person's own capital. One who plants a vineyard expects to care for the vine so that one can eat the fruits of the labor. One who owns and cares for sheep expects to obtain some benefit from the sheep and not simply do so for no return.

Paul defends his message with the Law of labor and reward. God forbade the Israelites from using oxen as slave labor by muzzling their mouths as they worked. To compensate oxen for "treading out the corn," the Israelites would allow them to eat the corn as they worked. Since God cares for oxen, how much more does God care for His ministers? Even the oxen fed from the same venue in which they labored. Even so, a traveling minister should also obtain support from the same venue: the churches that send them out. Who goes to war at his own charges? Who goes to the mission field at his own charges?

Those who plow and those who thresh do so in the hope that these labors will produce a crop that they can enjoy. Their labor earned their food. Now, since Paul as a traveling minister was not working in a carnally productive vocation, "preaching the gospel" would not literally produce food as a return. However, since the people to whom Paul wrote became believers in the gospel through his work in the ministry, for them to repay his spiritual labor in them with physical sustenance was certainly not unreasonable.

Given these analogies to provide the trust of Paul's message, these, along with the analogy of the priesthood in the temple in verse 13, serve to clarify what Paul meant in verse 14. "Even so" does not mean "tithes." "Even so" means the principle of sowing and reaping. God has ordained that "they which preach the gospel" should receive physical sustenance from those who receive the spiritual ministry. As the priests ministering in the temple received sustenance from the people to whom they ministered, "even so" the traveling gospel ministers should receive sustenance from the churches to whom they minister. Paul's message had nothing to do with "tithes" because of the nature of tithes in the law, but rather in the general sense of labor and return and in sowing and reaping. As a scholar of the Law, a student of Gamaliel, and a former Pharisee, Paul intimately understood the tithe laws and had no intention of communicating a "tithe" requirement in 1 Corinthians 9:13-14.

Conclusion and summary

In conclusion, we see that 1 Corinthians 9:13-14 fails as a proof text for New Testament tithing. This text is not about "tithes" for "pastors" or church elders. As Paul was the writer and referred to himself, this text is about traveling ministers. We saw from many other passages in the New Testament that "they which preach the gospel" is a clear reference to evangelists or missionaries—those who travel and preach the gospel. We saw that this passage could not mean that traveling ministers receive their sustenance in the form of "tithes" and that "even so" could not mean "in the same means and the same method" because the specifics of the Law would preclude such an assumption when taken to their full evaluation. 1 Corinthians 9:13-14 in context is part of the whole chapter that teaches the principles of reward from labor and reaping from sowing.

SECTION VI: EPILOGUE

Truth or Tradition

We have examined every text in the Bible that mentions laws, practices, and customs regarding tithes. We have analyzed every known passage taken to imply tithing for the realm of the church. We have scrutinized both the Old and New Testaments. Unless God is in the business of inspiring works other than the Bible, we simply have found no Biblical proof for the modern monetary income tithe doctrine.

How can it be, then, that so many churches that claim to believe the Bible teach a doctrine that the Bible itself never presents in any remotely similar form? Many intelligent pastors and theologians preach the modern church tithing doctrine and other, more fundamental doctrines, such as salvation by grace through faith, with equal zeal. If the former doctrine is not Biblically correct, what exactly went wrong?

Understand that no one believes or teaches anything in a vacuum. One believes something because one receives an influx of **information** and digests it according to nature, desires, logic, and existing information. Many people believe something specifically because they were **taught** such by someone else, whether a parent, a pastor, a professor, or a politician. This person, in turn, may have been taught the same information from previous lips. The effect, then, is that some beliefs are not based completely on closely examining facts and evidence firsthand, but rather on the propagation of **tradition**.

The longer tradition is transposed down the chain of people and time the more likely people will assume it to be true by an article of faith. Then, instead of examining the tradition according to the data available, one uses the tradition itself as the lens to examine the data. This problem is evident with the modern monetary income tithe doctrine. One finds "proof" for the doctrine in the Bible by gleaning isolated verses that merely mention any form of the word *tithe*. One already approaches the text with an assumption about what "tithing" must mean, and injects this assumption into the text of the Bible.

The question then, is what is the primary source of the tradition of the modern understanding of Biblical tithing? Can we find the origin of the tradition and trace its development over time? Is it possible to run a successful church ministry without teaching the modern tithe doctrine? This section attempts to demonstrate a brief, but accurate history of the idea of tithes in the history of the church. This study will begin with the completion of the Biblical canon in the first century A.D. to the present. We will then attempt to explore several fundraising tactics and principles for a church with a proper focus and emphasis on grace and the leading of the Holy Spirit.

19. The Early Church

How We Got Where We Are

The first century—the Apostles in Scripture

If one were to thumb through the pages of the writings of the early church, one would be hard pressed to find much, if anything, regarding tithes in the context of the church. In fact, such an idea did not appear to take hold in history until the fourth century, A.D.[1] During the time of the Apostles, no mention is made of tithing as a command for the church. In previous chapters of this book we have examined the faulty claims that certain texts **implicitly** teach the doctrine. These claims were simply wishful thinking from the bias of the doctrine itself.

Giving to meet needs was prevalent and abundant. People sold expensive assets and used the funds to meet needs (Acts 2:44-45). Churches took up collections to relieve the famine in Jerusalem. The Apostles instructed members of the church to give cheerfully (2 Corinthians 9:7), compassionately (1 John 3:17), proportionately (1 Corinthians 16:2), and laboriously (Acts 20:35), but not from compulsion (2 Corinthians 9:7). They were to give to enemies (Romans 12:20-21), lovingly to the poor (1 Corinthians 13:3), to the saints (1 Corinthians 16:1), to the needy (Ephesians 4:28), and to destitute brothers and sisters (James 2:15-16). The attitude of the early church, the direction of the Apostles, and the leading of the Holy Spirit

---

1. Sir William Smith and Samuel Cheetham, eds., *A Dictionary of Christian Antiquities* (Hartford: The J. B. Burr Publishing Company, 1880), s.v. "tithes."

appeared to be targeting all needs of believers and ensuring that they are met. The Apostles acted as a distribution center and clearinghouse for gifts and aid, but not as a collection agency that formed a budget at their own discretion.

Luke 10:4-7

4: <u>Carry neither purse</u> [for money], <u>nor scrip</u> [for food], nor shoes: and salute no man by the way.
5: And into whatsoever house ye enter, first say, Peace *be* to this house.
6: And if the son of peace be there, your peace shall rest upon it: if not, it shall turn to you again.
7: And in the same house remain, <u>eating and drinking such things as they give: for the labourer is worthy of his hire</u>. Go not from house to house.

When Jesus first commissioned the twelve disciples and the seventy disciples, He told them not to take anything with them that would function in the marketplace. Jesus referenced the Law of compensating a laborer, but in this context it was that of being fed directly in a house that received a disciple. Jesus did not tell the disciples to administer collections from saints to raise their own support. He told them that their support would come from the hospitality of those who would provide them food and shelter on their journey. In other words, in the original commission, Jesus did not instruct the disciples to raise funds from people and budget them at their discretion; He told them that their needs would be met **directly**.

Luke 22:35

35: And he said unto them, When I sent you without purse, and scrip, and shoes, lacked ye any thing? And they said, Nothing.

Although the disciples likely felt uneasy at the original instructions of Jesus regarding their preliminary Gospel ministry, He probed them about their success. They admitted that they lacked nothing under His terms. Am I suggesting that this original commission applies to ministers of the church today? No! However, the instructions of Jesus to these early disciples demonstrate that the purpose of the Gospel ministry and the church itself is not meant to be any form of enterprise or business. Neither the earthly ministry of Jesus, nor the history of the early church in the Acts of the Apostles, nor the instructions in the epistles illustrate the church as an organization whose purpose is to raise funds from members through coercion like a business and use them to build an empire or establish glamorous real estate in the eyes of the secular world. The church is not about impressive assets, buildings, and attractions; it is about genuine members, a mission, and a message.

Acts 20:33-35

33: <u>I have coveted no man's silver, or gold, or apparel</u>.
34: Yea, ye yourselves know, that <u>these hands have ministered unto my necessities, and to them that were with me</u>.
35: I have shewed you all things, how that <u>so labouring ye ought to support the weak</u>, and to remember the words of the Lord Jesus, how he said, <u>It is more blessed to give than to receive</u>.

When the Apostle Paul spoke to the elders at the church of Ephesus, he gave them instructions that many church elders today often disregard. He told them that he "coveted no man's silver or gold." How many today who teach the Biblically incorrect modern monetary income tithe doctrine can confess this same statement?

Although certainly many ministers are ones of integrity and honestly preach what they believe out of ignorance, other dishonest ones will hide the fact that they truly covet this "silver and gold" and fear personal discomfort if their church's "tithes and offerings" were to decline or fail. They hide this fear under the garb of religious piety and would rather their congregation fear a curse from God for not "tithing" even in abject poverty to prevent any disruptions to the current empire and the parameters of their salaries. When many church ministers quote Paul's words "It is more blessed to give than to receive," they most often present them to the congregation as a provocation for "offerings" to the church budget rather than in their original context of a commission to the **elders** to labor with their hands to support others.

The Apostle Paul spoke about the fact that his "hands have ministered unto [his] necessities, AND to them that were with [him]." In other words, He supported himself **and others** with his own hands. He did not follow with a statement such as "Men, and brethren, these things ought not be so!" He commissioned the **elders** at Ephesus to do the same as he and "to support the weak." As chapter 17 of this book explained, church elders functioned just as other members of the church did—they worked secular jobs and earned a living from it. Paul told the members of the church to compensate elders who labored in the Word and doctrine, meaning that elders who performed this "second job" should receive compensation for this, as well.

Chapters 17 and 18 of this book also explained the difference between elders and evangelists (or missionaries). Elders would live in a location just as other church members and would "feed the flock of God." Evangelists and missionaries would travel and "preach the Gospel." These "Gospel preachers" should receive adequate compensation to deal with their travel expenses and such, but could also find themselves doing additional manual labor in the mission field.

The first century—Jewish Christians before A.D. 70

The question of whether any early Christians practiced tithing is mostly a question of the nationality or religious leaning of these early Christians. No doubt, some of the early Christians **did**, in fact, practice tithing. The ones who practiced tithing were mostly Jewish Christians.

Galatians 2:11-14

11: But when Peter was come to Antioch, I withstood him to the face, because he was to be blamed.
12: For before that certain came from James, he did eat with the Gentiles: but when they were come, he withdrew and separated himself, fearing them which were of the circumcision.
13: And the other Jews dissembled likewise with him; insomuch that Barnabas also was carried away with their dissimulation.
14: But when I saw that they walked not uprightly according to the truth of the gospel, I said unto Peter before *them* all, If thou, being a Jew, livest after the manner of Gentiles, and not as do the Jews, why compellest thou the Gentiles to live as do the Jews?

Peter the Apostle lapsed for a time into fear of persecution from the religious leaders of his own kin. He began to teach Gentiles to live according to the Jewish laws and customs. These would include regulations from the Torah and any extra regulations added at the time such as those from the Mishnah. Undoubtedly Peter taught Gentile landowners to tithe of their produce and herds. However, no evidence

411

exists of any Apostles telling people to give tithes to the church; any Gentile converts to Judaism or Jewish-compelled Christianity would have been instructed to deliver appropriate tithes to the Levitical cities for the Levites.

The Apostle Paul learned of Peter's double standard and harshly corrected him. Paul did not tell Peter to tell his converts to switch their tithes from the Levitical cities or the Temple to a local church assembly. He did not tell him to teach tithes of monetary income instead of agricultural increase. He told him to stop teaching the Gentiles to live as the Jews.

The writer to the Hebrews faced a similar problem as Paul did. Many Jews who converted to Christianity did not understand the effects of the work of Messiah on the Temple system and the Levitical priesthood. The writer to the Hebrews explained the Jesus Christ was superior to angels, to Moses, to Abraham, to the Levitical priesthood, and to the Law. His high priestly sacrifice of Himself did what the Law could not do—permanently cover sins. His sacrifice was once for all time; therefore, His sacrifice eliminated the need of a perpetually functioning earthly priesthood supported by tithes. He is a priest forever after the order of Melchizedek, and Abraham's one-time tithe to this order validated the priestly nature of Christ's one-time sacrifice.

In a real sense the epistle to the Hebrews was prophetic. Being written before the destruction of the Temple, the epistle invalidated the operating ministry of the Levitical priesthood before the destruction of the Temple itself did shortly thereafter. Jesus, the Messiah Himself

Who predicted the utter destruction of the Temple that would end the Levitical priesthood performed the work necessary that would make it irrelevant. Thus, the legal reign of the Mosaic Law ended at Christ's resurrection, but He slammed the door shut to all rational temptation in A.D. 70. Those who taught tithing taught it in the context of Judaism or adherence to the Mosaic Law, and not as a practicum of the Christian church itself.

The evidence of the lack of "tithes" as a practice for the early Christian church is not buried in caves or hidden in volumes of antiquity. Modern theologians and historians who examine the history of this period discover the truth of the origin of the modern concept of "tithing." Henry Clarke states concerning the church of the first century: "Those who preached the Gospel lived by the Gospel, but this Scriptural statement did not mean, as some assert, that they were to live on the payment of tithes, otherwise it would have been stated."[2] Chapters 17 and 18 of this book deconstructed the arguments similar to those that Clarke addressed that certain New Testament passages claim a link to the Old Testament tithes for funding church ministers. Clarke continues: "The Jewish Law, as regards the payment of tithes, was not binding on Christians, no more than the custom of bigamy and polygamy adopted by the Israelites is binding on the Christian

---

2. Clarke, *A History of Tithes*, 4.

church."[3] Clarke then states emphatically: "There is no injunction in the New Testament binding Christians to pay tithes to their ministers."[4]

The first century—early church voices

In the first century, Jewish and Christian historians lived during the time of the apostolic church to record historical events and teachings. Surely if the sprouting Christian church practiced a form of "tithing" these historians would have recorded such ordinances.

Josephus, an early Jewish historian, lived during the period of the early church (A.D. 37-100). Of the known works of Josephus, the only references to tithes are of those found in the Law as a matter of history.[5] He made no mention of tithes in the context of the Christian church or of the New Covenant in any respect, and neither did he derive an "application" whatsoever.

Clement of Rome was a bishop in the early Roman Christian church. His birth is unknown, but he died around A.D. 101. Around A.D. 95 he wrote two epistles to the Corinthian church. Concerning Christian charity, he wrote: "Let the rich man provide for the wants of the poor; and let the poor man bless God, because He hath given him

---

3. Ibid.
4. Ibid.
5. See Flavius Josephus, *Josephus: The Complete Works*, trans. William Whiston (Nashville: Thomas Nelson, 1998). Josephus records regulations of the Levitical tithe in *Antiquities* 4.4.3, the tithe of the Levites to the priests in *Antiquities* 4.4.4, and the reforms of King Hezekiah in *Antiquities* 9.13.3. Not once in any of his recorded works did he extract anything from the tithes mentioned in the Old or New Testaments to the context of the church.

one by whom his need may be supplied."[6] In one instance he compared the offerings of the Law to services that God commissioned people to do in the context of the church. Of these, he encouraged to be performed "not thoughtlessly or irregularly, but at the appointed times and hours;"[7] however, each person was to "give thanks to God in his own order."[8] He contrasted this with "the daily sacrifices offered, or the peace-offerings, or the sin-offerings and the trespass-offerings... [that were] in Jerusalem only."[9] Not once in Clement's available writings did he ever mention "tithes."

Ignatius of Antioch was a bishop in the church of Antioch and a disciple of the Apostle John. Ignatius was harshly critical of Judaism and attempts to bind Christians to the regulations of the Torah. In his Epistle to the Philadelphians, he declared that "if any one preach the Jewish law unto you, listen not to him."[10] Similarly, in his Epistle to the Magnesians, he asserted that "if we still live according to the Jewish law, we acknowledge that we have not received grace."[11] Ignatius says nothing about "tithes" or the like in any of his **twenty epistles**.

Barnabas of Alexandria (most likely not the same Barnabas who traveled with the Apostle Paul) was a Jewish Christian who wrote an

---

6. Philip Schaff, *ANF01. The Apostolic Fathers with Justin Martyr and Irenaeus* (Grand Rapids: Christian Classics Ethereal Library, 2002), 29.
7. Ibid., 31.
8. Ibid.
9. Ibid.
10. Ibid., 135.
11. Ibid., 104.

epistle around A.D. 100 staunchly to warn Christian converts about Judaism. Barnabas spoke concerning the Law: "For He hath revealed to us by all the prophets that He needs neither sacrifices, nor burnt-offerings, nor oblations... He has therefore abolished these things, that the new law of our Lord Jesus Christ, which is without the yoke of necessity, might have a human oblation. [Emphasis added]"[12] Not once in the Epistle of Barnabus is any mention of "tithes."

The second century—the early "church fathers"

Mathetes (meaning "disciple") was an anonymous early church apologist who wrote an epistle to "Diognetus" in A.D. 130. In this epistle he noted that "the Christians do not observe the same forms of divine worship as do the Jews."[13] Contrasting the "madness" of Gentile Christian generosity, he observed that the Jews were "thinking to offer these things to God as if he needed them."[14] These Gentile Christians "are poor, yet make many rich; they are in lack of all things, and yet abound in all," possibly referencing 2 Corinthians 6:10.[15] Mathetes makes no reference to "tithes" or the like.

Polycarp was a bishop in Smyrna who lived from about A.D. 69 to 155 and was a disciple of the Apostle John. The Apostle John said concerning giving: "But whoso hath this world's good, and seeth his brother have need, and shutteth up his bowels *of compassion* from

---

12. Ibid., 212.
13. Ibid., 46.
14. Ibid.
15. Ibid., 48.

him, how dwelleth the love of God in him?" (1 John 3:17). The Apostle John never mentioned anything to do with tithing in his writings included in the Biblical canon. Likewise, nothing exists in any of Polycarp's writings that mentions tithing.

Justin Martyr was a Christian apologist who lived from A.D. 100 to 165. Not once did he extol the practice of tithes as a church command. In one place he records the statement of Jesus to the Pharisees concerning their "tithe of mint and rue" only within the context of blasting their hypocrisy and making a mockery of God.[16] Next, he references the tithes of Abraham to Melchizedek only within the context of circumcision as unnecessary for Christians.[17] Third, he mentions again Abraham's tithe to Melchizedek in the context of circumcision being unnecessary for the church and Hezekiah not being a priest.[18] Finally, he references the tithes of the Pharisees again when accusing them of ignoring the prophets and the Law.[19] These four times are the only times that Justin Martyr mentions anything to do with "tithes" in all his writings.

Irenaeus was a bishop in Gaul who lived from about A.D. 115 to 202 and was a disciple of Polycarp. Irenaeus stated concerning Christ and the Law that "instead of the law enjoining the giving of tithes, [He told us] to share all our possessions with the poor."[20] This statement

---

16. Ibid., 320.
17. Ibid., 321-322.
18. Ibid., 334.
19. Ibid., 415.
20. Ibid., 797.

references Jesus' admonition to the rich young ruler to sell all that he had and give to the poor. It also reflects the voluntary practice of the church in the Acts of the Apostles.

Irenaeus continued:

"And for this reason they (the Jews) had indeed the tithes of their goods consecrated to Him, but those who have received liberty set aside all their possessions for the Lord's purposes, bestowing joyfully and freely not the less valuable portions of their property, since they have the hope of better things [hereafter]; as that poor widow acted who cast all her living into the treasury of God."

Some church tithing advocates will emphasize the words "not the less valuable portions" and infer that Irenaeus was claiming that "tithing" was hence "the minimal standard." However, "those who have received liberty" who do this "freely" nullifies this loose inference. Irenaeus was not claiming a "minimal" command to tithe, but was merely stating that the liberal practice of the early Christian church resulted in giving whose total material value exceeded that which would have occurred had the tithes of the Law been an established ordinance for the church. How many church tithing advocates using this statement to defend their teaching would allow the statement itself its full value and practice "set[ting] aside all their possessions"? Not once in any of the writings of Irenaeus did he extract anything about tithes from the Bible as a command for the church. Rather, the voluntary practice of "those who have received liberty" should give generously and abundantly.

The "Pastor of Hermas" is an unknown second-century parable book with disputed authorship. This book contains admonitions to generosity such as the following: "Give heed, therefore, ye who glory in your wealth, lest those who are needy should groan, and their groans should ascend to the Lord."[21] No mention is made of "tithes."

Tatian was an Assyrian Christian writer who lived from about A.D. 110 to 180. His major known writings are his *Address to the Greeks*—a treatise attacking Greek paganism—and his *Diatessaron*—a harmony account of the four gospels. The only mentions of "tithes" in his known writings are twice in the *Diatessaron*: once recording Jesus' parable of the Pharisee[22] and the publican and the other recording Jesus' woes on the religious leaders.[23]

Tertullian, a Christian writer who lived from about A.D. 160 to 220, was the first to introduce such writings originally in Latin; the previous writings up to this point were mostly in Greek and translated into Latin. For this reason Tertullian is known as "the father of Latin Christianity." He mentions "tithes" in X contexts. First, he ridicules

---

21. Philip Schaff, *ANF02. Fathers of the Second Century: Hermas, Tatian, Athenagoras, Theophilus, and Clement of Alexandria (Entire)* (Grand Rapids: Christian Classics Ethereal Library, 2004), 23.

22. Ernest Cushing Richardson and Bernhard Pick, *The Ante-Nicene Fathers: The Gospel of Peter, The Dietessaron of Tatian, The Apocalypse of Peter, The Visio Pauli, The Apocalypses of the Virgin and Sedrach, The Testament of Abraham, The Acts of Xanthippe and Polyxena, The Narrative of Zosimus, The Apology of Aristides, The Epistles of Clement (Complete Text), Origen's Commentary on John, Books I-X, and Commentary on Matthew, Books I, II, and X-XI*, vol 9 of *The Ante-Nicene Fathers: Translations of the Writings of the Fathers Down to A.D. 325*, ed. Alexander Roberts, Sir James Donaldson, Arthur Cleveland Coxe, and Allan Menzies (New York: Charles Scribner's Sons, 1903), 93.

23. Ibid., 105.

the pagan Greeks with "the tithe of Hercules" as an example.[24] Second, he references the Pharisees who were "tithing paltry herbs," but strictly in the context of them repressing the people with their religious hypocrisy.[25] Third, he recalls Christ as Priest after the order of Melchizedek, but extracts no application from Abraham's tithe to Melchizedek.[26] Not once did Tertullian ever instruct the church directly to practice "tithing."

Some assume that Tertullian **indirectly** referenced tithing when he said of the offerings of Cain and Abel: "He [God] accepted what he [Abel] was offering in simplicity of heart, and reprobated the sacrifice of his brother Cain, who was not <u>rightly dividing</u> what he was offering."[27] The assumption is that Cain did not "rightly divide" a "tithe" and was rejected for not giving enough.

Several problems exist with the interpretation. First, the wording says nothing about a "tithe" as assumed. Second, the context of this statement is in Tertullian's argument that Jews no longer have an obligation to practice circumcision or to observe the Sabbath. Third, "rightly dividing what he was offering" can refer to quality rather than quantity. If the rejection of Cain's offering had nothing to do with blood atonement, it most certainly could have to do with Cain not giving to God quality produce. Abel by faith offered "of the <u>firstlings</u>

---

24. Philip Schaff, *ANF03. Latin Christianity: Its Founder, Tertullian*, ed. Allan Menzies (Grand Rapids: Christian Classics Ethereal Library, 2006), 41.
25. Ibid., 670-672.
26. Ibid., 771-773.
27. Ibid., 242.

of his flock" (Genesis 4:4), whereas Cain offered "of the fruit of the ground" (Genesis 4:3). No mention is made about whether Cain's offering represented **firstfruits**. He likely did not give the first and best as a reflection of the later laws of **firstfruits**. Chapter 7 of this book clearly explained the difference between firstfruits and tithes, and no real proof exists that Tertullian was speaking of "tithes" in the context of Cain's offering.

Clement of Alexandria was a Christian theologian in Alexandria, Egypt who lived from about A.D. 150 to 215. He was a teacher of Origen and began to introduce Platonic Greek philosophies and gnosticism into his Christian theology. He mentions the "first-fruits and tithes" from an inscription on a statue to the Greek god Apollos[28] and the historical "tithes," "sacrifices," and "pascal feast" of the Jews.[29] He mentions the Old Testament commands of tithes, firstfruits, Sabbaths for the land, and Jubilee. Concluding from these regulations, he states: "We now therefore understand that we are instructed in piety, and in liberality, and in justice, and in humanity by the law."[30] In no instance does Clement suggest that Christians have the same obligations—only that the Law expresses humanitarian moral "gnosis" from God. Many Christian purists today would be logically hard pressed to regard a gnostic such as Clement of Alexandria as a defender of the Christian faith.

---

28. Ibid., 552-553.
29. Ibid., 588.
30. Ibid., 601.

The third century—the seeds of the Catholic tree

The first and second centuries are entirely absent of any reasonable defense of the modern idea of an obligation to tithe of one's monetary income to the church. Those who would glean such insight from this earlier period would be scraping the bottom of the barrel for hidden treasure. One sees what one desires to see, and discovering anything remotely resembling a teaching of "tithing" for the church requires that one already assume such a teaching and wear rose-colored glasses to see specificity where there only exists ambiguity.

Toward the end of the third century the seeds begin to be planted toward creating a state-run church. Notably, it is here also that the seeds of the church tithing doctrine begin to make their way into the same soil. Coincidence? Is there a direct, but subtle connection between the origin of the church tithing doctrine and efforts to form the church into a state religion? Are tithes *always* a function of government taxation whether the government is "religious" or not?

According to church historian Edward Blackhouse, "to... the third and fourth centuries, may possibly be referred the origin of tithes."[31] This teaching, however, did not start to develop until late in the third century. Church leaders, theologians, and writers were beginning to forsake the virtues of local, separate assemblies and wanted to unite the church under a central leadership. Perhaps persecution had led to this desire to consolidate. Naturally, if the church expected to

---

31. Edward Blackhouse, *Early Church History: To the Death of Constantine*, 6th ed., ed. Charles Tylor (London: Headley Brothers, 1906), 235.

centralize its influence, it would also need to centralize its form of funding.

Origen was a Greek and Hebrew scholar and a teacher in Alexandria, Egypt. He lived from about A.D. 185 to 254. Taking gnostic doctrine from his mentor Clement of Alexandria, he further developed this approach to theology and Scripture. Although he wrote commentaries on most of the Bible, he maintained an allegorical approach to interpretation over a literal one. He even introduced a form of reincarnation into his Christian theology.

Despite Origen's outright heresy, he never taught "tithes" as a church ordinance. The closest one could *infer* from Origen comes from his trademark allegorical approach to the Scriptures where he treated Christianity as "the spiritual Israel" and that the church leaders can "be called our levites and priests."[32] Otherwise, Origen only taught Christian generosity in general.

Cyprian was a third-century Christian writer who converted to the current form of Christianity from paganism. He eventually became bishop of Carthage, although the election for this position was disputed. During this time in the third century church leaders became more sheltered from secular activities to perform "ministry." Cyprian saw the church "clergy" as people who needed to shield themselves totally from the world. Cyprian began to draw closer correlations between the church "clergy" and the Levitical priesthood than that of the "spiritual" correlation of Origen. He matched church "bishop" with

---

32. Richardson and Pick, 298.

high priest, "elder" or "presbyter" with other priest, and "deacon" with Levite.[33] He asserted that the "clergy" should not be "tied down by worldly anxieties and matters; but in the honour of the brethren who contribute, <u>receiving as it were tenths of the fruits</u>, they may not withdraw from the altars and sacrifices, but may serve day and night in heavenly and spiritual things. [Emphasis added]"[34] The words "as it were" can indicate that the "clergy" at the time were not really receiving "tithes" but were receiving compensation for their religious studies in a similar fashion.

What Cyprian did not understand was that neither the Levites nor the priests ministered full-time in the Temple. They lived in allotted cities throughout the nation of Israel. They were not all teachers of the Law. Cyprian was reading the current evolution of the church—whether or not it actually resembled the apostolic version—into the Scriptures themselves.

Cyprian's assertion that the "clergy" receive "as it were" tithes is not a definite proof of actual early church "tithing" at this time, but his statement planted the seeds from which the fruit of this doctrine grew later. Cyprian's statement did not yet represent the teaching of a unified church—only that from the area of which he had influence through his office.[35] Another problem with using Cyprian's teaching as

---

33. Kelly, 255.
34. Philip Schaff, *ANF05. Fathers of the Third Century: Hippolytus, Cyprian, Caius, Novatian, Appendix* (Grand Rapids: Christian Classics Ethereal Library, 2004), 650.
35. Kelly, 255.

proof of early church "tithing" is that Cyprian also taught and practiced the current idea of asceticism in church leadership, instructing fellow "clergy" to care for the poor and keep their material possessions to a minimum.[36]

Conclusion and summary

In conclusion, we have examined the teachings of the Apostles in the canon of Scripture and the historic example of the generosity of the early church. We have seen that these Apostles did not teach any type of tithing obligation for the church and did not carry any related laws from the Torah. Paul rebuked Peter when he tried to teach that the Gentiles had to obey Jewish laws.

Early church Jewish historian Josephus did not teach tithing. First century church fathers Clement of Rome, Ignatius of Antioch, and Barnabas of Alexandria did not teach tithing, but encouraged cheerful, voluntary, and abundant giving. They also taught, as did their Apostle mentors, that the Mosaic Law was not binding on Gentile Christians. Jesus had done away with the Law.

Second century church fathers did not teach tithing either. Mathetes contrasted the generosity of the Gentile Christians with the Jewish sacrifices. Polycarp, a disciple of the Apostle John did not teach tithing just as his teacher did not. Justin Martyr only referenced tithes with respect to Jewish hypocrisy and was staunchly against requiring Christians to follow the Mosaic Law. Some attempt to quote a statement from Irenaeus to support Christian tithing, yet his

---

36. Ibid.

statement really expresses Christian stewardship in everything rather than a mandate to tithe. As Gnosticism arose in the second century, the closest one could infer tithe teaching from those church fathers who dabbled in gnosticism involves their spiritualizing the Old Testament.

Only until the third century did the roots for the modern tithing doctrine begin. These roots formed as church leaders attempted to expand their power and influence. Cyprian is the primary one who introduced that concept that the church leaders were similar in function to the Levites and priests and that they should receive regular donations "as it were the tenths of the fruits." Despite these late teachings, the so-called "clergy" were supposed to live virtually in poverty and to give what they received generously to the poor. During this time the idea of wealthy church leaders increasing their own personal estates would have been taboo.

The fact that none of the Apostles and none of their personal students taught any kind of tithing duties for Christians proves that the Scriptures themselves never instructs Christians so to do. The fact also that sparse roots for such a doctrine arose as late as the latter third century demonstrates that this doctrine itself is far removed from the original Scriptures. The idea of a church tithe has a correlation to the idea of a state religion because the Mosaic Law itself existed as a code of laws for a theocracy.

20. The Reign of the Church-State

Blessed be the Tithe that Binds

The fourth century—an emerging state religion

The third century planted trace seeds of the church tithing doctrine that quickly produced fruit in the fourth century. The fourth century saw the official beginning of the Catholic Church as a state religion and consequent teachings of "tithes" for the church "clergy." The correlation between these two is startling.

Chapter 8 of this book exposed the fact that "tithes" have a tradition in government entities. Ancient cultures practiced tithe-related standards regarding their rulers. Tithes were only "religious" in nature if the government itself was a religious entity. The Levitical tithes were agricultural funds for the family of civil servants who comprised the nation's theocratic system of government. When the nation of Israel introduced a king into the bureaucracy, an extra tithe became necessary to support him.

As one would expect from history, the roots of a system of tithing in the Christian church are that of the union of church and state. The leaders of the Christian church began to see the need to fund their enterprise through a form of taxation, and this system of "tithes" would resemble—albeit remotely—the nation of Israel rather than the voluntary church of the diaspora. Henry Clarke asserted that the origin of "tithes" as a mandatory custom of the church was derived from Levitical laws in the Torah rather than clear teaching from church instructions in the New Testament.[37] Interestingly, one would expect that actual instructions to the **church** itself would be the foundational doctrine for church funding. However, because the nation of Israel was a theocratic government, the new Catholic state religion attempted to claim its succession as the new Israel rather than as the decentralized, non-national church spread around the world.

A monetary tithe for "clergy" most assuredly has its roots in the history and structure of the Catholic Church. Constantine Emperor of Rome removed the ban on "Christianity" and his zealous heir Theodosius enforced "Christianity" as the only religion permitted in the empire.[38] Before Constantine's reign "clergy" did not receive established salaries from their religious endeavors; however, Constantine implemented this practice.[39] Nevertheless, these salaries did not come from compulsory "tithes" until later in church history.

The Rev. John Hunt of the nineteenth century reiterated this common understanding of Christian history and the relationship between tithes and legal authority in *Religious Thought in England*. Examining this history, he relayed the following:

Under the Christian dispensation, for the first four hundred years, no tithes were paid. The devotion of the first Christians was so great that their liberality was unbounded. They even sold all their possessions and laid the money at the Apostles' feet. We read of tithes in the third and

---

37. Clarke, *A History of Tithes*, 4.
38. Thomas H. Greer and Gavin Lewis, *A Brief History of the Western World*, 9th ed. (Belmont, CA: Thomas Wadsworth, 2004), 150.
39. Frank Viola and George Barna, *Pagan Christianity?: exploring the roots of our church practices* (Carol Stream, IL: Tyndale House, 2008), 178.

fourth centuries as being paid to emperors and lords of the soil.[40]
[Emphasis added]

Indeed, for anyone who studies the writings of early church fathers and the social and political events that occurred during these centuries the conclusion is inescapable. If tithing had been a doctrine that the Apostles commissioned to the Gentile Christians of the early church, it would assuredly have appeared in the church epistles and early writings despite the explosive generosity. The absence of such witnesses brings the claims of later writings into question and renders them dubious.

The Apostolic Constitutions are a collection of writings of church ordinances compiled toward the end of the fourth century that allegedly claim to be teachings directly from the Apostles themselves. Henry Clarke maintains that they were written by secluded Catholic monks and falsely claim their authorship to implement a system of tithes in the context of the Catholic church.[41] Many early Catholics and most Protestants today (even tithe-teaching ones) utterly reject the authenticity of the Apostolic Constitutions. These Constitutions instruct the church to "[l]et [the bishop] use those tenths and first-fruits, which are given according to the command of God, as a man of

---

40. John Hunt, *Religious Though in England from the Reformation to the End of the Last Century: A Contribution to the History of Theology*, vol. 1 (London: Strahan & Co., 1870), 144-145.
41. Clarke, *A History of Tithes*, 6.

God."[42] The Apostolic Constitutions contain frequent references to "tithes" in the context of the church; however, it is also replete with the garb of Catholic sacramentalism and authority hierarchy. Perhaps modern Protestants that advocate church tithing would do well to study the attempts of the early church-state to impose a form of Old Testament tithing. They should evaluate their own understanding of the Scriptures to see if God has indeed entrusted the church itself to exact tithes for its own funding.

The origin of tithing in the Catholic Church is linked strongly to the idea that the bishops fill the same office of the Levitical priests of the Old Testament. The Apostolic Constitutions claim that the Apostles spoke to the church clergy: "You, therefore, O bishops, are to your people priests and Levites, ministering to the holy tabernacle, the holy Catholic Church; who stand at the altar of the Lord your God, and offer to Him reasonable and unbloody sacrifices through Jesus the great High Priest. [Emphasis added]"[43] Apparently, according to these writings, the Apostles had flip-flopped on the effects of the sacrifice of Christ Himself and the individual priesthood of the believer. The epistle to the Hebrews strongly emphasizes that Christ's sacrifice ended the necessity of continual sacrifices that the Old Covenant instituted (Hebrews 9:6-7,11-15,24-26; 10:11-14). Paul the Apostle

---

42. Philip Schaff, *ANF07. Fathers of the Third and Fourth Centuries: Lactantius, Venantius, Asterius, Victorinus, Dionysius, Apostolic Teaching and Constitutions, Homily, and Liturgies* (Grand Rapids: Christian Classics Ethereal Library, 2004), 604.
43. Ibid., 605.

stated that Jesus Christ Himself was "the mediator between God and men" (1 Timothy 2:5). However, the Apostolic Constitutions argues that the church bishops "are to the laity prophets, rulers, governors, and kings; the mediators between God and His faithful people,.... who bear the sins of all, and intercede for all. [Emphasis added]"[44] Naturally, these "priests" would be "rulers, governors, and kings" because the Catholic church was establishing itself as a state-run religion. Why not exact a tithe-tax from the people if you are the *de facto* government?

The fifth century—voluntary mandates

The fifth century saw more spurious attempts to inject the idea of "tithes" for the church, similar to that of the so-called Apostolic Constitutions. Much like these Constitutions, church statists who wanted to fund the Catholic Church with mandatory "tithes" made other attempts at forgery to attribute tithe-teaching to persons regarded as authoritative and influential. History reveals these attempts for what they are. Official compulsory tithes for the whole of the Catholic church did not yet begin, but the fight was on.

Augustine of Hippo was a theologian and a philosopher who lived from A.D. 354 to 430. He was born into a pagan family, but later converted to Christianity and became a bishop in the Catholic Church. He is well-known today for his contention with Pelagius—a Greek and Latin scholar, theologian, and philosopher. Augustine taught that the grace of God was wholly necessary and entirely sufficient for

---

44. Ibid.

salvation, whereas Pelagius taught that one could achieve salvation on one's own efforts with or without the grace of God. These soteriological ideas represent polar opposites in a debate that still rages in Christianity. Today, the prevailing evangelical view of soteriology in most Catholic and non-Catholic churches is a form of "semi-pelagianism" where the grace of God is wholly necessary for salvation, but is not wholly sufficient.

In writings that are **known** to be rightly attributed to Augustine, "tithes" are mentioned only in the historical context of understanding the Levitical system in the Jewish law. He did admonish the rich to give "more" than the Jewish religious leaders, but he did not set their "tithes" as a doctrinal requirement.[45] According to Henry Clarke, Augustine most likely did not teach mandatory "tithes" in the Christian context, given the body of his known works.[46] One loose writing not found in the body of known works by Augustine claims to be from him and harshly teaches that God will reduce those who do not "tithe" to abject poverty.[47] A later manuscript, according to Clarke, falsely asserts laws from eleventh-century Anglo-Saxon king Edward the Confessor that claimed his authority to exact tithes from the people

---

45. St. Augustine, *St. Augustin on Sermon on the Mount, Harmony of the Gospels and Homilies on the Gospels: Nicene and Post-Nicene Fathers of the Christian Church 1887*, vol 6 of *St. Augustin on Sermon on the Mount, Harmony of the Gospels and Homilies on the Gospels Kessinger Publishing's rare reprints*, ed. Philip Schaff (Whitefish, MT: Kessinger Publishing, 2004), 367-368.
46. Clarke, *A History of Tithes*, 19.
47. Smith and Cheetham, s.v. "tithes."

through the guidance and teaching of Augustine.[48] Another story that English authorities propagated for their right to "tithes" was that Augustine established the practice in Oxfordshire; however, many regard this story as a "tale" and not fact.[49] Because many church leaders until the Middle Ages regarded Augustine highly, those who wanted a doctrine or law implemented would seek to claim support from him.

Jerome, a church priest and apologist who lived from about A.D. 347 to 420, is well-known for translating the Greek and Hebrew Bible into Latin—the Latin Vulgate. The idea of "tithes" to support the church "clergy" was a fresh and evolving idea in the fifth century, and was certainly not yet a unified Catholic doctrine. Jerome began to propagate an idea similar to that of Cyprian in that the church "clergy" were successors of the Levites and priests and fulfilled the same "office." He reasoned: "I, if I am the portion of the Lord, and the line of His heritage, receive no portion among the remaining tribes; but, like the Priest and the Levite, I live on the tithe, and serving the altar, am supported by its offerings. [Emphasis added]"[50] Obviously, Jerome did not understand the New Covenant that Jesus Christ introduced through His work as our High Priest. The Levitical Priesthood is now

---

48. Clarke, *A History of Tithes*, 19.
49. Sir Henry Craik, ed., *English Prose: Sixteenth Century to the Restoration*, vol. 2 of *English Prose: Selections with Critical Introductions by Various Writers and General Introductions to Each Period* (London: MacMillan and Co., 1920), 170.
50. St. Jerome, *NPNF2-06. Jerome: The Principal Works of St. Jerome*, ed. Philip Schaff, trans. The Hon. W. H. Freemantle (Grand Rapids: Christian Classics Ethereal Library, 1982), 211.

obsolete because there is no further need of a human priesthood to mediate between God and man. The so-called church "clergy" are not supposed to "serve at the altar;" Christ already performed the sacrifice of Himself once for all time.

Despite Jerome's fallacy of "tithes and offerings" for the "clergy," he still taught and practiced the customary asceticism. Immediately following his statement above, Jerome admonished: "Having food and raiment, I shall be content with these, and as a disciple of the Cross shall share its poverty. [Emphasis added]"[51] Regardless of a "cleric"'s position on "tithes" during these early centuries of the church, they all seemed to teach self-poverty for church leadership, bestowing to the poor and others anything that they received that they did not need specifically for life. How many church leaders today who hammer a "tithing" mandate today practice the same asceticism?

The sixth century—a failed council

Prior to the sixth century no unified doctrine of "tithes" for the church existed. Some leaders taught such an obligation while others taught a higher, but voluntary form of charity with all possessions. All seemed to teach "poverty" for the "clergy."

In the early sixth century, _Caesarius, Archbishop of Arles_, may have articulated the first assumption of entitlement of the Catholic Church to tithes from its members.[52] He desired to establish Arles as a

---

51. Ibid.
52. Roundell Palmer Selbourne (Earl of), _Ancient Facts and Fictions Concerning Churches and Tithes_, 2nd ed. (London: Macmillan, 1892), 47.

Section VI: Epilogue

"Christian community" and defined the occupations of the citizens there as government occupations to obligate them to pay "tithes" to this church-government community.[53] The efforts of Caesarius to create a regional church-government with a tithe-tax to fund it demonstrates all the more clearly the fact that tithes have always been a function of government taxation, and that this same principle represents the indisputable source of the doctrine today.

Toward the later part of the sixth century other forces were at play to force tithe-taxes on people who did not want them to feed the appetite of a growing state religion. The Council of Tours in A.D. 567 strongly pushed for **voluntary** "tithes" by stating of this practice: "we most earnestly press this upon you."[54] The Provincial Council of French bishop at Mascon in A.D. 586 was the first official council of any Catholic Christian church that made any mention of "tithes" as a requirement.[55] According to Henry Clarke, this council attempted to appeal to authority from early church history by blurring the distinction between what these early church fathers called "offerings" and "oblations" with "tithes."[56] Thus, the fact that no record of the apostolic church and that of the first two centuries contained neither

53. William E. Klingshirn, *Caesarius of Arles: The Making of a Christian Communi-ty in Late Antique Gaul*, vol. 22 of *Cambridge Studies in Medieval Life and Thought: Fourth Series* (Cambridge: Cambridge University Press, 1994), 172-173.
54. William Easterby, *The History of the Law of Tithes in England: Being the Yorke Prize Essay of the University of Cambridge for 1887* (Cambridge: Cambridge University Press, 1888), 3.
55. George Miller, *History, Philosophically Illustrated, from the Fall of the Roman Empire, to the French Revolution, Volume 1*, 3rd ed. (London: H. G. Bohn, 1852), 93.
56. Clarke, *History of Tithes from Abraham to Queen Victoria*, 14.

accounts nor commands to members about "tithing" did not stop Catholic church leadership from attempting to rewrite history. The plan appeared to be to inject current practices of a runaway state religion into early Christian history to convince members that this empire represented the true church and practiced the teachings of the Apostles.

The Council of Mascon in A.D. 586, however, was not a universal council for the whole Catholic Church, and many church leaders did not immediately accept it or reference it for defense of doctrine. Archbishop Agobard of Lyons did not cite it for the policies of his region.[57] Around the time of this council, some adopted a **voluntary** practice of giving "tithes," and the council itself was largely ignored as binding.[58] The **real** beginning of compulsory "tithes" in the Catholic church did not begin until much later.

The seventh century—the church becomes a landlord

The seventh century also saw the rise of church manors. Wealthy church devotees donated land to build church parishes so that they would not need to travel long distances to attend services.[59] The result of this practice was that the church became more unified and owned land upon which wage earners lived. Living on church land eventually became another source of tithe-taxes. The policies of Caesarius of Arles would take greater shape in a much larger context.

---

57. William and Cheetham, s.v. "tithes."
58. Ibid.
59. Clarke, *History of Tithes from Abraham to Queen Victoria*, 20.

Section VI: Epilogue

The eighth century—thank the king for tithes

The very first official church council to require "tithes" throughout the reaches of the Catholic Church did not take place through a voluntary assembly of religious leaders. Remember that tithes **always** had to do with a form of government taxation. This important fact is especially pronounced by the events of the eighth century—the first century thus far for **real** "tithing" for the church.

King Charlemagne of France actually accomplished what no zealot was able to do in the church for seven centuries. In 787, Charlemagne made the payment of "tithes" an actual law. Just prior to this year, Charlemagne had conquered the Lombard kingdom to join his French kingdom with part of Italy. Pope Hadrian I seized this opportunity and colluded with the king to craft edicts that would "renew the faith."[60] Naturally, the Scriptural "proof" for a church right to "tithes" for clergy maintenance came strictly from the Mosaic Law, and not the actual New Testament instructions.

Because of Charlemagne's rule, Pope Hadrian was able to climb in influence and power. In A.D. 785, soon prior to Charlemagne's laws, Pope Hadrian attempted to force the Anglo-Saxon people to pay "tithes." These people did not appreciate the blatant taxation and expressed staunch opposition.[61] It would take years for the compulsory acts of King Charlemagne and Pope Hadrian to function without significant resistance.

---

60. Easterby, 10.
61. Clarke, _History of Tithes from Abraham to Queen Victoria_, 32.

The Council of Friuli in A.D. 791 expressly urged tithe-taxes in Italy. This council regarded Malachi chapter 3 as the greatest passage in Scripture to teach tithing.[62] Perhaps the trend of granting land to the church on which was built monasteries encouraged church leaders to think of the church in terms of buildings, and thus a "storehouse." During this time "abbots" were closer to the common people of the church and practiced more generosity than did the bishops.[63] Sensing that more poor would benefit through the work of abbots, many people tried to fulfill their new legal requirement by letting the abbots handle their tithes; however, the bishops disapproved this practice and later made it illegal.[64]

On December 25, A.D. 800, the pope crowned Charlemagne with the title "Holy Roman Emperor." Obviously, the pope appreciated Charlemagne's efforts to finalize a legal church-state to which the king and the pope would reign over the wealth and the spirituality of the people by force of arms. Undoubtedly many saw at that time the frightening events unfolding that ultimately led families to become pilgrims to the New World. Consolidating church and state where the church had legal power to tax and punish civilians supplied the groundwork for royal and religious tyranny.

---

62. William and Cheetham, s.v. "tithes."
63. John Allen, *State Churches and the Kingdom of Christ: An Essay on the Establishment of Ministers, Forms and Services of Religion by Secular Power, and on its Inconsistency with the Free, Humbling, Spiritual Nature of the Christian Dispensation* (London: William and Frederick G. Cash, 1853), 139.
64. Ibid.

The ninth century through the Middle Ages—the reign of the Catholic Church

The conquests and policies of Charlemagne created a new era for the Catholic Church. Church leaders became more than ecclesiastical elders—they were now high-ranking government officials. The pope was no longer a "spiritual" leader—he was now a powerful politician. The collusion of Pope Hadrian and King Charlemagne granted to the pope the power to create civil and criminal laws under the guise of church authority.

Award-winning church historian Diarmaid MacCulloch discusses the rise of parishes in his large treatise *Christianity: The First Three Thousand Years*. He addressed the introduction of tithes during this period around the first millennium as followed:

As parishes were organized, it became apparent that there were <u>new sources of wealth for churchmen</u> as well as for secular landlords. The parish system covering the countryside <u>gave the Church the chance to tax the new farming resources</u> of Europe by demanding from its farmer-parishioners <u>a scriptural tenth of agricultural produce, the tithe</u>. Tithe was provided by many more of the laity than the old aristocratic elite, and was another incentive for extending the Church's pastoral concern much more widely.[65] [Emphasis added]

Although the Catholic Church was incorrectly injecting a quasi-Levitical system on farming citizens, the tithe-taxes initially began according to a more proper understanding of the tithes that the Levitical laws described. In 1059, Pope Nicholas II issued the first

---

65. Diarmaid MacColloch, *Christianity: The First Three Thousand Years* (New York: Viking, 2009), 369.

tithe-tax law that bore the force of government coercion. The pope forced the people to render "tithes" to the Catholic Church and that the bishops would have sole discretion for their use; the penalty was excommunication.[66] Originally, the force of tithes was from agricultural produce—similar to the actual Levitical laws—but eventually evolved into tithes of monetary profits and wage earnings.[67]

The title "Holy Roman Emperor" became a coveted title that many Catholic kings sought. However, to obtain this title, a king would have to please the pope by somehow "advancing" the Roman Catholic Church. Through the centuries after Charlemagne, kings would find themselves at odds with the pope and the feelings would be mutual. The emperors taught and practiced a "divine right of kings" and the popes likewise believed in "apostolic succession." Popes would fear the force of arms of the kings and would threaten with excommunication from the church. The kings would fear this excommunication, but threaten with the authority of the monarchy. Such contention ultimately led King Henry VIII to part from the Catholic Church and establish his own state religion—the Anglican Church. The Anglican Church became the basis for the state Church of England and the state Church of Ireland in the respective countries.

In the years following Charlemagne the church acquired more land through the direct taxation of "tithes." The legal tithes were divided into three parts, and sometimes four parts for maintaining the church,

---

66. Allen, 140.
67. Ibid.

the "clergy," the poor, and the bishop. As the church-state grew through acquisitions of the land from other countries, efforts to expand the requirement of tithe-taxes to the people of these nations were met with fierce resistance, even to the assassination of King Canute IV in 1086.[68] Another attempt by the church to enforce Norman peasants to pay tithe-taxes about 100 years later was met with an open letter warning of morbid physical violence to the church leaders if they did not cease and desist from the tithe-taxes and remain to perform their religious duties.[69]

Another 100 years passed—the mid thirteenth century—before the church had its way and subjugated Norman peoples to pay tithe-taxes. The fear of peasant revolts led the Catholic Church to secure and guard its property from vandalism. The feudal system began when landowners granted to the church land to be caretakers while the church granted protection in return.[70] How many common theologians today understand that the medieval **feudal system** of land originated from a church **tithing** doctrine?!

In 1590, the Council of Trent under Pope Pius IV claimed the right of the Catholic Church to certain authority, giving church decrees essentially the same weight as inspired Scripture. Of course, the council also staunchly enforced the obligation of tithe-taxes with the penalty of excommunication.

---

68. Ibid., 141.
69. Ibid., 142.
70. Ibid.

Thomas Aquinas—the Catholic apologist

Fitting with the dogma of a state religion and papal authority, _Thomas Aquinas_, an apologist for the Catholic Church, constructed his apologetic in _Summa Theologica_. In this work, he defended church "tithing" against stated objections. Concerning tithes "as a matter of precept" he answers five objections with quotations from Scripture or logic.

His first stated objection is that the tithe laws do not apply to Christians because they were abrogated ceremonial and judicial aspects of the Mosaic Law.[71] His answer is that Malachi 3:10 expresses a moral aspect that demonstrates that whenever there are "those who minister the divine worship," they must be supported by a similar system of tithes.[72]

His second stated objection is that under the age of grace, Jesus Christ and the apostles never taught the church to practice tithes.[73] His answer is that Jesus' teaching that one should be paid for work establishes a moral binding of tithes and that the church has the authority to exact them.[74]

---

71. Thomas Aquinas, "Whether men are bound to pay tithes under a necessity of precept?," _Summa Theologica, Volume 2_, trans. Fathers of the English Dominican Province (Charleston, SC: BiblioBazaar, 2008), 306.
72. Ibid., 308.
73. Ibid., 307.
74. Ibid., 310.

Section VI: Epilogue

His third stated objection is that prior to the Law, the patriarchs (Abraham and Jacob) seemed to give tithes voluntarily, not by law.[75] His answer is that before the Law, the patriarchs obeyed a divine unwritten law out of "prophetic instinct."[76]

His fourth stated objection is that because there were three different types of tithes in the Mosaic Law—the Levitical tithe, the Festival tithe, and the poor tithe—and the first applied to an obsolete Levitical priesthood, then necessarily all three tithes no longer apply.[77] His answer is that the New Testament commands care for both the poor and ministers and that the ministers have the obligation and authority to distribute to the poor; therefore, at least the first and third tithes must apply.[78]

His fifth stated objection is that under the age of grace, a necessity to pay tithes would be inconsistent because such would be debts, which would subject people to sin.[79] His answer is that, while the Apostle Paul abstained from his moral right to receive support for his ministry, the church has the authority to exact tithes in certain conditions, and those disobeying such commands could face damnation.[80]

Aquinas answers an objection to an obligation to tithe "of all things" (rather than simply agricultural produce according to the

---

75. Ibid., 307.
76. Ibid., 310.
77. Ibid., 307-308.
78. Ibid., 311.
79. Ibid., 308.
80. Ibid., 311.

Mosaic Law) by quoting Jacob's vow to God.[81] Even he recognized that Jacob's vow was voluntary, but he attempted earlier to craft it into some obedience to a hidden divine law so as to nullify the plain language of the Mosaic Law. Aquinas, then, obligates church "laity" to commit tithes of all property from a loose interpretation of Jacob's vow over the exhaustive and clear wording of the tithe laws in the Torah!

As many evangelical Protestants attempt to do today, Aquinas did centuries earlier. He forced another defense of church tithes by claiming that 1 Corinthians 9:11 (sowing spiritual things and reaping carnal things) enforces an obligation to give **tithes**.[82] He also argues that the church, composed of people spread across regions, could not thrive if those who lived by trades rather than by farming were under no obligation to pay tithes.[83] This argument is akin to arguments today that if members of a local church were not required to give a fixed portion of their income, how could such a church survive and establish a budget. Of course, when the Scripture does not support one's emotions or logic, one often attempts to force the Scriptures to agree.

Aquinas further attempted to defend the idea of an obligation to pay tithes "of all things" rather than agricultural produce because the Pharisees paid tithes of garden herbs not required under the Law, yet

---

81. Thomas Aquinas, "Whether men are bound to pay tithes of all things?," *Summa Theologica, Volume 2*, trans. Fathers of the English Dominican Province (Charleston, SC: BiblioBazaar, 2008), 312.
82. Ibid.
83. Ibid., 313.

Jesus commended their deed.[84] However, the fact that Jesus appreciated the effect of their additional "charity" provides no proof that the Scriptures require church members to pay tithes of all sustenance not listed in the Law (**assuming** that Christians were actually under the Law).

Aquinas blankly asserts that the "clergy" inherit the same office of the Levites, and therefore have the same right to receive tithes for sustenance.[85] He also assumes that the "clergy" have a right to receive tithes because of Paul's statement concerning sowing spiritual things and reaping carnal things.[86] As chapter 18 of this book explained, such an assumption is ridiculous because the ones to which Paul was referring were traveling ministers, and taking "even so" to its necessary conclusion requires the tithing ordinances of the Mosaic Law itself.

Answering an argument that because the Levites had to pay tithes to the priests, the "clergy" would likewise need to pay tithes, Aquinas, acting as a good Catholic apologist, quotes a statement from a pope rather than Scripture to alleviate the so-called "clergy" from such an obligation if the Mosaic Law were to be consistently applied to the church.[87] Aquinas ignores the distinction between Levites and priests in the Old Testament, and simply refers to the "clergy" as a whole as

---

84. Ibid., 314.
85. Thomas Aquinas, "Whether tithes should be paid to the clergy?," *Summa Theologica, Volume 2*, trans. Fathers of the English Dominican Province (Charleston, SC: BiblioBazaar, 2008), 315.
86. Ibid., 316.
87. Ibid., 318.

"ministers of the altar and sowers of spiritual things among the people."[88] He obligates certain clergy to pay tithes only from land that is private property and not owned by the church.[89] However, if Aquinas were to be consistent with the Mosaic Law from which he claims the "clergy" succeed the Levites and priests, no provision is made in the Law for Levites or priests to own private land. Thus, Aquinas and many modern church tithing advocates want to have their cake and eat it too—church ministers that have **both** a divine right to receive tithes **and** the legal ability to obtain private real estate.

Aquinas also replies to an objection that the poor should receive tithes, but not pay tithes.[90] He states: "Tithes should be employed for the assistance of the poor, through the dispensation of the clergy. Hence, the poor have no reason for accepting tithes, but they are bound to pay them."[91] Modern evangelical church tithing advocates implicitly use similar logic when they obligate the poor members of their churches to pay "tithes" to minister to their own care. This teaching directly contradicts the regulations in the Mosaic Law that demonstrate that only landowners tithed but that the poor were fed from these tithes. This teaching also directly contradicts the procedures of the Mosaic Law wherein those who tithed gave them **directly** to the poor, not "through the dispensation of the clergy." The Levites and priests

---

88. Ibid.
89. Ibid.
90. Ibid., 317.
91. Ibid., 319.

did not collect all tithes and distribute them as needed. The practice of the Apostles to distribute goods and money to the poor in the church had nothing to do with the Levitical system of the Mosaic Law and had nothing to do with tithes.

The dilemma of the modern church tithing advocate is that he or she agrees with much of the logic and Scripture twisting of Thomas Aquinas. However, Aquinas was a Catholic apologist through and through. The church-state had grown over the centuries from a faulty dogma of incorporating the Mosaic Law into the sphere of Christianity to a statist monster that introduced extra-Biblical teachings and requirements through papal decrees and royal force of law. Believing that this "Holy Roman Empire" was God's sanctioned incarnation of Christianity, Aquinas strove to force the Scriptures to prove what the church was practicing. His arguments are strikingly similar to those used by many modern Protestants; yet these Protestants do not understand the inherent connection between such arguments and the support of a state religion.

Conclusion and summary

In conclusion, we have examined the history of the Catholic Church in its connection to the teaching of a tithing doctrine. We have seen how this doctrine evolved as the structure of the church evolved into a unified religion that became a part of the government. Emperor Constantine ended the persecution of Christianity, but he laid the groundwork for a religious tyranny.

Considered a product of the fourth century, the so-called Apostolic Constitutions evolved from secluded traditions and claimed tithe teaching from the Apostles themselves. These Constitutions utterly contradicted much of what the Apostles said in the Scriptures about the destruction of the Levitical system and the priesthood of believers. Those who desired to fund a growing universal church attempted to forge words from the Apostles to compel people to yield their wealth and obey these "clergy" as governing officials.

Some assume that Augustine of Hippo taught tithing because a few sermons attributed to him command it. However, the authenticity of these sermons is disputed. Jerome, however, taught Cyprian's idea of "tithes" for the "clergy" while still teaching and practicing asceticism.

The sixth through the eighth centuries saw attempts by local bishops to enforce tithe-taxes for the regional church, but these attempts were met with contention. Wealthy landowners donated or sold land to the church for parishes, and the church attempted to exact tithes from people who lived on this land as rent fees. The first official, legal tithe laws for the Catholic Church came under the iron fist of King Charlemagne and his assistance of Pope Hadrian.

Thomas Aquinas, a medieval Catholic apologist argued in his *Summa Theologica* for the system of tithes that the church imposed on the people. His appeal to church authority and his Scripture twisting demonstrates many arguments that tithing advocates use today. However, such a system of tithe laws grew from a unified church-state that evolved and departed from Biblical roots.

21. The Reformation and the Modern Church

Dissent and Assent

The Reformation—a challenge to state religion

The Reformation certainly acted as a challenge to the Catholic Church in more ways than one. Of prime importance was questioning the supremacy of the pope. Contending with papal authority and embracing *sola scriptura* (Scripture alone) naturally led reformers to break the matrix and challenge doctrines that the pope and members of the clerical hierarchy under him taught that appeared to contradict Scripture.

Gutenberg's printing press was a new invention that was making information more readily available *en masse* once a work was compiled. This invention allowed those with differing opinions to find an audience for which to express them. The Catholic Church no longer maintained a domain of monopoly on information dissemination through scribes who would copy liturgical works in Latin for use by the elite. Dissenters could print works such as translations of the Bible with marginal notes that challenged papal authority or the divine right of kings and smuggle them to curious citizens. The Catholic Church initially dealt harshly with the dissenters of the Reformation era, but their attempts to squelch these "apostates" were like trying to get rid of malaria in a swamp by killing each individual mosquito with a fly swatter. The more the church tried to persecute the dissenters, the greater the Reformation spread because this persecution created greater public awareness of such teaching. The appeal of reading the original Scriptures to determine truth became more compelling than simply trusting mysterious human agents to harbor it.

Remember that the Catholic Church emerged as a self-acclaimed successor to the Old Covenant theocracy. The "clergy" were allegedly successors to the Levitical system of government. Naturally, the teaching of "tithing," which was nonexistent in the first few centuries of a disunified church, gradually became imposed after Christianity became a state religion. Questioning the papal and priestly authority of this Catholic Church in light of Scripture itself led to reexamining the role of the Mosaic Law in the auspices of the New Testament church and the effects of the death and resurrection of Christ on the Law.

Martin Luther on Moses and tithes

Martin Luther, known as "The Father of the Great Reformation," broke the church-state mold by challenging the role of the Mosaic Law on the Christian. In a 1525 sermon entitled "How Christians Should Regard Moses," Luther emphatically stated in a subheading that "The Law of Moses Binds only the Jews and not the Gentiles."[92] Luther explained the view of his opponents as followed:

> I say this on account of <u>the enthusiasts</u>. For you see and hear how they read Moses, extol him, and bring up the way he <u>ruled the people with commandments</u>. They try to be clever, and think they know something more than is presented in the gospel; so they minimize faith, contrive something new, and boastfully claim that it comes from the Old Testament. <u>They desire to govern people according to the letter of the law of Moses</u>, as if no one had ever read it before.[93] [Emphasis added]

---

92. Martin Luther, *Martin Luther's Basic Theological Writings*, 2nd ed., eds. Timothy F. Lull and William R. Russell (Minneapolis: Fortress Press, 2005), 126.
93. Ibid.

No doubt "the enthusiasts" of the Mosaic Law were the Catholic apologists of Luther's day. As a state religion, the Catholic Church "[desired] to govern people according to the letter of the law of Moses." The tithing doctrine crept into the unified church as part and parcel of the general teaching that ruling members of the church were the new Levites and priests.

Luther continued by opposing this viewpoint. He declared:

> But we will not have this sort of thing. <u>We would rather not preach again for the rest of our life</u> than to let Moses return and to let Christ be torn out of our hearts. We will not have Moses as ruler or lawgiver any longer. <u>Indeed God himself will not have it either</u>.[94] [Emphasis added]

Luther apparently saw a contrast between the Old Covenant of the Law and the New Covenant of grace. Indeed, the issue of the Law concerns what Jesus Christ actually accomplished on the Cross. If the Law binds Christians, then the work of Christ on the Cross was fruitless. It was mere symbolism with no real merit.

Colossians 2:13-14

13: And you, being dead in your sins and the uncircumcision of your flesh, hath he quickened together with him, having forgiven you all trespasses;
14: Blotting out the handwriting of ordinances that was against us, which was contrary to us, and took it out of the way, nailing it to his cross;

The Mosaic Law as a unified whole applied only to the nation of Israel. This is not to say that **nothing** in the Mosaic Law applies to the

---

94. Ibid., 127.

lives of Christians. Certainly doctrines in the epistles to the church contain moral statements that overlap ordinances in the Law. However, Christians do not follow such principles by virtue of them being in the Law, but rather by them being expressed in the New Covenant. For example, the United States and Canada have their own codes of law and constitutions. Both provide penalties for murder. However, a Canadian citizen does not refrain from murder because the United States enforces such a law, but because his or her own country has the law.

Mosaic Law adherents claim that if the Mosaic Law no longer applies, then one is free to murder and steal and commit other immoral crimes. The flaw in this argument is that the New Testament itself teaches against such sins. The Mosaic Law is not the only code that contains provisions for these crimes. Correlation does not prove causation. While it is true that the same God gave both the Old and New Covenants, one is not subject to the latter by virtue of being also subject to the former. The Old Covenant was a code of laws for a national theocracy. The New Covenant is a system of doctrines for those individuals whom Christ has redeemed. A Gentile Christian refrains from murder because the New Covenant condemns murder and also compels him or her to be subject to a secular government that also punishes murder.

Luther continues: "Moses has nothing to do with us. If I were to accept Moses in one commandment, I would have to accept the entire

Moses."[95] This statement is key to understanding the issue of Law. The Jews of Israel could not cherry pick favorite portions of the Law because they were subject to the entire code. Christians have their own constitution from God in the New Testament. Accepting the Mosaic Law as authoritative requires that the entire body of this Law be authoritative as well. Christians who claim that the Mosaic Law applies to the church commit to themselves a disservice, because they themselves do not come close to following even a majority of the ordinances in the Law. Whether intentional or not they engage in the very cherry picking that they condemn.

Luther elaborated on his argument: "Thus the consequence would be that if I accept Moses as master, then I must have myself circumcised, wash my clothes in the Jewish way, eat and drink and dress thus and so, and observe all that stuff."[96] Indeed, to argue otherwise is foolish. To follow fragments of the Law is not to obey the Law itself. The New Covenant stands as its own "law" regardless of any similarities. To claim to be obligated to tithe because the Law commands it automatically subjects the claimant to follow every word of the entire Law.

James 2:10-12

10: For whosoever shall keep the whole law, and yet offend in one *point*, he is guilty of all.
11: For he that said, Do not commit adultery, said also, Do not kill. Now if thou commit no adultery, yet if thou kill, thou art become a transgressor of the law.

---

95. Ibid.
96. Ibid.

12: So speak ye, and so do, as they that shall be judged by the law of liberty.

James explained this truth clearly. One cannot claim to follow the Law by keeping only parts of it. If one violates any provision of the Law, one is a *lawbreaker*, regardless of any portion one has successfully followed. James then commissions Christians to teach such moral truths as refraining from murder and theft, but as being subject to "the law of liberty." This Christian "law of liberty" condemns murder and theft just as the Mosaic Law does, but a Christian avoids killing and stealing according to "the law of liberty," not according to the body of the Mosaic Law itself.

Luther plainly stated: "So, then, we will neither observe nor accept Moses. Moses is dead. His rule ended when Christ came. He is of no further service."[97] Luther, then, regarded any obligation to tithe according to what the New Covenant itself taught about it—exactly zero. Nowhere in any of Luther's writings did he ever express tithing as an obligation for Christians. Why? Because Gentile Christians are not subject to the Law of Moses. The Mosaic Law commanded the Jews of Israel to tithe. The New Testament doctrines to the church do not. Therefore, Christians have no obligation to practice any form of a tithe.

---

97. Ibid.

Luther understood that the tithe of the Mosaic Law was not a "moral principle," but that it represented a form of taxation from a government entity. He explained as followed:

> If I were emperor, I would take from Moses a model for [my] statutes; not that Moses should be binding on me, but that I should be free to follow him in ruling as he ruled. For example, tithing is a very fine rule, because with the giving of the tenth all other taxes would be eliminated. For the ordinary man it would be easier to give a tenth than to pay rents and fees.[98] [Emphasis added]

Luther understood something that many in Christendom today do not—tithes were taxes paid to a legal government entity. Luther spoke of the tithe from Moses in the context of **government**. He also referred to the "rents and fees" that became prevalent in church districts that grew from the intrusion of Catholic tithes.

As a bonus reminder, Luther also understood the tithe as the Mosaic Law taught it: "Suppose I had ten cows; I would then give one. If I had only five, I would give nothing. [Emphasis added]"[99] Luther recognized that the tithe-tax of Moses was purely agricultural, and that it was not truly 10% of a substance, but only every tenth unit counted.

Luther then lamented the conditions of his own pagan **government** and church-state, contrasting it with the Law:

> But as things are now, I must pay the Gentile tax even if the hail should ruin my entire crop. If I owe a hundred gulden in taxes, I must pay it even though there may be nothing growing in the field. This is also the way the pope decrees and governs.[100] [Emphasis added]

---

98. Ibid., 128.
99. Ibid.
100. Ibid.

Luther clearly contrasted the agricultural tithe of the Mosaic Law with the monetary taxes of the king. If monetary income were a source of tithe payments, one's agricultural tragedies make no difference. Luther's statement about the pope hinted that the authority figures of the Catholic Church enforce certain laws in the name of Moses that were actually far removed from what Moses himself said. Such is the same with anyone today who attempts to use Moses to defend the unscriptural idea that one owes 10% of one's monetary income to one's local church.

Finally, Luther later clearly stated in no uncertain terms that the Gentile Christians have no obligation to tithe:

> But the other commandments of Moses, which are not [implanted in all men] by nature, the Gentiles do not hold. Nor do these pertain to the Gentiles, such as the tithe and others which I wish we had too. Now this is the first thing that I ought to see in Moses, namely, the commandments to which I am not bound except insofar as they are [implanted in everyone] by nature [and written in everyone's heart].[101] [Emphasis added]

Luther reiterated the fact that laws against lying, stealing, and murder existed elsewhere besides the Mosaic Law and were natural laws. The Gentiles are bound to obey these natural laws, but not because they were bound by them in the Mosaic Law. Tithes were not natural laws and were not "written in everyone's heart." Laws such as these "do [not] pertain to the Gentiles." Once again, Luther's reference to tithes were in respect to **government**. He considered the tithe of

---

101. Ibid., 129.

Moses to be desirable as a means of government taxation **only** because it was superior and less of a burden than the taxes imposed by the king and the pope. Nowhere did Luther obligate Christians to practice tithing and nowhere did he present tithes as a concept outside the subject of governments and taxation.

John Calvin on tithes

John Calvin did not teach tithing for Christians, despite the claims of some that he did. Calvin ridiculed the Catholic Church's claim to Mosaic tithes:

> Wherefore the Papal priests draw a silly inference, when they claim the tithes for themselves, as if due to them in right of the priesthood... Nor does that expression of the Apostle, which they no less dishonestly than ignorantly allege, help them at all, "The priesthood being changed, the right also is at the same time transferred." (Heb. vii. 12.) The Apostle there contends, that whatever the Law had conferred on the Levitical priests now belongs to Christ alone, since their dignity and office received its end in Him. These blockheads, just as if they had robbed Christ, appropriate to themselves the honour peculiar to Him... as Paul correctly infers that a subsistence is now no less due to the ministers of the Gospel than of old to the priests who waited at the altar, (1 Cor. ix. 14;) but under this pretext they unjustly lay hands on the tithes, as if they were their owners, and with still greater imprudence accumulate landed properties and other revenues.
>
> It is probable that when the Roman Emperors first professed themselves Christians, either induced by just and proper feelings, or out of superstition, or impressed with a pious solicitude that the Church should not be without ministers, they gave the tithes for the maintenance of the clergy; for whilst the Roman State was free, the people used to exact tithes from their tributary nations. And this was the case, too, where there were kings; for the Sicilians paid tithes before the Romans obtained dominion over them.[102] [Emphasis added]

---

102. Jean Calvin, *Commentaries on the Four Last Books of Moses: Arranged in the Form of a Harmony*, 2nd ed., trans. Charles William Bingham (Edinburgh: The Calvin Translation Society, 1853), 278-279.

Calvin's references to tithes in the Mosaic Law and to those taught by the Catholic Church during his time all had to do with laws enforced by a governing entity. He referred to the tithes of kings and of "the Roman State." He concluded that the early Roman Empire attempted to apply the tithes of Mosaic Law to the church "by just and proper feelings, or out of superstition," but to do so was incorrect. The church ministers "unjustly lay hands on the tithes" because the Scriptures do not authorize them to do this. Calvin also understood the inconsistency of the "clergy" that claimed the right to receive tithes as successors of the Levites, yet also "with still greater imprudence" bought real estate, which the Mosaic Law specifically granted the Levites no such privilege.

Many assume that Calvin advocated church tithing because he appeared to write favorable about the Mosaic Law. Naturally, Calvin was really a pioneer of the concept of "systematic theologies" by his *Institutes* and his commentaries on the Bible. Other prior theologians scarcely dealt with the entire Bible other than to translate or print it. Therefore, Calvin's commentaries on the Old Testament might lead some to believe that he advocated the whole Mosaic Law as binding to Christians. However, this is simply not the case.

Calvin spoke of using the Mosaic Law to govern a nation in an unfavorable light:

This I would have rather passed in silence, were I not aware that many dangerous errors are here committed. For there are some who deny that any commonwealth is rightly framed which neglects the law of Moses, and is ruled by the common law of nations. How perilous and seditious these views are, let others see: for me it is enough to demonstrate that they are stupid and false. We must attend to the well known division which distributes the whole law of God, as promulgated by Moses, into the moral, the ceremonial, and the judicial law, and we must attend to each of these parts, in order to understand how far they do, or do not, pertain to us. Meanwhile, let no one be moved by the thought that the judicial and ceremonial laws relate to morals. For the ancients who adopted this division, though they were not aware that the two latter classes had to do with morals, did not give them the name of moral, because they might be changed and abrogated without affecting morals. They give this name specifically to the first class, without which, true holiness of life and an immutable rule of conduct cannot exist.[103] [Emphasis added]

Calvin emphatically explained above that the Mosaic Law as a whole is not binding upon Gentile nations. Such a view is "perilous and seditious" and "stupid and false." He splits the Mosaic Law into moral, ceremonial, and judicial parts, and argues that only the moral portion is universal. This moral portion is "the common law of nations." It is that part of the law that concerns civility such as provisions against lying, theft, and murder, just as Luther explained as that portion of the Law "implanted in all men by nature." Tithes and feasts were part of the ceremonial portion of the Law, which Calvin here declares "[do not] relate to morals" and "might be changed and abrogated without affecting morals."

Calvin later explains:

The ceremonial law of the Jews was a tutelage by which the Lord was pleased to exercise, as it were, the childhood of that people, until the fullness of the time should come when he was fully to manifest his wisdom to the world, and exhibit the reality of those things which were then adumbrated by figures (Gal. 3:24; 4:4). The judicial law, given them

---

103. John Calvin, *The Institutes of the Christian Religion: Vol. 3 of 3.*, trans. Henry Beveridge (Charleston, SC: Forgotten Books, 2007), 444-445.

as a kind of polity, delivered certain forms of equality and justice, by which they might live together innocently and quietly... Therefore, as ceremonies might be abrogated without at all interfering with piety, so, also, when these judicial arrangements are removed, the duties and precepts of charity can still remain perpetual.[104] [Emphasis added]

As mentioned previously, Calvin claimed that the Catholic Church received tithes unjustly because Jesus Christ as Priest after the order of Melchizedek ended the Levitical priesthood. In Calvin's *Institutes*, he most certainly did not claim tithes as part of the Law that would pertain to anyone outside the Jewish nation of Israel. The tithes and feasts were "ceremonies [that] might be abrogated without at all interfering with piety."

Calvin refers to the basic common denominator among what is divinely acceptable for the laws of nations: "equity."

Equity, as it is natural, cannot be the same in all, and therefore ought to be proposed by all laws, according to the nature of the thing enacted. As constitutions have some circumstances on which they partly depend, there is nothing to prevent their diversity, provided they all alike aim at equity as their end.[105] [Emphasis added]

Though the inference is more subtle, the nature of the teachings of Calvin regarding tithes and the Mosaic Law is very similar to what Luther clearly and emphatically taught. The only provisions of the Mosaic Law that apply outside the nation of Israel are indirectly those portions that express the very moral framework of running a nation

---

104. Ibid., 445.
105. Ibid., 446.

with civil justice—not the ceremonial or judicial specifics. Such specifics must include the tithe ordinances.

John Wesley on tithes

John Wesley did not teach tithing for Christians. He taught "stewardship" in everything, but no obligation to tithe (similar to the teaching of the early church fathers). In a sermon called "The Good Steward," he declared:

Do not stint yourself, like a Jew rather than a Christian, to this or that proportion. Render unto God, not a tenth, not a third, not half, but all that is God's, be it more or less; by employing all, on yourself, your household, the household of faith, and all mankind, in such a manner that you may give a good account of your stewardship, when ye can no longer be stewards; in such a manner as the oracles of God direct, both by general and particular precepts; in such a manner, that whatever ye do ye may be "a sacrifice of a sweet smelling savour to GOD," and that every act may be rewarded in that day, when the Lord cometh with all his saints.[106] [Emphasis added]

In the same sermon, Wesley specifically addresses money:

God has entrusted us...with a portion of worldly goods; with food to eat, raiment to put on, and a place where to lay our head; with not only the necessaries, but the conveniences, of life. Above all, he has committed to our charge that precious talent which contains all the rest,—money: Indeed it is unspeakably precious, if we are wise and faithful stewards of it; if we employ every part of it for such purposes as our blessed Lord has commanded us to do.[107] [Emphasis added]

Wesley taught the concept of stewardship, such that one's giving is of the purpose to meet needs, not of adhering to any relative amount

---

106. John Wesley, *Sermons on Several Occasions, Volume 1* (New York: Carlton & Phillips, 1855), 448.
107. John Wesley, *The Works of the Rev. John Wesley: With the Last Corrections of the Author*, vol. 6 (London: Wesleyan Conference Office, 1872), 139.

given. He taught that we are accountable for **all** our possessions to use them in a way that honors God. Nowhere in any of Wesley's sermons or writings did he teach an obligation of Christians to practice tithing. Nowhere did he teach a "minimum requirement" such that all Christians would be obligated to render 10% or more of all income to a church's disposal.

English tithe rents

As mentioned earlier, church authorities tried for centuries to impose religious obligations to members to pay tithe-taxes to the church-state. With the failure of religious persuasion, the church-state had to resort to legal enforcements to raise these revenues. Wealthy church members who desired a nearby parish in which to worship donated or sold land to church authorities. The losers in these transactions were any peasants who lived on land that the church acquired. The church, having legal deed to the land, could charge rents on subjects and promulgate these rents as religious "tithes." The tag team of Charlemagne and Pope Hadrian allowed the church to acquire new land through conquest rather than voluntary acquisition and to enforce tithe-taxes through legal acts upon the conquered subjects.

Tithes as land rents existed throughout the history of most nations that had been under the legal influence of the Catholic Church. Of particular interest is the history of such tithe rents in England and other related countries in the United Kingdom. As Thomas Aquinas defended, such tithes evolved into a taxation that actually obligated the poor to pay rather than provided for their livelihood.[108]

In a January-April, 1835 edition of England's *The Monthly Review*, the researchers presenting the article about a bill in the Parliament related to tithes for the Church of England discuss a short history of tithes in the kingdom. The article attempted to unravel the ignorant assumptions of the time. In the article, such bold statements appear:

> There is not one doctrine or fact which unsophisticated minds have believed, but has been impugned and contradicted: not even the plainest and most forcible. Nay, we should say that the simpler and more manifest that they are, with so much the greater pertinacity have they been opposed. We may instance the case of tithes. <u>Nothing, according to the nature of the thing, nor its true history, can be plainer, than that the law created them</u>, and that whatever has been created by the law <u>may be disposed of</u> by the same authority.[109] [Emphasis added]

Still in the position of compulsory legal tithes to central authority, the writers of this article understood much of the subject of tithes what today's church members and theologians do not understand. According to the article's history, Abraham gave tithes voluntarily and from his war spoils—not of his own possessions.[110] They also recalled that Jacob's vow was voluntary and not in obedience to a law.[111] Regarding the Mosaic Law, they understood that it expressed four tithes (the

---

108. "On Tithes," *The Monthly Review* 1, no. 1 (1835): 164.
109. Ibid., 151-152.
110. Ibid., 152.
111. Ibid.

Levitical tithe and the priestly tithe considered separate), and that these tithes were all of agricultural produce alone.[112]

Concerning Christianity, the article defends that Jesus Christ and the Apostles in the New Testament writings never presented an obligation for tithes to the church, that fund raising was voluntary, and that the Apostles committed to manual labor along with their ministry.[113] They, as informed and honest historians, reiterated the indisputable fact that a doctrine of tithes did not enter the church mainstream until the fourth century.[114] Even at this time, what was called a "tithe" was not really a strict calculation, but still varying voluntary contributions.[115] Attempting to find the origin of tithes throughout the world, the article claims that tithes were "given either to their kings, their priests, or their gods."[116]

The article contrasts the Levitical system with that of the church: "Under the former dispensation, God gave tithes—under the latter, all things in his church are left to charity and Christian freedom."[117] Tithes in England first became an obligation to those who were subject to the lands of parishes.[118] These were rent charges expected under the guise of religious tithes.

---

112. Ibid., 152-153.
113. Ibid., 153.
114. Ibid.
115.Ibid.
116. Ibid.
117. Ibid., 154.
118. Ibid., 155.

Section VI: Epilogue

The article examines the role of the Reformation in the role of tithes and the Catholic church-state:

> Well then, who were those that were the donors of this property, and to whom was it given? Not certainly the present generation or the present Church. If the possessions and rights so granted were inalienable, <u>how did the Protestants receive them, since all the world knows they were given by Catholics to Catholics?</u>[119] [Emphasis added]

We know the answer to that question from reading the words of Luther, Calvin, and Wesley. None of them believed a Biblical mandate existed for a tithe-tax to a Christian entity. Subject to the state-run Church of England, the writers of the article surmised: "We venture to predict, that neither ignorance, prejudice, nor self-interest, will long be able to withstand the force of reason and truth on this subject."[120] Indeed, the truth about tithes exists for all to glean, if they would simply examine tradition in light of the facts of Scripture and history.

From the time that tithe-taxes became law through about a millennium, such rents were primarily from agricultural sources. Naturally, the original justification for this fact was the Mosaic Law itself. However, fragments of enforcement of monetary tithes arose. The church-state became discontent with the annoyances of obtaining revenue dependent upon the conditions of the weather. In 1836 the United Kingdom (England and Wales) passed the Tithe Commutation Act to "update" the tithing system to one that dealt primarily in monetary sources.

---

119. Ibid., 158.
120. Ibid., 159.

This Act was a response to the Tithe War that occurred in Ireland from 1831 through 1836. The populous of Ireland was primarily Catholic at the time, yet the state Anglican Church of Ireland required the non-Anglican landowners to pay tithe-rents to this Church. Although the Catholic Emancipation Act had passed in 1829, the Anglican state continued to exercise authority to exact these tithe rents to non-members and to threaten seizures of goods for noncompliance. The Roman Catholic Church, already at odds with its Anglican cousin, encouraged opposition.

The six-year war—more a landowners' revolt—began with acts of civil disobedience and turned to violence when the acts were met with police action. Because the cost of using police force to quell the rebellion became far greater than the revenue that would have come from the tithe rents, the desperate government passed the Tithe Commutation Act in an attempt to ease the rebellion. Effectively, while converting sources of tithe rents from complex regulations on various types of produce to monetary sources, the Act reduced the overall burden of the tithe rents themselves. Eventually, in 1869, the Catholics were exempted from paying tithe rents to the Anglican Church.

Ironically, the conflict between these two inherently state-run religions demonstrated the true nature of these tithe rents. Originally justified as a divine ordinance upon Christians to sustain ministers, they became exposed for what they truly were as well as their intentions—a tax upon citizens to fund the government. The question then becomes one of what happens to the doctrine of tithes in the separation of church and state.

Charles Haddon Spurgeon wrote about the situation in the United Kingdom in his pastoral periodical *The Sword and the Trowel*:

We never ought to have paid tithes to those who teach a religion we do not believe, and we shall always do our utmost to get rid of the oppressive exaction. If it be said that tithes do not pay the clergy, we may ask, how are they paid? Do they work without pay, and receive the tithes for doing nothing? So much the worse is the case. It is said that tithes belong to God, but that no more proves that they belong to the parson than to the Methodist minister, since one may be as much sent of God as the other. It is a piece of robbery and no better.[121] [Emphasis added]

Although Spurgeon and several other nineteenth century revival ministers were not against the idea of "tithes" for true church ministers, they did not preach "tithes" as a compulsory obligation upon church members. They simply referenced "tithes" as possible examples of voluntary giving standards. The weight that churches today place on a "tithe" as an absolute "minimum" for giving required by God or a practice whereby one must faithfully calculate from one's income was simply not characteristic of non-Catholic, non-state Protestant churches of this period. Compulsory "tithes" were still a product of state religions.

Modern pressures of society to disestablish the church from government led the United Kingdom to begin to dissolve the tithe laws that were becoming anachronistic. Because those who lived on land

---

121. Charles Haddon Spurgeon, ed., *The Sword and the Trowel* (London: London Metropolitan Tabernacle, 1873), 569.

owned by others were subject to tithe rents, The Tithe Act of 1891 transferred the obligations to pay tithe-taxes from the land occupiers to the landowners. Essentially, the tithe rents became a form of monetary property tax. The Tithe Act of 1936 finally eliminated tithe-taxes on property and the fading link to state religion. Small traces of tithe rents existed and the Statute Law (Repeals) Act—as late as 1998—abolished them.

The nineteenth century—revival fires

Evidence from writings exists that indicates that the monetary income tithing doctrine did not take shape in non-Catholic or non-state churches until the mid-nineteenth century. In fact, Paul Merritt Bassett from Nazarene Theological Seminary attempted to trace sermons on the subject and could not find any until immediately prior to the Civil War.[122] The period was the first Great Awakening with a renewed emphasis on spreading the Gospel.

Obviously, missions work requires appropriate funds. The early New Testament church demonstrated abundant generosity and the traveling evangelists received contributions to aid these endeavors. However, some of the preachers of the Great Awakening began to preach obligations to their congregations to give in the form of "tithes."

Rather than take the Catholic Church approach of the obligation being as under the Mosaic Law, the Protestants focused on the idea

---

122. Miller, 294.

that "tithing" was required outside the Law as a matter of God's eternal commands.[123] In other words, the obligation of Christians to "tithe" is not because the Mosaic Law itself is binding, but rather because Abraham and Jacob gave tithes before the Law. The argument is that "tithing" is part of God's eternal "moral law" that exists independently of the Mosaic Law that implemented it. Such an idea is at odds with early Protestants such as Luther and Calvin who included tithes in the category of "ceremonial law" that was only binding on the theocracy of Israel. The argument of tithes from the records of Abraham and Jacob are discussed in chapters 1 and 2 of this book.

Baptist confessions—an example of doctrinal evolution

Like the early Protestants, the early Baptists opposed the state-run Catholic Church. Modern Baptists claim a lush history of doctrinal confessions through the recent centuries. Some confessions of faith are more exhaustive than others. However, if the modern idea of income tithing were a "timeless moral principle" that was of utmost importance to Christianity, one would think that early Baptist confessions of faith would have allotted appropriate sections of these doctrinal statements to express such an obligation. The lack of such a thing is telling, and the evolution of the confessions to the forms we see today demonstrate that this "timeless moral principle" was only recently recognized.

Baptists claim the Waldensians as part of the Baptist doctrinal lineage. The Waldensians compiled two confessions: one in 1120 and

---

123. Ibid.

another in 1544. Neither of these confessions express even the faintest mention of "tithing."

The first official confession bearing the name "Baptist" was the *London Baptist Confession of 1644*. If tithing were an important non-Catholic Christian doctrine at this time, this exhaustive and lengthy confession of faith certainly would have had ample opportunity to present it. On the contrary, the confession does not at all mention tithes. Further, it makes the following statement in section XXXVII about maintenance for ministers:

That the due maintenance of the Officers [Ministers] aforesaid, should be the free and voluntary communication of the Church, that according to Christ's ordinance, they that preach the Gospel, should live of the Gospel and not by constraint to be compelled from the people by a forced Law.[124] [Emphasis added]

Apparently the Baptists at the time, like the Protestant Reformers, believed that God had ordained church ministers to receive **support** from the congregation, but that this support was "free and voluntary" and "not by constraint to be compelled." Perhaps they recognized—like Luther and Calvin—that the Catholic Church at the time inappropriately claimed the status of God's theocracy, and that tithes, a matter of Law, were a tax that the state church imposed on citizens of the land.

In 1689 another Baptist Confession was issued. Likewise, this statement of faith makes no mention of tithing and contains no

---

124. William Joseph McGlothlin, *Baptist Confessions of Faith* (Philadelphia: American Baptist Publication Society, 1911), 184-185.

references to tithing verses in the Bible despite the sheer number of Biblical references. Chapter XXVI section 10 makes the following statement about maintenance for ministers:

> The work of Pastors being constantly to attend the Service of Christ, in his Churches, in the Ministry of the Word, and Prayer, with watching for their Souls, as they that must give account to him; it is incumbent on the Churches to whom they minister, not only to give them all due respect, but also to communicate to them of all their goods according to their ability, so that they may have a comfortable supply, without being themselves entangled in Secular Affairs; and may also be capable of exercising Hospitality towards others; and this is required by the Law of Nature, and by the express order of our Lord Jesus, who hath ordained that they that preach the Gospel, should live of the Gospel.[125] [Emphasis added]

In contrast to the Catholic Church's interpretation of 1 Corinthians 9:13-14 as a proof text for church tithing, the London Baptist Confession of faith links this to "the Law of Nature." This "law of nature" is that law of laboring and receiving a just reward. Rather than expressing this obligation to meet the needs of ministers in the form of "tithes," the Confession provides no specific amounts. The people of the church supply the ministers "according to their ability."

In 1742 the American Baptists in Philadelphia presented their confession of faith. They actually adopted the exact text of the 1689 London confession, and added two sections: "Chapter XXIII. Of Singing Psalms" and "Chapter XXXI. Of Laying On Of Hands." If, after 53 years had elapsed, the Philadelphia church had recognized an important doctrine of church tithing, they surely could have included it

---

125. Ibid., 266-267.

in their additions to the confession. However, they obviously believed that singing psalms and laying on of hands were more important matters.

In 1770 some Methodists joined with some General Baptists to create "The New Connection of General Baptists." This "New Connection" comprised six short articles. Article 2 is entitled "On the Nature and Perpetual Obligation of the Moral Law" and explains that this "moral law" is "of perpetual duration and obligation, to all men, at all times, and in all places or parts of the world."[126] This article declares that "the ten commandments" express this universal "moral law,"[127] yet this article does not include anything about "tithing." In fact, "The New Connection" does not mention "tithing" at all.

The Baptists in New Hampshire crafted their own confession in 1833. Again, this _New Hampshire Confession_ mentions nothing of "tithing." This Confession's statement on the maintenance of ministers is found in section "xiii. Of a Gospel Church":

That a visible Church of Christ is a congregation of baptized believers, associated by covenant in the faith and fellowship of the Gospel; observing the ordinances of Christ; governed by his laws; and exercising the gifts, rights, and privileges invested in them by his word; that its only proper officers are Bishops or Pastors, and Deacons, whose qualifications, claims, and duties are defined in the Epistles to Timothy and Titus.[128] [Emphasis added]

---

126. Ibid., 165.
127. Ibid.
128. John H. Leith, ed., *Creeds of the Churches: A Reader in Christian Doctrine, from the Bible to the Present*, 3rd ed. (Louisville, KY: Westminster John Knox Press, 1982), 338.

The epistles to Timothy and Titus, like all of the Apostle Paul's epistles, make no mention of church tithing. Though some claim that the "double honor" in 1 Timothy 5:17 implies "tithes," The New Hampshire Confession of 1833 certainly makes no mention of such thing. 1 Timothy 5:17 and "double honor" for elders is explained in detail in chapter 17 of this book.

The Southern Baptist denomination effectually began in 1858 with the Southern Baptist Theological Seminary's *Abstract of Doctrinal Principles*. This Abstract makes no mention of "tithing" even in 1858! This first confession even makes no specific mention of how the church ministers are to receive sustenance. The relevant section of the Abstract is section XIV on "The Church":

> The Lord Jesus is the Head of the Church, which is composed of all his true disciples, and in Him is invested supremely all power for its government. According to his commandment, Christians are to associate themselves into particular societies or churches; and to each of these churches he hath given needful authority for administering that order, discipline and worship which he hath appointed. The regular officers of a Church are Bishops, or Elders, and Deacons.[129]

The first official confession of the Southern Baptist Convention after the Theological Seminary's Abstract was the very first *Baptist Faith and Message* in 1925. The Southern Baptist Convention has since revised the original under the same title. The introduction (2), recognizing that no statement of faith is "complete" or without "infallibility" advises that future Baptists of the convention are "free to

---

129. "The Abstract of Principles," *Founders Ministries*, (n.d.), http://www.founders.org/journal/fj01/abstract.html (accessed April 24, 2010).

revise their statements of faith as may seem to them wise and expedient at any time."[130]

Section 12 entitled "A Gospel Church" makes a statement similar to the Abstract where the church's "Scriptural officers are bishops or elders and deacons."[131] Section 24 discusses "Stewardship" by making the following statement:

> God is the source of all blessings, temporal and spiritual; all that we have and are we owe to him. We have a spiritual debtorship to the whole world, a holy trusteeship in the Gospel, and a binding stewardship in our possessions. We are therefore under obligation to serve him with our time, talents and material possessions; and should recognize all these as entrusted to us to use for the glory of God and helping others. Christians should cheerfully, regularly, systematically, proportionately, and liberally contribute of their means to advancing the Redeemer's cause on earth.[132] [Emphasis added]

Not once does this first Statement of Faith and Message mention any form of "tithing." It lists 11 Scripture references to support its position on "Stewardship." None of these texts are ones that mention tithes.

The introduction to the first Faith and Message permitted revisions as Baptists saw fit. Naturally then, instead of drafting a new statement, future Southern Baptists Conventions simply followed the allowance and edited the original statement. We will examine some relevant changes to this statement over time along with the reasons for these changes.

---

130. Leith, 345.
131. Ibid., 348.
132. Ibid., 352.

The 1963 edition of the Baptist Faith and Message made no change to the content of the "Stewardship" section—only slight rewording and rearranging of a few words. Although the slight wording changes still did not introduce anything about "tithing," the list of Scripture verses changed. The 1963 edition simply added four Scripture references to the list of references: Genesis 14:20, Leviticus 27:30-32, Malachi 3:8-12, and Matthew 23:23.[133] All four of these new passages are ones that explicitly mention tithes. Obviously, the intention of these changes was to introduce some form of "tithing" obligation to church members as an expression of "stewardship." The Southern Baptist Convention in 1963 believed that the Bible taught that Christians were obligated to practice "tithing" whereas the Convention of 1925 did not!

The 2000 edition of the Baptist Faith and Message did not change anything in the "Stewardship" section. This most recent edition still does not explicitly mention "tithing" in any of the text of the statement, but still contains the four added "tithing texts" from the 1963 edition. The wording of the "Stewardship" section, therefore, does not inform Southern Baptists what they are to do with their "tithes" outlined in the supporting Scripture references. Strictly following the Baptist Faith and Message, a Southern Baptist could reasonably justify "us[ing] [their 'tithes'] for the glory of God and helping others" by giving these alleged "tithes" to "para-church"

---

133. Douglas K. Blount and Joseph D. Wooddell, eds., *The Baptist Faith and Message 2000: Critical Issues in America's Largest Protestant Denomination* (Lanham, MD: Rowman & Littlefield Publishers, 2007), 140.

entities or non-profit charitable organizations. However, many Southern Baptists today would quickly quote Malachi 3:8-12 to crush such an argument. Unfortunately for the Southern Baptist Convention, their Baptist Faith and Message is still woefully inadequate and out-of-date to express the current tithing doctrines taught in many Southern Baptist churches.

Presbyterian confessions

The Presbyterian Church claims its roots during the Protestant Reformation with the leadership of John Knox in Scotland and England in the mid-sixteenth century. Several confessions that follow can be regarded as Presbyterian confessions. We shall observe the Presbyterian confessions and follow the introduction of a tithing doctrine.

The Scot's Confession of 1560 was a statement by the Parliament of Scotland as it reflected the Reformation views of Knox and his followers in bitter struggle with the Catholic Church. Remember that the Catholic Church at the time maintained heavy governmental and doctrinal enforcement of tithe-taxes. If the early Presbyterian reformers—themselves defectors from the Catholic Church as a movement—believed that tithing were an essential doctrine of the Presbyterian Church, one would think that their first confession of faith (issued by the Parliament, no less!) would specifically cover such an issue. The Scot's Confession defines the true church as one that performs "the right administration of the sacraments of Christ Jesus" and ensures that "ecclesiastical discipline [is] uprightly ministered, as

God's word prescribes."[134] Nowhere does this Confession mention "tithing" in any form.

The Heidelberg Catechism of 1563 was developed to teach Reformed doctrine on a stream of Sunday worship sessions in a question and answer format. The portion of the catechism dealing with "Thankfulness" would have been the likely portion to insert a reference to "tithing." However, neither here nor anywhere in the catechism is any such mention.

The Second Helvetic Confession of 1566 was created in Switzerland as the country saw the adoption of Presbyterian reformation doctrine through the likes of Urlich Zwingli and Heinrich Bullinger. This Confession proclaimed that "restitution and compassion, and even almsgiving, are necessary for those who truly repent."[135] Chapter 28 of the Confession is entitled "Of the Possessions of the Church." No mention of tithes occurs here, but rather "the liberality of the faithful who have given their means to the Church" and part of these resources were "especially for the succor and relief of the poor."[136] If any institution of the church abuses the resources, "the relief of the poor must be arranged dutifully, wisely, and in good faith."[137] This Confession never prescribes "tithes" for the

---

134. Dennis Bracher, ed., "The Scot's Confession (1560)," *Creeds and Confessions,* 2006, http://www.crivoice.org/creedscots.html (accessed May 15, 2010).

135. Dennis Bracher, ed., "The Second Helvetic Confession (1566)," *Creeds and Confessions,* 2010, http://www.crivoice.org/creed2helvetic.html (accessed May 15, 2010).

136. Ibid.

137. Ibid.

maintenance of the church, but does emphasize the use of "the liberality of the faithful" for "the relief of the poor."

The Westminster Confession of Faith, drafted in 1646, is a well-known statement, and many Presbyterian churches today use it as an official statement of faith. In fact, this Confession has been so well received in Presbyterian churches that virtually no official confessions have arisen since then. The Westminster Confession contains nothing about the resourceful maintenance of the church and nothing about "tithes." Any Presbyterian church today that uses the Westminster Confession of Faith as the church's official statement would have to supplement it with something else if the church wished to have an official statement on the matter of tithes.

As Presbyterian churches formed distinct denominational groups within the last century, a few new statements have appeared mainly to clarify doctrine in major modern events. *The Barmen Declaration of 1934* was a brief statement among several Reformed churches in Germany to clarify that they opposed the rise of Nazism and its anti-Semitic dogma. No mention of tithing occurs in this statement as it merely addresses issues of church and state.

The Confession of 1967 was a Presbyterian statement to respond to the rise of secular influence in the church and to reaffirm historic Reformed teaching. The Confession contains such sections as "The Mission of the Church" and "The Equipment of the Church." However, in neither of these sections or in the entire confession is any mention of "tithes" or of any formal method for funding the church.

In 1990, as an effort to rejoin the northern United Presbyterian Church with the southern Presbyterian Church U.S.A, the two denominations created *A Brief Statement of Faith* as part of the collaborative *Book of Confessions*. This very brief statement is mostly a statement of praise to the Godhead and makes no mention of "tithes."

Essentially, no organized body of Presbyterian churches expressed an official statement of faith that referenced tithing at all. Nevertheless, many Presbyterian churches today preach and practice "tithing" as an essential doctrine from covenant theology. A closer look at Presbyterian history will show where such a doctrine formed.

The Presbyterian Church originated first in Scotland, then spread to England and Ireland. In Ireland, the Catholic Church and the Presbyterian Church fought over control of the government. Essentially, the obligation of "tithes" was still a standard legal requirement of the church-state, and the church that obtained control of the government was the one that claimed the tithe-taxes from the citizens.

Church historians note that a church doctrine of tithes in the United States did not begin until the mid-to-late 1800's. This was also a period revival and evangelistic endeavors. As conflicts such as the Civil War incurred taxes and churches were facing poverty, the idea of an obligation to pay tithes of one's income to the church spread as a way to fight a church's inability to raise enough funds through charitable contributions. During this time, Christians who espoused Covenant

Theology and some form of subjection to the Mosaic Law embraced the income tithe doctrine as a Scriptural mandate; Presbyterians were among the first to lead this charge.[138]

The United States had more freedom of religion at the time than did imperial Europe. On the flip side of this freedom came the lack of public funding that a state-run church enjoyed.[139] This new "resurgence" of tithe teaching changed it from the original Scriptural concept of an agricultural "land rent" by only landowners to a form of sacred monetary income tax.[140]

Some church historians noticed a new focus on tithing especially from the Presbyterian Church. Scottish Presbyterian William Garden Blaikie authored a journal in 1880 called *The Catholic Presbyterian*. Comparing Gideon's ephod with the Presbyterian Church, he warned that what can start as good things can become "poisonous plants in the garden of the Lord."[141] Concerning the new tithe doctrine in the Presbyterian Church, Blaikie writes:

Again, we find the tithe-principle introduced into the Church, as if the Church had gone back to the twilight condition of pre-Christian times, and was coincident with a governmental polity... This tithe-principle stands directly in the way of the Christian principle that all we have is the Lord's, and that we should strive to give directly to evangelisation

---

138. James David Hudnut-Beumler, *In Pursuit of the Almighty's Dollar: A History of Money and American Protestantism* (Chapel Hill, NC: The University of North Carolina Press, 2007), 54.
139. Victor V. Claar and Robin J. Klay, *Economics in Christian Perspective: Theory, Policy and Life Choices* (Downers Grove, IL: InterVarsity Press, 2007), 86.
140. Ibid.
141. William Garden Blaikie, ed., *The Catholic Presbyterian, vol. 9* (London: James Nisbet & Co., 1880), 4.

and the case of the Lord's poor as much as possible, knowing no limit to our communications of good. In spite of this truth, <u>we find large portions of the Presbyterian Church adopting this tithe system</u>, and advocating it by preaching and printing. <u>It is a human legalism, calculated to make all giving mechanical, and to check the flow of Christian fraternity.</u>[142] [Emphasis added]

Blaikie sounded an alarm for a doctrine that was creeping into the Presbyterian Church, and predicted that it would lead to laziness for those who should give more[143] and gimmicks for the church over time:

But <u>do not let the Church put its seal of approbation on a tenth, and make that the godly fraction</u>. The expedient will be a boomerang, and eventually injure the Church itself, even though at present it may have a <u>temporary success</u>.
<u>Alas for these temporary successes!</u> How they lure Christians to all sorts of unchristian schemes! They are excuses for Church fairs and Church raffles, and Church puppet-shows. They are the excuses for pulpit buffoonery, for sensational advertising, and for a degrading subservience to a godless daily press.[144] [Emphasis added]

Blaikie then calls upon the Presbyterian Church to abandon such gimmicks and return to proper Scriptural teaching:

When will the Church rise to the level of its Divine dignity, and <u>trust its blessed Lord and Head for all that it needs in His own ordained way?</u> When will it cease to approve of any scheme or method which shocks the common mind and secularises religion, and to salve over the inconsistency or enormity by enlarging on the worldly success or the immaculate orthodoxy that issues from it, or is connected with it? Of <u>what avail is success if it kills the Church's purity</u>; and of what avail is orthodoxy of creed if it be proclaimed by a harlequin diverting the populace?
It is a common thing to hear <u>these follies defended by those who ought to know better</u>, with an enumeration of the additions made to the Church by

---

142. Ibid., 4-5.
143. Ibid., 4.
144. Ibid., 5.

their means! as if the end would justify the means; as if all sorts of slang and vulgarity and irreverence were legitimate in the Church, if only it helped to increase the Church roll![145] [Emphasis added]

The Presbyterian Church of the United States held a *General Assembly* in 1890. Several questions were discussed in the meeting— one of which was the new doctrine of income tithes for church fund raising. Being an emerging teaching, the Assembly did not observe a conclusive and universal opinion. According to the report:

[S]ixty-eight Presbyteries of the seventy-one on the roll have set up papers on the law of the tithe as a means of raising the funds of the church. All the shades of opinion expressed could not be presented without giving the papers in full, some of which are voluminous.[146]

The opinions in the General Assembly were varied, but the majority did not see a "tithe" as a command for the church. The following is a breakdown of the 68 opinions on the subject:[147]

- 51 believed there was no tithing obligation
- 16 believed it was a "suggestion"
- 35 did not believe it had any place in the teaching of fund raising
- 10 believed such an obligation existed
- 7 believed that the church should enact measures to enforce it
- 3 argued against measures of enforcement
- 6 abstained from answering

---

145. Ibid., 5.
146. *Minutes of the General Assembly of the Presbyterian Church in the United States* (Richmond, VA: Presbyterian Committee of Publication, 1890), 26.
147. Ibid., 26-27.

⅄ 1 was ambiguous

Even as this tithing doctrine was spreading in the Presbyterian Church in the United States, over half the opinion was that tithing had no place in the church **at all!** At the time of the minutes, the General Assembly in 1890 could not produce a definitive statement other than that of abundant and voluntary Christian charity, of which all ultimately supported.[148]

However, over time the General Assembly would reflect more agreement of a tithe obligation. According to the minutes of the General Assembly in 1921:

> Pastors all over the Church are <u>faithful in teaching</u> the Stewardship of life and possessions, and there is a commendable <u>increase in the number of members who tithe or give a definitive portion of their income</u>, yet not half the churches seem to be paid in full their apportionment for their benevolences. They have, however, almost universally paid their pastors' salaries fully and promptly, and in a few instances small salary increases are reported.[149] [Emphasis added]

The tithe teaching and its accumulated defense from Scripture passages seemed to contribute to this increase in members paying "tithes" out of a perceived divine obligation. The General Assembly later stated the following in its report of the minutes:

> <u>Fears have been felt in some quarters that the financial side of the Presbyterian Progressive Program was over-emphasized</u>, but in view of the facts given in the reports for the past year these fears are seen to be groundless. As God's people have grown in their grace of giving and have <u>brought in larger measure of tithes into His house</u>, God has, according to the unfailing promise of His work, <u>opened to us the windows of heaven</u>

---

148. Ibid., 27.
149. *Minutes of the Sixty-First General Assembly of the Presbyterian Church in the United States* (Richmond, VA: Presbyterian Committee of Publication, 1921), 64.

and poured out a blessing so rich and full that it has been felt throughout the whole Church.[150] [Emphasis added]

Years before this, the struggle over a tithing issue was what Paul meant in the New Testament by "even so" in 1 Corinthians 9:13-14. Although the idea that this taught a tithing obligation was a minority view in 1890, eventually Presbyterians accepted that this taught tithing and an obligation to it for the church. Having accepted such an interpretation, the door became open once again for exploring the Mosaic Law for the details. The General Assembly of 1921 proceeded to use Malachi 3:8-10 as proof of the blessings of increased funds through tithe teaching, assuming that "the storehouse" and "mine house" referenced is now the Church. Perhaps this "success" is one of the "temporary successes" that William Blaikie warned about. Perhaps we must stay tuned to see if his predictions have come true, or will come true, for Presbyterian churches as well as other churches. Indeed, if the modern monetary income tithe doctrine is a fallacy in Scriptural interpretation, the blessings acquired by the teaching of certain compulsory giving (contrary to 2 Corinthians 9:7) may be short-lived for an individual church or a denomination dependent on such a formal methodology.

Conclusion and summary

In conclusion, we have examined the history of the modern monetary income tithe doctrine from the medieval Reformation to the

---

150. Ibid.

present. One of the issues to which the Reformers, such as Luther and Calvin, objected was the tithe-taxes of the Catholic Church and its departure from what the Scriptures actually taught about tithes. Both Luther and Calvin believed that the Mosaic Law was God's constitution for Old Testament Israel, and that Christians were not obligated to follow its ceremonial and judicial facets, including tithing. John Wesley taught abundant, voluntary stewardship, yet some today quote his statements and inject into them a perceived defense of "tithing." The views of these Reformers on the Mosaic Law indicate a significant difference from the Covenant Theology taught in modern circles.

From the Reformation to the nineteenth century, bitter struggles arose between state-run Catholic churches and state-run Protestant churches over the ability of the government to exact tithe-taxes to pay salaries of the establishment clergy. A Tithe War was fought, and following its conclusion over decades, the tithe-taxes phased out.

Subsequent to the end of state-church tithe-taxes, revivals arose in England and the United States. Free churches that did not enjoy public funding began to explore the idea of a tithing obligation apart from government enforcement. Examples of the evolution of the tithing doctrine include Baptists and Presbyterians. Statements of faith that these churches claimed did not originally include a doctrine imposing tithing. The Southern Baptist Church's Faith and Message eventually injected Scripture references to reflect the growing opinion among leaders of a tithing obligation. The General Assembly of the

Presbyterian Church of the United States saw weak support in its early years, yet teaching of Presbyterian pastors over time prompted members to follow. As this definitive—but by no means exhaustive—history of tithe teaching in the church age has demonstrated, the modern monetary income tithe doctrine most certainly has not enjoyed a benevolent history of support, and its enforcement has been proven to have its roots in a theocratic government tax—exactly what the Levitical system represented.

22. A Primer on Giving

Practical Suggestions for Grace Giving

Now comes the *pièce de résistance*. If you have been reading this book from cover to cover, you have engaged in an in-depth analysis of the entirety of what the Bible has to say about the subject of *tithing*. You have also encountered a brief history of this issue as the church has battled over it. In many cases this issue has involved the very lives of people. If this study has changed your mind about the subject of tithing, you may be asking yourself, "Even if this is all true, how can a legitimate, New Testament church survive without a predictable, reliable source of funds that would come as a result of the modern monetary income tithe doctrine?"

Gaining a proper perspective of the church

Although this chapter attempts to provide some answers to this question, I will admit upfront: **there is no perfect guarantee** for a church's financial survival. No mathematical formula exists from the

486

Bible or anywhere else that combines both voluntary, cheerful giving and a forward-looking budget of the church to **guarantee** that a church or its leadership will be able to pursue all desired endeavors or even to survive as a whole. God has promised that the gates of hell will not be able to withstand "the church" itself (Matthew 16:18), but He does not guarantee the earthly "success" of any particular local assembly or that it will remain a unified assembly.

Romans 8:35-37

35: Who shall separate us from the love of Christ? *shall* tribulation, or distress, or persecution, or famine, or nakedness, or peril, or sword?
36: As it is written, For thy sake we are killed all the day long; we are accounted as sheep for the slaughter.
37: Nay, in all these things we are more than conquerors through him that loved us.

As long as we as Christians are in this world we should anticipate the possibility of persecution that could threaten even our very lives, much less financial success an assembly. Although citizens of the United States of America recognize that political attacks on religious freedom have been increasing, they have still been quite accustomed to the freedoms they have enjoyed by law thus far. The temptation then becomes to treat a local church assembly as just another state-recognized corporation in form and function, and to expect that it should be able to succeed in its mission using the same financial strategies that a business uses to maximize profits for investors or shareholders.

A ministry, not a business

One thing must be made clear to gain a proper perspective of the form and function of the church: **God never intended the church to be a business**. Although a church may register itself as a corporate entity, its purpose for existing is not to entangle itself in the mindset of promoting itself for this purpose. The "pastor" or "elder board" is not a CEO, and members of the congregation are not employees. The mission is to spread the gospel of Jesus Christ throughout the world, not for any local assembly to make a name for itself for secular popularity. The goal is to promote Jesus Christ Himself, not the name of "First Baptist Church of Metropolis." The purpose is to share the gospel, not to build empires of educational institutions, campuses, gymnasiums, coffee shops, and other attractions. Although nothing is inherently wrong with any of these things, and they can be tools for spreading the gospel if used appropriately, the proper perspective is that they are possible means to an end, and not the end itself.

Dr. Bob Griffin is teaching elder at Sovereign Grace Church in Casper, Wyoming. He has been involved in pastoral ministries, church planting, and missionary endeavors for over forty years. Among his educational portfolio, he holds a B.S. from the University of Wisconsin and a D.Min. in Pastoral Theology from Trinity Theological Seminary in Newburgh, IN. Dr. Bob Griffin does not believe that Christians are required to practice any form of tithing.

I asked Dr. Bob about his view of the church in light of his disagreement with the modern monetary income tithe doctrine. In no uncertain terms he declared: "There is NO, NADA, ZERO, ZILCH command or evidence of Old Testament tithing being any part of the New Testament church program of financing." He also stated emphatically: "We are not a business. God's people need to see the 'fields white unto harvest,' and that will move a redeemed soul." As an elder whose financial well-being depends at least partially on the gifts of church members, Dr. Bob recognizes the whole purpose of the church: to spread the gospel, not to build an earthly empire. He stressed to me that his fundraising is geared to missions rather than "buildings, salaries, or programs that drain the church world-wide to provide 'fluff' and 'comfort' and 'extravagance' here in America."

Many Christians will pay lip service to the virtues of the Apostle Paul and all the selfless suffering he endured to carry the gospel to Gentile nations; however, they will believe that they have a right from God to their own financial success and equate their views of following God's will with the guarantee of a life of comfort. Although a government may recognize legal rights to life, liberty, and property, we should recognize these as blessings from God, not something that we can demand of Him. We have no guarantee from God of security from religious persecution or violations of rights from an intrusive government. The church must keep its eyes on its divine purpose, not on any present circumstances, because circumstances can be misleading.

Understanding the motive

Those who need to raise funds for a cause must properly understand motivation for giving. Undoubtedly, one who is attempting to secure donations to meet intimate needs has been at the other end of the spectrum in the past. A fundraiser should also have experience as a giver donating to a worthy cause. A fundraiser should ask himself or herself, "What causes **me** to give?" **A disconnect of mind and heart between the giver and the receiver will surely diminish pure motivations for giving!**

Especially for the church and Christian ministry, one should pay special attention to motive, the Holy Spirit, and the parameters of the Bible. Fundraising is **not** a mathematical formula. Is is not a mechanical process where a methodology or a list of steps will produce exactly the same result as an experiment in a laboratory. People are not machines; they have unique, individual personalities and wills. Christians also have the leading of the Holy Spirit.

R. Scott Rodin, President of Palmer Theological Seminary and of the Christian Stewardship Foundation, is a prolific author of books on Christian stewardship and fundraising topics. In *Stewards in the kingdom*, he argues for the role of the Holy Spirit in Christian fundraising. Berating contemporary Christian fundraising schemes, he describes the tactics as follows:

> We are told that if we use the right words, build an emotionally compelling case, use a specific number of sentences in each paragraph and a certain arrangement of paragraphs in every letter, and address our envelopes in certain ways and mail our letters at certain times, we will increase our response by x percent....

We need to ask ourselves in the face of all this, why then do we ask our donors to pray in consideration of their giving?... We must either accept the worldly view that our role as fundraisers is to motivate, or we acknowledge the powerful role of the Holy Spirit through prayer that we ask of our donors and stop placing on our shoulders the responsibility to move people to give.[151] [Emphasis added]

Rodin is right on the money (pun intended). How can Christians expect God to bless a ministry or endeavor if it is treated more as computational sales maneuvering rather than as a sacred trust in God? The element of **faith** is essential, and by this is not meant faith in the reliability of marketing tactics. If the giver is supposed to have faith in giving, the receiver is also to have faith in receiving. **The Holy Spirit is the channel between the faith of both ends.**

Being transparent and honest

People are more apt to give if they can see **their gifts in action**. A church shrouding its monetary affairs in secrecy is destined for failure. Statements such as "Your duty is to give to God and not to know what the church does with its money" are not reassuring. Those who give to a cause want to know that their donations actually do what they are supposed to do.

Any church leadership that expects members to give regularly should also be transparent about how funds are used. A periodic financial statement available to any member who asks should be foundational. Including at least a brief weekly or monthly summary of

---

151. R. Scott Rodin, *Stewards in the kingdom: a theology of life in all its fullness* (Downers Grove, IL: InterVarsity Press, 2000), 209.

total income, total salary paid, and amounts dispensed for certain projects aids in assuring the congregation that the church practices good accounting procedures and remains accountable. Expecting members to reveal their financial status by discouraging anonymous cash gifts in favor of marked envelopes while also shielding the church's budgetary information is the epitome of financial irresponsibility.

If any generous person reasonably expects assurance that a charitable non-profit organization is not embezzling contributions, why should he or she expect anything less from a church whose intent of existence is to promote a gracious God and spread the gospel? **Financial transparency and honesty are minimal and essential to the health of a church.** Transparency and honesty naturally pave the way for the next strategy: targeting needs.

Targeting needs

1 John 3:17

17: But whoso hath this world's good, and <u>seeth his brother have need</u>, and shutteth up his bowels *of compassion* from him, how dwelleth the love of God in him?

An effective strategy for acquiring needed funds is to express to donors a need clearly and succinctly. **One is more apt to give when one can share in the joy of seeing a legitimate need fulfilled.** It is often not enough to know that there is "a cause," but rather to know **what** this cause is.

Specificity invokes generosity. Be specific about the need and include as much information as possible. If the following information is available, do not shy away from providing it:

The total funds necessary to meet the need. God will not strike a church elder dead if he presents the congregation with a monetary figure. In fact, I can personally attest that I feel led to give more when I see the amount of the need realized. Providing monetary statistics is part of targeting needs and offers the givers a realistic goal. For example, Dr. Bob Griffin's church had a goal in 2010 to raise $5,000 over the course of two Sundays for missions work in Baja California, Mexico. I would surmise that a goal encourages more funding because the target is known and the ability to meet the goal is tangible. **Being unaware of a goal deprives the giver of determining a proportionate gift according to his or her ability.** Some may feel the heartfelt burden of shouldering the goal as if they were the only donors. If the goal for a need was $5000 and the church had 100 members, a reasonable donor would not expect that everyone give exactly $50. A Spirit-led donor would not trust everyone else (in good taste, of course) and desire to **ensure** that the need is met by giving significantly more than a calculated average.

The name of the recipient person or organization. People do not want to give into a black hole. They want to know who receives the gift so that they could **see their efforts in action**. Perhaps providing a way for the givers to include their contact information with their gifts and with a way to receive personal letters will encourage greater giving by making the needy recipient more **personal** to the individual giver.

⅄ *The exact use, or list of uses, for which the funds will apply.* State the effect of the funds in a positive way that connects the giver to the receiver. For example, for a fundraising inquiry in a church bulletin, Dr. Bob's church described a remote need on a foreign field as an "exciting way to get some basic Bible training to pastors who are woefully under-prepared for ministry." If possible, arrange for the recipient to notify each giver what the recipient was able to do with the gift. For example, if the recipient were a missions organization that distributes Bibles to third-world countries, the organization could send the giver a personal letter thanking him or her for the gift of $200 and explain that this amount purchased 50 printed New Testaments and placed them in the hands of 50 unsaved individuals. Little can be more encouraging than **seeing how giving produces results** that can lead to the salvation of others, making giving this mere money "easy."

⅄ *The amount of any funds received beyond the goal and for what they will be used.* If people are led to **give** "above and beyond," they would be encouraged knowing that the need **received** "above and beyond." An announcement that the fund for the need received **twice** as much as the total presented is a joy for all to share, regardless of how much each person gave. If the need met can put such extra to further use, allow the recipient to receive this excess. By no means should the church leadership hide this excess and squander it. If the recipient does not need the excess and cannot make appropriate use of it, perhaps the church could present a list of possible uses and vote on where to disburse the extra funds.

Dr. Bob Griffin told me that third-world missions endeavors are the primary goal and motivation for fundraising at his current church. Such a benevolent purpose encourages church members to give generously because they know that their contributions go directly to meet real needs and not to improve the structural appeal of a place of worship. The expenses of his church are kept low by agreement of the congregation and 75% of the church's budget is apportioned and guaranteed for third-world missions projects. Of the funds raised for missions work, the congregation is informed of specific amounts needed and used for each part of a project. For example, in a Baja project, Dr. Bob delineated $1,000 for a church roof, $1,000 for a room addition, $1,000 for funding for a second church, $500 for medical supplies for a nursing home, and $1,000 to send elders on-site both to preach and work.

Establishing personal relationships

This strategy essentially extends from that of targeting needs. Once a target is established, a greater focus can be placed on building a "personal relationship" between the giver and the receiver. Mutual family members and intimate friends on good terms are more apt to lend each other helping hands than to total strangers. According to professional fundraiser Dr. Wesley E. Lindahl, "The basis of effective fundraising is relationship building, and this is true for church fundraising as well. It is the sense of love and belonging to one's religious community that creates the bond of devotion to the mission of the church."[152]

Breaking a project down into smaller, constituent parts can also tug on the heart strings of individual members to set personal goals. For instance, in such a case as $1,000 for a church roof, a generous church member could personally volunteer to designate this amount from savings for this specific project. A follow-up report to the church of the success of this part of the project with a slide show portraying the construction of the roof along with a personal letter of thanks to the donor can encourage the giver not only in the current endeavor but also in future endeavors. However, the church must be wise to keep such praise cordial and not to encourage emotional competition for recognition. Giving must be from a pure motive.

Dedicating entire sermons to meeting specific needs

Motivation is key to successful fundraising. Proper motivation can enhance, whereas improper motivation can detract. Proper motivation would include emphasis on the joys and blessings of giving and sharing in the pleasure of being a part of meeting needs. A wealth of coherent Scripture will convict a heart more so than a proof text without proper expounding on context. I will present some Scriptures for fundraising shortly.

---

152. Wesley E. Lindahl, *Principles of Fundraising: Theory and Practice* (Sudbury, MD: Jones and Bartlett Publishers, 2010), 205.

Improper motivation includes scare tactics, generalities, and commands that "beg the question." Statements that focus on **obligation** to give but **discretionary freedom** for church leadership are not reassuring. Givers need to feel that that their joyful giving is instrumental in the spread of the Gospel and not that they are a labor force to be milked for funds under the heavy hand of God. A break from a sermon series to emphasize the need and the joys of giving can be especially powerful, notable, and timely.

Sermons on giving can apply both to specific projects as well as to general funds. The pastor can dedicate an entire sermon to giving and express the need for fulfilling operating costs in the church budget. If the need lies in a projected lack of funds to pay for an essential such as electricity, provide the amount of the cost. The congregation needs to be aware of actual needs, not simply their "duty" to give to the ministry.

A sermon that focuses on meeting the local church expenses can also provide statistics on gospel endeavors. Such statistics can include the "results" of these needs. For instance, if the church needs to raise an amount of money to cover the month's electricity bill, the sermon can list the total number of people saved last month to demonstrate what this electricity makes possible. Remember that the focus should not be geared toward the **success** of the local church, but toward its **goal**. The goal is to spread the gospel, not to maintain a comfortable "worship house." Facilities for worship are a **means** to the goal.

Perhaps a need to fund expenses can be accompanied with an extended plan for missions funding or other needs. The elder delivering the sermon can promise that gifts received in excess of the need can go toward other projects. A possible project suggestion could also be a fund dedicated toward meeting the emergency needs of members or their families. The more noble the cause, the more gifts will come in excess. The church elders should continue to praise God and the congregation that this church is "a giving church."

Scriptures for fundraising and meeting needs

Obviously if you have read through this book, you know that there are quite a few Scripture passages discussed that are **not** proper nor hermeneutically sound for an applicable sermon on giving. The Bible, however, does not lack in passages that most certainly **are** appropriate. Most of these verses are in the New Testament—not surprisingly in the church epistles. Some Old Testament verses are also applicable and beneficial for analogy.

⋏ *Genesis chapter 23.* The children of Heth graciously offered Abraham a free burial cave for his wife Sarah. Abraham graciously refused to take it for free and offered payment for it. Abraham paid them the estimated worth of the land. He understood the joy of giving to those from whom he would receive, even if he had no obligation. When we freely partake of the benefits of the grace of God in His ministry, we as God's people should desire to give back what we feel is its worth and according to our own capacity to give.

498

Section VI: Epilogue

▲ *2 Samuel 24:18-25.* Araunah offered king David a threshingfloor for free to build an altar for God. David refused to accept this property for sacred use without payment and sacrifice. Araunah provided a good example of charity for ministry. David provided a good example of regard for the care of others. He did not use his position as king to exclude himself from the common practice of exchange and value. We should follow David's example in that, whether great or small, we all treat the ministry with the same attitude of sacredness and sacrifice.

▲ *Proverbs 17:8.* "A gift *is as* a precious stone in the eyes of him that hath it: whithersoever it turneth, it prospereth." A giver truly receives a blessing when the gift is cheerful and voluntary. To give something without restraint makes the gift feel much more valuable than something required—as if it were a rare gem. God promises prosperity to the giver in such a way that the giver will truly enjoy the act of meeting a need over keeping the extra for unfulfilling use.

▲ *Proverbs 19:6.* "Many will intreat the favour of the prince: and every man *is* a friend to him that giveth gifts." Although someone of high esteem will receive many requests for favor, **everyone** loves a generous giver. Someone with fame and fortune can be assured of a multitude of admirers. This admiration falls short of the universal admiration for one who gives liberally. Kindness of heart far exceeds the prestige of high office. Know that when you give generously your regard and worth excels above rulers and kings!

▲ *Proverbs 19:17.* "He that hath pity upon the poor lendeth unto the LORD; and that which he hath given will he pay him again." God places the poor and needy of utmost importance. In fact, He treats generosity to the poor as generosity to Him. God will reward those who meet the needs of the poor. Whether He rewards this liberality with physical, mental, spiritual, or financial means, God will not let the generosity of His people go unnoticed.

⋏ *Matthew 5:42.* "Give to him that asketh thee, and from him that would borrow of thee turn not thou away." Jesus taught His disciples in the Sermon on the Mount to give indiscriminately to those who have needs. In the context of this verse, Jesus is speaking to Jewish disciples of how to treat their Roman Gentile overlords, such as the soldiers. He told them that if a soldier compelled them to carry their equipment for a mile of their journey, they should volunteer to go two miles. At this time the Jews harbored great disdain for the Romans and desired freedom from the bondage of their empire. Jesus further taught them to love their enemies. One who is generous will meet needs for their own sake and not discriminate. Church members should desire to give generously to any need for which they are able without picking favorites.

⋏ *Luke 6:38.* "Give, and it shall be given unto you; good measure, pressed down, and shaken together, and running over, shall men give into your bosom. For with the same measure that ye mete withal it shall be measured to you again." Jesus taught the same principle in Proverbs 19:6 that everyone lover a giver and in Proverbs 19:17 that God Himself regards those who give to the needy. According to John Gill, the illustration used here is that of filling a container of a dry substance (such a flour). A person will try to fit as much as possible into the container to save space. The person will pour the flour in causing a heap. The person will then press the flour down and shake the container to level it out. The process will continue until either the source runs out or the container is entirely full. Jesus taught that generosity given will yield generosity returned such that one will not be able to handle it all. It will be more than enough to fulfill and will persist to "run over."

⋏ *1 John 3:17.* "But whoso hath this world's good, and seeth his brother have need, and shutteth up his bowels *of compassion* from him, how dwelleth the love of God in him?" As many times as God emphasized His regard for meeting the needs of the truly poor in the Law, He reiterated this message through the Apostle John. One can claim to be a disciple of Jesus in word and doctrine, but **actions** are what demonstrate the love of God. If you have ought to give to a need and are made aware of a need, you cannot demonstrate the love of God by ignoring it. To the Jews, generosity and compassion was often expressed in the figure of speech of loosely moving bowels. The "bowels," or the inner seat of a person, represents the softest, most pliable and moving part of a person. The emotion is compassion that this tender part feels. If someone tries to refrain from allowing the "bowels of compassion" from their natural (regenerate) action of fulfilling the need, this action is in direct contrast to the love of God. To love God is to meet the needs of the brethren.

These are but a scant few of the many verses in the Bible that express the fulfillment, joy, and reward of giving to the needy. Plenty of motivation for giving to both the needs of the church and to missions work can be found from the pages of Scripture without taking a passage about tithing out of context to bully the congregation into paying an income tax to the church. Does the church desire humble hearts, voluntary giving, and pure lovers of God and His truth, or fearful subjects yielding a tax to the church to escape the judgment of God. I am sure that even the novice student of the Word can determine which method would be more effective to meeting the goal of the church and pleasing to God.

The Scriptures cannot be broken

John 10:35 says that "the scripture cannot be broken." 2 Peter 1:20 also says that "no prophecy of the scripture is of any private interpretation." If one is tempted to disregard Scriptural convictions and teach contrary to what one believes for "practical" reasons, how can one expect God to bless such efforts? The Scriptures command not to "bear false witness," and do not state that God will overlook dishonesty for "practical" propositions. God is not a wishy-washy Being Who weighs one's obedience to His commands with one's reasoning and intentions and absolves the wrongdoing if done for "good intentions."

The laws, courts, and justice systems do not work this way either. If one commits a crime, the law prescribes an appropriate punishment to fit the crime. One cannot argue in a court of law that ten years of generous giving to "Save the Children Fund" rightfully precludes the legal punishment for an act of murder. Why should we expect God to act any differently in His dealings with His people. We should seek to obey what He says in His Word, not think that we can ignore it and propose better.

Indeed, if the Scriptures do not teach the modern monetary income tithe doctrine, how can one expect God to bless and withhold chastening if one teaches that people are **obligated** to follow a **command** that God never gave, and attribute it to God with full knowledge of such a reality?

Philippians 4:8-9

8: Finally, brethren, <u>whatsoever things are true, whatsoever things *are* honest</u>, whatsoever things *are* just, whatsoever things *are* pure, whatsoever things *are* lovely, whatsoever things *are* of good report; if *there be* any virtue, and if *there be* any praise, <u>think on these things</u>.
9: <u>Those things, which ye have both learned, and received, and heard, and seen in me, do</u>: and the God of peace shall be with you.

We should think on what is both true and honest. We should place truth above all else perceived as pragmatic according to worldly standards. Paul told the Philippians that the things that the thing that they had **learned** from him, they should do. Paul never taught "tithing." He taught untainted generosity. We should teach what we **know** to be true. If we discover that what we previously believed is not truth, we should not teach what we know is not true. We should ponder the **true** and **honest** things. We should strive to learn **truth**, and we should be **honest** with others. Teaching one thing while believing another is not being honest. Dishonesty is contrary to God's Word.

Conclusion and summary

If this book has opened your eyes and mind to a Scriptural reality, you have a choice to make. You can continue to advocate, promote, or teach doctrine as Biblical that you now know is not, or you can determine to advocate, promote, or teach what you reasonably **know** and believe the Word of God expresses. The correct answer is not to violate your conscience or to be dishonest. You may have more studying to do or more questions to ask. This book cannot claim to teach all truth or answer all questions about this important subject. Only you yourself know what you need to do and what your next challenge will be. Whether or not you agree with everything in this book is least of importance; what matters is that you always seek to maintain your integrity and follow what **you** know is right, good, and **true**.

> **I John 3:18**
> 18: My little children, let us not love in word, neither in tongue; but in deed and in truth.

RECOMMENDED READING

Clarke, Henry William. *A History of Tithes*, 2nd ed. London: Swan Sonnenschein & Co, 1894.

Clarke, Henry William. *The History of Tithes from Abraham to Queen Victoria*. New York: George Redway, 1887.

Croteau, David A. *You Mean I Dont Have to Tithe?: A Deconstruction of Tithing and a Reconstruction of Post-Tithe Giving*. Eugene, OR: Pickwick Publications, 2010.

Greene, George W. *No More Tithing*. Omaha: Nehemiah Publishing, 2000.

Kelly, Russell Earl. *Should the Church Teach Tithing?: A Theologian's Conclusions about a Taboo Doctrine*. New York: Writers Club Press, 2000.

MacArthur, John. *The MacArthur Bible Commentary*. Nashville: Thomas Nelson, 2005.

Moore, Rory. *The Tithe That Binds*. Buford, GA: Faithful Publishing, 2006.

Narramore, Matthew E. *Tithing: Low-Realm, Obsolete & Defunct*. Graham, NC: Tekoa Publishing, 2004.

Parker, Joel P. *Tithing in the Age of Grace*. Bloomington, IN: Trafford Publishing, 2006.

Webb, Michael L., and Mitchell T. Webb. *Beyond Tithes & Offerings*. Edited by Sharon Y. Brown. Tacoma, WA: On Time Publishing, 1998.

Wells, A. Bruce. *Tithing: Nailed to the Cross*. Bloomington, IN: AuthorHouse, 2007.

BIBLIOGRAPHY

Acharya S. *Suns of God*. Kempton, IL: Adventures Unlimited Press, 2004.

Achtemeier, Paul J., ed. *HarperCollins Bible Dictionary*, Rev. ed. New York: HarperCollins, 1996.

Alcorn, Randy. *Money, Possessions and Eternity*, Rev. ed. Wheaton, IL: Tyndale House Publishers, 2003.

Alcorn, Randy. *The Treasure Principle*. Sistera, OR: Multnomah, 2001.

Alexander, Pat, and David Alexander, *Zondervan Handbook to the Bible*, 3rd ed. Grand Rapids: Zondervan, 1999.

Alter, Robert. *The Five Books of Moses: A Translation with Commentary*. New York: W. W. Norton & Company, 1996.

Allen, John. *State Churches and the Kingdom of Christ: An Essay on the Establishment of Ministers, Forms and Services of Religion by Secular Power, and on its Inconsistency with the Free, Humbling, Spiritual Nature of the Christian Dispensation*. London: William and Frederick G. Cash, 1853.

Aquinas, Thomas. *Summa Theologica, Volume 2*. Translated by Fathers of the English Dominican Province. Charleston, SC: BiblioBazaar, 2008.

Attridge, Harold W., and Wayne A. Meeks, eds. *The HarperCollins Study Bible*, Rev. ed. New York: HarperCollins, 2006.

Augustine (St.). *St. Augustin on Sermon on the Mount, Harmony of the Gospels and Homilies on the Gospels: Nicene and Post-Nicene Fathers of the Christian Church 1887*. Vol 6 of *St. Augustin on Sermon on the Mount, Harmony of the Gospels and Homilies on the Gospels Kessinger Publishing's rare reprints*. Edited by Philip Schaff. Whitefish, MT: Kessinger Publishing, 2004.

Ayers, Philip. *A Proverb a Day Keeps the Devil Away*. Longwood, FL: Xulon Press, 2008.

Babbs, Arthur Virgil. *The Law of the Tithe As Set Forth in the Old Testament: Illustrated, explained, and enforced from Biblical and extra-Biblical Sources*, 2nd ed. New York: Fleming H. Revell Company, 1921.

Balentine, Samuel E. *Leviticus*. Vol. 3 of *Interpretation Commentary Series*. Louisville, KY: Westminster John Knox Press, 2002.

Barnes, Albert. *Notes, Explanatory and Practical, on the Epistle to the Hebrews*. London: Routledge, Warne, and Routledge, 1860.

Barton, John, and John Muddiman, ed. *The Oxford Bible Commentary*. Oxford: Oxford University Press, 2001.

Batten, Loring Woart. *A Commentary on the First Book of Samuel*. New York: Macmillan, 1919.

Bebslin, *Tithing and Winning Souls*. Longwood, FL: Xulon Press, 2009.

Berlin, Adele, Marc Zvi Brettler, and Michael A. Fishbane, eds. *The Jewish Study Bible: Jewish Publication Society Tanakh Translation*. Oxford: Oxford University Press, 1999.

Biddle, Daniel A. *The Secret of the Seven Pillars - Building Your Life on God's Wisdom from the Book of Proverbs*. Longwood, FL: Xulon Press, 2007.

Blackhouse, Edward. *Early Church History: To the Death of Constantine*, 6th ed. Edited by Charles Tylor. London: Headley Brothers, 1906.

Blaikie, William Garden, ed. *The Catholic Presbyterian, Vol. 9*. London: James Nisbet & Co., 1880.

Blavatsky, Helena Petrovna. *The Secret Doctrine*. Vol. 2 of *The Synthesis of Science, Religion, and Philosophy*. Adyar, India: Quest Books, 1993.

Blount, Douglas K., and Joseph D. Wooddell, eds. *The Baptist Faith and Message 2000: Critical Issues in America's Largest Protestant Denomination*. Lanham, MD: Rowman & Littlefield Publishers, 2007.

Bonar, Andrew Alexander. *Commentary on Leviticus*. Lafayette, IN: Sovereign Grace Publishers, 2000.

Brewer, Mark A. *What's Your Spiritual Quotient?*. Shippensburg, PA: Destiny Image Publishers, 2008.

Bromiley, Geoffrey W. *The International Standard Bible Encyclopedia*, Vol. 4, Rev. ed. 1979. Reprint. Grand Rapids: William B. Eerdmans, 1995.

Brott, Rich, and Frank Damazio. *Family Finance Handbook: Discovering The Blessings Of Financial Freedom*. Portland: City Christian Publishing, 2004.

Brown, George W., comp. *Gems of Thought on Tithing*, 2nd ed. Cincinnati: Jennings & Graham, 1911.

Bruce, Frederick Fyvie. *The Epistle to the Hebrews*. Rev. ed. Grand Rapids: Wm. B. Eerdmans Publishing, 1990.

Burkett, Larry. *Giving & Tithing*. Chicago: Moody Publishers, 1998.

Calmet, Augustin. *Calmet's Dictionary of the Holy Bible*. Edited by Charles Taylor. London: Holdsworth and Ball, 1832.

Calvin, Jean. *Commentaries on the Four Last Books of Moses: Arranged in the Form of a Harmony*. 2nd ed. Translated by Charles William Bingham. Edinburgh: The

Calvin Translation Society, 1853.

Calvin, John. *The Institutes of the Christian Religion: Vol. 3 of 3*. Translated by Henry Beveridge. Charleston, SC: Forgotten Books, 2007.

Carpenter, Eugene E., and Philip Wesley Comfort. *Holman Treasury of Key Bible Words: 200 Greek and 200 Hebrew Words Defined and Explained*. Nashville: Broadman & Holman, 2000.

Chapman, A. T., and A. W. Streane. *The Book of Leviticus in the Revised Version*. Vol. 4 of *Cambridge Bible for schools and colleges*. Cambridge: Cambridge University Press, 1914.

Claar Victor V., and Robin J. Klay. *Economics in Christian Perspective: Theory, Policy and Life Choices*. Downers Grove, IL: InterVarsity Press, 2007.

Clarke, Henry William. *A History of Tithes*, 2nd ed. London: Swan Sonnenschein & Co, 1894.

Clarke, Henry William. *The History of Tithes from Abraham to Queen Victoria*. New York: George Redway, 1887.

Colenso, John William. *The Pentateuch and book of Joshua critically examined*. London, Longmans, Green, and Co., 1873.

Collier, Fred. *Doctrine of the Priesthood Vol 8 No. 1 - New Light on the Ancient Hebrew/Christian Doctrine on Deity — Part 1*. Salt Lake City: Collier's Publishing, 1991.

Craigie, Peter C. *The Book of Deuteronomy*. Grand Rapids: William B. Eerdmans Publishing, 1976.

Craik, Henry (Sir), ed. *English Prose: Sixteenth Century to the Restoration*. Vol. 2 of *English Prose: Selections with Critical Introductions by Various Writers and General Introductions to Each Period*. London: MacMillan and Co., 1920.

Curtis, Edward Lewis, Samuel Rolles Driver, Albert Alonzo Madsen, Alfred Plummer, and Charles Augustus Briggs. *A Critical and Exegetical Commentary on the Books of Chronicles*. Vol. 10 of *The International critical commentary on the Holy Scriptures of the Old and New Testaments*. New York: Charles Scribner's Sons, 1910.

Davis, Kenneth C. *Don't Know Much About® The Bible: Everything You Need to Know about the Gook Book but Never Learned*. New York: HarperCollins, 1998.

Dobson, Edward G., Charles L. Feinberg, Edward E. Hindson, Woodrow Michael Kroll, and Harold L. Willmington. *King James Version Bible Commentary*. Nashville: Thomas Nelson, 2005.

Douglas, J. D., and Merrill C. Tenney, eds. *New International Bible Dictionary*. Grand Rapids: Zondervan, 1987.

Driver, Samuel Rolles. *A Critical and Exegetical Commentary on Deuteronomy*, 3rd ed. Edinburgh: T & T Clark, 1902.

Dummelow, John Roberts, ed. *A Commentary on the Holy Bible*. New York: The Macmillan Company, 1920.

Dunn, James D. G., and John William Rogerson, ed. *Eerdmans Commentary on the Bible*. Grand Rapids: William B. Eerdmans Publishing, 2003.

Easterby, William. *The History of the Law of Tithes in England: Being the Yorke Prize Essay of the University of Cambridge for 1887*. Cambridge: Cambridge University Press, 1888.

Elwell, Walter A., and Philip W. Comfort, ed. *Tyndale Bible Dictionary*. Wheaton, IL: Tyndale House Publishers, 2001.

The Essential Study Bible: Contemporary English Version. New York: American Bible Society, 2007.

Evans, Grant, and Maria Tam, eds. *Hong Kong: The Anthropology of a Chinese Metropolis*. Honolulu: University of Hawaii Press, 1997.

Fairbairn, Patrick, ed. *The Imperial Bible-Dictionary*. London: Blackie and Son, 1866.

Fields, Michael. *FirstFruits: Revelation for Increase & Excellence*. Longwood, FL: Xulon Press, 2008.

Free, Joseph P., and Howard Frederic Vos. *Archaeology and Bible History*. Rev. ed. Grand Rapids: Zondervan, 1992.

Goodspeed, Edgar Johnson. *The epistle to the Hebrews*. New York: Macmillan, 1908.

Greer, Thomas H., and Gavin Lewis. *A Brief History of the Western World*, 9th ed. Belmont, CA: Thomas Wadsworth, 2004.

Hagee, John. *Financial Armageddon*. Lake Mary, FL: FrontLine, 2008.

Halley's Bible Handbook with the New International Version, 25th ed. Grand Rapids: Zondervan, 2000.

Hanson, Buddy. *What's Scripture Got to Do with It?*. Tuscaloosa, AL: Hanson Group, 2005.

Hayes, Doremus Almy. *The New Testament epistles: Hebrews, James, First Peter, Second Peter, Jude*. New York: The Methodist book concern, 1921.

Hazard, Marshall Custiss, and Henry Thatcher Fowler. *Books of the Bible*. Boston: The Pilgrim Press, 1903.

Henry, Matthew. *Matthew Henry's Concise Commentary on the Whole Bible*. Nashville: Thomas Nelson, 1997.

Holman Illustrated Bible Dictionary. Nashville: Holman, 2003.

Horton, Fred L. and Fred L. Horton, Jr. *The Melchizedek Tradition: A Critical Examination of the Sources to the Fifth Century A.D. and in the Epistle to the Hebrews*. Vol. 30 of *Society for New Testament Studies Monograph Series*. Cambridge, UK: Cambridge University Press, 2005.

Hudnut-Beumler, James David. *In Pursuit of the Almighty's Dollar: A History of Money and American Protestantism*. Chapel Hill, NC: The University of North Carolina Press, 2007.

Hunt, John. *Religious Though in England from the Reformation to the End of the Last Century: A Contribution to the History of Theology*. Vol. 1. London: Strahan & Co., 1870.

Hyles, Jack. *Jack Hyles Speaks on Biblical Separation*. Hammond, IN: Hyles-Anderson Publications, 1984. The Jack Hyles Website, http://jackhyles.net/separate.shtml (accessed February 6, 2010).

Ibn Ezra, Abraham ben Meïr. *The Commentary of Abraham ibn Ezra on the Pentateuch*. Edited by Jay F. Shachter. Hoboken, NJ: Ktav Publishing House, 2003.

Jeremias, Joachim. *Jerusalem in the Time of Jesus*. Translated by F. H. Cave and C. H. Cave. London: SCM Press Ltd., 1969.

Jerome (St.). *NPNF2-06. Jerome: The Principal Works of St. Jerome*. Edited by Philip Schaff. Translated by The Hon. W. H. Freemantle. Grand Rapids: Christian Classics Ethereal Library, 1982.

Josephus, Flavius. *Josephus: The Complete Works*. Translated by William Whiston. Nashville: Thomas Nelson, 1998.

Josephus, Flavius. *The New Complete Works of Josephus*. Rev. ed. Edited by Paul L. Maier. Translated by William Whiston. Grand Rapids: Kregel Publications, 1999.

Kelly, Russell Earl. *Should the Church Teach Tithing?: A Theologian's Conclusions about a Taboo Doctrine*. New York: Writers Club Press, 2000.

Kendall, R. T. *Tithing*. Grand Rapids: Zondervan, 1983.

Klingshirn, William E. *Caesarius of Arles: The Making of a Christian Community in Late Antique Gaul*. Vol. 22 of *Cambridge Studies in Medieval Life and Thought: Fourth Series*. Cambridge: Cambridge University Press, 1994.

Kugel, James L. *Traditions of the Bible: a guide to the Bible as it was at the start of the common era*. Cambridge: Harvard University Press, 1998.

Lansdell, Henry. *Studies in tithe giving, ancient and modern*. London: Society for Promoting Christian Knowledge, 1906.

Leith, John H, ed. *Creeds of the Churches: A Reader in Christian Doctrine, from the*

Bible to the Present. 3rd ed. Louisville, KY: Westminster John Knox Press, 1982.

Lindahl, Wesley E. *Principles of Fundraising: Theory and Practice*. Sudbury, MD: Jones and Bartlett Publishers, 2010.

Lindsay, Thomas Martin. *Church and the Ministry in the Early Centuries*. London: Hodder and Stoughton, 1903. http://www.ccel.org/ccel/lindsay/early_church.html. Also available in print form and as a PDF eBook.

Little, Christopher R. *The revelation of God among the unevangelized: an evangelical appraisal and missiological contribution to the debate*. Pasadena: William Carey Library, 2000.

Littledale, Richard Frederick. *Plain reasons against joining the church of Rome*. London: Society for Promoting Christian Knowledge, 1886.

Luther, Martin. *Martin Luther's Basic Theological Writings*. 2nd ed. Edited by Timothy F. Lull and William R. Russell. Minneapolis: Fortress Press, 2005.

MacArthur, John. *1 Corinthians*. Nashville: Thomas Nelson, 2007.

MacArthur, John. *The MacArthur Bible Commentary*. Nashville: Thomas Nelson, 2005.

MacColloch, Diarmaid. *Christianity: The First Three Thousand Years*. New York: Viking, 2009.

MacDonald, William. *Believer's Bible Commentary*. Nashville: Thomas Nelson, 1995.

McGlothlin, William Joseph. *Baptist Confessions of Faith*. Philadelphia: American Baptist Publication Society, 1911.

McKenzie, John L. *Dictionary of the Bible*. 1965. Reprint, New York: Touchstone, 1995.

Meakin, Budgett. *The Land of the Moors: A Comprehensive Description*. London: Swan Sonnenschein & Co., 1901.

Menzies, Allan, ed. *The Ante-Nicene Fathers: Translations of the Writings of the Fathers Down to A.D. 325*. 5th ed. New York: Charles Scribner's Sons: 1903.

Milgrom, Jacob. *Leviticus: A Book of Ritual and Ethics: A Continental Commentary*. Minneapolis: Fortress Press, 2004.

Miller, George. *History, Philosophically Illustrated, from the Fall of the Roman Empire, to the French Revolution, Volume 1*. 3rd ed. London: H. G. Bohn, 1852.

Miller, Stephen M. *The Complete Guide to the Bible*. Uhrichsville, OH: Barbour Publishing, 2007.

Mills, Watson E., and Roger Aubrey Bullard, eds. *Mercer Dictionary of the Bible*.

Macon, GA: Mercer University Press, 1990.

Minutes of the General Assembly of the Presbyterian Church in the United States. Richmond, VA: Presbyterian Committee of Publication, 1890.

Minutes of the Sixty-First General Assembly of the Presbyterian Church in the United States. Richmond, VA: Presbyterian Committee of Publication, 1921.

Moseley, Dan, ed. *Joyful Giving: Sermons on Stewardship.* St. Louis, MO: Chalice Press, 1997.

Newsom, Carol Ann, and Sharon H. Ringe, ed. *Women's Bible Commentary,* expanded ed. Louisville, KY: Westminster John Knox Press, 1998.

Olford, Stephen F. *The Grace of Giving: A Biblical Study of Christian Stewardship,* 3rd ed. Grand Rapids: Kregel Publications, 2000.

"On Tithes," *The Monthly Review* 1, no. 1 (1835): 151-169.

Oppenheimer, Aharon. *The 'am ha-aretz: A Study in the Social History of the Jewish People in the Hellenistic-Roman Period.* Vol. 8 of *Arbeiten zur Literatur und Geschichte des hellenistischen Judentums Arbeiten Zur Geschichte Des Antiken Judentums Und Des Urchristentums.* Translated by I. H. Levine. Leiden: E. J. Brill, 1977.

Pfeiffer, Charles F., and Everett F. Harrison, eds. *The Wycliffe Bible Commentary.* Chicago: Moody Press, 1962.

Pink, Arthur W. *Tithing.* Grand Rapids: Christian Classics Ethereal Library, 2007. http://www.ccel.org/ccel/pink/tithing.html. Also available in print form and as PDF and Microsoft Word eBooks.

Revel, Bernard. *The Karaite halakah: and its relation to Sadducean, Samaritan and Philonian Halakah.* Philadelphia: Cahan Printing Co., 1913.

Richardson, Ernest Cushing, and Bernhard Pick. *The Ante-Nicene Fathers: The Gospel of Peter, The Dietessaron of Tatian, The Apocalypse of Peter, The Visio Pauli, The Apocalypses of the Virgin and Sedrach, The Testament of Abraham, The Acts of Xanthippe and Polyxena, The Narrative of Zosimus, The Apology of Aristides, The Epistles of Clement (Complete Text), Origen's Commentary on John, Books I-X, and Commentary on Matthew, Books I, II, and X-XI.* Vol 9 of *The Ante-Nicene Fathers: Translations of the Writings of the Fathers Down to A.D. 325.* Edited by Alexander Roberts, Sir James Donaldson, Arthur Cleveland Coxe, and Allan Menzies. New York: Charles Scribner's Sons, 1903.

Ritchie, John. *Feasts of Jehovah: Foreshadows of Christ in the Calendar of Israel.* Grand Rapids: Kregel Publications, 1982.

Rodin, R. Scott. *Stewards in the kingdom: a theology of life in all its fullness.* Downers Grove, IL: InterVarsity Press, 2000.

Ryken, Leland, Jim Wilhoit, Tremper Longman, Colin Duriez, Douglas Penney, and

Daniel G. Reid. *Dictionary of Biblical Imagery*. Downers Grove, IL: InterVarsity Press, 1998.

Schaeffer, Francis A. *A Christian View of the Bible as Truth*, 2nd ed. Vol 2 of *The Complete Works of Francis A. Schaeffer: A Christian Worldview*. Wheaton, IL: Crossway Books, 1985.

Schaff, Philip. *ANF01. The Apostolic Fathers with Justin Martyr and Irenaeus*. Grand Rapids: Christian Classics Ethereal Library, 2002.

Schaff, Philip. *ANF02. Fathers of the Second Century: Hermas, Tatian, Athenagoras, Theophilus, and Clement of Alexandria (Entire)*. Grand Rapids: Christian Classics Ethereal Library, 2004.

Schaff, Philip. *ANF03. Latin Christianity: Its Founder, Tertullian*. Edited by Allan Menzies. Grand Rapids: Christian Classics Ethereal Library, 2006.

Schaff, Philip. *ANF05. Fathers of the Third Century: Hippolytus, Cyprian, Caius, Novatian, Appendix*. Grand Rapids: Christian Classics Ethereal Library, 2004.

Schaff, Philip. *ANF07. Fathers of the Third and Fourth Centuries: Lactantius, Venantius, Asterius, Victorinus, Dionysius, Apostolic Teaching and Constitutions, Homily, and Liturgies*. Grand Rapids: Christian Classics Ethereal Library, 2004.

Scharfstein, Sol. *Torah and Commentary: The Five Books of Moses: Translation, Rabbinic, and Contemporary Commentary*. Jersey City: KTAV Publishing House, 2008.

Selbourne (Earl of), Roundell Palmer. *Ancient Facts and Fictions Concerning Churches and Tithes*, 2nd ed. London: Macmillan, 1892.

Shuler, J. L. *Helps to Bible Study*. Hagerstown, MD: Review and Herald Pub Assoc., 1990.

Smith, William (Sir), and Samuel Cheetham, eds. *A Dictionary of Christian Antiquities*. Hartford: The J. B. Burr Publishing Company, 1880.

Smith, William. *Smith's Bible Dictionary*. Nashville: Thomas Nelson, 1986.

Sproul, R. C. *Now, That's a Good Question!* Wheaton, IL: Tyndale House Publishers, 1996.

Spurgeon, Charles Haddon, ed. *The Sword and the Trowel*. London: London Metropolitan Tabernacle, 1873.

Spurling, Marshall B. *Ladder: Math Code 2*. Longwood, FL: Xulon Press, 2006.

Stedman, Ray C. *Hebrews*. Vol. 15 of *The IVP New Testament commentary series*. Westmont, IL: InterVarsity Press, 1992.

Steele, Daniel, and John Wesley Lindsay. *Leviticus and Numbers*. Vol. 2 of *Commentary on the Old Testament*. New York: Hunt and Eaton, 1891.

Stewart, Elmer Bryan. *The Tithe*. Chicago: The Winona Publishing Co., 1903.

Taylor, Richard A., and E. Ray Clendenen. *Haggai, Malachi*. Vol. 21A of *The New American Commentary*. Nashville: Broadman & Holman, 2004.

The Book of Jasher. Translated by Mordecai Manuel Noah. New York: M.M. Noah & A.S. Gould, 1840.

The Book of Jubilees: or The Little Genesis. Translated by Robert Henry Charles. London: Adam and Charles Black, 1902.

The Chronological Study Bible. Nashville: Thomas Nelson, 2008.

Tooke, Andrew. *Tooke's Pantheon of the Heathen Gods and Illustrious Heroes*. Baltimore: Cushings & Bailey, 1851.

Townsend, George, ed. *The Old Testament: Arranged in Chronological Order*. 2nd ed. London: C. and J. Rivington, 1826.

Trim, James Scott. *The Tithe of YHWH*. Hurst, TX: Worldwide Nazarene Assembly of Elohim, 2009.

Vine's Complete Expository Dictionary of Old and New Testament Words. Nashville: Thomas Nelson, 1996.

Viola, Frank, and George Barna. *Pagan Christianity?: exploring the roots of our church practices*. Carol Stream, IL: Tyndale House, 2008.

Walton, John H., and Victor H. Matthews. *The Ivp Bible Background Commentary: Genesis-Deuteronomy*. Downers Grove, IL: InterVarsity Press, 2000.

Walvoord, John F., and Roy B. Zuck, ed. *The Bible Knowledge Commentary: Old Testament*. Vol. 2 of *The Bible Knowledge Commentary: An Exposition of the Scriptures*. Colorado Springs: David C. Cook, 1983.

Wangenye, Stan. *God's Will still is Prosperity*. Longwood, FL: Xulon Press, 2009.

Webb, Michael L., and Mitchell T. Webb. *Beyond Tithes & Offerings*. Edited by Sharon Y. Brown. Tacoma, WA: On Time Publishing, 1998.

Wesley, John. *Sermons on Several Occasions, Volume 1*. New York: Carlton & Phillips, 1855.

Wesley, John. *The Works of the Rev. John Wesley: With the Last Corrections of the Author*. Vol. 6. London: Wesleyan Conference Office, 1872.

Whitehead, Bert, and Carrie Wally. *Spirit of the Tithe*. Haverford, PA: Infinity Publishing, 2004.

Wiersbe, Warren W. *With the Word: The Chapter-by-Chapter Bible Handbook*. Nashville: Thomas Nelson, 1991.

Winston, Bill. *The Power of the Tithe*. Oak Park, IL: Bill Winston Ministries, 1999.

Williams, George, *The Student's Commentary on the Holy Scriptures*, 6th ed. Grand
Rapids: Kregel Publications, 1981.